SOCIAL CHANGE THEORIES IN MOTION

This book assesses how theorists explained processes of change set in motion by the rise of capitalism. It situates them in the milieu in which they wrote. They were never neutral observers standing outside the conditions they were trying to explain. Their arguments were responses to those circumstances and to the views of others commentators, living and dead. Some repeated earlier views; others built on those perspectives; a few changed the way we think. While surveying earlier writers, the author's primary concerns are theorists who sought to explain industrialization, imperialism, and the consolidation of nation-states after 1840. Marx, Durkheim, and Weber still shape our understandings of the past, present, and future. Patterson focuses on explanations of the unsettled conditions that crystallized in the 1910s and still persist: the rise of socialist states, anti-colonial movements, prolonged economic crises, and almost continuous war. After 1945, theorists in capitalist countries, influenced by Cold War politics, saw social change in terms of economic growth, progress, and modernization; their contemporaries elsewhere wrote about underdevelopment, dependency, or uneven development. In the 1980s, theorists of postmodernity, neoliberalism, globalization, innovations in communications technologies, and post-socialism argued that they rendered earlier accounts insufficient. Others saw them as manifestations of a new imperialism, capitalist accumulation on a global scale, environmental crises, and nationalist populism.

Thomas C. Patterson is Distinguished Professor of Anthropology Emeritus at the University of California, Riverside, and the author of a number of books, including *Karl Marx, Anthropologist, From Acorns to Warehouses: The Historical Political Economy of Southern California's Inland Empire*, and *Inventing Western Civilization*.

This book is a valuable explanation and critique of explanations of social change in the last three centuries. The theme is how power influences, and is influenced by, theories of social change—a fascinating angle for examining the structural changes that have occurred in the modern world-system since the 18th century.

Christopher Chase-Dunn, Institute for Research on World-Systems,
University of California, Riverside

For the past five decades, Tom Patterson has been one of the most stimulating and original thinkers in the field of anthropology. This excellent book reflects such exciting thinking, as it critically examines many of the explanations for global change that have been advanced in the last two centuries. Moreover, it can be profitably read not only by anthropologists but by all social scientists.

Jeremy A. Sabloff, The Santa Fe Institute

Tom Patterson makes today's crises more intelligible by taking a long-term perspective, exploring how social theorists with different ideological orientations diagnosed the changes that capitalism produced in their own eras. Supremely lucid and richly contextualised accounts of ideas and debates provide readers with a truly worldwide vision of modern history, combined with the strongest intellectual incentives to continue thinking not only about how to understand our world but also about how to change it.

John Gledhill, FBA, FAcSS, Emeritus Professor of Social
Anthropology, The University of Manchester

In this far-ranging and erudite work, Patterson carries out a dialogue among a wide array of theorists within the Marxian and social science traditions, from Rousseau and Smith to Marx, and from Weber and Luxemburg to Fanon and Foucault. Throughout, he considers not only Western Europe and North America, but also theories and theorists connected to the Global South and to agrarian societies. Far from a history of social thought for its own sake, Social Change Theories in Motion speaks to a twenty-first century world riven by economic, social, and cultural crisis.

Kevin B. Anderson, University of California, Santa Barbara

This book is a welcome, timely contribution to our collective understandings of what can be learned from by placing key theorists of social change in relationship to the historical conjunctures that they were observing and analyzing. As such the book is a reminder and guide for how to think about and speak to the contemporary crises and efforts to erase historical memories of critique.

Nina Glick Schiller, Emeritus Professor,
Social Anthropology, University of Manchester and
the University of New Hampshire

Social Change Theories in Motion

Explaining the Past, Understanding the Present, Envisioning the Future

Thomas C. Patterson

DISTINGUISHED PROFESSOR EMERITUS OF ANTHROPOLOGY
UNIVERSITY OF CALIFORNIA, RIVERSIDE

Routledge
Taylor & Francis Group

LONDON AND NEW YORK

First published 2018 by Routledge
2 Park Square, Milton Park, Abingdon, Oxon OX14 4RN
52 Vanderbilt Avenue, New York, NY 10017

Routledge is an imprint of the Taylor & Francis Group, an informa business

© 2018 Taylor & Francis

Library of Congress Cataloging-in-Publication Data
A catalog record for this book has been requested

ISBN: 978-0-815-35299-0 (hbk)
ISBN: 978-0-815-35295-2 (pbk)

Typeset in Minion
by codeMantra

In Memory of Ananth Aiyer
Student, Teacher, Colleague, Friend

Contents

Preface–Author's Note   x

Introduction   1

1   The Language of Change: Motion in Time   13
  Change as Recurrence and Renewal 14
  Change as Teleology, Change as Growth 17
  Change as Progress, Change as Becoming Modern 20
  Change as Development, Change as Modernity 26
  Change as Human Nature, Change as Nature 30
  Discussion 35
  Notes 37

2   Modern Industrial Capitalist Society, 1820–1914   38
  Karl Marx: Historical Materialist, Communist 39
  *Émile Durkheim: Conservative Centrist Theorist of Social
     Nature 49*
  Max Weber: Critic, Nationalist, Historical Political Economist 57
  Discussion 67
  Notes 69

**3   Imperialism and the National, Colonial, and Agrarian
     Questions, 1890–1929**   71
  Imperialism: Conquest Abroad, Repression at Home 72
  *The National Question: Nations, Nationalism, and National
     Minorities 85*
  *The Colonial Question: Settlers, National Minorities, and
     Indigenous Peoples 95*
  The Agrarian Question: Peasants and Rural Economic Change 99
  *From Social Evolution to Uneven and Combined
     Development 106*
  Discussion 109
  Notes 113

4 Capitalism in Crisis and the Search for Social Order, 1918–1945   115

Economic Crises, Cycles, or Evolution? 116
Capitalism in Crisis: Social Reform or Socialist Revolution? 120
Rural Class Structures and Alternative Paths of
   Agrarian Development 129
Articulation, Integration, and the Constitution of
   Multi-Nation Nation-States 138
Crisis, Conflict, and the Quest for Social Order 142
Discussion 151
Notes 152

5 The Cold War, Decolonization, and the Third World, 1945–1970   153

Theories of Economic Growth and Modernization 155
Underdevelopment, Dependency, and the Modern World
   System 164
Unequal Exchange, the Imperialism of International Trade, and
   the Political Economy of Multinational Corporate Capital 172
Modes of Production in Third World Societies 177
The Transition Question from Feudalism to Capitalism 182
Precipitants of Transitions 188
   Anti-Colonialism, National Liberation Movements, and New
      Nations 188
   Rural Development, Social Revolution, and Peasant
      Communities 194
   Transitions between Capitalism and Socialism and Vice Versa 199
Discussion 200
Notes 201

6 The World in Crisis, 1970–2017   203

An Overview of Social Formation in an Age of Continual
   Crises 206
Neoliberalism and the Current Crisis 212
   Neoliberalism as a Theory of Society 212
   Neoliberalism as an Ideology 213
   Neoliberalism and its Political Agenda 214
Globalization and the New Imperialism 217
   Globalization Theory 217
   The New Imperialism and Global Capitalism 222
Postmodernism, Postmodernity, and Governmentality 232
   Postmodernism 232
   Postmodernity 233
   Governmentality 236

The Dissolution of Socialism, the Rise of Post-Socialism 239
Nationalism, the Nation, and Nation-States 247
   Nationalism and the Nation 248
Post-coloniality, Nationality, and Modernity 251
Crisis, Identity, and Populism 255
Global Capitalism and World Environmental Crisis 262
Discussion 266
Notes 270

References   271
Index   305

Preface–Author's Note

I regularly taught a course on theories of social change for fifty-three years before retiring in 2016. It was the first course I ever taught. The content changed steadily over the years, thanks to students. They continually amazed me, taught me, and sparked my curiosity, taking it, and me, in unimaginable directions. They still inspire me. I will not attempt to list all of them for fear of missing a name; there are too many, and besides, they know who they are.

Writing has never been a solitary activity for me. I share drafts with students and friends. I read paragraphs to them over the phone or over cups of coffee. I look forward to their comments and criticisms. I especially want to thank Wendy Ashmore—my colleague, inspiration, and partner, who has high standards and sets a high bar. She has read and commented on every word of the manuscript—often more than once. I also want to thank Alexandra Andrejevich, Carole Nagengast, Chris Chase-Dunn, and Bob Paynter, who improved the clarity of the arguments and text.

Introduction

Historical memory is dangerous to authoritarian regimes because it has the power to both question the past and reveal it as a site of injustice.

(Giroux 2017:23)

Losing it in times of crisis and manufactured ignorance is even more dangerous!

This book looks at how theorists have understood and explained social and political-economic changes and developments that have occurred since the mid-1700s. Economic historian Karl Polanyi (1957[1944]) called these developments "the great transformation." This tumultuous period witnessed the rise of The Enlightenment; the appeal to reason and anti-authoritarian sentiments that challenged and eventually eroded the authority of the aristocracy and the Church; the steady implementation of the Scientific Revolution that brought technological innovations and new understandings of nature in its wake; and the crystallization of the Industrial Revolution, entrepreneurial manufacturing, and industrial capitalism. It was the time when imperialist countries established far-flung colonies around the world, when they waged wars with one another and with their colonial subjects, and when political and economic crises begun to erupt with astonishing frequency. These processes, set in motion during the eighteenth century by some accounts and in the 1500s by others, have had profound and long-lasting consequences. Theorists have typically formulated their explanations of these changes in terms of concepts and ideas that were already part of the intellectual baggage they inherited from previous generations. While some analysts recycled earlier accounts, others refined them, and a few came up with novel insights about the processes of change that had been unleashed. The latter usually transform the ways we think, talk, and write about these processes.

One thing is certain. Theorists have rarely, if ever, been neutral, objective observers disengaged from or standing completely outside the social relations and changes they were attempting to explain. They were participants whose views either gave voice to the sentiments of a group in hierarchically organized sets of social relations or were fundamental in structuring their understandings. What distinguishes the groups from one another is their relation to power—briefly, their capacity to set agendas and produce intended outcomes or effects and their place or location in structures of power. Thus, power relations inflect knowledge. What this means is (1) that the social locations of groups both shape and constrain their understanding of the social and cultural worlds they inhabit and (2) that analysts from different locations in those groups may experience, know, privilege, and clearly understand certain features of the dynamics of the power structures at the same time they may deny, not understand, or be invested in ignoring other features.

From the early 1800s onwards, advocates of what we now call "standpoint theory" have argued that analysts from social locations that are disadvantaged or marginalized in power structures often have clearer understandings of the dynamics of what is taking place than their counterparts from more dominant groups. In other words, they experience and know things that members of dominant groups either do not know, take for granted, or deny altogether. They know first-hand the effects of oppressive social relations, and, at the same time, they have to accurately understand and function in social and cultural milieu shaped by dominant worldviews. These analysts are potentially able to disassociate their experiences and perceptions from those of more privileged groups. Moreover, they have no particular reason to maintain or perpetuate understandings of the world that legitimate and rationalize privilege and oppressive social relations—i.e. the ones that groups with dominant or authoritative social locations in power structures take for granted and seek to reproduce (Wylie 2004, 2012).

An example of standpoint theory in action is the master-slave relationship described in Georg Hegel's (1967[1807]:228–240) *The Phenomenology of Mind*. The master rules his property, the slaves, and depends on them to provide the goods and services he requires; he also lives in mortal fear that his property will revolt, thereby depriving him not only of the means to satisfy his desires but also his very existence. The slaves know this, but the master does not know that they know. By gaining knowledge and deeper understanding of the relationship, the slaves continually attempt to adjust the balance of power to the best of their ability, given the circumstances and the conditions in which they live.[1] To paraphrase philosopher Michel Foucault, knowledge is power! To quote another analyst of the human condition, "Philosophers have only *interpreted* the world in various ways; the point is to *change* it" (Marx 1976[1845]:5). While the question of praxis—the active process by which human beings establish relationships with objects in the external world and with one another—is not a central concern in this book, it always looms as a subtext just over the horizon.

Another example, perhaps more germane to this work, is the still unresolved dialectic between two standpoints of what was happening in Western Europe in the mid-eighteenth century. Jean-Jacques Rousseau (1973[1750], 1973[1755]) and Adam Smith (1976[1776]) gave voice to the sentiments and views of groups with different positions in the social structure: respectively, a class of downwardly mobile artisans whose ability to shape their own destiny was slipping away rapidly (if indeed it ever existed) and emerging "middle" class fractions composed of increasingly competitive entrepreneurial manufacturers and merchants. Both sought to understand and assess the implications of (1) the emerging autonomy and domination of the economic realm in the form of a self-regulating market in Western Europe and (2) how the profit motive gained primacy in shaping interpersonal and social relations. Rousseau, the critic of what others would soon call civilization, described the emerging social order and its increasingly influential middle class in historical terms. The sociohistorical process involved the dissolution of community, living outside of society, theft, the pursuit of private interests at the expense of community, courting those in power and the wealthy (both of whom were hated and despised), viewing freedom only as a means of acquiring possessions, and living only in the opinion of others. Smith, state official and advocate for the new middle class, portrayed the development of this emergent commercial or civil society in terms of the unfolding of natural laws and of a human nature shared by all human beings; economic progress fueled by man's natural disposition to better his own condition through the growing division of labor and his natural propensity to truck, barter, and exchange one thing for another; the growth of towns and cities; and the self-interested acquisition of riches and novelties to keep up with the popular images of his position. In Smith's view, this whole process was fueled by the hidden hand of the market, free trade, and minimal interference from the state (e.g. Gray 2000; Löwy and Sayre 2001; Sandel 1984). In their analyses, both Rousseau and Smith focus on the autonomy of the individual, property, exchange, equality, new power relations, and the possession and consumption of commodities deployed as symbols of a newly acquired status that distinguished their owners from those of other groups in the society (Goldmann 1973).

The standpoints of Rousseau and Smith manifest two cultures, two worldviews, two understandings of the past and present, and two visions of the future. By the 1830s, these were increasingly called romanticism and liberalism, respectively, in various media. Seen through a different lens from the one used in the preceding paragraph, both touch on the issue of modernity. A modern society (read: Western society) is one that promotes novelties and new commodities, and modernity is the result. The views of Smith and other advocates of modernity and modernization are invariably pulled toward the future because of their commitment to continuous growth and innovation. They see existing social forms as provisional because of the dynamism of modern society that constantly throws the institutions and practices into conflict with one another— for example, the polity against the economy and culture against instrumental rationality. Past societies (read: traditional societies) have no relevance for modernization theorists because of their orientation toward the future (Kerr 1960; Kumar 2006). Smith, the proponent of both liberalism and modernity, praised the self-regulating market, the steady stream of new goods and services, the mechanization of the world, the conquest of nature as its raw materials were transformed into commodities, and the new kinds of work and knowledge the market provided to those seeking employment. Modernity was moral in Smith's view: It did not harm the innocent, and it not only benefited one's self but also one's family, friends, and community as well as one's benefactors, whose contributions should be gratefully recognized. Rousseau had an alternative reaction to modern capitalist civilization and its free market. He noted the dissolution of social bonds, disenchantment of the world, theft, exploitation, inequality, expropriation of customary rights, destruction of valorized forms of work and leisure, imposition of industrial discipline, and insignificance and stifling effects of its arts and sciences. He lamented the loss of the very basis for preserving any sort of perspective distance on the kind of society that was emerging. The historiographical categories used to organize what was needed were rapidly being erased and replaced "from start to finish with the ideology of progress as linear, inevitable, and beneficent" (Löwy and Sayre 2001:241). For Rousseau, the immorality of modernity was that it deadened empathy and feelings of compassion for others, and this destroyed individual authenticity; it was a cry to resist the usury and commercialism of the Antichrist, the beast, embodied by contemporary society (Thompson 1963: jacket). Thus, modernity for advocates of liberalism implies the growing wealth and autonomy of the individual; for the proponents of romanticism, it implies growing inequality and a rapid descent into a Hobbesian state of nature with its war of all against all.[2] The turmoil of the late 1700s spawned other political ideologies, worldviews, and philosophies as well.[3] The most prominent of these were conservatism, anarchism, and socialism. Proponents of each were engaged in an ongoing dialog with one another as well as with liberals and romantics.

Conservatism is sometimes described as a "situational ideology" provoked by the threat or onset of rapid, potentially upsetting social change (Burke 1993[1790]). Conservatives remind us that some traditional institutions and practices are desirable or even necessary for the maintenance of social order. They raise the experience of life to the very condition necessary for life itself, emphasizing the importance of community rather than detached individuals. They appeal less to tradition itself than to the eternal truths they claim are embodied in those traditions; they often buttress their arguments with images of natural laws and an immutable human nature (Crowther 1997; Muller 1997:3–31).

The anarchists had a vision of a society that is neither authoritarian nor coercive (e.g. Godwin 1976[1793], 1998[1794]; Proudhon 1966[1840]). Instead, their concern is with individual liberty, which people acquire as they free themselves from their history and from the circumstances of their everyday lives. In their view, society and the state exist independently, and because the state claims political authority and a monopoly on the means of coercion, it impinges on the ability of individuals to fulfill their needs (i.e. freedom). As a result, in some critiques of modern capitalist society, the link between social-class position and the state is important. Many anarchists hold beliefs about innate human nature: People are naturally inclined toward mutual aid, cooperation, respect, communal relations, and voluntary associations rather than toward resorting to coercion or violence. The collectivist anarchists view social solidarity in terms of mutual aid and networks of linked but autonomous communities—that is, a federation organized from below. Over the years, anarchists have used various strategies and tactics to build a less authoritarian and coercive society (Chomsky 2003; Clark 1984:117–140; Ostergaard 2006).

The socialist movement began to crystallize during the early 1800s in reaction to the individualism, competition, and importance of private property in the increasingly capitalist society—e.g. Robert Owen (1991[1817]) and Henri de Saint-Simon (1976[1804–25]), among others. Initially, these socialists did not recognize the necessity of class struggle and instead attributed the ills of society to prevailing moral, religious, and political ideologies of the day. They advocated founding a science of human society as well as intentional communities and co-operatives. The plight and centrality of the working class became more apparent during the 1830s and 1840s, and the tensions among socialists over the adequacy of alternative explanations, strategies, and tactics intensified (Bottomore 2006; Stedman Jones 1991; Sweezy 1991).

Immanuel Wallerstein provides an accessible survey of the political debates among the proponents of the different standpoints (Wallerstein 2011:1–19). In the second half of the nineteenth century, Karl Marx, Émile Durkheim, and Max Weber engaged with the political philosophies and social theoretical perspectives sketched in the preceding paragraphs. They also provided textured analyses of the kind of industrial capitalist society that was developing at the end of the nineteenth century in an era marked by the concentration and centralization of capital, the consolidation of national states, renewed imperialism, and growing class conflict. Because they have influenced most subsequent theorists of social change and development, their perspectives are still relevant today. In fact, their views have been continually reworked for the last hundred years to explain changes associated with the development of world capitalist society. It is not erroneous to claim that virtually all the important statements made about social change and development during the twentieth century build directly or indirectly on these theorists' writings or on the debates they provoked.

Marx, Durkheim, and Weber wrestled in different ways with modernity, which proclaimed that change was directional; that old forms of society would be continually replaced by more modern ones; and that the only really significant differences were those that differentiated modern societies from traditional ones or more civilized societies (again, read: the West) from less civilized, traditional, or primitive ones. Modernization theorists, like Walt Rostow, masked the extent of social and cultural differences in the world. In their view, traditional peoples would either follow the road to capitalism that the West had taken earlier, though perhaps at a slower pace, or they would be condemned to extinction. The engine driving progress was the West—its superior technology and the capacity of its elites. The rest of the world's population—the masses in the industrial capitalist countries themselves and the members of traditional societies elsewhere—lacked agency and were either destined to follow the West's lead or forever doomed. Weber (1958[1904–1905]), for example, argued that all the world's religions except Protestantism actually impeded the growth of rational institutions and economic development.

In the industrializing countries, politicians, business leaders, and academics concerned with structuring and disciplining the labor force and repressing opposition to those efforts were always more receptive to the liberal ideas of Durkheim,

Weber, and their successors as well as to those of neoclassical economic theorists. Neoclassical theories were developed between the 1870s and the 1930s in order to explain issues such as the structure of the market; the maximization of utility or profit; the intersection of supply and demand; the allocation of scarce resources; the determination of prices, outputs, and income distribution; equilibrium and business cycles; or growth and development. Neoclassical economists, such as Alfred Marshall (1920[1890]), celebrated the market—i.e. the purchase and sale of goods and services by rational property owners. They assumed that (1) individuals and firms (they are identical in this reductive view) always act rationally and have rational preferences between alternative possible outcomes that can be identified and associated with particular values, (2) individuals seek to maximize utility and firms to maximize profit, (3) individuals and firms act independently in the market on the basis of possessing all relevant and accurate knowledge, and (4) every transaction in a free market is beneficial and just.

The Depression of the 1930s damaged the reputation of neoclassical theories, which could not account for (1) the economic crisis itself, (2) the behavior of capitalist economies under those conditions, and (3) why the market could not lift the capitalist economies out of the Depression (Wolff and Resnick 1987:7–41). John Maynard Keynes's writings from the late 1920s onward, especially *The General Theory of Employment, Income and Money* (1936), were critical of the neoclassical theorists' assumptions. He questioned concepts of "supply-side economics" (Say's Law) and market equilibrium and argued, instead, that unemployment was not the result of moral problems or laziness but rather imbalances in the demand for goods and services. Keynes urged governments to put under-utilized savings to work in order to reduce unemployment. This involved reducing interest rates (monetary policy) and investing in infrastructural development (fiscal policy) to reduce the amplitude of business cycles. Two questions concerned with the autonomy and power of the state came up repeatedly in newspapers and popular literature: Was the power of the state separate from that of the dominant class? Did it have the capacity to pursue its own interests or those of the society as a whole, even when they came into conflict with the interests of the dominant class?

The period from the 1920s to the 1970s was a time of conflict and crisis—two world wars; innumerable smaller ones; and global economic crises, some more widespread and severe than others. The other part of this historical dialectic was the effects of the Russian Revolution, national liberation or revolutionary movements in many colonial countries, and, eventually, decolonization for more than a third of the world's population. The successes of these collective undertakings were buttressed by alternative visions of what societies not dominated by capitalist or colonial social relations might be like; Lenin and others imagined societies with more egalitarian social relations and circumstances in which individuals had opportunities to fulfill their needs and achieve the real potential of being human. Because the people acting collectively to initiate change did so under conditions not of their own choosing, their actions often had unanticipated or unintended consequences because of the uncertainties of processes over which they had less than full control. The events of the mid-twentieth century showed what revolutionaries and anthropologists had long known: The actually existing political-economic, social, and cultural differences mattered. These differences were infinitely more important than theoretical distinctions drawn between modern and traditional societies that oversimplified and distorted reality. The diversity of societies also showed that the history of humanity could no longer be viewed as a mere extension of what had happened in Europe and North America.

As the events of the mid-twentieth century showed, the world was racked by contradictions, protest, and civil unrest that neither the Weberians, the Durkheimian functionalists, nor the social evolutionists, who had resurfaced, could adequately conceptualize and explain. It was also a time when Marxist theorists and those from peripheral and "less-developed" countries most successfully challenged the hegemony of liberal explanations of change and development. This did not, however, mean that the Durkheimian and Weberian strands of social theory disappeared during the mid-twentieth century. In fact, modernization theorists kept them alive and well. These theorists combined the dichotomy between traditional and modern types of society with Weber's views about rationality, bureaucracy, and political parties. Modernization theorists argued that power resided in the upper levels of an organization and agreed with Durkheim's claim that the state was the central nervous system of modern society—i.e. its prime mover and organ of moral discipline. Because power involved both the capacity to produce certain results and to command but never to completely control subordinate members, agency was the possession of the political elite. Modernization theorists linked this conceptualization of the dominance of the political realm of society with Keynesian political-economic theory. Recall that the Keynesians did not believe that an unregulated market system had the capacity to exploit the full productive potential of a society and instead argued that the state should intervene in the economy in order to stabilize demand, fluctuations in the financial sector, and prices.

The discussions that occurred in the wake of World War II produced theoretical perspectives that were more diverse and more finely textured than those crafted later as the capitalist classes and global capitalism re-established the hegemony of their discourse in the 1980s and 1990s—i.e. with the dissolution of socialism and the Eastern Bloc. Thus, many contemporary descriptions of the world today are stunningly similar to liberal accounts from the Age of Robber Barons after the American Civil War. Today, the World Bank and the International Monetary Fund have adopted neoclassical perspectives on the economy, combined them with neoliberal perspectives and policies, and recycled them to produce theories of globalization. They place the motor of change in capitalist countries, in the domestic and foreign markets that have been created, in their technologies, and in the power of their leading classes. The core capitalist areas—the United States, the European Union, and the Far East—are seen as organizing the world economy and controlling the activities of the other states. Both policy makers and academics view the significant cultural and social differences of the day largely in terms of those between the capitalist (civilized) West and the cultural Other (an analytical category, like traditional or primitive, that homogenizes diversity) who resides in less-industrialized or de-industrialized parts of the capitalist world or on its periphery. These people will either be enveloped by modern social relations as globalization, cultural imperialism, and postmodernity proceed along their current path or be left awash in their wake.

Contemporary theorists, like Manuel Castells (1996), examine the potential benefits of new information and automation technologies, and their role in transforming the global economy; at the same time, many continue to ignore the prophetic statements of Norbert Wiener, one of the pioneers of electronic communication, automated control systems, and robotics in the 1940s:

> … the automatic machine, whatever we think of any feelings it may have or may not have, is the precise economic equivalent of slave labor. Any labor which competes with slave labor must accept the economic conditions of slave labor. It is perfectly clear that this will produce an unemployment situation in comparison with which the present recession and even the depression of the thirties will seem like a pleasant joke. This depression will ruin many industries—possibility even the industries which have taken advantage of the new potentialities. However, there is nothing in the industrial tradition, which forbids an industrialist to make a sure and quick profit, and to get out before the crash touches him personally. Thus the new revolution is a two-edged sword.
>
> (Wiener 1954[1950]:162)

Other analysts, like Benedict Anderson (1983) and Michael Bray (2015), write about the resurgence of nationalism; the rise of nationalist, populist, or fascist movements; and the dangers they pose—intensified boundary-marking and protection or ethnic cleansing. Others, like Michael Hardt and Antonio Negri (2000), see the declining influence of states and growing importance of supranational organizations that monitor economic policies, and strive to make those policies more receptive to free trade—e.g. the G7 or the World Trade Organization. Some explore the influence of "too big to fail" transnational corporations on the social and economic policies of states. Other neoliberal theorists and politicians—e.g. the former Prime Minister of Great Britain (Margaret Thatcher) and former president of the United States (Ronald Reagan)—proclaimed that society does not exist: It is an illusion, merely an aggregate of self-interested individuals who engage in market exchange to satisfy their every need and desire. In 2010, the U.S. Supreme Court even decreed that corporations are individuals!

Ignoring state and corporate policies whose purpose is to impede or prevent workers from organizing unions or class-based political parties, still other commentators on the human condition decry efforts to organize collectively and argue that most of the world's population lacks the power or the will to initiate structural changes that will address issues ranging from the myriad faces of inequality to the consequences of environmental destruction, global climate change, and repeated denials of a factual basis for knowledge itself. At best, in their view, agency involves individual acts of resistance in which individuals mark themselves or their bodies in ways that establish an identity that they might possibly share with others in a world that is increasingly shaped by consumerism and Janus-faced desires to be simultaneously different from and the same as others.

This Book and Its Organization

The processes of social change set in motion by the development of capitalism have had profound, long-lasting consequences and implications. They affected the views of late-nineteenth-century theorists—like Marx, Durkheim, and Weber—who sought to explain them as well as those of later theorists, who have had to cope with both the changes that occurred and with the views of their predecessors. As a result, our understanding of social change in the twentieth century has developed through a series of ongoing dialogs, both imagined and real, between theorists with different points of view.

Social theorists have usually viewed change either as a quantitative alteration in the form of society or as the replacement of one type of society by another. However, this statement is complicated by the fact that most of them—including Marx, Durkheim, and Weber—have portrayed the *idea* of change in terms of analogies, metaphors, and synonyms that convey subtle differences of meaning and evoke a wide range of images. For example, they have depicted change as movement, growth, unfolding, emergence, metamorphosis, maturation, succession, progression, alteration, modification, refashioning, evolution, mutation, transformation, progress, development, advancement, enhancement, gain, improvement, and modernization.

Chapter 1 briefly explores the language—the analogies, the metaphors, and the subtle differences of synonyms—used to portray change as motion in time. These are palimpsests constructed over the last 2,500 years; they have continually gained and lost nuances of meaning during the process of sedimentation. Analysts have produced a series of seemingly contradictory explanations of change, both of what happened and the processes involved. Is social change directional or not? Is it the unfolding of some potential deepness in the soul of society that culminated in some final end-product, like civilization, or merely a series of oscillations and cycles? Is it a slow, gradual, continuous process or a sudden metamorphosis? Is it a consequence of motors internal to society itself or of external forces and events that impinge from outside to modify, direct, or disrupt the normal course of development?

Chapter 2 examines theories that Marx, Durkheim, and Weber formulated between the 1840s and early 1920s to account for the development of industrial capitalism and modern industrial society. Their theories are important today because they have had a continuing influence on virtually all subsequent writers who have dealt with issues of social change. Each of them made use of the theories discussed in the preceding chapter. Marx argued that classical political economists ignored the historical specificity of capitalist social relations when they failed to distinguish between different kinds of class structures and forms of exploitation. Durkheim was concerned with the rise of individualism, the cult of the individual, and the breakdown of traditional social relations in industrial society. In his view, the real foundations of society resided in the religious, moral, and legal institutions that regulated behavior rather than in the social relations shaped by market exchange and an economy that had become separated from other realms of the social being. Weber focused his attention on the historical political economy and the role of national economic policies and the state; he considered the interplay of increasing industrialization, instrumental rationality, and notions of scientific progress and efficiency in more detail as they penetrated into realms of life—values, habits, customs, and traditions. Additionally, in the wake of World War I, he feared the "iron cage" of industrial organizations and state bureaucracies, on the one hand, and what he saw as the irrationality of mass movements, on the other.

Chapter 3 explores how social theorists conceptualized the consequences of the interrelated formation of industrial capitalism, nation-states, and a new kind of imperialism between the 1880s and 1914. This development fueled economic expansion and territorial acquisition as the states scrambled for overseas markets and investment opportunities and vied with one another to gain territorial possessions and to extend their political power into regions, such as Africa or Asia, where the indigenous populations were too numerous to crush and too culturally different to be easily assimilated. As the imperial states consolidated their overseas empires, their relations with the inhabitants of their new territories shifted from occurring in ministries of foreign relations to occurring in offices of colonial affairs and departments of the interior. The statuses of the formerly autonomous inhabitants of those possessions shifted to those of colonial subjects, indigenous or tribal peoples, or national or racial minorities. There was a resurgence of nationalism surrounding the efforts to achieve political unification in the Balkans, Germany, and Italy; the struggles to free Poland from Russia and Hungary from Austria; and the nascent attempts of the newly constituted colonial subjects, especially in Asia, to free themselves from their imperial overlords. Nationalism and xenophobia were also fueled in imperial states—like the United States, which had its origins in settler colonies—by the tens of millions of people from Eastern and Central Europe who emigrated in search of work and eventually found it in racially and ethnically stratified labor markets. The lives of rural peoples and colonial subjects on the margins of capitalist economy and society were transformed as capitalist production relations penetrated the countryside.

Chapter 4 examines how analysts explained the processes of change unleashed by imperialist expansion in the late nineteenth century and the crises these processes provoked—the ones that underpinned the two world wars, the Great Depression, and socialist revolutions during the first half of the twentieth century. Analysts had different standpoints. Liberal theorists building on neoclassical economic models saw the crises as the result of forces that were external to the nation-state. Marxians viewed them as fundamental features of capitalism, which had both economic and political dimensions. World War I left unsettled conditions in its wake, and the political map of the world was re-drawn as territories changed hands, and new countries appeared. It was a time of revolutionary turmoil. Civil wars waged in Mexico, Russia, China, Bavaria, and Hungary. A variety of socialist states emerged—some lasting a few months, others continuing for decades. The imperialist nation-states had to confront old issues: the incorporation of new peoples into their polities; the rise of nationalist movements, especially in the colonies; the penetration of capitalist social relations into the countryside; and the expansion of capitalism at home and abroad. The socialist states that developed in the Soviet Union and later in China had to deal with these issues as well as industrialization and the transition to some variety of socialism. This involved confronting the issue of the articulation of socialist, capitalist, and pre- or non-capitalist sectors of their economies and societies, and establishing policies, institutions, and practices that would facilitate social transformation into a socialist society. The closing section of the chapter raises the specter of how the philanthropic foundations established in the United States influenced and shaped understandings of the processes of social change.

Chapter 5 looks at how social theorists grappled with the issues of change after World War II in a milieu shaped by the Cold War politics and national liberation movements. The United States precipitated the Cold War in 1946 to contain the expansion of socialism. The Cold War pitted the West against the Soviet Union, the socialist states established in Eastern Europe, and socialist and communist parties in their own countries. Nationalists seized opportunities provided by the weakness of the colonial powers after the war to proclaim their independence or to launch popular struggles for political autonomy. By 1960, 1.3 billion people—a third of the world's population—had gained independence, and the number of independent countries in Africa and Asia increased from a handful to more than fifty. Decolonization created a Third World out of the non-aligned states that attempted to be neither capitalist nor socialist. It pitted the poor countries of the emerging Third World against the capitalist colonial powers and quickly became the major arena of Cold War struggle. From 1946 onwards, liberal analysts underpinned theories of capitalist economic growth and modernization by recycling social evolutionism and the ideas of progress and modernity. By contrast, Third World and Marxian writers pointed out that the world economy was characterized by uneven development and that the poor countries were not, in fact, becoming more similar to the capitalist ones. In addition, both theorists and activists investigated national and rural class structures in the colonies, their linkages, and their potential as agents of reform or revolutionary social change. Social scientists with an evolutionary perspective saw analogies between the contemporary conditions of the Third World countries and those that had prevailed in the West during the transition from feudalism to capitalism.

Chapter 6 reviews how theorists have explained the crises that have occurred almost non-stop on a worldwide scale since the mid-1970s. Liberal and neoliberal analysts argue that existing theories do not adequately account for what happened because of a major break with the past in the last quarter of the twentieth century. This break was marked by the widespread adoption of neoliberal social thought and policies, the globalization of capitalism, the dissolution of socialism, the emergence of the postmodern condition and postmodernity, and rapid technological innovations in robotics and information-sharing devices (including computers, the internet, and cell phones). Marxian commentators depict the changes in terms of capital accumulation on an increasingly global scale—the new imperialism—and do not view them as so epochal or transformative. They debate whether or not the global hegemony of the United States, which was established during World War II, has persisted or waned since the 1970s. On a related tack, it is clear that the National Question—issues of national identity and ideology in a context shaped by state formation and modernity—continues unabated. Nationalist, populist, and fascist movements have thrived in this milieu, and their governments continue to intervene in the politics of other countries as they have done for more than two centuries. But these movements once again raise issues of identity and question what happens when identities intersect as they always do. The final issue examined is concerned with the relationship between the ongoing environmental crisis and global capitalism; its focus is on the fact that the fundamental relationship between capitalists is competition, and cooperation among them is merely historically contingent.

Notes

1 Former slaves, like James McCune Smith (2006[1841]) and Frederick Douglass (1857), were well aware of the dialectic of the master-slave relationship. W. E. B. Du Bois (1969 [1903]), for example, described the "double-consciousness" of subjugated communities whose members have multiple simultaneous identities.

2 There were two major strands to romanticism, both reactions to the Industrial Revolution and the aristocratic social and political norms of The Enlightenment. One sought a return to or revival of a bygone golden age or condition; the other provided underpinnings for the French and Haitian Revolutions and for others that erupted around the world between the 1820s and the 1850s (Thompson 1997).

3 The concept of ideology is contemporaneous with the rise of industrial capitalism and the proliferation of political perspectives that were given names in the 1820s and 1830s. It has two meanings: a positive one signifying "a worldview" (a set of values, beliefs, etc. constituting a comprehensive outlook of the world) and a pejorative one suggesting "false thinking" or "false consciousness" (justification or promotion of a set of political beliefs). This points to a dialectic between the two meanings and to close connections with the concepts of "worldview" (a set of values and beliefs that constitute a comprehensive outlook on the world) and "philosophy" (a body of knowledge). Antonio Gramsci saw "the distinction between philosophy and ideology as a quantitative one, related to the level of social, political and historical coherence of conceptions of the world" (Thomas 2010:278). Ferruccio Rossi-Landi (1990:18–21) provided a useful visual image of their relationship to one another and to the concept of worldview. He represented them in terms of a clockface with false consciousness (minimal seriousness, consciousness, or generality) at 6 o'clock, philosophy (maximum seriousness, consciousness, and generality) at noon, ideology as worldview at 3, and ideology as false thinking at 9 o'clock. The clock's hand can move either clockwise or counterclockwise. As it sweeps around the face, its movement is simultaneously positional and relational, depicting the precipitation of a worldview and its crystallization into a philosophy or of false consciousness into false thinking.

1

The Language of Change
Motion in Time

There have been moments when established explanations of social change no longer provided satisfactory accounts of what had happened or what was taking place. One of these moments occurred during the widespread contacts between Africans, Asians, and Europeans during the middle half of the first millennium B.C. (Bernal 1987; Jaspers 1953[1949]). A second coincided with the restructuring of the world economy that began in the mid-fourteenth century (Abu-Lughod 1989; Needham 1969). A third occurred in the aftermath of the crystallization of industrial capitalist society and empire from the late eighteenth century onwards (Hobsbawm 1968; Pomerantz 2000). Recognizing the novelty of these moments impelled commentators to develop new vocabularies to describe and explain changes that had been set in motion. Social theorists have typically formulated and refined their explanations of change in terms of concepts and ideas that were already part of the intellectual language they inherited from previous generations. While some analysts recycled earlier accounts, others refined them, and a few came up with truly novel insights about the processes of change. The thesis of this book is that the changes set in motion during the nineteenth century have had profound, long-lasting consequences and implications. They not only affected the views of the late-nineteenth-century analysts and critics—like Karl Marx, Émile Durkheim, and Max Weber—who sought to explain what was happening. The views of Marx, Durkheim, and Weber have, in turn, influenced the perspectives of their successors as they have struggled to understand the world we live in.

Let us briefly consider what the word "change" means. On the one hand, it can mean a movement or shift from one place to another, usually with the implication that a passage of time occurred. On the other, it can mean a substitution of one thing for another; the succession of one thing by another; flux or flow, implying a continuous series of movements or actions; and growth, metamorphosis, or transformation—the appearance of new characteristics. These metaphors and synonyms involve spans of time and imply the existence of a past, a present, and a future. Some images suggest directionality or movement toward an end-product—e.g. development, progress, growth, or modernization. They may invoke (1) causal-mechanical descriptions or explanations of successions of events that investigate the extent to which the past causes the present, (2) teleological accounts that treat past and present temporalities (the condition of being temporary) as either descriptions *or* explanations of movement toward some future end or goal, or (3) present-oriented accounts that seek to shed light on how the past and the future are continually reconstructed in the present. Other accounts may not involve directionality. Of course, the idea and the reality of change raise other questions as well: Does it occur slowly, gradually, and continuously, or is it punctuated, discontinuous, and variable in rate—i.e. a series of revolutions? Is change in the past different from change in the present?

In this chapter, I want to briefly examine the more influential theories that have been proposed to explain social change and development and to consider the circumstances in which they emerged. Nineteenth- and twentieth-century social theorists have built on the images, analogies, metaphors, and synonyms used by earlier analysts to describe processes of change in the explanation of capitalist development and imperialism. These models still influence how we understand the processes being described.

Change as Recurrence and Renewal

Ionian commentators who lived in Asia Minor on the edges of the Persian Empire during the middle half of the first millennium B.C. sought to account for the origins of world they lived in. The poet Hesiod (c. 750–650 B.C.) imagined a world that began in complete chaos, which begat a genealogy of gods, each connected with a part of the physical world and each struggling violently with the others in a Hollywood-style family drama that underpins the world as it is coming to be. As you recall, Zeus eventually triumphs in this drama by destroying the powers that threatened the world and by establishing order among the remaining gods. In another poem, Hesiod describes the world differently as successive degradation from a golden age in which humans intermingled on almost equal terms with the gods in conditions of peace, prosperity, and harmony (order) to a current one beset by pain and evil (Curd 2012). In both images, society is a world in flux, completely under the control of external forces. Similarly, Homer, who was Hesiod's contemporary, depicted the trials and tribulations of human beings who lived nearly five centuries earlier at the time of the Trojan War. They too had little effective control over their lives in a world that, as depicted by Homer, was saturated by gods. Hesiod and Homer were poets who envisioned a world structured by social order and disrupted by social changes emanating from above.

The pre-Socratic philosophers, who lived in Ionia fifty to two hundred years later, were already engaged in a dialog with their predecessors and with each other. They were less concerned with explaining the creation of the existing world (cosmogony) than with understanding it as a totality in time and space (cosmology). This totality (*kosmos* or ordered arrangement) was an organized whole whose structure and development, while not immediately apparent, could be discovered through rational inquiry and observation. It was inherently intelligible and not subject to super-natural intervention (Curd 2012). The philosophers did, however, agree with their predecessors to the extent that both saw the present state of affairs as deriving from some initial situation or set of conditions, and both believed that change operates "according to the order of time." For Anaximenes (585–528 B.C.), air was the base material found everywhere; it was acted upon by the natural forces of compression and decompression. Compaction transformed air successively into wind, clouds, water, and stone; the force of decompression caused stone to turn into water, water into clouds, clouds into wind, and wind into air. Because one material was more basic than others, change was not necessarily directional; it could be sequential, but it could also be cyclical, periodic, and random, accidental, or not fixed by necessity (i.e. contingent) (Graham 2003; White 2008). The appearance of human beings merely represented the latest stage in the development of the cosmos.

Heraclitus of Ephesus (544–483 B.C.) attempted to answer two questions posed by his predecessors: What causes change? What is the mechanism that drives change? While he built on some of their arguments, he rejected others, most noticeably their notion of a single generating substance (Baert 2006; Graham 2008). Heraclitus argued (1) that the cosmos was a "unity of opposites"—simultaneously change and non-change (continuity)—recalling his remark that a road that goes downhill is, at the same time, one that goes uphill; (2) that the cosmos is in a continual state of flux because of the continually shifting interrelation of change and permanence; (3) that the world is changed through transformations ordered in and by time; (4) that time is responsible for the existence of a stable world; (5) that the cosmos exists through the transformation of substances into one another; (6) that the substances are not permanent; and (7) that fire is simultaneously the most unstable (changeable) and the most enduring of his predecessors' generating substances, and it is also the one into which everything else turns. In other words, both change and permanence are constant and continually interacting features of the cosmos, and both may occur simultaneously at different levels of the totality; this was the basis for his comment that no one could step twice in the same river so long as the water flows continuously over their feet from one instant to the next, even though it may do so in a seemingly unchanging stream bed. Philosopher Daniel Graham (1997:44) notes that Heraclitus's

> transcendent insight is to see that constancy and flux, like all other opposites, are interdependent: constancy requires ongoing change and ongoing change produces stability. But stability and change are not ontologically equivalent: stability is supervenient [i.e. something additional] on change, so that change is prior to constancy, process is prior to substance.

To describe this theory, Heraclitus fell back on the familiar language of life and death as well as of recurrence and renewal. In doing so, he laid the foundations for future debates about the nature of human society and of social change.

Democritus (460–370 B.C.) was also concerned with questions about the composition of the cosmos and the reason for change. He conceptualized the universe as infinite, a totality composed simultaneously of both small irreducible, unchangeable particles (atoms) and voids (non-particles or bodies). Atoms inexplicably concentrate in particulars regions of the cosmos, form a vortex, collide with increasing frequency, and adhere together to produce worlds like ours.

In the process, like things, both inanimate and animate, were attracted to one another. This provided an explanation of the beginnings and growth of human society. At the beginning, human beings foraged individually and lived lives of hardship; they gradually came together and formed communities for mutual aid. With their hands, language, and shrewd minds, they created arts and crafts to satisfy their growing needs. In this view, human beings are interdependent. Moreover, they are analogous to city-states. The gradual process of change that occurred was not without difficulties because there were both good men and evil ones, and strife between them undermined the ability of the community to provide for the common good. In Democritus's view the way to avoid strife and maintain order was to redistribute wealth from the rich to the poor (Cartledge 1999; Cole 1967:107–147; Hussey 1985:119–120).

The social milieu in which Democritus and his Ionian contemporaries— notably the historian Herodotus (484–425 B.C.) and tragedian Aeschylus (525– 456 B.C.)—wrote was shaped by the Persian colonization of Asia Minor, the Ionian revolt against the Persian state, the subsequent destruction of Ionian cities during the disastrous defeat they suffered in 494 B.C. at the hands of the Persians and their allies, and the subsequent re-incorporation of the Ionians into the empire. It was a time of crisis for many Ionians. It was also a time when the Greeks were clarifying ideas about their identity and their relationships with their neighbors. They busied themselves with inventing the identities/concepts of Greeks, barbarians (all non-Greeks), and Persians and creating images of them (Ste. Croix 1972, 1981; Hall 1989). Their quest involved considering alternative accounts of the human past, alternative accounts of their non-Greek-speaking contemporaries and what they could teach them about Greek society and the human condition more generally, and alternative visions of what the best future might be.

Theories of change that involve notions of recurrence and renewal gain currency in times of flux (Trompf 1979). For example, between the fourteenth and sixteenth centuries, the nature of commerce, the distribution of wealth, and uses of the past were transformed in the Mediterranean world. Historical scholarship enjoyed a resurgence in both Mediterranean North Africa and Europe as thinkers struggled to explain what had happened to the traditional social order. Civil servants, clerics, politicians, and merchants began to study ancient texts and monuments (Ibn Khaldun 1967[1377]; Rowe 1965; Weiss 1988). They revived the ideas of writers from Classical Antiquity whose views were preserved in the copyists' archives of monasteries and medieval universities and gradually subsumed Muslim knowledge and science into a common Renaissance European culture (Makdisi 1981; Rodinson 1987[1980]:23–44). Many intellectuals believed they could regain the freedom lost during the Middle Ages by retrieving and developing the capacities possessed by the ancient Greeks and Romans. In the process, they not only portrayed the artisans and writers of the classical world as models of excellence to be emulated but also began to see history as a series of cyclical ups and downs—recurrences caused by outside forces impinging on a relatively fixed human nature. One writer, Niccolò Machiavelli (1469–1527), described it in the following way:

Usually provinces go most of the time, in the changes they make, from order to disorder and then pass again from disorder to order, for worldly things are not allowed by nature to stand still. As soon as they reach their ultimate perfection, having no further to rise, they must descend; and similarly, once they have descended and through their disorders arrived at the ultimate depth, since they cannot descend further, of necessity they must rise. Thus they are always descending from good to bad and rising from bad to good.

(Machiavelli 1988[1525]:185)

Recurrence theories of history—the idea that history repeats itself or that change is cyclical—have been around for more than two thousand and five hundred years (Caponigri 1968; Trompf 1979). Oswald Spengler, who had studied Heraclitus, invoked these theories when he wrote the widely read *Decline of the West* (1918–1922) in the wake of World War I and the disastrous consequences of the Treaty of Versailles for Germany. Arnold Toynbee began his twelve-volume *A Study of History* (1934–1961) during the Great Depression of the 1930s; he argued that civilizations are born as a response to challenges. They grow when their creative minorities successfully meet new challenges, and they decline when these elite "makers and shakers" become enamored with their past successes and fail either to recognize or to confront new challenges. Theories of cyclical change also involve characterizations of present conditions and comparisons with those that prevailed or that are presumed to have characterized particular societies or periods of time in the past—like the Middle Ages (e.g. Cantor 1991; Diamond 2005).

Change as Teleology, Change as Growth

Not every analyst of change in ancient Greece agreed with the atomic theory of the pre-Socratics or with Heraclitus's view that the world was ordered by a continual state of flux.[1] For example, Empedocles (c. 490–430 B.C.) claimed that change was merely an illusion, and Plato (427–347 B.C.) argued that ideas, not flux, were the ordering principle for the reality of objects in the world. Aristotle (384–322 B.C.) was concerned with the causes of change and observed that his predecessors and contemporaries had variously attributed them to luck (Empedocles), necessity and spontaneity (Democritus), intelligence (Anaxagoras), god (Socrates), and form (Plato) (Johnson 2005; Woodfield 1976). He complained that their answers were reductive in the sense that they sought to explain the cosmos and living things solely in terms of matter, motion, and necessity. Aristotle pointed out that they did not distinguish clearly between inanimate objects and living things. He also observed that they were actually asking two different kinds of questions. One question involved explaining the causes of *kinesis* (the growth, alteration, or movement of a material), and the other was concerned with explaining the final cause of the motion—i.e. its purpose, goal, aim, or function in a state of completion, or *telos*—a Greek word that philosopher Monte Johnson (2005:64–88) suggests is better translated as "that for the sake of which" or "the cause for the sake of which." Because change, causes, and purposes exist in inanimate as well as animate nature, complete explanations must answer the two questions for both the cosmos and living organisms.

Aristotle argued that nature is inherent in a body and that the body moves according to the principles it embodies. He discerned four principles of change: (1) locomotion or change of place in space, (2) generation and destruction, (3) growth and diminution—a change in quantity, and (4) alteration or qualitative change. In his view, the circular rotation of celestial objects and the eternal moving and resting of terrestrial bodies, which seek to imitate them, are explained by the realization of the principle of locomotion. This is also true of those inanimate elements that move from one cosmic realm to another and evince the principle of continual generation and destruction—e.g. seasonal rainfall in the Mediterranean world and its complex interrelations with the aspirations of farmers. Animals, which provide many of Aristotle's examples of teleology, manifest all of the principles of change. In general, he argues that living organisms benefit from their organs and their developmental and temporal motion—e.g. the function or purpose of the development of the eye from embryo to adult is to see, and the function of a person's walking after dinner is to aid in the digestion of food in the near run and to promote health in the long run. The former demonstrates the development of an organ through time, and the latter demonstrates a sequential order of actions through time. Both facilitate survival and reproduction.

Recall that in *Politics*, Aristotle regards human beings as "political animals" whose principle relationships occur in the household or the city. In his view, the city is a totality that has an existence prior to its interdependent parts—i.e. a city can exist without citizens or households as long as it has a legitimate governor. Its purpose is self-sufficiency, and it comes into existence for the sake of a good life, a contemplative life, so that its citizens can devote themselves to the study of the cycles of nature's growth, decline, and renewal. In Aristotle's words,

> Every state is a community of some kind, and every community is established with a view to some good; for everyone always acts in order to obtain that which they think is good. But, if all communities aim at some good, the state or political community, which is the highest of all, and which embraces all the rest, aims at good in a greater degree than any other, and at the highest good.
>
> (*Politics* 1252ª1–6)

> He who thus considers things in their first growth and origin, whether a state or anything else, will obtain the clearest view of them. In the first place there must be a union of those who cannot exist without each other; namely, of male and female, that the race may continue (and this is a union which is formed, not of choice, but because, in common with other animals and with plants, mankind have a natural desire to leave behind them an image of themselves), and of a natural ruler and subject.
>
> (*Politics* 1252ª24–31)

Out of these two relationships [i.e. with wife and slave] the first thing to rise is the family.

(*Politics* 1252^{b}10)

When several families are united, and the association aims at something more than the supply of daily needs, the first society to be formed is the village.

(*Politics* 1252^{b}16–18)

When several villages are united in a single complete community, large enough to be nearly or quite self-sufficing, the state [city] comes into existence. Hence it is evident that the state is a creation of nature, and that man is by nature a political animal.

(*Politics* 1252^{b}28–29, 1253^{a}2–3)

Further, the state [city] is by nature clearly prior to the family and to the individual, since the whole is of necessity prior to the part.

(*Politics* 1253^{a}19–20; Aristotle 1984 [c. 350 B.C.]:1986–1988)

In this view, the city-state unfolded in a fixed sequence of stages from coming-to-be and passing-away. When one state decayed or degenerated, it was replaced by another. For Aristotle, the processes necessary for the formation of states in general could be studied scientifically, while the historically specific events that affected the development of particular states could not because there could be no science of the accidental (Nisbet 1969:38–40).

Aristotle and his successors schooled in classical Greek and Roman philosophy exerted a profound influence over early and medieval writers concerned with human society and social change (Furley 1999). St Augustine's (A.D. 354–430) *City of God* was the most influential fusion of Greek views on the growth and decay of society with the biblical account of humanity's relation to God. Augustine was not concerned with the history of the Roman world per se but rather with the problems that the imperial state confronted and, more importantly, with the possibilities that might be open to human beings in the future. However, in order to understand the problems and options available, he believed that it was necessary to know how the world had come to be the way it was. This meant examining Roman history in terms of the same theory of growth and decay employed by other writers of classical antiquity: "There is a process of education, through the epochs of a people's history, as through the successive stages of a man's life, designed to raise them from the temporal and the visible to an apprehension of the eternal and the invisible" (*City of God*, Bk. X, Ch. 14; Augustine 1984 [early fifth century]:392). For Augustine, conflict between the baser and nobler sides of human nature was the motor that drove human history and promoted the growth and decay of society. It began when Cain murdered Abel, and it was exhibited again at the founding of Rome when Romulus murdered his brother Remus.

When Augustine fused the growth analogy with the biblical account, he was forced to argue, unlike his pagan predecessors, that there was only one cycle of human existence. It began with Adam and would culminate with an eternal, unchanging state of grace. This meant that human history could be divided into three great epochs: pre-Christian, post-Christian, and the future. While the pre-Christian epoch corresponded to nature, and the post-Christian epoch was marked by the rule of law, the future would be an eternity marked by grace, a time of continuous unchanging morality, justice, and service (Deane 1963:91–92).

Augustine's reworking of the growth analogy dominated Western ideas about social change until the twelfth-century Renaissance (Burns 1988; Burns and Goldie 1991; Lerner and Mahdi 1963). Clerics and scholars had translated all but one of Aristotle's works between 1120 and 1270 as well as a number of Arabic works on science and medicine, which were written largely in the wake of the Spanish Reconquest of the Iberian Peninsula in 1492. These had a major impact on theological writing, and the dominance of the Augustinian worldview waned with the influx of both Classical and Arabic writers into the canon. The Scholastic philosophers of Western Europe on the periphery of the Arab world and Ireland, where Greek continued to be taught in monasteries during the Middle Ages, were leaders in the effort to reconcile Christian theology with the new knowledge. While the Franciscan friars defended Augustine, the Dominicans made extensive use of various Aristotelian and Neoplatonic works after the twelfth century. Scholars and merchants combined elements of Judeo-Christian, Arab, and Persian thought. They believed that humanity could regain the freedom it had lost in medieval times by retrieving and developing capacities that the ancient Greeks and Romans had possessed nearly two thousand years earlier. In the process, medieval scholars began to see history as a series of cyclical ups and downs—recurrences caused by outside forces impinging on a relatively fixed human nature. The idea that historical change was cyclical had been widespread among certain circles of Hellenistic society. What the social theorists of Renaissance Europe actually did was portray the artisans and writers of Greece and Rome as models of excellence worthy of emulation. In the process, they revived and recycled ideas and works that were virtually extinguished in Western Europe after Rome was sacked in 410.

Change as Progress, Change as Becoming Modern

The fifteenth to eighteenth centuries were tumultuous times. They were marked by a number of processes that mutually shaped and reinforced one another. These included (1) the formation of merchant empires and overseas colonies in the Americas, Africa, and Asia by the countries of Northern and Western Europe (Tracy 1990); (2) the rise of anti-authoritarian sentiments, skepticism, and appeals to reason or rationality rather than to religion, faith, or belief, which challenged and eroded the divinely ordained authority claimed by the churches and aristocracy, especially after the Protestant Reformation of the sixteenth century in Northern and Western Europe (Israel 2001; Popkin 1979); (3) the "scientific revolution"—also known as the "conquest of nature" or the "death of nature"—beginning in the late 1550s in Europe, which involved the assimilation of a new understanding of nature into the wider culture and society because of the desire of the emerging commercial classes for technological innovations and the erosion of barriers separating intellectuals and artisans (Forbes 1968; Jacob 1988; Merchant 1980; Zilsel 2003); and (4) the rise of industrial capitalism (the Industrial Revolution and industrial society), which, from about 1750 onward, involved new forms of manufacture that were based on the continual adoption of technological innovations, new forms of social relations, and the hardening of the distinction between city and countryside (Hobsbawm 1968).

This period—referred to sequentially by historians as Later Middle Ages, the Renaissance or Early Modern Europe (or the Late Renaissance, Reformation, and Counter-Reformation), and The Enlightenment (the Age of Reason)—was marked by almost continuous conflicts between Catholics, Lutherans, Calvinists, and other Protestant fringe movements from the 1520s onward. Some claim that the religious wars and the major intellectual turmoil that erupted first in the Dutch Republic and the Calvinist states of Germany were "Europe's prime engine of cultural and educational change" (Israel 2001:23). These were fueled in no small part by the development of efficient printing presses and the publication of books translated into various vernaculars and national languages (Anderson 1991; Febvre and Henri-Jean Martin 1976). Besides the ideological and political strife that formed the backdrop of everyday life, there were probably no more than a few decades between 1550 and 1830 in which peace prevailed, and wars were not being waged somewhere in the world. The impact of these disputes was not limited to intellectuals or to the soldiers and sailors who died in the battles. More than one aristocrat and preacher of the day lamented that "even the common people were susceptible to new ideas" (Israel 2001:1, 8–9)!

One thing that distinguished some writers of the late sixteenth century from their immediate predecessors was that they began to periodize human history. In effect, they invented the Middle Ages as a period of time and a set of cultural beliefs that differed not only from those of their present but also from those of the Greek and Roman worlds of Classical Antiquity (Rowe 1965). Thus, scholars laid the foundations for a "perspective distance" from the past and a distinction between the past and the present that was based in facts that were observable in the modern world rather than on traditions passed down from earlier times (Baron 1938, 1939; Maravall 1986[1975]; Panofsky 1957). They soon began to apply this perspective distance to societies they encountered in other parts of the world (Kinser 1971).

Change as progress was a worldview endorsed by those who saw themselves benefiting from emerging structures of power relations.[2] From this view, progress implied a form of uni-directional change in which "mankind has slowly, gradually and continually advanced from the original condition of deprivation, ignorance, and insecurity to constantly higher levels of civilization, and that such advancement will, with only occasional setbacks, continue through the present into the future" (Nisbet 1980:10). This metaphor of change simultaneously (1) rejects the classical writers' imagery of change as growth; (2) accepts their understandings of past and present temporalities but not their vision of the future ones—i.e. the idea of repeated decline, renewal, and recurrence; and (3) accepts Augustine's representations of the human condition in past and present times, his notion of change as an unfolding of human potential under circumstances directed by an eternal force emanating from within or without, and his vision of what an unchanging future temporality might or could be like as long as the engine continues to operate unimpeded and without being derailed (Rotenstreich 1971).

In the late 1570s, José de Acosta (1540–1600), the King of Spain's Jesuit emissary to the Pope, constructed a typology of non-Christian societies based on the kinds of idolatries their members practiced and on the methods needed to bring about their conversion. Monarchies like China and Japan had writing and governments; consequently, their members could be converted through peaceful teaching. There were also illiterate barbarians, like the Aztecs and the Incas in the Americas, who had governments and fixed places of residence but lacked the intelligence and reasoning ability of the ancient Greeks and Romans; their conversion required a strong Christian ruler who would enforce their adherence to Christianity. Finally, there were savages, like the inhabitants of the Amazon basin, who lacked laws, government, and permanent settlements; their conversion could only be accomplished by force and required the collaboration of soldiers and missionaries (Rowe 1964:16–18). Acosta proceeded to outline how one social type changed into another. He argued that

> Famous authors maintain by plausible conjectures that for a very long time these barbarians had no kings nor any regularly constituted state organization but lived promiscuously in bands after the fashion of the Floridans, the Brazilians, the Chiriguaná and numerous other Indian nations, who have no regular kings but hastily improvise leaders as the fortune of war or peace requires and try out whatever behavior lust or anger suggest. With the passage of time, however, men outstanding for strength and diligence began to rule by tyranny, as Nimrod did in times past. Increasing gradually [in power], they constituted the state organization which our people found among the Peruvians and Mexicans, an organization which, though barbarous, was very different from the barbarism of the rest of the Indians. Reason itself, therefore, leads to the conclusion that this savage kind of men has proceeded principally from barbarous and fugitive men.
>
> (Acosta quoted by Rowe 1964:19)

In Acosta's view, the development from savagery to barbarism occurred only in the New World, presumably because there was nothing in the biblical account resembling the stage of primitive savagery. This slot was filled by images of wild men, savages, and other fabled beings who dwelt in forests or in legendary, previously unknown lands (e.g. Bernheimer 1952; Dudley and Novak 1972). By the end of sixteenth century, writers were portraying savages as naked cannibals with increasing frequency (Forsyth 1983).

While many sixteenth-century writers did not believe that Acosta's typology actually represented historical development or a genealogical sequence that unfolded over time, Louis Le Roy (c. 1510–1577)—humanist, professor of classics, diplomat, and advisor to the French king—did. In 1575, he referred to Plato's claim in *Protagoras* that the first human beings were naked forest-dwellers and drew an obvious inference, stating that the ancient inhabitants of Europe must have been as rude and as uncivilized as the contemporary forest-dwelling savages discovered by the Portuguese and Spaniards in Africa and the Americas (Defert 1982; Moser 1998). They were

> ... not civil by nature, nor governed by discipline, nor conjoined in habitations, neither do they sowe or plant; helpe themselves little or nothing with manury [manual] trades; exchange in their bargaining one thing for another, not knowing the use of money; but living without houses, townes, cities... dwelling in fields....
> (Le Roy quoted in Hodgen 1964:199)

These forest-dwellers progressed from their primitive, original condition to a more advanced one by means of intellectual, moral, and social progress. In this civilizing process, they passed through a series of stages:

> Now whereas men have taken nourishment, first of tame beasts, before either of graine or of fruits: there is no doubt but that pasturage, grasing, and shepheardie, were before husbandry and tillage.... The tillage and planting of the earth have bin both invented after pasturage, and unto both have bin added hunting, fowling, and fishing.
> (Le Roy *Vicissitudes* quoted in Hodgen 1964:466–467)

Earlier in 1568, Le Roy had used the verb *civiliser* (to civilize) to describe the process by which change from a primitive natural condition—primitive in the sense of the first in a series or sequence—to a more advanced one by means of moral, intellectual, and social progress (Huppert 1971:769).

A few years later in 1586, his contemporary—Jean Bodin (1530–1596), a political theorist and another advisor to the French king—used the idea of progress to propose a theory of universal history (Bodin 1945[1596]:291–302). He argued that human history was divided into three periods, each more civilized than the last. Each period was dominated by the peoples of a particular region. The Oriental peoples—the Babylonians, Persians, and Egyptians—dominated the first two millennia because of their innovations in religion, philosophy, and mathematics as well as their ability to unravel the secrets of nature. The Mediterranean peoples—the Greeks and Romans—reigned for the next two millennia because of their practical knowledge, gifted statesmanship, and politics. Finally, the Northern nations came to the fore because of their skill in warfare and their mechanical inventions. Shifts in history's center of gravity were the result of geographical and climatic conditions acting on peoples who had different instincts, desires, and capacities for self-preservation. In other words, Bodin laid the foundations for a theory of historical development that is still dominant in many parts of the world today: Civilization began in the Holy Land, passed to Greece and Rome, and then reached its highest levels in the nations of Northern Europe (and, later, the United States).

For Le Roy and Bodin, progress meant that knowledge and the arts gradually increased through time as a result of observation and experience. The then recent discoveries of places and things unknown to the peoples of Classical Antiquity challenged Renaissance claims alleging the superiority of Greek and Roman civilization; as a consequence, these claims also called into question the validity of cyclical theories of change. These challenges laid the foundations for the Quarrel between the Ancients and the Moderns—a debate partly concerned with whether modern society was superior to the societies of ancient times. It examined the question of whether modern peoples were more advanced because they were able to incorporate and elaborate the ideas and discoveries of their predecessors (Baron 1959; Jones 1961; Moulakis 2011). One question it failed to answer was how progress actually took place.

Two Crown intellectuals—Francis Bacon (1561–1626) and René Descartes (1596–1650)—provided answers to this question in the early seventeenth century. They argued that reason was a uniquely human attribute that differentiated people from animals and nature. If reason were applied systematically, they held, then custom and superstition could be eliminated, nature conquered, and social institutions improved. Reason was an abstract skill that did not depend on particular bodies of knowledge. Rather, it was an instrument that any human being—properly schooled in the scientific method—could apply. When properly applied, reason became the engine of progress.

In the *New Organon* (1620), Bacon saw reason as the application of a set of procedures that we now call the scientific method; it resembled a judge and jury sifting through piles of evidence to establish the facts of the case. Descartes wrote about reason in a slightly different way. In *Discourse on [Scientific] Method* (1637), he noted that half-savages began to behave rationally when they made laws to regulate crimes and quarrels. It was at this point that they became civilized; in his view, the application of reason was a civilizing process. He then argued that civilized (or modern) societies were both rationally organized and superior to their less rational predecessors and contemporaries. Their members applied reason to nurture progress and change, unlike the savages and barbarians of static, backward societies.

The growth of reason was a sign of modernity. It freed people from the restraints of tradition. Rationality untainted by human passions, ethics, or historical considerations was the distinctive feature of the countries of Northern Europe; it distinguished them from their predecessors and from their more primitive contemporaries. After all, as the argument went, the growth of reason and the increased rationality of the European states had already underwritten overseas expansion and technological innovation, such as advances in printing, military ordnance, and navigational instruments.

It would facilitate the conquest of nature, which would, in turn, unleash rapid, beneficial, and profitable changes, and offer unlimited opportunities in the future.

Seventeenth-century commentators carried this view to its logical conclusion: Modern society, which was the result of rationality, was clearly superior to earlier forms. Consequently, modernity was a goal that should be pursued. In 1651, Thomas Hobbes (1588–1679) described what might happen if this goal were not encouraged:

> Whatsoever there is consequent to a time of Warre, where every man is Enemy to every man; the same is consequent to the time, wherein men lived without other security, than what their own strength, and their own invention shall furnish withall. In such a condition, there is no place for Industry; because the fruit thereof is uncertain: and consequently, no Culture of the Earth, no Navigation, nor use of the commodities that may be imported by Sea; no commodious Building; no Instruments of moving, and removing such things as require much force; no Knowledge of the face of the Earth; no account of Time; no Arts; no Letters; no Society; and which is worst of all, continuall feare, and danger of violent death; And the life of man, solitary, poore, nasty, brutish, and short.
>
> (Hobbes 1968[1651]:186–187)

Hobbes's perspective made it difficult to idealize earlier stages of society that lacked agriculture, commerce, and security, and whose members acted instinctively rather than rationally (Meek 1976:17).

In his essay "On Cannibals" (1588), written more than fifty years earlier, Michel de Montaigne (1533–1592) had already commented critically on what progress, civilization, and modernity had brought in their wake (Diamond 1992; Montaigne 1965[1588]).[3] He criticized the civilized societies of Europe when he compared them, unfavorably, with travelers' descriptions of the American Indians that portrayed them as generous, honest, and not desirous of others' goods. In his view, these noble savages resembled the original human community. He used nudity as a metaphor for the original societies living in freedom, according to "nature's first laws," while clothing marked the counterfeit world of civilized societies in which social relations were veiled and deceptive. He viewed the destruction of American Indian societies and the moral decay of his own as signs of the sickness of civilized society. He observed that his contemporaries used their concepts of savages and barbarians (which originally included any people that did not speak Greek and was later used by the English to describe the Irish, who moved from place to place and hence were hard to tax) to create an unambiguous dichotomy between their own civilized societies and other nations they typically portrayed as wild, cruel, or brutal. He argued that rather than prejudice, reason should be used to judge what constituted barbarity. He questioned whether the cannibalism of the Tupinamba, which reputedly involved the ritual eating of the dead, was as barbarous as the tortures used by his fellow citizens and countrymen—e.g. tearing human beings apart on the rack, slowly roasting them over an open fire, or having them bitten and mangled by packs of dogs. He was also struck by the musings of a Tupinamba at Rouen:

> ... that there were among us men full and gorged with all sorts of good things, and that their other halves were beggars at their doors, emaciated with hunger and poverty; and [that] they thought it strange that these needy halves could endure such injustice, and did not take the others by the throat, or set fire to their houses.
>
> (Montaigne 1965[1588]:159)

Change as Development, Change as Modernity

Concepts of modern society are always framed in terms of the present with a vision to what could happen in the future; as a result, they have little or no concern for the past because it has no relevance for understanding the present. The present is merely a transition to something that will progress and develop in the future. Modern society is a historical structure in constant flux that always occupies an imaginary landscape set in the future and that only partly overlaps with the progressive or forward-moving parts of the present. This stage of development is temporary, always in the process of creating and recreating itself, hopefully without recasting the nightmares of the past and the present in the future. It occupies a time-span always in motion. Its hallmarks are commerce, industrial capitalism, and science: the mass production and consumption of novelties, the expansion of markets and the creation of new ones, and ever-changing technologies. If problems emerge during the process of modernization, there will always be technological and scientific fixes that can be implemented to ensure that the imaginary of the immediate future comes into being.

Rationalism and utilitarianism have been the guiding ideologies of modern society that underpin concepts of modernity (Kumar 2006). Here, rationalism means that the human mind and human society are natural. They are rational in the sense that they are an ordered system of causes and effects governed by natural laws that can be discovered through the application of reason (i.e. the scientific method); this excludes goals (*telos*) and values from consideration. Rationalists understand causal laws in terms of hidden forces and necessities—e.g. Newton's gravity—that can be discerned because of our own capacity to reason. They see human beings as rational actors who maximize pleasure in a world of scarcity (Hollis 2006). Utilitarianism asserts that the rightness of a choice or decision can be determined by whether it produces the best consequences out of the range of possible alternative courses of action available. There is a value component: Is goodness calculated only in terms of the satisfaction of pleasure, or do other things besides happiness serve as measures? Finally, who determines the rightness of an act—a few individuals or the whole society (Frey 2006)?

There were already strong reactions to Bacon, Descartes, and Hobbes by the early eighteenth century as industrial capitalism and bourgeois culture[4] began to take root in northwestern Europe. Giambattista Vico (1688–1744), Neapolitan social critic, constructed one alternative to Hobbes's perspective on the progress of human society. In *The New Science* (1970[1725]), he argued that it was impossible to talk about society as whole; instead, it was necessary to focus on what happened in particular societies and on how the various aspects of those societies were interconnected. While he viewed society as similar to an organism composed of interrelated parts and made use of the growth analogy, he based his arguments on relativist claims related to a particular society rather than assertions about human society as a whole. Contrary to Hobbes, he argued that political institutions were not imposed by a social contract and that social institutions were not the product of some innate human nature that was forever fixed in time nor were they part of the state of nature. In his view, "... this world of nations has certainly been made by men, [and] it is within these modifications that its principles should have been sought" (Vico 1970[1725]:76). In his view, the customs and laws of a particular society—its social institutions—were the product of a long historical development that resulted from the fact that human nature changed with the passage of time. Social institutions appeared in a fixed order: "... first the forests, after that the huts, then the villages, next the cities, and finally the academies" (Vico 1970[1725]:36). Furthermore, social institutions determined both the form of the ideas or culture of people and the order in which these ideas appeared. In his words, "the order of ideas must follow the order of institutions" (Vico 1970[1725]:36). Vico also asserted that, while there were parallel developments in different societies, human nature was not uniform from one society to another because of the specificity of the circumstances that fostered intellectual advancement and eroded it. Thus, the growth of reason could not be the motor of social change or indicate the historical development of society, as Descartes and others had claimed. Instead, the development of society and the mind were parts of the same historical process.

Jean-Jacques Rousseau's (1712–1778) critique of modern society was, if anything, even harsher. In *A Discourse on the Moral Effects of the Arts and Sciences*, he charged that people were morally corrupted, both by the civilizing process and by life in the commercial societies that were slowly crystallizing across the globe as their elites steadily severed customary, mutually recognized obligations to the members of the lower classes and replaced them with social relations based on market exchange. He wrote that while "the politicians of the ancient world were always talking about morality and virtue; ours speak of nothing but commerce and money"; to the citizens of Geneva, he wrote, "you are merchants, artisans, bourgeois, always occupied with your private interests, your work, commerce, profits; you are people for whom freedom is only a means toward untrammeled acquisition and secure possession" (Rousseau 1973[1750]:16; 1962[1764]:284). At the same time, he accepted Hobbes's claim that it was possible to systematically examine the original condition of humanity and the development of society. History would (1) provide a corrective to what politicians said by focusing on what they actually did; (2) strip away the later, human-made accretions to show what people were like before civilization was introduced; (3) reveal the errors and prejudices of ancient and modern writers regarding the original nature of humankind and the origins of social and political inequality; and (4) further "people's reflective self-identification and self-location within time, space, and a context of others," which had the potential to expand their vision of human possibilities of thinking of themselves not as "passive observers" but rather "as active participants" (Barnard 2003:162).

Rousseau (1973[1755]) outlined his critical anthropology in the *Discourse on the Origins of Inequality*. Some distinctive features of his historical-dialectical perspective were (1) human nature as a historical process associated with the emergence of human beings from nature through the creation of culture and their transformation of nature through social labor; (2) the interactions of human beings with one another and with their external (natural) world as shaped by successively different, historically specific sets of social relations; (3) a recognition of both the existence and anteriority of social forms other than modern bourgeois society; and (4) a historicized conception of "man" as a subject who was not always identical with "bourgeois man" of modern society.

In Rousseau's view, the historical development of society rested on the growing importance *in society* of the bonds created by mutual affection, dependence, self-esteem, and self-interest. He called these sentiments *amour-propre* and believed that the development of self-esteem and pride occurred as a result of the public recognition of personal qualities of excellence valued by the community. However, life in the community broke down when sharing was disrupted, and production became increasingly based on new forms of social relations—i.e. the division of labor—that the community could no longer replicate. *Amour-propre* came to signify vanity rather than pride, competition for public esteem, and the life of the individual rather than that of the community. The steady metamorphosis of *amour-propre* into growing individuation and alienation was the motor driving this historical development. The "dynamic of civil society compel[led] all the actors to foster actively the proliferation of needs in others" and fostered a system of social relations constructed as exchange relations that promoted "universal disorder, competition, and exploitation" (Horowitz 1987:109, 116). In Rousseau's words,

> Civilized man ... is always moving, sweating, toiling and racking his brains to find still more laborious occupations. ... He pays court to men in power, whom he hates, and to the wealthy, whom he despises; he stops at nothing to have the honour of serving them; he is not ashamed to value himself on his own meanness and their protection; and, proud of his slavery, he speaks with disdain of those, who have not the honour of sharing it. ... [T]he source of all these differences is ... [that the civilized or bourgeois] man only knows how to live in the opinion of others.
>
> (Rousseau 1973[1755]:104)

The Scottish historical philosophers—e.g. Adam Smith and Adam Ferguson—held different views about historical development from Hobbes or Rousseau, even though both of the latter theorists influenced the former. They did not believe that the formation of society was predicated on reason in order to protect life, liberty, and property. Smith (1723–1790) asserted that exchanges between individuals were the foundation for the development of both sociability and morality. These exchanges served as mirrors by which individuals gained the approval of others; they were the way in which individuals constituted themselves as members of society and satisfied their needs through their "propensity to truck, barter, and exchange one thing for another" (Smith 1976[1776], vol. 1:117, 405). The progress of society was thus a natural, law-driven process tied to the natural dispositions of human beings and to an increasing division of labor associated with population growth and changes in the mode of subsistence. The first societies were foragers, then herders, then farmers, and finally individuals who pursued various activities after the division of labor emerged—e.g. herders and farmers in the countryside and artisans who no longer produced their own foods and settled in towns to pursue their crafts and barter their goods with others (Smith 1982[1762–1763]). This sequence followed the appearance of property and "the natural course of things." In addition to their views about the natural sociability of human beings, property, scarcity, exchange, and the immutability of human nature, the Scottish philosophers also believed that society was developing in a desirable direction.

Smith was principally interested in the material and technical advantages that result from raising the productivity of labor. He accounted for the development of a technical division of labor in which the various members of a society pursued different activities, each producing commodities that were ultimately bartered or exchanged for money in the market. In his view, society was organized like a modern factory. He distinguished three economic classes on the basis of their source of revenue: capitalists derived their income from stock, landowners derived their income from rent, and laborers derived their income from wages. The classes had their origins in the functional differentiation of stock, land, and labor as factors of production in an emerging technical division of labor rather than in innate human differences or historical circumstances. Any uneven distribution of wealth and property among the various classes resulted from the differential contribution of stock, land, and labor to the growing economy—i.e. the increasing division of labor and the expanding market. Smith further believed that despite the inequalities that develop in societies with an expanding division of labor, the relations between the classes normally remain harmonious.

However, Smith's discussion concerning the appearance of a social division of labor—i.e. the crystallization of a class structure in which the members of one group appropriate either the labor power or goods of one or more classes of direct producers—was problematic. Because he conflated the technical and social divisions of labor, he was unable to discern how class structures actually emerged and how the various classes came to occupy particular places in a system of social production and have varying degrees of control over the conditions of their production, their labor power, and the goods they produced. It also prevented him from examining seriously the antagonistic relations that develop between classes. In other words, Smith was not as clear as Rousseau about the disruptive effects of a social division of labor.

For Smith, there was a complex relationship between politics and economics. Political economy was concerned with supplying people with the subsistence or revenues they needed to sustain themselves and providing the state with the revenues it required for public works and other expenditures—defense, justice, and "supporting the dignity of the sovereign." Thus, law and government were central concerns. He implied that the hidden hand of the market—humankind's continual effort to achieve order through exchange—could be thwarted and that it operated only under certain conditions: when exchange was possible and when it was free from state restrictions and control. Hence, the role and form of the government—to maintain social order and provide the stability required for extending the division of labor, accumulating capital, and protecting the diverse forms of property ownership—must change from one stage of development to the next. Because of the increasing liberalization of politics in the 1770s, Smith believed that a centralized form of government with separate judicial and executive branches was a necessary precondition for the continued growth of modern civil society. Henri de Saint-Simon (1760–1825) coined the term "industrial society" to describe a particular configuration of functionally interrelated and interdependent social institutions that was emerging in northwestern Europe in the early nineteenth century. He and the other founders of utopian socialism—Charles Fourier (1772–1837) and Robert Owen (1771–1858)—called for the creation of an exact science to understand the disruptions taking place. Each identified a pre-existing moral, religious, or political theory as the main obstacle to restoring social harmony, and each had a vision of the future rooted in a new kind of social order.

Change as Human Nature, Change as Nature

Nineteenth-century writers increasingly emphasized that progress was inevitable and that it occurred through successive stages of intellectual and social development. They called it "evolution" in order to convey the idea of continuous change through time. The ideas immediately underlying social evolutionist thought did not have their origins in the work of Charles Darwin (1809–1882) but rather in that of Smith and his contemporaries in France and Scotland. Nevertheless, several shared an intellectual ancestor with Darwin: Thomas Malthus (1766–1834), who asserted that while human populations grew geometrically, their food supplies increased arithmetically, thereby creating a world of growing scarcity. The social evolutionists claimed that the human and natural worlds were governed by the same kind of immutable laws. While they saw human nature as uniform, they also believed that human progress was uneven in a double sense: Civilized societies were evolving (developing) more rapidly than non-civilized ones, and the pace at which a particular society had developed varied during the different stages of its evolution. This conclusion was frequently used to buttress assertions about the existence of social, cultural, or racial hierarchies.

Since the evolutionists did not constitute a single, coherent school of thought, let us consider the works of Lewis Henry Morgan (1818–1881) and Herbert Spencer (1820–1903). Morgan conceptualized evolution in terms of the growth and progress metaphors used by Smith: "... the gradual evolution of the mental and moral powers in their experience, and of their protracted struggle with opposing obstacles while winning their way to civilization" and "the slow accumulation of experimental knowledge" (Morgan 1963[1877]:5). Progress was the operation of human nature, and Morgan emphasized the importance of mutual aid rather than competition in the process. Spencer viewed it in terms of the gradual, relentless unfolding of natural principles operating on a cosmic scale and saw human society as a living organism or system with numerous parts or structures rather than as a layer-cake composed of an economic base and social and political superstructures.

For Morgan, what distinguished one people from another was their respective level of social development rather than their physical appearance or the quality of their intellect. He understood their historical development in terms of a series of stages—from savagery (foraging) to barbarism (farming) to civilization. Technological innovations that transformed the modes of subsistence and the kinds of social institutions inextricably linked with them were the motors of motion and progress. In his view, the dietary improvements that ensued fueled both the physical expansion of the brain and improvements in beliefs and social institutions. In *Ancient Society*, he called this "the growth of intelligence through invention and discovery" (Morgan 1963[1877]:18–19). In a phrase, he subscribed to a base-superstructure model of society in which changes in the economic base brought about changes in political organization as well as in cultural beliefs and practices. The change from a socially to a territorially-based political organization occurred with the appearance of food-producing economies, which enabled people to live in cities and to acquire private property, and which also underwrote the increasing importance of the monogamous family and the diminished status of women (Morgan 1963[1877]:264, 330).

Morgan was concerned with the processes underlying the rise of civilization rather than the sequence of stages that occurred. He was acutely aware that civilization was ultimately the product of a series of fortuitous circumstances:

> Its attainment at some time was certain; but that it should have been accomplished when it was, is still an extraordinary fact. ... It may well serve to remind us that we owe our present condition, with its multiple forms of safety and happiness, to the struggles, the heroic exertions, and the patient toil of our barbarous, and more remotely, our savage ancestors. Their labors, their trials and their successes were a part of the plan of the Supreme Intelligence to develop a barbarian out of a savage, and a civilized man out of this barbarian.
>
> (Morgan 1963[1877]:563)

Morgan also employed a concept of uneven development so that at any given moment in time, some peoples were more advanced than others, and tribes either advanced by borrowing from neighboring, more developed cultures or were held back by their geographical isolation and circumstances.

While Morgan never doubted the superiority of Christianity, capitalism, and U.S. democracy, he was also imbued with a profound sense of honesty, fairness, and equality. He discussed the growth of private property in the final section of *Ancient Society*. On the one hand, he believed that social classes were disappearing in the United States. On the other, he was critical of the greed and profit motive that gripped some of his contemporaries—most notably the "robber barons" and "captains of industry" who made fortunes from financial deals, railroads, industry, and public utilities in the wake of the Civil War. While Morgan saw civilization as beneficial, he also believed that the rise of civilization had, in fact, destroyed something valuable—the values and beliefs of those past and present-day peoples who knew neither private property nor the profit motive. He foresaw a day when the social class system and the concentration of private property in the hands of a wealthy few would be overthrown:

> A mere property career is not the final destiny of mankind. ... Democracy in government, brotherhood in society, equality in rights and privileges, and universal education foreshadow the next higher plane of society to which experience, intelligence, and knowledge are steadily tending. It will be a revival, in a higher form, of the liberty, equality, and fraternity of the ancient gentes [clans].
>
> (Morgan 1963[1877]:561–562)

Spencer believed that the inorganic, the organic, the societal (superorganic), and the psychological realms of the cosmos were always in motion and subject to a combination of the same immutable laws of evolution and dissolution. His theory of change started with the notion that societies are always in flux and combined this with Hobbes's view of the state of nature in which individuals are continually competing with one another for scarce resources in order to maximize pleasure and avoid misery. In his view, simple societies were often nomadic and composed of a number of more or less identical elements: economically self-sufficient individuals or households that were not dependent on one another because the communities lacked a division of labor and, hence, had poorly developed exchange relations. They also lacked formalized political organization altogether or had only rudimentary forms of political control. As a result of their seeming homogeneity and simplicity, Spencer viewed this kind of society as unstable and easily subject to the winds of change (Spencer 1880[1862]:347).

Population growth was the motivating force that drove simple societies together. Aggregation into larger communities unleashed two further processes: differentiation and integration as a division of labor and exchange relations crystallized in the new, larger social entity. Spencer viewed the new, more heterogeneous communities—in the sense of their being more internally differentiated and having denser webs of interconnections—as more stable than the constituent parts that preceded them. He referred to the processes of aggregation, differentiation, and integration as compounding. Doubly compound societies had permanent settlements (i.e. cities) and recognized political leaders as well as more developed divisions of labor and social, political, and ecclesiastical hierarchies. Trebly compound societies had even more overarching forms of political organization and functioned as centers for their social aggregates. Compound societies were even more stable than their more homogeneous precursors due to the increasing density of the division of labor and the webs of social relations connecting their constituent elements. This ultimately led to the possibility of some sort of equilibrium that would endure until some more powerful force disrupted and dissolved the aggregation. The disintegration of a society set in motion new processes of aggregation, leading to the reintegration of its fragmented but enduring components. Thus, while phases of structuring and destructuring over an extended period of time can appear as rhythmic oscillations, gyrations, or cycles, long-term processes operating simultaneously are driving the totality as a whole toward some kind of equilibrium, with even denser and more numerous interconnections between its components (Turner 1985:35–42).

The importance of population pressure diminished as human society became more complex. Spencer (1852:267) described this in the following manner:

> The gradual diminution and ultimate disappearance of the original excess of fertility could take place only through the process of civilization; and, at the same time, the excess of fertility has itself rendered the process of civilization inevitable. From the beginning, pressure of population has been the proximate cause of progress. It produced the original diffusion of the race. It compelled men to abandon predatory habits and take up agriculture. It led to the clearing of the earth's surface. It forced men into the social state; made social organization inevitable; and has developed the social sentiments. It has stimulated to progressive improvements in production, and to increased skill and intelligence. It is daily pressing us into closer contact and more mutually-dependent relationships. And after having caused, as it ultimately must, the due peopling of the globe, and the bringing of all its habitable parts into the highest state of culture—after having brought all processes for the satisfaction of human wants to the greatest perfection— after having, at the same time, developed the intellect into complete competency for its work, and the feelings into complete fitness for social life—after having done all this, we see that the pressure of population, as it gradually finishes its work, must gradually bring itself to an end.

Thus, the evolution of human society—i.e. the rise of civilization—was law-driven and merely one aspect of the general tendency toward progress in the cosmos. Human society had evolved slowly under contradictory circumstances.[5] On the one hand, following Hobbes, each society attempted to achieve the highest degree of happiness, which brought them into conflict with other communities and actually hindered the development of civilization. On the other, each society had a desire to diminish the misery of inferior creatures—laborers, children, and primitive communities—by ameliorating their conditions of existence; this actually promoted the evolution of the social state. As a result, civilization could emerge only when the sympathetic circumstances based on the amelioration of misery outweighed the earlier unsympathetic ones rooted in the war of man against man.

Spencer (1876:576–596) believed that all societies—except for simple ones inhabiting remote, sparsely populated regions—came into conflict with neighboring groups. As a result, they developed institutions and practices for defending themselves and for attacking their enemies, on the one hand, and for providing for the sustenance and other needs of their members, on the other. The two forms of organization, the militant and the industrial, co-existed in every society. In some societies, like Japan, the militant organization was predominant and shaped various aspects of everyday life; in other societies, like the Pueblos or the towns of the Hanseatic League from which the Dutch Republic rose, the industrial organization predominated and affected other parts of the social structure.

In social evolution, there was a trend from the militant to the industrial type as a result of the growing importance of altruism—i.e. individuals became steadily more interdependent because of increasing social differentiation. As a result, militant organizations were more prominent during the earlier stages of social evolution, and industrial organizations became more important as the evolutionary process unfolded. Spencer (1876:596) contrasted the militant and industrial types in the following way: While the individual existed for the benefit of the state in the militant type, the state existed for the benefit of the individual in the industrial type. He also hinted that there might be a third type of society, one in which "work is for life"—i.e. for enjoyment and self-expression.

Toward the end of his career, Spencer recorded his thoughts about various aspects of modern industrial society; these notes focused mainly on institutional structures rather than any potential for social change. For example, in describing the impact of the factory system and the new forms of industrial organization associated with it, he remarked that

> The wage-earning factory-hand does, indeed, exemplify entirely free labour, in so far that, making contracts at will and able to break them after short notice, he is free to engage with whomsoever he pleases and where he pleases. But this liberty amounts in practice to little more than the ability to exchange one slavery for another; since, fit only for his particular occupation, he has rarely an opportunity of doing anything more than decide in what mill he will pass the greater part of his dreary days.
>
> (Spencer 1896:515–516)

Spencer's views were very influential in the United States and Europe, where they underwrote claims that the differences between individuals, societies, races,

nations, and even corporations were rooted in human nature or even in nature itself, both of which were ripe with notions of teleology and steady progress. This is
the ideology of Social Darwinism, which saw and interpreted the world through
a lens called "the survival of the fittest" (Jones 1980). Because the Social Darwinists believed that all things progressed naturally from lower to higher or more
advanced forms, they constructed various kinds of hierarchies to portray the
developmental relationships of those elements. The "fittest" forms found at the
top of their hierarchies were those deemed more perfect or those deemed to have
progressed further up the evolutionary ladder. For example, Darwin (1874:142),
who also happened to be a Social Darwinist, remarked that "... a nation which
produced during a lengthened period the greatest number of highly intellectual,
energetic, brave, patriotic, and benevolent men, would generally prevail over less
favored [i.e. less civilized] nations."

Discussion

Modern theorists of social change and development—including Marx,
Durkheim, and Weber—were both influenced by earlier theories of change and
critical of them. Marx built on Heraclitus's dialectical understanding of the cosmos and human society, and appreciated the significance of theories that described change in terms of progress, evolution, or directionality. However, Marx
was ultimately much less interested in the evolutionary schemes of Morgan or
Spencer than he was in Darwin's (1859) *On the Origin of Species by Means of
Natural Selection*, which he believed provided a way of looking at the dialectically constituted, historical contingency of the natural world of which human
societies were one part (Marx 1985[1860]). Durkheim drew on the organic analogy and responded to Spencer's evolutionism. He would also arrange societies
along an axis of simplicity and complexity, and treated simpler communities as
representatives of the developmentally earlier stages of complex society. While
Weber undoubtedly believed in the superiority of industrial capitalist society,
evolutionism was never a significant feature of his social thought. Contemporary
analysts, both modernization and Marxist theorists, have portrayed the penetration of capitalist social relations in Third World countries in terms of progress,
development, and cyclical growth.

Marx, Durkheim, and Weber conceptualized society in different ways. Marx
argued that it was the natural condition of human beings and that human beings
were social animals whose real essence or nature was realized only in a social
collectivity; human nature was constrained by the historically constituted traditions it encountered, and it was modified as new relations of production and
needs developed. For Durkheim (1938[1895]:102), society was an emergent phenomenon that was borne by its individual members and that had an existence
independent of them: In his words, "When the individual has been eliminated,
society alone remains." In Weber's (1978[1922]:14) view, categories like "society"
referred only to the likelihood that individuals would act in certain ways under
certain conditions:

> When reference is made in a sociological context to a state, a nation, a corporation, a family... or to similar collectivities, what is meant is... only a certain kind of development of actual or possible social actions of individual persons.

Durkheim and Weber also believed that human nature was malleable rather than fixed, as their contemporary Sigmund Freud seemed to claim.

Marx, Durkheim, and Weber were also critical of the political-economic theories of society and change devised by Smith and his successors. For example, Marx argued that these early theorists ignored the specificity of capitalist relations of production, distribution, and exchange. Durkheim (1888:29) agreed that the economists distorted reality by removing "... all circumstances of time, place and country in order to conceive of the abstract type of man in general; but in that ideal type itself, they neglected all that did not relate to strictly individual life." Weber rejected economistic conceptualizations of society because these abstracted individual actors from the capitalist social relations that structured their lives and avoided ethical and political questions or subordinated them in favor of economic ones (Clarke 1982: 190, 204).

Durkheim and Weber had important relationships with two strands of thought that appeared in the 1870s and crystallized in the 1880s. One was Neo-Kantianism, and the other was marginal utility or neoclassical economics. The Neo-Kantians were dissatisfied by the alternatives afforded by idealism and materialism and sought to bridge the gap between liberalism and socialism by reviving and engaging with Kant's philosophical discussions from the late eighteenth century (Benton 1977). Durkheim was interested in themes suggesting that philosophy could be viewed as a science; this raised issues about the place of values and ethics in such an endeavor. Weber accepted the claims of other Neo-Kantians that the natural and human sciences needed different methodologies and that a distinction needed to be drawn between facts and values.

Marginal utility theory was the other strand of social thought that exercised Durkheim and Weber. Marginal utility theorists—like Alfred Marshall (1920[1890])—rejected the classical political economy developed by Smith and his successors in order to develop a theory of prices that would account for the rational allocation of scarce resources in the market. They claimed that

> the economic institutions of capitalist society can be abstracted from their social and historical context and can be considered as the rationally developed technical instruments appropriate to the optimal allocation of scarce resources....
>
> In its theory of price, marginalism explains the formation of prices as an expression of the individual rationality of economic agents, competitive exchange serving optimally to reconcile the conflicting interests of these individuals so as to reconcile individual and social rationality. On the basis of this analysis marginalism then proceeds to demonstrate that all capitalist economic institutions are, in the purest and most abstract form, the most perfect expressions of individual rationality....
>
> (Clarke 1982:156–157)

In Durkheim's eyes, economic exchanges that occurred in the market constituted the fundamental problem of modern society because the social relations that were established between individuals in the marketplace were not effectively constrained by the moral ethics of a wider community. Weber rejected the marginal utility theorists' claim that economic rationality was natural. In his view, it was only one possible value-orientation in modern society; however, while economic rationality provided an important starting point for the development of industrial capitalist society, it had the capacity to undermine other ideals, such as independence, self-sufficiency, community, or national security.

In the next chapter, we will examine in more detail how Marx, Durkheim, and Weber extended some of the metaphors and models of change outlined in this chapter in their efforts to explain the rise of industrial capitalist society.

Notes

1 My discussion of Aristotle and teleology has benefited enormously from philosopher Monte R. Johnson's (2005) *Aristotle on Teleology*. There is a debate about teleology. Some view it as causation, and others view it as explanation. His careful historical survey suggests a middle course, which avoids claims that teleology is merely "backward causation" or that it is merely the attribution of human characteristics to animate or inanimate things (anthropomorphism).

2 Briefly, (1) power can be viewed as the capacity of some entity (a person, class, community, or state) to produce an intended outcome; (2) the possession of power may be based on relations of domination or merely reflect the ability to act; (3) it may be deployed across a range of contexts or be limited to what can be done at a particular time and place; and (4) in contexts shaped by conflicting interests, power may involve only the ability to set an agenda, or it may be wielded to shape ideas and beliefs (Lukes 2006).

3 Montaigne's ancestors were international merchants who had purchased a title estate near Bordeaux. He was a civil servant, like his father. The composition of his family was diverse: His mother's family were Spanish Jews; several siblings were Huguenots; Montaigne himself was Catholic. He wrote "On Cannibals" at a time when wars—pitting the nobility against the monarch, townspeople, and peasants, and Catholic against Protestant—were sweeping across Western Europe. In one week in August 1573, more than ten thousand Protestants were massacred in Rouen and Paris. Montaigne's tolerance of religious differences and his opposition to the excesses of all factions led him to occupy a critical middle ground during the wars. His tolerance was buttressed by his insatiable curiosity about the customs of American Indians. He read published accounts and visited the Tupinamba, who had been kidnapped, brought to Rouen in the 1550s, and housed in an "ethnographic garden" on the edge of town. They were abandoned by their keepers and left to fend for themselves during the war.

4 Briefly, bourgeois culture is a worldview that subordinates the economic to the social sphere of life; that makes certain assumptions about the nature of truth, taste, civilization, culture, and refinement; and that seeks to establish its place in society through the conspicuous consumption of mass-produced, high-quality luxury items and forms of sociability and elite conversation manifested materially, for example, in the sitting rooms and salons of the early twentieth century. It emulates traditional forms of wealth and status; its focus is urban and urbane; it is consumerist; and it is conservative because its goal to establish, maintain, and reproduce the distinctions between itself and other such worldviews, ideologies, and philosophies in class-stratified societies (Berger 1972; Lowe 1982).

5 This suggests that Spencer conceived of an interplay of teleology and contingency and that we must distinguish between his seemingly teleological explanations and teleological description.

2
Modern Industrial Capitalist Society, 1820–1914

What is modern industrial capitalist society? When did it appear? Henri Saint-Simon coined the term "industrial system" to describe the combination of business, scientific, technological, and intellectual endeavors already apparent in France by 1820. The concept united the production of goods for the market, new machines, the men and women who used them, scientific insights, businessmen, and bankers. Saint-Simon's question was: What kind of political organization best fostered and promoted the growth of industrial society? The term "capitalism" appeared a few years later to contrast the class of individuals who held wealth from those who labored for them (the proletariat). This emerging social order was based on the industrial production of commodities and "the ideas and beliefs which seemed to legitimate and ratify it: ... reason, science, progress, and liberalism" (Hobsbawm 1979:xix). The advocates of this new social and economic order believed that growth and progress rested on unrestrained competitive private enterprise and the absence of government interference. However, the reign of unrestrained competitive capitalism was short-lived. It was eroded by the rapid expansion of domestic consumer markets in the 1860s and 1870s, the growth of large-scale producers, new sources of power, and the rise of international rivalries between different national industrial economies. These led the various industrial states to intervene to protect their national economic interests. In the late nineteenth century, the distinction between developed and underdeveloped rapidly assumed its modern form, and spectra of political parties—capitalist, working-class, collaborationist, nationalist, fascist, and oppositional—appeared in the core industrial countries (Hobsbawm 1979:337–343).

A number of nineteenth-century writers analyzed the changes taking place. Three perspectives came to dominate discussions by the early years of the twentieth century—those of Karl Marx, Émile Durkheim, and Max Weber. Their legacies still influence contemporary analyses. Marx and Weber framed their analyses in terms of capitalism; Durkheim used the concept of industrial society to buttress his views. Marx wrote between the mid-1840s and 1882. Durkheim and Weber wrote a generation later from the mid-1880s until about 1920. Consequently, they captured two different moments in the development of industrial capitalist society. As a result, more than one commentator has remarked that both Durkheim and Weber engaged in critical discussions with Marx's ghost. However, their reasons for engaging this specter were different.

Let us briefly review the contributions of each before considering their writings in more detail. Marx, the student of the historical development of capitalism on a world stage, sought a critical understanding; Marx, the political activist, sought to use critical understanding to change the world, to permit alienated individuals to become less estranged, human social and natural beings in the world that was crystallizing from the interplay of capitalism's laws of motion, shifts in the balance of force, and contingency. There was a dialectical tension between Marx's two sides. Durkheim urged the separation of scholarship from politics. He argued that the malaise of modern industrial society—its anomie (the absence of socially accepted standards and values)—was pathological. The condition was a consequence of the fact that the old moral order was dissolving more rapidly than the formation of a new one. This new moral and social order would be a self-regulating equilibrium embodying market exchange and the emerging division of labor; the national state, in Durkheim's view, was the institution best-suited for solidifying the new order. Weber argued for the uniqueness of capitalist development in the West and its "imposition from above." He sought to understand the ways in which one group asserts control over another and why "the personal subjective standards by which the first judges the behavior of the second render[ed] it consequential" (Jones 2003:231). He too saw the impossibility of separating either science or politics from the reality of everyday life in national states and worried about the growing threats posed by practical rationality, in which the egoistic interests of the individual come to the fore in decision making and the iron cage of bureaucracy (Kalberg 2003:173). Let us now look in more detail at their analyses of industrial capitalism and industrial society.

Karl Marx: Historical Materialist, Communist

Karl Marx (1818–1883) grew up in the Rhineland in western Germany, the inhabitants of which were influenced by The Enlightenment, the French Revolution, and socialist thought. He was a voracious reader—Homer, Shakespeare, Voltaire, Rousseau, Kant, and Saint-Simon, whom he would discuss with his father, future father-in-law, and the director of his high school. Later, at the University of Berlin, he became familiar with the moral ethics of the Saint-Simonian socialists—especially their concern with the future of the "poorest and most numerous class," the property-less and exploited industrial workers. These concerns influenced his subsequent reading and critique of Hegel's *Philosophy of Right* (Marcuse 1960[1941]; Marx 1975[1844]). It also led him to the nascent socialist movement in Berlin and the group now known as the Young Hegelians. While Marx believed that the socialist and subsequent communist movements contained a new understanding of the kinds of social relations that were developing in industrial capitalist society, he maintained a life-long critical stance toward such views, particularly when they failed to base their moral claims on a theoretically informed conception of reality (Bottomore 1988:4–5).[1]

Marx (1975[1844]:270–282) launched his critique of political economy in *The Economic and Philosophic Manuscripts of 1844*. He developed two arguments that he would elaborate on in subsequent works. First, he took Hegel's observation that the essence of humankind is created through labor and moved it from the realm of pure thought to the language of political economy. By laboring to transform nature, humanity not only produces wealth but also develops the uniquely human qualities and forms of social life that distinguish it from animals. In his words, man (sic.) "... sees himself in a world he has created" (Marx 1975[1844]:277). Second, Marx extended Feuerbach's notion of alienation to describe the real conditions of industrial society. While workers should be developing their human potential through labor, in fact, they are unable to do so because of the economic class structure of industrial society—a class of property owners and a much larger class of property-less workers. Because workers do not own the products of their labor, they are estranged from the commodities they create; they are estranged from one another and separated from meaningful relationships because they compete with one another in the labor market as isolated individuals in search of the jobs they need to sustain themselves; and they are alienated from their ability to satisfy their creative potential—i.e. their essence as human beings. In Marx's view, alienation, which also existed in pre-capitalist and non-capitalist societies, was never greater than it is in industrial capitalism.

In the mid-1840s, Marx and his lifelong collaborator Frederick Engels (1820–1895) initially tackled the question of the historical development of human society. They equated different forms of property with various stages in the development of the division of labor. Briefly, the first form of property was tribal property; subsistence was based on foraging, herding, or agriculture; the division of labor was elemental; and there may have been chieftains and slaves. The second form was ancient or communal property, which results from the union of several tribes into a city; the communally held property of the city bound its citizens together; and there were social-class relations between citizens who came to hold private property and retain access to communal property and slaves, acquired through war or barter, who did not. The third form was feudal or estate property, which was also communal property and was worked not by slaves but rather by enserfed peasants who occupied the land and by the two estates (the lords and clergy) who claimed it as property and derived their incomes from the serfs (the third estate) from whom they exacted tribute, taxes, rent, labor, or time. Tensions surfaced and persisted between the countryside and the towns, which were centers of industry and commerce. Marx and Engels called the fourth form civil society or the modern form; it emerged as production and commerce extricated themselves from existing property relations (Marx and Engels 1976[1845–1846]:32–93). Marx and Engels soon came to call these forms of property "modes of production" (e.g. Marx and Engels 1976[1848]).

Marx elaborated on their "mode of production" concept in the 1850s, most famously with his layer-cake architectural metaphor of an economic base composed of the forces of production and the social relations of production, with legal and political superstructures and associated forms of human consciousness (i.e. culture) (Marx 1970[1859]:263–264; 1973[1857–1858]). Modes of production manifest themselves in the relations, institutions, and practices of societies as they inherit them from the past, reproduce and re-create them under new circumstances in the present, and strive to reproduce them or to create something new in the future. What distinguished real societies manifesting different modes of production was exploitation, which Marx described as

> the specific economic form in which unpaid surplus labor [or goods] is pumped out of the direct producers. [It] determines the relationship of domination and servitude, as this grows directly out of production itself and reacts back on it as a determinant. On this is based the entire configuration of the economic community arising from the actual relations of production, and hence also its specific political form.
>
> (Marx 1981[1864–1894]:927)

The collective expression of exploitation is the relationship between different groups in the community—its social-class structure and the ways in which it is embodied and inscribed in the beliefs, practices, and organization of everyday life (Ste. Croix 1984:100):[2]

> ... a class (a *particular* class) is a group of persons in a community identified by their position in the whole system of social production, defined above all according to their relationship (primarily in terms of the degree of *control*) to the conditions of production (that is to say, to the means and labour of production) and to other classes. The individuals constituting a given class may or may not be wholly or partly conscious of their own identity and interests as a class, and they may or may not feel antagonism towards members of other classes as such. Class *conflict* ... is essentially the fundamental relationship between classes, involving *exploitation* and resistance to it, but not *necessarily* either class consciousness or collective activity in common.
>
> (Ste. Croix 1984:100)

Most importantly, class is a relationship and lived experience,

> and class happens when some men (*sic.*), as a result of common experiences (inherited or shared), feel and articulate the identity of their interests as between themselves, and as against other men (*sic.*) whose interests are different from (and usually opposed to) theirs. The class experience is largely determined by the productive relations into which men (*sic.*) are born—or enter involuntarily. Class-consciousness is the way in which these experiences are handled in cultural terms: embodied in traditions, value-systems, ideas, and institutional forms. If the experience appears as determined, class-consciousness does not. We can see a logic in the responses of similar occupational groups undergoing similar experiences, but we cannot predicate any law. Consciousness of class arises in the same way in different times and places, but never in just the same way.
>
> (Thompson 1963:9–10)

From the mid-1840s onward, Marx tackled questions concerning the dynamics of change, the motors of change, and whether different modes of production had different laws of motion. In the *Manifesto of the Communist Party*, he and Engels wrote that the dynamic of

> the history of all hitherto existing society is the history of class struggle ...
> [as] oppressor and oppressed stood in constant opposition to one another,
> carried on an uninterrupted, now hidden, now open fight, a fight that each
> time ended, either in a revolutionary re-constitution of society at large, or
> in the common ruin of the contending classes.
>
> (Marx and Engels 1976[1848]:482)

Marx turned his attention again to the dynamic of history a few years later in *The Eighteenth Brumaire*. He referred to something Hegel wrote, to the effect that all facts and personages occur twice and indicated that Hegel "forgot to add: 'the first time as tragedy, the second as farce'" (Marx 1979[1852]:103). A few lines later, he wrote that while people

> ... make their own history, they do not make it just as they please; they do
> not make it under circumstances chosen by themselves, but under circum-
> stances directly encountered, given and transmitted from the past. The
> traditions of all the dead generations weigh like a nightmare on the brain
> of the living. And just when they seem engaged in creating something that
> never yet existed, precisely in such periods of revolutionary crisis they anx-
> iously conjure up the spirits of the past to their service and borrow from
> them names, battle-cries and costumes in order to present the new scene of
> world history in the time-honoured disguise and this borrowed language.
>
> (Marx 1979[1852]:103–104)

Thus, in the span of a few years, he raised important issues about the dynamics of change: Is change uni-directional or a two-way street? Are some modes of pro-duction more prone to change than others? What is the interrelation of structure and agency? Are the laws of motion the same in different modes of production? What is the interplay of the laws of motion, if there are any, and contingency? Is change continual or episodic? What is a crisis? Let us consider what he thought about possible answers.

Marx wrote a series of articles for the *New York Daily Tribune* in the mid-1850s that dealt with the complexity of Indian society, village communities, and the subversion of traditional property relations, and the creation of new ones under British colonial rule. He developed the idea of an asiatic mode of production. This has been much debated since then because he described societies manifest-ing the asiatic mode of production in two ways; the accounts are usually viewed as mutually exclusive. However, if they are not sequential and mutually exclusive, then a democratic (his earlier tribal form of property) form and more hierar-chical tributary form exist side by side. The former consists of self-sufficient, independent village communities; the latter consists of several village communities that are enmeshed in social relations with some sort of overarching entity that attempts to assert but does not necessarily succeed in claiming ownership of village lands, leaving the villages as mere possessors of their means of production. Marx also described asiatic societies, like other pre-capitalist ones, as being relatively impervious to change, oscillating between democratic and hierarchical forms because of the instability of the latter and the resistance and resilience of the former (Marx 1973[1857–1858]:472–474; 1977[1863–1867]:478–479). The mode of production seems analogous to trains with squeaky wheels in a railroad yard that do not run smoothly in the same direction, often stop, and frequently back up. Marx never identified the dynamic or law of motion for the asiatic mode of production; however, anthropologists Stanley Diamond (1974:255–280) and Christine Gailey (1987) subsequently called these cycles of centralization and collapse "kin/civil conflict." They pointed to various cultural practices, like ridicule or non-compliance, that hinder or thwart altogether assertions of control over the means of production or promote their dissolution and disintegration.

An important focus of Marx's work from the late 1850s onward was explaining the dynamics of the capitalist mode of production; the engines, processes, conditions, and events that propelled its formation; and the laws of motion that shaped its subsequent development. This led him to examine capitalist formations at two different levels: one abstract and the other concrete. For example, at the more abstract level, Marx (1977[1863–1867]:772–780) described the developmental logic of capital in terms of accumulation: the steady concentration and reproduction of capital on an ever-expanding scale and the centralization of capital into a steadily smaller number of increasingly large production units (e.g. corporations). There are elements of both developmental necessity (directionality) and contingency (accidents) in his arguments. He noted that the development of capitalist societies in England, France, Germany, and Russia followed different pathways and that, at the time he wrote, there were several potential alternative routes for the development of capitalism in the United States in the immediate future, given the then existing property relations and balance of force.

The concept of "developmental contingency," elaborated on by biologists Richard Levins and Richard Lewontin (1985:94–96) in another context, provides a useful, shorthand account of Marx's views about historical change. The concept captures the interrelations and interplay of necessity and contingency. To paraphrase, development is a historical process in which the effects of a force cannot be specified in a general or abstract way; they can only be specified in the particularity of the conditions and relations that exist at a given time and place. A consequence of this is that the formation of an ensemble of social relations and their associated milieu can appear "as a temporal sequence of events in which the exact order is critical" (Levins and Lewontin 1985:95). A second consequence is that subtle variations among societies can have the potential to affect what happens or does not happen next in this sequence. Still another consequence is that the transition from one to another depends as much on the conditions that prevailed at the time of the transition as on how the conditions and relations of the whole emerged. In Marx's (1989[1877]:201) words, "Events of striking similarity, taking place in different historical contexts, led to disparate results. By studying each of the developments separately, and then comparing them, one may easily discover the key to this phenomenon." Finally, in some instances, the possible outcomes for a particular course of change are often quite constrained. As a result, they play themselves out with almost law-like regularity or predictability in some moments (e.g. what happens when someone rolls a bowling ball down an alley; average bowlers usually do not know how many pins will be knocked down, and they can only begin to estimate this at some point after the ball is released and before it makes impact). At other moments, when the balance of forces are more nearly equal, people have a real potential or capacity to make their own histories; whether they have chosen to do so or succeeded in doing so is related to other issues, such as accurate assessments of the balance of force and the possibilities inherent in alternative courses of action.

At the more concrete level, Marx analyzed the development of capitalist economies, mostly in the national states of northwestern Europe, especially England. He compared these economies with one another and with the trajectories of capitalist formation in Russia and the United States. He explored the transition from feudalism to capitalism and attempted to understand the processes of transformation and alternative trajectories of development that were appearing on the margins of the capitalist world, particularly in South Asia and the Far East. He distinguished three kinds of capitalist: moneylender, merchant, and industrialist. The first two are divorced from the sphere of production. Moneylender or banker capitalists derive income from making loans and charging interest. Merchant capitalists purchase commodities in one place and sell them for a greater price in another. Industrial capitalists derive income from the production of commodities. For Marx, the distinctive features of the capitalist mode of production occur precisely in the sphere of production and the formation of a free-labor force separated from its means of production (the process called primitive accumulation). Thus, the capitalist mode of production and Western capitalist society had a number of features that distinguished them from other social forms, the most important of which involved the generalized production of commodities that are exchanged for money in the market.

The opening sentence of Marx's (1977[1863–1867]:125) *Capital* is "The wealth of societies in which capitalism prevails appears as an 'immense collection of commodities'; the individual commodity appears as its elementary form." His nearly three thousand-page analysis begins with a discussion of commodities—objects produced for exchange rather than for use or consumption by their makers. This contrasted with the views of Adam Smith and other classical political economists who argued that the concentration of commodities in Western society was the result of humanity's natural propensity "to truck, barter, and exchange." Marx instead situated the development of capitalism and the motor for change in the realm of human history rather than in some universal human nature or the unfolding of some inchoate principle of nature. Thus, he begins his analysis with production rather than exchange (circulation).

In industrial capitalist societies, production is organized by how commodities are distributed and how they circulate or are exchanged in the market. The commodities produced by the employees of a capitalist who owns the means of production are the property of the capitalist. In the market, the owner of a commodity confronts the individuals who possess other, different commodities. When they exchange one commodity for another, the value of a commodity is always expressed in terms of a definite quantity of another—e.g. a coat equals three beaver pelts, one hundred dollars, or ten hours of labor valued at $10 an hour. Thus, any given commodity has a dual character. On the one hand, the commodity satisfies a particular need of the individual who purchases it; it has use value. On the other, it has exchange value for the capitalist who owns the commodity produced by the worker, because its value is only realized when it is sold in the market.

The industrial capitalist uses a certain amount of capital (the money form) in the production process to purchase raw materials, tools, and labor power to produce a particular commodity. However, one of the commodities he purchases to produce the commodity has a unique property. That is the labor power of the workers, whose wages the capitalist pays in return for their knowledge and activity during the time they labored to produce the commodity. The worker produces a given product that has value, which the capitalist—as the owner of both the means of production and the goods produced—realizes only when that commodity is sold in the market. In other words, it is the workers, and only the workers, who create value. To obtain the value of the commodities, the capitalist must sell them for a profit—i.e. more money than he initially invested in materials, tools, and wages. The difference between the value of his initial investment and the value of commodities when they are sold is the "surplus value" created by the workers. The capitalist uses the money he received to purchase the commodities he needs to produce more of the particular commodity and to satisfy his personal needs and those of the firm; the workers use their wages to purchase the commodities required to satisfy their needs. Note that the form of value changes during the production-exchange-distribution-consumption cycle: the money form, the commodities (raw materials, labor) to produce the particular commodity, and the money form once it is sold.

Capitalists producing the same commodity compete with one another for customers in the market. The value of the commodity they produce depends on the average amount of labor that is socially necessary to produce it. A capitalist can increase his profits at the expense of his competitors by increasing productivity—i.e. extending the length of the workday; paying lower wages; purchasing machines that perform the same tasks of production as their workers but do so with greater productivity; re-organizing the whole production process with increased technical divisions of labor that simultaneously involves new forms of cooperation and replaces more skilled workers with less skilled but more specialized ones toiling as extensions of new machines in some form of assembly-line production; and creating new markets. The desire for increased profits and productivity was the impetus for the mechanization of factories and the continuous stream of new machines and new forms of organization in factories. These, in turn, underwrote the production of new kinds of commodities and the creation of new needs by the persons who used or consumed them. They simultaneously created new kinds of jobs, replaced workers with clever machines destroying the old forms of production in their wake, and opened up whole new spheres of production. This constant, systematic tendency to transform production and make it more efficient rests, of course, on steady progress in science and technology. These are motors for change at an ever-accelerating rate. Marx and Engels (1976[1848]:487) wrote that

> The bourgeoisie [i.e. the capitalists] cannot exist without continually revolutionizing the instruments of production, and thereby the relations of production, and with them the whole relations of society. Conservation of the old modes of production in unaltered forms, was, on the contrary, the first condition of existence for all earlier industrial classes. Constant revolutionizing of production, uninterrupted disturbance of all social conditions, everlasting uncertainty and agitation distinguish the bourgeois epoch from all earlier ones.

These are capitalism's laws of motion: (1) the concentration of capital in ever-expanding quantities and (2) the centralization of the increasingly large masses of capital in the hands of fewer and fewer but larger capitalist firms. This was especially true after the 1850s as gigantic corporations began to appear and shifted production from consumer to capital goods. The latter were essential for the production of other commodities, like those of the steel companies that manufactured steel for railroad companies that used it to make rails and locomotives. Because the new capital goods technologies were expensive, any capitalist wishing to use them had to invest significant amounts of capital to increase output and to gain a greater share of the market and profits. Not every firm was able to do so, and the weaker ones were either absorbed or driven out of business. This fueled the formation of progressively larger companies and the appearance of monopolies.

Capitalist production is vulnerable to periodic crises because of competition within and between different economic sectors and their growing interdependence. Marx (1978[1884]:468–574) sketched an incomplete theory of the periodic crises of the capitalist economic system. It was based on the tendency of the rates of profit to fall. Because profit is the driving force of capitalist activity, the individual producer must lower the cost of his commodity below its average value in the market in order to compete successfully with other firms producing the same item. He reduces the unit cost by mechanizing production and by raising productivity. While his profits increase initially, his actions simultaneously lower the social value of the commodity and diminish the profit rates of his competitors. The tendency for the rate of profit to fall affects not only his weaker competitors but also the entire economic sector defined by the commodity they produce. Investment in the sector declines, leading to under-consumption, excess productive capacities, wage squeezes, and layoffs. Besides eliminating the weaker capitalists, falling rates of profit also stimulate investment in other economic sectors.

Marx also raised questions about the conditions and processes that underwrote the formation of industrial capitalism. Initially, in the 1840s, he followed Smith and argued that the rise of industrial capitalists who extended commercial networks promoted commodity production and dissolved the natural economy that dominated in the countryside by restructuring labor processes and rural putting-out industries. They removed production from the guild-imposed limitations of the towns and eventually transformed the power and class relations of the existing feudal order. Two decades later, Marx revised his assessments of the merchants, characterizing them instead as a conservative fraction of the ruling class bent on accumulating the money form of capital, spending it on conspicuous consumption, and preserving the conditions and social relations, both at home and abroad, that permitted them to maintain their lavish lifestyles. They preserved the old mode of production and worsened the circumstances of the direct producers (Marx 1981[1864–1894]:379–455). By the late 1850s, Marx had begun to refine his understanding of tribal social formations and define them as communities whose members had largely retained possession of their land and other means of production. Thus, his later appraisal of the rise of industrial capitalism was that village communities were separated from their means of production and were forced to work for wages in order to survive, that domestic markets for food and locally produced goods appeared, and that some smaller owner-operated shops were able to establish themselves as independent producers that employed wage-workers from the emergent proletariat (Marx 1981[1864–1894]:873–878). In his view, legislation by the state, beginning with the enclosure acts of the late fifteenth century, drove this process in England.

Marx and Engels were acutely aware of the relationship between colonialism and the expansionist nature of industrial capitalism: its constant need for new markets, its quest for raw materials and cheap labor power, and its capacity to transform those societies enmeshed in European colonial relations. They linked their critiques of colonial expansion and Western industrial society:

> The bourgeoisie, by the rapid improvement of all instruments of production, by the immensely facilitated means of communication, draws all, even the most barbarian, nations into civilization. The cheap prices of its commodities are the heavy artillery with which it batters down all Chinese walls, with which it forces the barbarians' intensely obstinate hatred of foreigners to capitulate. It compels all nations, on pain of extinction, to adopt the bourgeois mode of production; it compels them to introduce what it calls civilization into their midst, i.e., to become bourgeois themselves. In one word, it creates a world after its own image.
>
> (Marx and Engels 1976[1848]:488)

In the 1870s, Marx turned his attention once again to societies on the periphery of the Western capitalist world. He exchanged with correspondents and took copious notes on government reports, historical accounts, and ethnographic descriptions of non-capitalist societies, both historical and those on the margins. Sociologist Kevin Anderson (2002, 2010) suggests that Marx's goal was to gain a clearer understanding of what was happening in order to update the manuscript for the second volume of *Capital*, which is broadly concerned with the circulation of capital. His interest in primitive societies, and especially the Russian communes, was deeply influenced by the events surrounding the formation and destruction of the Paris Commune in 1871 (Marx 1986[1871]; Shanin 1983). Marx's studies of the village communes in Russia made him realize that the expropriation of the peasants—i.e. separating them from their means of production—would not necessarily proceed in the same manner as it had in England. He wrote,

> At the core of the capitalist system, therefore, lies the complete separation of the producer from the means of production ... the basis of this whole development is the *expropriation of the agricultural producer*. To date this has not been accomplished in a radical fashion anywhere except England..... But *all the other countries of Western Europe* are undergoing the same process....
>
> Hence, the "historical inevitability" of this process is *expressly* limited to the *countries of Western Europe*....
>
> In this Western movement, therefore, what is taking place is the *transformation of one form of private property* [founded on personal labor] *into another form of private property* [capitalist private property, which rests on wage labor]. In the case of the Russian peasants, however, *their communal property* would have to be *transformed into private property*.
>
> (Marx 1992[1881]:71 emphasis in the original)

In a phrase, different trajectories of capitalist development were unfolding. Marx could envision a society without private property and a class-based division of labor—characteristics of primitive communities—combined with the productive capacities of capitalism; however, given the historical conditions that prevailed in Russia, a survival and further development of the commune depended on a particular kind of revolution (Shanin 1983:111–117).

By 1882, Marx and Engels saw Russia as the potential revolutionary vanguard of Europe. They posed the following question:

> Can the Russian *obshchina* [village community], a form of primeval common ownership of land, even if greatly undermined, pass directly to the higher form of communist ownership? Or must it, conversely, first pass through the same process of dissolution as constitutes the historical development of the West?

The only answer possible today is this: If the Russian Revolution becomes the signal for a proletarian revolution in the West, so that the two complement each other, the present Russian common ownership of land may serve as the starting point for communist development.

(Marx and Engels 1989[1882]:426)

In other words, socialist revolution might begin in Russia rather than in the Western industrial countries. This was important. Marx and Engels rejected the idea held by the advocates of progress and evolution that social change was unilinear and occurred through a fixed progression of stages; they reasserted the importance of class struggle and the social and historical circumstances in which it was taking place. They also implied that socialism might be an end-product of uneven development and different developmental trajectories.

In sum, Marx's view of the world is historicist in the sense that he believes it is impossible to understand something fully unless one knows how it comes to be. It was important to understand both the processes involved and their succession. History was the intertwined development of human beings, of ensembles, of social relations, and of nature itself. The most significant features of his historical science and theory of change were (1) the rejection of atomist reductionism and the adoption of dialectical holism; (2) the adoption of a notion of totality as a multi-leveled, contingent, and dialectically structured unity that exists in and through the connections and contradictions shaping the interactions of parts with one another, with the totality, and with the greater whole of which they are a part; (3) a profound appreciation of variation and its importance; and (4) the interplay of developmental necessity and chance. Marx's dialectical-historical view of history saw human society as a process of becoming, which led him to consider factors such as contradiction; the balance of force among opposed groups; and the interplay of teleology, developmental contingency, and chance, and to employ concepts like alienation, modes of production, exploitation, social-class structures, class struggle, and social revolution (Patterson 2009:93–116).

Émile Durkheim: Conservative Centrist Theorist of Social Nature

Émile Durkheim (1858–1917) was, not surprisingly, the product of nineteenth-century French social thought. One influence on him was French anti-Semitism and hatred of Germany in the wake of the Franco-Prussian War, which he experienced first as an orthodox rabbi's son in Alsace-Lorraine on the border next to Germany and then in the 1890s as a relatively outspoken critic of the French government's decision to convict and imprison Alfred Dreyfus, a French army officer from an Alsatian Jewish family, for allegedly selling military secrets to the German embassy in Paris. A second was Saint-Simonian socialism, which recognized the impact of the Industrial Revolution on existing social relations and its role in the emerging plight of the working masses, claimed the moral and religious foundations of social cohesion, and called not only for funding of social scientific research but also for creating a priestly class to establish a moral order more responsive to the emerging circumstances. A third influence was Auguste Comte's quest to discover the abstract principles, starting with the human mind, that govern phenomena rather than merely discovering the natural laws that cause those phenomena as well as his view of a yet-to-be-born sociology that would stand as the pinnacle of science. A fourth was Charles Renouvier, a French Neo-Kantian and Saint-Simonian socialist, who argued for determinism in the natural world; indeterminism in the relations between autonomous (biological) individuals as a result of the freedom of conscience presupposed by moral action; the formation of associations of individuals independent of the state; and public, secular education. A fifth influence was historian Fustel de Coulanges's *The Ancient City* (1864) and its preoccupation with the family as the basic building block of human society; religion as a source of moral action; the religious origins of institutions like private property, law, and the state; and the identity of religion with society itself. A sixth was the conceptual language and concerns raised by German philosopher-psychologist Wilhelm Wundt: who suggested the mind as a process rather than a substance; new syntheses (wholes) formed by re-arrangements of component parts; or historical process as the progressive unfolding of individuality from an initial primitive stage in which the individual was indistinguishable from the group. A seventh and final influence was the evolutionism and organicism of Herbert Spencer (Bourdeau 2013; Gisberg 1959; Jones 2003:218–220; Lukes 1973:90–91, 140).

France was in turmoil, near civil war, from the mid-1880s until the outbreak of World War I: Rampant anti-Semitic and anti-German sentiments, always present just below the surface, erupted in the early-1890s with the Dreyfus Affair; threats of an imminent *coup d'état* were ever-present; strikes led by anarchist- and socialist-led unions were frequent; a corruption scandal over the Panama Canal implicated more than five hundred members of parliament and six ministers, including a national hero and future prime minister; there were occasional bombings; the president was assassinated in 1895; a repressive anti-terrorist law passed in the same year severely curtailed freedom of speech; and, responding to the wishes of industrialists, the government unleashed the military on striking workers and killed more than more four hundred during a single strike in 1909. These are the circumstances in which Durkheim wrote. In his view, traditional forms of collective authority, social consciousness, and moral order had broken down with the rise of industrial society and the division of labor. They were replaced by a "cult of the individual" dedicated to a new social category—the individual. This category emphasized the personal dignity of the individual, individuated beliefs, individualism, and a lack of interest in all that lay beyond the self. The natural milieu individuals shared was their occupation; however, the bonds created by these dispositions were not really social because individuals had steadily fewer sentiments in common. Those they shared emphasized their differences rather than their commonalities. Individualism was now the core of the collective conscience of modern industrial society (Durkheim 1964[1893]:172, 190).

Durkheim was profoundly disturbed by what he perceived as the pathologies of the modern industrial society of France and by its seeming loss of any collective conscience or moral compass. It had not developed normally. He intended to find and develop a set of institutions and practices that would restore social order and overcome the pathologies of the existing social milieu. I described him as a "conservative theorist" in the title to this section; however, his political sympathies did not lie with the conservative parties, which were anti-Semitic and intent on restoring the monarchy and strengthening the role of the Catholic Church in education. Nor did Durkheim's sympathies lie with the working-class anarchists, socialists, and Marxists whom he distrusted, whose activities he saw as unruly and prone to violence, and whose views he systemically portrayed as economic determinist and out of touch with the moral problems of industrial society. He believed that the public confused his view with those of the socialists and that the conflation had cost him university positions he sought in Paris (Llobera 1981; Mauss 1958[1895–1896]). In today's terms, he was a moderate liberal, supporting secular, state-sponsored education and defending the legitimacy of an autonomous, liberal-democratic state that would promote the rights of the individual (Hearn 1985; Vogt 1991). In a phrase, he believed that the promise of the French Revolution was largely unrealized because of the civil unrest and wars that had disrupted everyday life in France since the 1790s; France "… did not know how to create organs which could give these ideas life, institutions in which they could be embodied" (Durkheim 1977:305).

His goal was to explain what happened during the transition from traditional, pre-industrial societies to modern industrialist nations. What were the bonds that united people into a community? He contrasted the individualism—the absence of a moral center in the chronically unstable, crisis-ridden industrial society of France—with the circumstances that prevailed in primitive society, in which there was a set of beliefs, ideas, and rules that dictated everyday life and that were held with an intense, almost religious fervor. Durkheim referred to this as the collective conscience of the community and the form of cohesion it produced as "mechanical solidarity." While the members of a community changed over time, the collective conscience was more stable. He did not mean that this unity of interests and responsibilities yielded sameness or uniformity or that individuals were virtually identical or indistinguishable from their kin and neighbors. He did mean that these shared sets of beliefs yielded consensus and solidarity. For example, think of the interplay of individuality and unanimity in the performance of a piece of jazz music: The improvisation and virtuosity of the soloist always gives way to the form or chorus performed by the ensemble as a whole in order to achieve the aim of its collective project (Cladis 2005:384; West 2001:150–151).

In *The Division of Labor in Society*, Durkheim (1964[1893]:156–229) portrayed the transition from mechanical to organic solidarity as a natural process: a slow, continuous evolution or growth over time, a conversion, rather than a metamorphosis or a revolution. By "division of labor," he meant the specialization of social functions rather than exclusively occupational specialization.

He saw the evolution as broadly linear and uni-directional: a natural growth from relatively homogeneous or simple to increasingly more complex. Briefly, bands (the simplest type of society) came together to form tribal confederacies in which a division of labor slowly emerged as each band in the aggregation assumed a particular function (e.g. religious functionaries) and differentiated themselves from the rest of the community. Further social differentiation (increasing social complexity) and functional interdependence occurred with the dissolution of the tribal confederacies and the formation of city-states, the principal subdivisions of which were territorial groupings rather than social ones; in the process, political leadership was differentiated from the institutions associated with kinship and religion, and the domestic religious cults of the bands and tribal confederacies were subordinated to state religions that were simultaneously more abstract and less pervasive in their control of everyday life. Two changes occurred during the next phase of the process: (1) specialized institutions concerned with government, religion, education, and economics developed, and (2) inter-regional differentiation of the economy produced an international division of labor. The modern industrial nations were freed even further from the religious and territorial constraints of earlier stages in the process. They witnessed the growth of large-scale, functionally specific institutions concerned with government, education, manufacturing, and commerce that operated across the state; these institutions were interrelated and subordinated to the state, which established the conditions for their cooperation (e.g. property) through procedural and restitutive (restorative) laws rather than repression or punishment. The division of labor promoted individuation; personalities shared only by others occupying the same space in the division of labor; and the growth of a market economy, which ultimately pitted one individual against another when they sought to buy or sell the same item in the market. Eight years later, Durkheim described this evolution not as a hierarchy or linear succession but rather as analogous to a tree

> with many branches diverging in greater or lesser degree. But, on this tree societies are found at differing heights, and are found at differing distances from the common trunk. It is on condition that one looks in this way that one can talk of a general evolution of societies.
>
> (Durkheim 2013[1901]:81)

In so doing, he left room for the simultaneous operation of a general law at one level and contingency at another. He also left space for deviation from the normal course of development and for the emergence of pathologies.

Thus, he compared different stages in the transition from primitive to modern industrial society. He noted several differences. For him, the collective conscience of primitive society had been dissolved and replaced by an organic solidarity in modern industrial society that was based on a division of labor among occupational specialists; market exchange relations; and only vestigial traces of a collective conscience, which was shared to some extent by other practitioners of the same occupation. In Durkheim's view, the division of labor in modern industrial society, especially as it was emerging in France, had actually produced less solidarity, not more. The division of labor occurred because the economy was separated from the social whole and had become the most important social realm. The capitalist had wedged himself "between worker and society, [and] prevent[ed] labor from being properly appreciated and rewarded according to its social value" (Durkheim 1958[1895–1896]:25). There was a lack of exchange and communication between the workers and the wider society, and this had devastating consequences. Instead of increasing cooperation, it created economic failures, class conflict, a breakdown in social regulation, and disequilibrium (Alexander 1982:153). This anomic state occurred because of rapid industrialization. There were no rules regarding the relations between social functions; there was a breakdown and growing disjunction between existing norms and the inability of groups to act in accord with their goals (Lukes 2006). As a result, the relations between capital and labor were unregulated. The inequalities resulting from unequal exchanges in the market imposed a forced division of labor that reflected wealth and family position rather than a natural distribution based on the talents and abilities of individuals (Durkheim 1964[1893]:354–370).

For Durkheim, industrial society was an abnormal development—a pathological form or deviation from the natural course of development. He did not believe that the real problems created by rapid industrialization were economic ones because capitalism had excluded economic life from the processes of communication by which the state regulated the rest of society. Economic relations were not part of the real foundations of modern society, which rested instead on a substrate composed of religious faiths; legal and moral regulations; political, literary, and occupational associations; and, curiously, financial systems (Aimard 1962; Bottomore 1984:115–116; Lukes 1973:499–500).

In *Suicide*, Durkheim (1951[1897]:152–171) argued that Christianity was an independent causal factor contributing to the anomic condition and uniqueness of the West. In his view, two processes unfolded during the Middle Ages: (1) the appearance of specialized institutions concerned with government, religion, education, and economics, and (2) inter-regional economic differentiation. In these circumstances, the Christian religion became even more abstract, composed of "articles of faith which are very broad and very general, rather than of particular beliefs and determined practices" (Durkheim 1964[1893]:289). By allowing more individual reflection, voluntary action, and rational investigation, Christianity facilitated the secularization of the state and the economy, and sowed the seeds for further individuation of the increasingly atomistic, rational individual.

The state emerged as the mechanical solidarity of primitive society was eroded by the increasing differentiation of social functions—i.e. Durkheim's division of labor. It was the central organ that coordinated the functions of the various parts of the social whole. By virtue of this central place, it was better able than individuals to grasp the significance of the whole and to provide the identity of interest required to achieve and maintain equilibrium (Alexander 1982:107–108). It became "... the essential cog in the machine, since it alone makes it function"

(Durkheim 1964[1893]:113). As society advanced, the state became a source of social control by virtue of its regulation of the moral exchange and communication that occurred between diverse individuals and groups (Alexander 1982:222–223). Its representatives asserted control accomplished by making administrative and restitutive laws that determined the normal functions of the different parts of the social whole and their interrelations with one another (Durkheim 1964[1893]:126–127).

The pathologies of modern society, the disequilibrium resulting from the absence of regulation in economic life, could be remedied, he believed, by reconstituting secondary professional or occupational groups, like the Roman or medieval guilds, that stood between the family and the state. These groups had been destroyed by the rise of modern industrial society, which now operated on a national scale rather than for local or regional consumption. The loss of occupational groups in modern society diminished the regulation of the economy and the marketplace, the maintenance of an occupational morality backed by collective authority, and a collective milieu that was worthy of loyalty (Wallwork 1972:103):

> A society composed of an infinite number of unorganized individuals, that a hypertrophied State is forced to oppress and contain, constitutes a veritable sociological monstrosity. For collective activity is always too complex to be able to be expressed through the single and unique organ of the State. Moreover, the State is too remote from individuals; its relations with them too external and intermittent to penetrate deeply into individual consciences and socialize them within. Where the State is the only environment in which men can lead communal lives, they inevitably lose contact, become detached, and thus society disintegrates. A nation can be maintained only if, between the State and the individual, there is intercalated a whole series of secondary groups near enough to the individuals to attract them strongly in their sphere of action and drag them, in this way, into the general torrent of social life.
>
> (Durkheim 1964[1893]:28)

In Durkheim's view, occupational groups would serve this function. They would also counterbalance any tendencies of the state to exert its control over individuals, on the one hand, and the growth of anomic individualism, on the other. Employers and employees would belong to different corporate organizations because their interests were antagonistic under the circumstances created by capitalism. Group life would be based on education and mutual aid, and the members of an organization would be related to one another by moral exchanges and communication. In other words, they would share ideas, sentiments, and practices, and the groups would regulate the actions of their members by virtue of the moral authority and force invested in them.

The formation of secondary groups was essential for providing linkage between the individual and the state. The question for Durkheim was how the groups could be instituted and maintained. His answer was that the state must participate in their formation. Thus, in *Professional Ethics and Civil Morals*, written in the late 1890s, he modified his earlier view that the state was the moral regulator and authority of society, and argued instead that

> the State is a special organ responsible for elaborating certain representations which are valid for the collectivity. These representations are distinguished from other collective representations by their higher degree of consciousness and reflection.... [T]he State does not execute anything. The Council of ministers or the sovereign do not themselves take action any more than Parliament: they give the orders for the action to be taken. They co-ordinate ideas and sentiments, from these they frame decisions and transmit these decisions to other agencies that carry them out: but this is the limit to their office. In this respect there is no difference between Parliament (or the deliberative assemblies of all kinds surrounding the sovereign or head of State) and the government in the exact meaning of the term, the power known as executive. The whole life of the State, in its true meaning, consists not in exterior action, in making changes, but in deliberation, that is, in representations. It is others, the administrative bodies of all kinds, who are in charge of carrying out the changes.... Strictly speaking, the State is the very organ of social thought. As things are, this thought is directed towards an aim that is practical, not speculative. The State, as a rule at least, does not think for the sake of thought or to build up doctrinal systems, but to guide collective conduct. None the less, its principal function is to think.
>
> (Durkheim 1992[1898–1900]:50–51)

The state was no longer merely the moral regulator of society as it had been in the ancient city or in medieval times. In modern society, it had become a representation of the collectivity and a moral community that forged rules and inspired loyalty. It had the capacity to create the conditions required for forging a new morality, one that involved secondary groups in the regulation of economic life and that dealt with the contradictions between the social norms of equality and the inequalities and injustices arising from the inheritance of property and talent (Durkheim 1992[1898–1900]:213, 220).[3]

During its early stages of development in the ancient city and medieval society, the state and the civic morality it promoted were intimately bound up with religion and religious beliefs:

> The destiny of the State was closely bound up with the fate of the gods worshipped at its altars. If a State suffered reverses, then the prestige of its gods declined in the same measure—and vice versa. Public religion and civic morals were fused: they were but different aspects of the same reality. To bring glory to the City was the same as enhancing the glory of the gods of the City....
>
> (Durkheim 1992[1898–1900]:55)

There were striking similarities between the moral community constituted by the early state and the one constituted by religion—that "unified system of beliefs and practices relative to sacred things" (Durkheim 1965[1912]:62). Both communities emphasized its sacred quality and were, in fact, merely two sides of the same coin. Society

> is worshipped by believers; the superiority of the gods over men is that of the group over its members. The early gods were the substantive objects which served as symbols to the collectivity and for this reason became the representation of it: as a result of this representation they shared in the sentiments of respect inspired by the society in the individuals composing it.
>
> (Durkheim 1992[1898–1900]:161)

Religion, which originated in the collective behavior of a society, was ultimately the source of virtually every institution in modern society—law, morality, contract, property, arts, and science—except economic activity. It helped people live together in a single moral community and adapt to the circumstances of their existence, and it was also a system of representations that explained the world in which they lived. It underpinned and strengthened society. However, religion was also a source of change, especially on those occasions in which individuals came together in a context of collective disorganization, and new collective representations and understandings emerged as a result of their participation and actions (Pickering 1984:385, 412–414; Wallwork 1984).

Durkheim (1886:61–69) believed that morality, religion, and law were the three important control mechanisms of society; they dictated the sentiments and ideas of a group, and regulated the actions of its members. Morality allowed people to live together; it "adapt[ed] individuals to one another, to assure thus the equilibrium and survival of the group" (Durkheim 1887:138). However, it was religion that really stood at the core of this triad; it was ultimately the historical source, the foundation, of the entire institutional apparatus of society. In Durkheim's view,

> Religion contains in itself from the very beginning, even if in an indistinct state, all the elements which in dissociating themselves from it, articulating themselves, and combining with one another in a thousand ways, have given rise to the various manifestations of collective life. From myths and legends have issued forth science and poetry; from religious ornamentations and cult ceremonials have come the plastic arts; from ritual practice were born law and morals.
>
> (Durkheim 1898:ii)

According to Durkheim "the religious nature of man ... [is] an essential and permanent aspect of humanity" (Durkheim 1965[1912]:13).

Durkheim's concern in *The Elementary Forms of Religious Life* (1912) was the problem of social order: What prevents a society, especially a modern democratic one, from collapsing into a struggle and pitting one individual against another? While the early state was indifferent to the individual, whose interests were subordinated to those of the collectivity, the individual broke away from the social mass in modern society and gradually acquired rights, property, and respect as the cult of the individual replaced the cult of the gods as an object of worship (Wallwork 1972:106–107). Durkheim (1992[1898–1900]:69–74) argued that it was the duty of the modern state to promote, protect, and define the emerging rights of the individual and, at the same time, to forge a civic morality that would engender and promote the loyalty of the increasingly autonomous person to the wider collectivity—i.e. the nation and humanity. These rights and the ethic on which they were based would ultimately be rooted in the realm of the sacred because only the beliefs and practices associated with sacred things, "set apart and forbidden," had the capacity to create social bonds. These bonds were more fundamental than the ones forged in the world of the profane—i.e. in the market.

Durkheim viewed society through an evolutionary lens.[4] To him, society was analogous to a biological system composed of functionally interrelated, increasingly specialized parts or spheres. The equilibrium or cohesion of this complex whole was maintained by shared norms (*collective conscience*) and the regular exchange of knowledge and information among the parts (i.e. the division of labor). However, the cohesion of society was gradually eroded by social differentiation as spheres—like the economy—became steadily more autonomous as well as by the breakdown of the moral order as the division of labor intensified, and individuals had steadily fewer things in common with those who functioned outside their own spheres of specialization (in Durkheim's terms, this was the rise of individualism, the shift from mechanical to organic solidarity, and the growing importance of market exchange). This was the pathology of modern industrial society—one that might be remedied.

Max Weber: Critic, Nationalist, Historical Political Economist

Max Weber (1864–1920)—a liberal nationalist—was raised in Berlin in the years following the unification of Germany in 1871 under the leadership of Prussian landowners. During this period, he witnessed the transformation of Berlin from a provincial administrative center to a cosmopolitan industrial metropolis, the crisis of the German agrarian economy, the rapid and uneven development of the world's most advanced industrial capitalist economy, the formation of the German overseas empire, the rapid growth of the working class, and a significant expansion of both state and industrial bureaucracies. A voracious reader as a child, he studied history, law, and political economy while at the university and wrote two dissertations—one dealing with commercial partnerships in medieval Europe and the other on land law in the Roman Empire (Weber 2003[1889]; 2008[1889]). Soon after completing his dissertations, he began to investigate current developments in the agrarian economy in Prussia, east of the Elbe River, under the growing impact of capitalist rationality (e.g. Mommsen and Osterhammel 1987; Tribe 1989a). This early work—focused on agrarian history, both ancient and modern—laid the methodological and conceptual foundations for his subsequent, comparative studies of societal histories, religion, political economy, and sociology.

The chaotic conditions in Germany underpinned a number of debates in which Weber participated. In the 1890s, these were often interwoven and sometimes conflated. It is useful to separate them before considering how he knotted them together. The first debate was the critique of positivism—broadly, that all knowledge of reality is based on experience; that the methodological procedures of the natural sciences are applicable to the study of cultural beings in society; that the goal of social inquiry is to establish law-like generalizations; that the explanation of cultural individuals can be reduced to the liberal, utilitarian origins of moral ethics and appetites postulated by Smith and others as part of a universal human nature; and that scientists should remain neutral with regard to value judgments and be objective observers with regard to their objects of inquiry (Hughes 1977:33–66; Kolakowski 1968:90–124). A second debate dealt with Neo-Kantian concerns about methodological and epistemological differences between the natural sciences, on the one hand, and the historical, cultural, and social sciences, on the other (Benton 1977:100–111). A third was a methodological squabble over the meanings of terms used to specify "economic activity and its representation" and the "derivation and elaboration of human needs and economic life." It raised issues over the meaning of understanding, values, and facts; the distinction between reality and concepts of reality; and the definition of reality through the use of ideal types conceptualized in terms of one another (Oakes 1987; Tribe 1995:76). A fourth debate was concerned with questions of economic policy: Should the political economy of Germany be based on free-market liberalism or state intervention and protective tariffs? How can the rapidly expanding number of wage-workers be integrated into the political economy of the national state? Weber had read widely and critically since childhood and engaged with a number of his predecessors and contemporaries—simultaneously interrogating and critiquing their work while clarifying and developing his own conceptual framework and analyses (e.g. Mommsen and Osterhammel 1987). In addition to Enlightenment authors concerned with reason and rationality, Weber read Marx, cultural critic Friedrich Nietzsche, liberal theorist John Stuart Mill, ancient historian Eduard Meyer, philosopher Heinrich Rickert, political economist Karl Knies, and Social Democratic politician Eduard Bernstein (Hennis 1987; Löwith 1982[1960]; Oakes 1987; Roth 1971a,b; Tenbruck 1987; Tribe 1989, 1995).

In *The Protestant Ethic and the Spirit of Capitalism*, Weber (1958[1904–1905]:17) thought that the rise of rational capitalism was "the most fateful force in modern life." This was not the first time he expressed this sentiment, nor would it be the last. However, before considering what he meant and how he arrived at this conclusion about the development of humanity, let us consider his historical-dialectical conceptual framework and understanding of reality. He was neither a positivist nor a reductionist; hence, in his view, the whole was greater than the sum of its parts. While recognizing that the methods and views of natural scientists were often quite different from those of cultural scientists, he understood that each yielded a partial picture of the worlds we inhabit and that, when they are brought together, we gain a greater understanding of the whole. To accomplish this, he used conceptual constructs called ideal types to clarify what underlay the superficial, often confusing appearances of empirical reality. They were logical arrays of possible components—like the multiple forms and meanings of rationality, value, or rational and non-rational capitalism he described (e.g. Albrow 1990:114–130; Brubaker 1984:1–48; Weber 1981[1923]:275–285). They could be assembled (at least theoretically) in various ways, taken apart, and re-assembled in new ways in order to understand and explain the contingency of historically specific societies and how they emerged: the configurations of social and economic relations; the cultures, traditions, habits, and psyches of their members; the socioeconomic interests and meanings that motivate them to do what they do; and the significance they attach to those actions (Swedberg 2005:119–121). He began to formulate this conceptual and methodological tool kit in the 1890s and set it in writing in the early 1900s, suggesting along the way that Marxian laws were actually ideal types (Weber 1949[1903–1917]; 1978[1922]:63–73).

Weber (1978[1922]:164–166) conceptualized capitalism in terms of several ideal types: (1) the profits realized by occasional trade and moneylending; (2) those gained by close connections with the political organizations or the state to finance wars or revolutions and to provide loans and supplies; (3) opportunities for profit guaranteed by the power of political authority; and (4) profits realized by the continuous purchase and sale of standardized commodities in a market, the financing of new enterprises, and engagement with the financial operations of the state. As you will recall from the preceding paragraphs, Weber's initial concerns were with whether capitalism existed, and in what forms it existed, in ancient Rome and medieval Europe as well as with the ongoing transformation of the agrarian economy east of the Elbe River in the late nineteenth century. On the one hand, he argued that trade and moneylending capital—i.e. his first three ideal types—were characteristic of the pre-modern societies he studied. On the other, he asserted that his fourth ideal type—capitalism distinguished by the regular provisioning of human needs as a result of continuous, rationalized industrial production and the sale of standardized commodities by private, profit-seeking enterprises—was typical of the industrializing countries of the West. He subsequently wrote that the more distinctive features of modern capitalism were (1) the appropriation of the means of production as the disposable property of private enterprises, (2) no limitations on a free market, (3) free labor in which individuals legally possess their labor power and are compelled to sell it on the market without restriction, (4) a rational technology that implies maximal mechanization, (5) calculable law, and (6) the commercialization of economic life (Weber 1981[1923]:276–278).

In 1896, Weber argued that capitalism in the ancient world was largely limited to "wealth used to gain profit in commerce [and moneylending]" (Weber 1976[1896]:48) and that the profit orientation of merchants and moneylenders was essentially grafted onto a natural economy based on production for use (Banaji 2002; Finley 1973; Love 1991:7–55). Capitalist enterprises that employed free wage labor and resembled those of the present day were rare and typically involved seasonal or irregular activities, such as harvests or state-sponsored construction projects. Weber suggested that pre-modern capitalism flourished in periods in which ancient states had recently acquired vast amounts of land through conquest and were in the process of redistributing spoils to their soldiers and allies. Furthermore, the institutions on which this early capitalism was based were very fragile; for example, the decline of the Roman Empire—marked by the disappearance of the standing army, salaried bureaucrats, inter-local commerce, administrative law, and cities—also witnessed the collapse of capitalist institutions (Weber 1976[1898]:409). Thus, the commercial and moneylending activities of antiquity had different consequences than those associated with the industrial capitalism that was shaping Western European national states in the nineteenth century.

Weber's (1989[1894]) next investigation of capitalism was his 1892–1893 study of the changes taking place in the rural-labor relations in East Prussia. He saw variations of the agrarian systems of the region as almost teleological "developmental tendencies." These marked the shift from a social order based on the superficially shared interests of estate owner and permanent estate worker to one firmly rooted in modern rational capitalism and the maximization of profits, in which the interests of owner and worker were antagonistic (Riesebrodt 1989; Tribe 1989b). Briefly, Weber argued that in the old system, the estates produced a combination of food grains and root crops: The aristocratic owners would sell grain harvested by permanent estate workers in the market, and the workers received a small portion of profits from the sale of grain as well as housing, use of marginal land for their own gardens, access to estate pastures, and other considerations in exchange for their labor on the estate. Because their labor was largely seasonal, the estate workers often went to western and southern Germany after the harvests and visited friends or relatives, engaged in some wage-work, and enjoyed what leisure time they had. In the new system, as the demand for more profitable grain crops grew, the estate owners increasingly planted grains on rented land or on the more marginal lands formerly used by estate workers, decreased the portion of profits the tenants received, and reduced the size of the payments in kind (use rights). As their living standards diminished, there was a massive exodus of rural workers to the industrial cities in search of more profitable work. Confronted with a rapidly shrinking labor force, the estate owners turned increasingly to Polish migrant farmworkers hired seasonally for the harvest.

Weber's analysis showed that the development of modern rational capitalism was marked by changes in the relation between domination and the economy, and by changes in the worldviews of both the landowning aristocrats and their tenants as they became enmeshed in capitalist productions. Labor relations, formerly based on voluntary contracts between owner and tenant in the natural economy of the estate, were replaced with legal, employer-employee contracts that turned the tenant into a rural proletarian who worked for wages and paid rent. In the process, these employees lost their economic independence as they were separated from the land and as their use rights to estate resources were replaced by monetary wages. This transformation was underwritten by legal measures that established the preconditions for development by allowing merchants to purchase or rent agricultural estates, which they ran in an economically efficient manner to maximize their profitability. Because the landed aristocrats were adopting bourgeois spending and consumption patterns, they had a steadily growing need for cash in order to maintain the style to which they were becoming accustomed. The values placed by tenants on economic independence and individualism were challenged in the new conditions, especially as these tenants moved to the industrial cities for better paying jobs and were exposed to the urban, market-oriented mentality of their new neighbors.

Weber touched on several urgent questions of the day in Germany in his report to the Association for Social Policy—the project's sponsor and a group of academic economists concerned with influencing policy and training government bureaucrats and ministers. These included (1) the consolidation of an overseas empire; (2) the recent legalization of the Social Democratic Party—which represented the interests of unionized industrial workers as well as various socialist and communist groups; (3) the rapid growth of modern rational capitalism and market exchange; (4) mounting class conflict; (5) the appearance of regionally specialized production on both national and international scales; (6) the transformation of agrarian social and economic relations in eastern Germany—what was being called "The Agrarian Question;" (7) international labor migration and the growing number of foreign nationals who were working in the country and toiling for lower wages than Germans—i.e. "The National Question;" and (8) the kinds of new political coalitions that might develop between the estate workers and peasants, on the one hand, and industrial workers, on the other. We will look in more detail at the Agrarian and National Questions in subsequent chapters.

Weber addressed several of the issues directly in his inaugural lecture as Professor of Economics at Freiburg University. He argued for the primacy of the interests of the German national-state in all discussions of economic and political policy: "The economic policy of a German state, and the standard of value adopted by a German economic theorist, can therefore be nothing other than a Germany policy and a German standard" (Weber 1989[1895]:198). He argued that it was not in the best interest of the national-state to have an economically declining class—i.e. the landowning aristocracy, the Junkers, who filled the state bureaucracy and had access to the German monarch—that remained politically dominant; this class was in an economic death-struggle because of the rapid development of rational capitalism. However, the German bourgeoisie, located in the towns and cities, had not yet consolidated the political power they believed was their due by virtue of their economic successes in the recent past. While this group was, in fact, the repository of real power interests, it was, like the German working class, politically immature and opportunist. Two years later, at the Social Evangelical Congress, Weber argued forcefully that Germany had to have an integrated national economic policy, not separate ones for the agricultural and industrial sectors (Weber 1989[1897]).

The social groups emerging in Germany represented the superposition and intersection of two contradictory forms of social stratification. Class stratification was based entirely on economic exchange in the marketplace as individuals bought and sold the property and skills they possessed. Individuals with the same class situation—i.e. belonging to same class—had roughly the same "probability of procuring goods, gaining a position in life, and finding inner satisfactions" (Weber 1978[1922]:302). The emerging class structure crosscut the existing stratified series of estates—traditional status groups—whose members shared legal rights and obligations that were different from those of people in the other estates. For example, the landed aristocracy of Prussia had one set of rights and obligations with respect to their tenants, while the tenants had different expectations and responsibilities toward the landowners. In Weber's view, while the social-class and estate structures competed for political power, class formation indicated that individuals and groups of individuals struggled to gain advantage as each sought to promote its own ideas and material interests (Clarke 1982:192–196).

One problem plaguing Germany in the 1890s was that the bureaucracy, which had become a social stratum unto itself, held political power and controlled the political and economic policies of the state. In order to promote the expansion of German influence, it was necessary to create the conditions required for the development of a political leadership that would effectively challenge the domination of the bureaucracy and recognize the primacy of the national state. This led to circumstances in which the property-holding bourgeoisie, the only group capable of providing leadership in a capitalist state, could emerge to challenge the rational-legal domination of the Junker bureaucracy, whose traditional rationality was oriented toward the maintenance of the existing social order (Bottomore 1984:125–127). This required the formation of a charismatic leader from the bourgeoisie who could break out of existing value orientations and behavior patterns, lay the foundations for new forms of action, disrupt established power relations, attract adherents from different segments of society, and show them that they had common interests. Weber (1946[1915]:280) remarked that such new "world images have, like switchmen, determined the tracks along which action has been pushed by a dynamic of interest."

In 1898, Weber produced his first comparative study of the agrarian conditions of ancient civilizations—Egypt, Mesopotamia, Israel, Greece, and Rome. In it, he repeatedly noted the interplay of religious and state institutions in shaping and constraining economic action. This was "the latent struggle between theocratic and secular political forces ... [that] influenced social and economic developments, especially in periods of general secularization or restoration" (Weber 1976[1898]:78–79). After a hiatus of seven years, he resumed his inquiry, this time into the economic ethics of world religions (i.e. those practical impulses toward economic action that derive from religion). The first was *The Protestant Ethic and the Spirit of Capitalism*, the controversial thesis of which was "that ascetic Protestantism helped form the mentality of modern, rational capitalism"

(Swedberg 1998:119). His argument was not that it caused modern capitalism but rather that the doctrines of some sects, notably the Puritans, provided religious rationales and reasons for thinking and acting in particular ways. These included (1) distinguishing between the members of a community and outsiders, (2) accepting the doctrine of predestination rather than salvation through absolution, (3) seeking salvation instead of damnation by working arduously to change the world in God's image, (4) taking both work and the work of God seriously as a calling or vocation, and (5) accepting the idea that any profits that ensued from one's work were signs of God's approval (Swedberg 1998:119–145).

The worldly asceticism adopted by the followers of Calvin and other charismatic Puritans provided a basis for challenging and ultimately undermining traditional notions of work. For Weber (1958[1904–1905]:78), the development of modern industrial capitalism seemed more like an adaptation rather than a revolutionary breakthrough because the economic ethic had gradually become so institutionalized in modern European society that

> it no longer needs the support of any religious forces, and feels the attempts of religion to influence economic life, in so far as they can still be felt at all, to be as much an unjustified interference as its regulation by the State.

He believed that industrial capitalism was a uniquely Western phenomenon and explored various dimensions of the historical circumstances in which it emerged. In 1915, he examined the relationship between the work ethics of various world religions and the conduct of the social strata that "most strongly influenced the practical ethic of their respective religions" (Weber 1946[1915]:268). He suggested that the various classes—warriors, peasants, merchants, artisans, and educated intellectuals—pursued different religious tendencies. Of these, the intellectuals and the business classes were the most open to rationalism, in contrast to the peasants, who were receptive to magical explanations of nature, or the warriors, who pursued worldly interests remote from mysticism. City-dwelling artisans, merchants, and entrepreneurs in China, India, the Middle East, and Western Europe were the most ambiguous in this regard and, at the same time, the most receptive to a variety of religious sects—Taoism, Buddhism, Sufism, and Puritanism. Yet what all of the civic classes had in common was a tendency toward a *practical* rationalism:

> Their whole existence has been based upon technological or economic calculations and upon the mastery of nature and of man, however primitive the means at their disposal. The technique of living handed down among them may, of course, be frozen in traditionalism.... [But] there has always existed the possibility—even though in greatly varying measure—of letting *ethical* and rational regulation of life arise. This may occur by the linkage of such an ethic to the tendency of technological and economic rationalism.
>
> (Weber 1946[1915]:284)

He proceeded to argue that while the religious prophets of Zoroastrianism and Islam, for example, directed their revelations of worldly action toward the peasant, noble, and warrior classes, the Puritan prophets directed their message of worldly asceticism toward the civic strata of Western cities, whose members were already receptive to arguments about the rationalization of everyday life (Weber 1946[1915]:287–289).

Because modern industrial capitalism was based on the rational organization of formally free labor attuned to the market, Weber also began to explore how this labor force "had gradually emerged as an entirely new form of social organization,... and where and under what conditions an autonomous urban bourgeoisie developed" (Mommsen 1989:149). In *The City* (1958[1921]), he examined the political and economic challenges to social stability that occurred during the development of Western cities, which emerged in the twelfth century. When the economic interests of their citizens clashed with those of local lords, they used political and military means to gain autonomy and to establish civic associations. Furthermore, "when the economic interests of the burghers urged them toward institutionalized association this movement was not frustrated by the existence of magic or religious barriers" (Weber 1958[1921]:114). The political equality of the associations was subsequently dissolved when affluent members monopolized municipal offices and excluded those who were unable to pay their share of the taxes. Nevertheless, the members who were excluded from office still viewed themselves and were viewed by the officials as citizens.

In the *General Economic History* (1981[1923]), Weber returned to his interest in the economic and political conditions that buttressed the rise of modern capitalism and the modern state. He argued that modern cities

> ... came under the power of competing national states in a condition of perpetual struggle for power in peace or war. This competitive struggle created the largest opportunities for modern Western capitalism. The separate states had to compete for mobile capital, which dictated to them the conditions under which it would assist them to power. Out of this alliance of the state with capital, dictated by necessity, arose the national citizen class, the bourgeoisie in the modern sense of the word. Hence it is the closed nation state which afforded capitalism its chance for development— and as long as the nation state does not give place to a world empire capitalism will also endure.
>
> (Weber 1981[1923]:337)

Thus, the national state was the only one in which modern industrial capitalism could flourish; they were exclusively Western. The bases of these modern states were rational law, which was made and applied by full-time jurists for a population with rights of citizenship, and a bureaucracy, which was staffed by full-time professional experts. Rational states were also national entities that had well-defined economic and political policies.

Mercantilism, which had appeared in England in the fourteenth century, was the first modern state economic policy; it brought the viewpoint of the capitalist entrepreneur into politics (Weber 1981[1923]:347–350). The rational state acted as if it were composed entirely of capitalist entrepreneurs who sought at every turn to maximize their gains at the expense of their opponents. The state became powerful by increasing the taxes derived from its citizens. Mercantilist economic policies had two features: They promoted class monopolies by granting import rights only to those with royal concessions, and they protected national industries. However, it did not provide the foundations for the development of modern capitalism because mercantilist policies disappeared. As a result, modern

> capitalistic development was not an outgrowth of national mercantilism; rather capitalism developed at first in England alongside the fiscal monopoly policy. The course of events was that a stratum of entrepreneurs which had developed in independence of the political administration secured the systematic support of Parliament in the 18th century, after the collapse of the fiscal monopoly policy of the Stuarts. Here for the last time irrational and rational capitalism faced each other in conflict, that is, capitalism in the field of fiscal and colonial privileges and public monopolies, and capitalism oriented in relation to market opportunities which were developed from within by business interests themselves on the basis of saleable services.
>
> (Weber 1981[1923]:350)

Weber was a liberal democrat, a critic of liberalism, and an activist policy advocate, as evidenced by his Freiburg address. He recognized the contradiction between democracy and liberalism: the former's primary concern with rule by the people, and the latter's with the rights of the desiring individual as constitutive of modern society. He rejected the natural rights, utilitarianism, and universal human nature arguments that dominated Anglophone liberal thought. In Germany, he opposed the traditional rationality of the Junkers and their allies, which looked backward and underpinned policies that were outmoded, given the new kinds of social relations, values, and psyches being forged in the country as a result of the dissolution of personal ties between individuals and their replacement with the impersonal relationships that promoted class conflict. What the Junkers had succeeded in accomplishing, however, was the professionalization of administration and the bureaucratization of the political structure. The bureaucracy was efficient and "had an inherent tendency to exceed its instrumental function, and to become a separate force within society, capable of influencing the goals and character of that society" (Beetham 1985:65).

Before World War I, Weber's goal was to curb the power of Junkers and the potential influence of the bureaucracy. To do so, he advocated an equilibrium model of a parliamentary liberal democracy—one that balanced various class and political party interests. It was pluralist in the sense that individuals and groups were pulled in diverse directions in order to maximize their goals under conditions of free competition; it was democratic in the sense that voting was a means of choosing between competing politicians to represent them and provide direction for the administration of government until the next election. Following the war, Weber reasserted a position he had held throughout his career: It was essential to strengthen the modern capitalist state. Doing so would preserve the integrity of the nation, which he defined largely in terms of literacy and a shared language and in terms of its international struggle for existence with other nation states. Because participatory democracy was all but impossible, except in the smallest of societies, democracy was reduced to a mechanism for selecting leaders—preferably charismatic leaders who possessed a vision of the future:

> Through the institution of the Reich presidency, [they might] ... rise to power even outside of the party machines and ... create sufficient room for maneuver for them to realize their most important political goals even if these differ from the intentions of the existing parliamentary majority.
> (Mommsen 1974:343–344)

This, of course, would involve the dissolution of old values and social relations and the formation of new ones; it would entail their adoption by the wider society and, ultimately, their acceptance and routinization by the administrative bureaucracies of both government and industry. While there was a sense of directionality in Weber's writing, there was neither certainty nor finality in what might happen. In his metaphor, there was always the possibility of another switchman down the track; thus, the future was always contingent and entailed redefining the relations between society, bureaucracy, the state, and the economy as he outlined in *Economy and Society* (Beetham 1994; Weber 1978[1922]).

At the same time, he saw democracy and the rights of citizens threatened from two directions in the modern industrial capitalist state. One threat was the increasing domination of economic and political life by large-scale organizations—i.e. by industrial corporations and the state bureaucracy. Weber feared that the growing instrumental rationality of the bureaucracy and the drive for mechanization would spread to all spheres of society—i.e. the modernization of culture, values, psyches, customs, and habits. These would constitute a metaphorical "iron cage," to use Talcott Parsons' translation of *stahlhartes Gehäuse*, from which there was no way out. "The individual is forced to live in [it], with its unrelenting demand that he or she work hard and methodically" (Swedberg 2005:132). The other threat was created by the irrational pressures that mass movements could exert.

Weber also considered human history to be an open-ended process. Disillusioned with deterministic evolutionary schemes of societal development, he constructed sociohistorical models of particular societies—i.e. his ideal types—that allowed him to consider the interplay of structures and historical dynamics and to explore the significance of concepts like rationality, bureaucracy, domination, legitimation, party, and charismatic leaders in order to suggest explanations of particular cases (Roth 1971c; Roth and Schluchter 1979:195–206).

Discussion

The Industrial Revolution—the rise of industrial capitalism and modern industrial society—was a protracted process that began to unfold several centuries ago. The process is still unfolding today. It is important to keep in mind that Marx began writing nearly half a century before Durkheim and Weber. As a result, each of the theorists witnessed different stages or moments in the process. Marx did not know Durkheim's or Weber's works; the latter either knew Marx's views from a few widely-circulated and translated works, like the first volume of *Capital* or *the Manifesto of the Communist Party*, or from the arguments of contemporary socialists who built on his work in different ways and who often had different assessments of current national and international conditions and questions. Although Durkheim and Weber were contemporaries with one another, they were either unfamiliar with what the other was writing or chose to ignore it. The three critics discussed in this chapter were clearly concerned with the formation of modern, industrial capitalist society and its consequences. All of them saw the modern world as a world in crisis. However, they understood the processes of change and circumstances forged in their wake in different ways. Their conceptual and theoretical frameworks were perhaps the most significant.

Besides capitalism and industrial society, the three critics also addressed other themes. One of these was the constitution of the individual subject. From his earliest works onward, Marx wrote about alienation and reification in industrial capitalist society. By this, he meant the estrangement of individuals from their means of production; from the goods they produce to satisfy needs; from one another as they compete in labor markets for the wages they require to purchase commodities to satisfy their needs; from themselves; and from their capacity to satisfy or realize their own human potential. In capitalist societies, the relation between individuals and the things they make is reified: "a relation between people takes on the character of a thing and thus acquires a 'phantom objectivity', an autonomy that seems so strictly rational and all-embracing as to conceal every trace of its fundamental nature" (Lukács 1971[1923]:83); people are transformed into things, and things are treated like people. Durkheim lamented the growing individualism—the cult of the individual—in modern industrial society. He attributed this to the separation of the moral sphere from market exchange relations and the economy from realms of the social being and to the secularization and individualization of religious life with the advent of Christianity in the West. Weber's attention was drawn to modern rational capitalism and market exchange; to how the economic ethic of ascetic Protestantism, which instilled in individuals the drive to take hard work seriously as a calling, to seek salvation through hard work, and to view profits as a sign of God's approval, laid the foundations for capitalism's development. He feared that the growing instrumental rationality and drive to mechanization would spread to other spheres of life and force individuals to live in the iron cage that was being created by modern industrial capitalism.

A second shared theme was modernity as increasing portions of humanity and everyday life were swept up into the relentless flux created by industrial society. Modernity presented an ever-changing, open-ended, and unlimited future. It is a self-propelled illusion of the future that also empties the past of history and the present of experience; it reduces them to flattened tradition and reduces time to mere chronometric ordering. Modernity found its energy in scientific progress, the Industrial Revolution, industrialization, the formation of the capitalist mode of production, the growth of instrumental rationality, and their spread to all corners of everyday life and the world. The locus of modernity has always been the city, the metropolis, and even civilization itself. For Marx, the city was where factories were located; it was a magnet attracting the proletariat—dispossessed peasants and serfs from the countryside—to markets and a new way of life. For Weber, the city was where the burghers attracted to ascetic Protestantism lived—a devoted labor force to the new kinds of contractual relation between employer and employee; it was also the place where workers went when rural-labor relations were dissolved, and they were replaced by contract migrant workers. For Durkheim, it was the ancient city where small homogeneous bands with different forms of mechanical solidarity came together and, over time, laid the foundations for the division of labor in society in all its manifestations. These increasingly heterogeneous spaces became motors of change with their markets, foreign trade, diversity, religious institutions, and centers of political power and control.

The explicit or implicit theories about the formation of national identities and the transformation of the countryside were a third theme. For Marx, the capitalist mode of production destroyed local cultural and linguistic differences and homogenized formerly disparate populations as the labor markets formed. The new national languages and cultures that formed laid the foundations for territorially-based absolutist states that subsequently underpinned the formation of national states—like England, France, or Germany in the 1870s. Moreover, Marx also recognized the existence of "peoples without history" in Eastern Europe—i.e. Slavic groups with distinctive cultures and languages that resided in territories dominated by the German-speaking aristocracy and bureaucracy. Durkheim also developed an implicit theory of national identity. He described social solidarity in ethnic or national terms as resulting from a community of beliefs and sentiments rooted in the shared historical experiences that occur when people participate in the same organizations. Nations appear when groups united by culture, language, and shared sentiments overlap, and merge with states. By distinguishing between nationality and the state, Durkheim also distinguished between distinctive nationalities, like the Finns or the Poles, that lacked their own states separate from those national states, like France or England, that were dominated by the members of a single nationality (Llobera 1994). Weber believed that nations exist when people share a common objective facto—language, values, culture, religion, and patterns of thought or political experience—and thought that it is a source of social cohesion and solidarity that finds its expression in an autonomous state. He also believed that while the idea of nationhood was found in all

Modern Industrial Capitalist Society · **69**

layers of the class structure, it was not held equally by all strata of the society. He asserted that

> certain sections of the community had a particular interest in it: the army and civil service in extending their power and prestige; the cultural strata in preserving or developing the character of national culture; the proper-tied class in the profits that accrued from overseas trade and colonization.
> (Beetham 1985:144)

The creation of colonies, colonial relations, and imperialism constituted a fourth theme investigated by Marx and Weber. While Marx seems never to have used the term "imperialism" in its modern sense, he did sketch the outlines of a theory to account for the geographical expansion of capitalism and its impact on non-capitalist societies. In his view, competition forced industrial capitalists to devise new methods of production to increase productivity; to develop new markets for their goods; and to locate the cheapest supplies of the raw materials, goods, and labor power they had to purchase. The industrial capitalists satisfied these needs initially by enmeshing pre-capitalist societies in their social rela-tions. Capitalist expansion was facilitated by imperial states that protected over-seas markets and prevented their colonial subjects from developing industries that would compete with those of the metropolitan country. As mentioned in the previous paragraph, Weber pointed out that different social strata gained pres-tige and had vested interests in imperialism—the propertied classes that profited from overseas expansion, the cultural strata, the military, and the civil service. All benefited symbolically and materially from the expansion of national culture into new territories.

In the next chapter, we will examine in more detail how Marx's successors and the contemporaries of Weber and Durkheim dealt with imperialism, nation-alism, the transformation of social relations in the countryside, and the related issues of indigenous peoples and colonial subjects.

Notes

1 For Marx, reality exists at two interrelated levels. The first superficial level consists of the independent existence, outward appearances, and essences of real objects and events experienced by the senses. The second consists of the generative structures, processes, and contradictions that underlie and shape the appearance of the surface. Marx's lifelong investigation was to clarify and understand the dynamics of the un-derlying generative structures and how they affected the relations of people and real objects.

2 Ste. Croix (1984:106–107) describes two forms of exploitation: direct and individual, and indirect and collective. "The first ... is of wage-labourers, slaves, serfs, and debt bondsmen, and also of tenants and ordinary debtors, by particular employers, mas-ters, landowners or moneylenders." The second is "effected through various organs of state ... for the *collective* benefit of (mainly) the propertied class.... [The state also] provide[s] for 'its own needs' by taxation, the extraction of compulsory services, and conscription" (Ste. Croix 1981:206).

3 Durkheim's view of the state contrasts markedly with that of Marx, who saw it simultaneously as an extension of ruling-class power and as an arena of class struggle.
4 Durkheim's theoretical framework was adopted in the 1920s by the British structural-functionalist anthropologists—Bronislaw Malinowski and A. R. Radcliffe-Brown—who were concerned primarily with indigenous, kin-organized communities in the colonies. While Malinowski elaborated on Durkheim's notion of *collective conscience* (culture in his terms), Radcliffe-Brown actively eschewed the idea of culture and focused instead on social relations. In the 1930s and 1940s, U.S. anthropologist Robert Redfield adapted Durkheim's evolutionary progression of social types to describe what he called the folk-urban continuum—the relations that exist between a city and a series of rural communities that have differentially adopted cultural patterns and practices emanating from the urban center. In the 1950s and 1960s, Durkheim's views of society would underpin those of the modernization theorists who wanted to ensure that Third World states would pursue capitalist economic, political, and social development strategies. They would also characterize modernization in terms of Weber's ideas about increased rationality, bureaucracy, and the importance of charismatic leaders.

3

Imperialism and the National, Colonial, and Agrarian Questions, 1890–1929

During the first half of the nineteenth century, the Industrial Revolution grew in petri dishes constituted by *relatively* autonomous nation-states through processes that involved the expansion of domestic markets, the growing exploitation of wage-workers, and the penetration of capitalist social relations into agricultural sectors of their economies. The appearance of capital-intensive industries—like steel, coal, and railroads—reflected both the concentration and centralization of capital as well as the growth of joint-stock companies (corporations) that required investments typically beyond the means of a single individual. However, the Industrial Revolution, and the appearance of industrial society, involved more than industrialization. After 1870, it coincided with (1) the consolidation of nation states (Germany, Italy, and the United States); (2) the massive dispossession of workers from the countryside and unprecedented migration, both within and between states, to industrial cities (Germany, Great Britain, and the United States); (3) the crystallization of new social-class structures; (4) the formation of national identities, nationalist movements, and nation-states (Germany and the United States); (5) imperialism and the construction of overseas colonial empires on a previously unknown scale (Belgium, France, Germany, Great Britain, and the United States); (6) the designation of indigenous peoples and colonial subjects; (7) the growth of trade unions in the industrialized countries as well as anti-colonial, nationalist, and armed resistance movements in the colonies (India, French Indochina, or the Philippines); and (8) the emergence and increasing importance of both economic and geopolitical competition and contradictions among the industrialized, imperialist nation states that underpinned virtually all of the wars in the twentieth century as well as today's conflicts.

In this chapter, let us consider how social commentators who wrote between the 1890s and the late 1920s—Marx's successors, Weber, Durkheim, and their contemporaries—analyzed modern imperialism. Until the 1890s, theories of empire were framed in political terms (Mommsen 1989).[1] Empires were aggregates of territories, states, or colonies under the authority of a single sovereign state, such as Great Britain. By the end of the decade, however, writers were no longer viewing imperialism as the product of exceptional rulers, like Alexander the Great or Napoleon; they were focusing instead on its economic basis—the material motives and class interests in those states where industrial capitalism flourished (Beer 2011[1897]:103; Conant 1898; Hobson 1965[1902]). The specter of imperialism raised three interwoven issues: (1) national identity, nationalism, and national minorities; (2) the creation of colonial subjects and indigenous peoples; and (3) the transformation of rural peoples residing in the "backward," economically undeveloped regions of the imperial states themselves. These have come to be known as the National Question, the Colonial Question, and the Agrarian Question.

Imperialism: Conquest Abroad, Repression at Home

While Marx did not develop a full-blown "theory of imperialism," he did write about the creation of world markets, capitalist states, and overseas colonies. Nonetheless, it is possible to glean retrospectively a developing line of argument from his writings (Anderson 2010). In *The Communist Manifesto*, he and Engels (1976[1848]:486–488) wrote about the constant need of modern industrial capitalists to find new markets for their goods, to draw all nations of the world into the orbit of the "civilized" industrial countries, and to tighten their interdependence and integration—i.e. "to create a world after their own image." The manifesto portrayed the modern industrial state as "a committee for managing the common affairs of the whole bourgeoisie [capitalist class]." In newspaper accounts written during the 1850s, Marx recognized that what was taking place in settler colonies and places where overseas markets were established was not entirely a result of the arrival of Western civilization—it also involved the interplay of historical processes and events that were unfolding independently in the overseas territories themselves. From the late 1850s onward, Marx was continually concerned with the interconnections between metropolitan countries and their colonies.

In *Capital*, Marx commented critically on Edward Wakefield's theory of colonization.[2] He pointed out that settler colonies, like those on the eastern seaboard of North America, were initially tied to the emigration policies of the mother country and that according to the arguments of Wakefield and his supporters, settlers potentially had the capacity to turn "public property" in the colony into private property, which they could work with their own labor to satisfy their own needs. In other words, immigrants who arrived as wage-workers today could potentially turn themselves into independent farmers tomorrow, thereby depriving the colony of its wage labor force. For Marx, the real concern of colonial administrators was how to destroy private property that rested on the labor of the individuals and how to turn their labor into a commodity. In his view, this involved nothing less than the creation and reproduction of the wage labor force itself, which, in the colonies, involved the transformation of colonial subjects and indigenous peoples into wage laborers (Marx 1977[1863–1867]:931–940).

Events in Europe and the United States during the 1860s and 1870s sparked new discussions on empires and colonies as well as on the meaning of the idea of imperialism itself (Cain 1999; Day and Gaido 2011; Koebner and Schmidt 1965; Sklar 1988:78–85). The events included the American Civil War (1861–1865), the Austro-Prussian War (1866), the Franco-Prussian War (1871), the Russo-Turkish War (1877–1878), and the scramble for colonies in Africa during the 1880s. They focused attention on militarism, the consolidation of nation-states, and colonial expansion. At the same time, there was a severe economic crisis in the industrial capitalist world, which lasted from 1873 to 1879. It involved declining rates of economic growth, bank failures, high unemployment in the industrial cities, and rampant corruption. It focused attention on the Colonial Question, the colonies themselves—their purpose, their nature, and their costs. There was a wide spectrum of opinion on these issues. At one pole, perhaps, were condemnations of economic and political liberals, cosmopolitan civilization, the absence of a common purpose, and cries for the landed aristocracy to reassert their moral leadership. A second position entailed reassertions of the deep union between the metropolitan countries and their overseas colonies, especially settler colonies like Canada or South Africa. The advocates of this view recognized that the strength of the empire and its internal stability rested on controlling its global commerce relative to that of other empires; however, in England, these advocates disagreed over how best to achieve this: with a federation of settler colonies, like South Africa, with the mother country, or by giving greater autonomy to the colonies by requiring them to raise revenues to finance their own expenditures, while the metropole defended the empire as a whole. A third position on the nature of their colonies, their purpose, and their costs revolved around questions of whether or not the governments of the metropolitan countries should provide subsidies for certain agricultural and industrial sectors of their economies or raise protective tariffs to maintain the position of those companies in domestic and world markets (Cain 1999:1–19). A fourth position, raised by socialists in the 1880s and 1890s, framed the Colonial Question in political-economic terms and argued that it was a feeble attempt by the industrial capitalist countries to export, under the pretext of bringing civilization, their own social problems—exploitation, unemployment, and poverty to other parts of the world, where indigenous peoples and societies were then attacked and destroyed. As a result, the socialists typically opposed colonialism (Day and Gaido 2011:9–10).

Opposition to imperialism and new understandings of its political-economic foundations crystallized in the years leading up to and following the Spanish-American War (1898–1899) and the Boer Wars (1895–1902). In the former, the United States seized control of all Spanish possessions in the Caribbean and Pacific—e.g. Cuba and the Philippines; in the latter, the British Empire defeated two politically independent Boer states in South Africa and subsequently incorporated them into the Union of South Africa. These wars added fuel to fire ignited by the events of the preceding forty years. The debates over imperialism brought attention to its interrelations with issues such as domestic tariffs, the growth of military expenditures in the industrial countries, colonial expansion, and the internal contradictions of industrial capitalism. The debates also raised the questions of whether imperialism represented a new stage of capitalist production or was merely a momentary phase that would pass. What were its implications for class struggle (Howard and King 1989:91)? They raised not only the geopolitical competition between sovereign states but also, more importantly, "the historical moment of capitalist imperialism ... when interstate rivalries become integrated into the larger processes of capital accumulation" (Callinicos 2009:15).

Two important analysts of imperialism at the turn of the century were Charles A. Conant (1861–1915) and John A. Hobson (1858–1940). In the days leading up to the Spanish-American War both pro- and anti-imperialist sentiments were fueled in the United States. Conant—journalist, banker, and financial and political advisor to U.S. Cabinet Secretaries—argued shortly after the war broke out that imperialism was a "natural law of economic and race development" created by the need to find outlets for the investment of excess savings at a more profitable rate than was assured by domestic investment (Conant 1898:326); in his view, imperialism was a consequence of excess savings. The 1902 work of Hobson—radical democrat, investigative reporter, and foreign correspondent—has perhaps been more influential in the long run.[3] His analysis emerged after an ill-fated, armed raid by British settlers in the Cape Colony of South Africa in late 1895 on two independent countries—the Transvaal Republic and the Orange Free State, the world's most important gold and diamond producing regions at the time. The raids' goals were to foment an uprising among the near majority of British immigrants in the two countries and to annex the countries into a British-controlled federation (later the Union of South Africa). Cecil Rhodes, Prime Minister of the Cape Colony and mining capitalist, organized the raid with the approval of Great Britain's Secretary of State for the Colonies. Hobson examined the shareholders in Rhodes's South Africa Company and found that about a quarter of the investors were foreigners. He suggested that there were connections between the unequal distribution of income in Great Britain, declining consumption of goods produced in the country because many of its residents could not afford to purchase them, declining production by domestic industries, ongoing quest for new overseas markets, and increased savings and foreign investment by the wealthy and by London banks (Cain 2002:59–124). Thus, he linked imperialism with the uneven distribution of income and wealth and argued that this laid the foundations for exporting excessive savings and foreign investment. The subsequent phases of the Boer Wars provided him with further evidence to elaborate his view.

In *Imperialism: A Study* (1965[1902]), Hobson wrote that the mainspring of a state's imperial policy was to find overseas markets for surplus goods and profitable investment opportunities in order to supplement the diminishing profits that could be expected and extracted from saturated home markets. Imperialist policies resulted from under-consumption and over-savings, and foreign investment provided an outlet for the surplus savings and unsold commodities that resulted from under-consumption:

> As one nation after another enters the machine economy and adopts advanced industrial methods, it becomes more difficult for its manufacturers, merchants and financiers to dispose profitably of their economic resources, and they are tempted more and more to use their Governments in order to secure for their particular use some distant undeveloped country by annexation and protection....
>
> Everywhere appear excessive powers of production, excessive capital in search of investment. It is admitted by all businessmen that the growth of the powers of production in their country exceeds the growth in consumption, that more goods can be produced than can be sold at a profit, and that more capital exists than can find remunerative investment.

It is this economic condition that forms the taproot of Imperialism. If the consuming public in this country raised its standard of consumption to keep pace with every rise of productive powers, there could be no excess of goods or capital clamorous to use Imperialism in order to find markets: foreign trade would indeed exist, but there would be no difficulty in exchanging a small surplus of our manufactures for the food and raw material we annually absorbed, and all the savings that we made could find employment, if we chose, in home industries.

(Hobson 1965[1902]:80–81)

Hobson noted that the primary advocates and beneficiaries of imperialist policies were large industrial firms and banking houses. They used war, militarism, and foreign policy to secure outlets for surplus goods and capital. As a result, the public finances of states committed to imperialist policies rose dramatically in the late nineteenth century; about two-thirds of the money raised from the general public, often through taxes on consumption, went to military expenditures and the payment of military debts. Such policies did not equally benefit all classes of the imperialist states because the tax burden fell disproportionately on the lower classes, whose members did not share in the overseas profits (Hobson 1965[1902]:105–106). Hobson concluded that the great industrial firms and banking houses promoting imperialist policies would grow steadily more parasitic on society as a whole and, consequently, would require increased protection by the state, not only from their own lower classes but also from capitalists in rival states.

Hobson's alternative to imperialism was to reduce the "mal-distribution of consuming power which prevents the absorption of commodities and capital within the country" and to "raise the general standard of home consumption and abate the pressure for foreign markets" (Hobson 1965[1902]:85, 91). He wrote,

It is not in the nature of things that we should spend our natural resources on militarism, war, and risky, unscrupulous diplomacy, in order to find markets for our goods and surplus capital. An intelligent progressive community, based upon substantial equality of economic and education opportunities, will raise the standard of consumption to correspond with every increased power of production, and can find full employment for an unlimited quantity of capital and labour within the limits of the country which it occupies. Where the distribution of incomes is such as to enable all classes of the nation to convert their wants into an effective demand for commodities, there can be no over-production, no under-employment of capital and labour, and no necessity to fight for foreign markets.

(Hobson 1965[1902]:92)

His "alternative to imperialist expansion was trade-unionism to raise domestic wages, and redistribution through progressive taxation of unearned [i.e. interest, rent, stock dividends, or inheritance] income" (Day and Gaido 2011:14).

By 1903, Rudolf Hilferding (1877–1941)—physician, journalist, socialist theorist, and twice Germany's Minister of Finance during the 1920s—was developing themes that were embryonic in Hobson and Marx and independent of the former (Bottomore 1981; Brewer 1990:88–108; Howard and King 1989:90–105). He suggested that

> in the modern system of protective tariffs the action of the capitalist class seems no longer to be handicapped by the multiplicity of diverging individual interests; it is much more organized, united, conscious action, which uses political [*staatlich*] means with enormous power to increase its profit ... [and] introduces the final phase of capitalism. To combat the fall in the rate of profit, this law of motion of capitalism, capital does away with free competition, organizes itself and through its organisation is put in a position to increase its influence through state power, placing it immediately and directly in the service of its interest in exploitation.
>
> (Hilferding 1902–1903:279–280, quoted by Howard and King 1989:95)

Hilferding expanded this argument over the next two years, eventually completing and publishing *Finance Capital* in 1910. He discussed four major themes and their interconnections: (1) money and credit as a way of minimizing the amount of "idle" money; (2) the growth of corporations (joint stock or shareholding companies) and the rise of cartels, monopolies, and trusts; (3) finance capital and economic crises; and, finally, (4) imperialism.[4] He argued that the formation of modern corporations laid the foundations for the development of monopolies and signaled the appearance of a new relationship between industrial firms and banks. Before corporations appeared in significant numbers in the last half of the nineteenth century, the size of an individual enterprise was limited by the personal wealth of its owner and his willingness to invest profits in the firm. However, the size of a corporation was limited only by the number of individuals who were willing to invest personal wealth in return for a share of the corporation. In Hilferding's view, the formation of corporations underwrote the concentration of capital needed to launch costly, gigantic enterprises—like modern steel mills. This meant that the relatively large number of small firms that competed with one another during the early stages of industrial capitalism were replaced by a small number of exceedingly large firms producing the same commodities. This also concentrated production because the new large firms usually produced the commodity more cheaply than their smaller, less efficiently organized competitors. As the competitors ceased to manufacture the same commodities, capital was centralized. The concentration and centralization of capital accelerated tendencies toward the formation of cartels or monopolies that were able to set prices artificially (Hilferding 1981[1910]:107–129, 305–307).

In Hilferding's view, banks—which concentrated the money form of capital—also underwrote the growth of monopolies because they supplied credit to industrial firms and became increasingly concerned with the long-term prospects of their clients. The banks would make loans to a particular company but not to their competitors in order to ensure profitable returns on their investments.

As monopolies emerged, industrial and banking capital, which had previously been distinct, fused into *finance capital*—i.e. the fraction of capital in which the banks and industry were united. The linkages between the banks and firms were cemented by interlocking directorates in which the high-level managers of one sat on the other's board of directors. Their interests quickly merged and became so intertwined in the process that they could not easily be disentangled (Hilferding 1981[1910]:170–182, 223–226). The mergers also resulted in one or a few very large financial groups in each country that controlled vast economic resources and underwrote the growing importance of (1) promoters' profit derived from selling shares in a corporation to generate wealth for further investment and (2) "separation between the ownership and control of production" (Bottomore 1981:5–6).

The rise of finance capital had other consequences as well. First, the financial groups that resulted from the fusion forced governments to enact tariffs that simultaneously protected the goods they produced from foreign competition in the domestic market and gave them greater control over the domestic market. Second, the rise of finance capital witnessed the transfer of profits from competitive to monopoly firms—i.e. the cartelized firms enjoyed increasingly high rates of profit at the expense of their smaller competitors. Third, as the monopolies increasingly dominated protected markets, consumers had a steadily diminishing number of sources from whom to purchase goods. Fourth, while high monopoly prices tended to reduce domestic sales, the monopolies had to increase exports in order to maintain their levels of production and rates of profit. Fifth, as monopoly control over national markets increased, investment in both the monopoly firms and their smaller competitors slowed; this led to an accumulation of capital in search of a safe investment that would yield maximum returns. Sixth, as a result, either un-invested capital was moved into undeveloped areas of the domestic economic territory with rich resources and cheap labor, the national economic territory itself was enlarged, or the capital was invested in foreign firms. Seventh, the finance capital groups in one country found that their interests were increasingly incompatible and irreconcilable with those of other countries as well as with the masses of people exploited by them.

Hilferding realized that imperialism transformed social relations at home and abroad. The class structure and role of the state within the national economic territory (the colonial country and its colonies) were modified. The social relations of the pre-capitalist societies enveloped by imperialist states were devastated by force or through policies that promoted dispossession, forced labor, and immigration from areas of the empires with large underemployed labor forces:

> The export of capital, especially since it has assumed the form of industrial and finance capital, has enormously accelerated the overthrow of all the old social relations, and the involvement of the world in capitalism. Capitalist development did not take place independently in each individual country, but instead capitalist relations of production and exploitation were imported along with capital from abroad, and indeed imported at the level already attained in the most advanced country.
>
> (Hilferding 1981[1910]: 322)

Rosa Luxemburg (1871–1919)—Marxist theorist, teacher, communist, and left-socialist activist—agreed with Hobson and Hilferding on several issues: the important roles played by the export of capital in imperialist expansion, violence, state-sponsored propaganda, and jingoism. While they viewed imperialism as a special form of capitalist society, Luxemburg saw it as militarism. It served to defend the national interests of one state from those of competing states and to consolidate the dominant position of industrial and financial capital vis-à-vis other classes and strata in the state. Imperialism was

> ... an instrument of class domination over the labouring population inside the country.... [It was] closely connected with colonialism, protectionism and power politics as a whole... a world armament race... colonial robbery and the policy of 'spheres of influence' all over the world... in home and foreign affairs the very essence of a capitalist policy of national aggression.
> (Nettl 1966, vol. 2:524)

Luxemburg discussed the relationship between capitalism and imperialism in *The Accumulation of Capital* (2003[1913]), paying much closer attention to the transformation of pre-capitalist economies in the colonies—i.e. the processes of primitive accumulation—than either Hobson or Hilferding. Her central thesis was that "the invasion of primitive [i.e. pre-capitalist] economies ... keeps the system alive" (Robinson 2003[1951]:xxxv). For her,

> Capitalism arises and develops historically amidst a non-capitalist society. In Western Europe it is found at first in a feudal environment from which it in fact sprang... and, later, after having swallowed up the feudal system, it exists mainly in an environment of peasants and artisans....
>   The existence and development of capitalism requires an environment of non-capitalist forms of production, but not every one of these forms will serve its ends. Capitalism needs non-capitalist social strata as a market for its surplus value, as a source of supply for its means of production and as a reservoir of labour power for its wage system.
> (Luxemburg 2003[1913]:348)

These pre-capitalist forms, or "natural economies" as she called them, were of no use to capitalists because they responded mainly to internal demands, produced no surplus, and had little use for foreign goods (Luxemburg 2013[1909–1910]:195–234). As a result, the capitalists had to transform or destroy all non-capitalist forms in order to gain possession of their resources, to acquire wage labor, to introduce commodities, and to separate trade from agriculture.

Thus, the world economy at the turn of the twentieth century was divided into two spheres: a static pre-capitalist sector and a dynamic capitalist sector. The motor driving the constantly expanding capitalist sector was the capitalists' continual need to transform the forces and means of production to ensure the highest possible rates of profits. As a result, uneven economic development was essential for the expansion of capitalism:

> From the very beginning the forms and laws of capitalist production aim to comprise the entire globe as a store of productive forces. Capital, impelled to appropriate productive forces for purposes of exploitation, ransacks the whole world, it procures its means of production from all corners of the earth, seizing them, if necessary by force, from all levels of civilization and from all forms of society.
>
> (Luxemburg 2003[1913]:338)

Because the capitalist mode of production could not exist in isolation and had to co-exist with non-capitalist societies for the accumulation of capital and the reproduction of the capitalist system to take place, capitalism could never become a universal form of society. Consequently, as it repressed its own workers and engulfed non-capitalist societies through expansion, it also sowed the seeds of an economic crisis and its own destruction because it was "... assimilating the very conditions which alone can ensure its own existence" (Luxemburg 2003[1913]:346):

> The more ruthlessly capital, by means of militarism, sets about the destruction of non-capitalist strata at home and in the outside world, the more it lowers the standard of living for the workers as a whole, the greater are the effects of day-to-day capital accumulation on the world state. It becomes a string of political and social disasters and convulsions, and under these conditions, punctuated by periodic catastrophes or crises, accumulation can go on no longer.
>
> (Luxemburg 2003[1913]:447)

The implication of Luxemburg's argument was that markets situated in areas with non-capitalist social relations rather than the exploitation of wage-workers, as Marx had argued earlier, were essential for the realization of surplus value and constituted the condition necessary for the accumulation of capital to occur (Tarbuck 1972:29–33). This interpretation had practical implications at the beginning of World War I. In 1915, Luxemburg asked whether the workers in capitalist countries should ally themselves with the capitalist classes of their nation-states or with the peoples of non-capitalist countries (Luxemburg 1972[1921]).

By 1915, Nikolai I. Bukharin (1888–1938)—Bolshevik activist, theorist, journalist, and cartoonist—was already pursuing themes developed a few years earlier by Hilferding and Luxemburg. The former, as mentioned earlier, formulated the theory of finance capitalism—the fusion of economic and politics—in the industrialized imperial states. In Bukharin's view, finance capital had developed so rapidly in the preceding five years that it was being replaced by "state capitalism" (Day 1982). He wrote that

The general pattern of the state's development is therefore as follows: in the beginning the state is the sole organization of the ruling class. Then other organizations begin to spring up, their numbers multiplying especially in the epoch of finance capitalism, the state is transformed from the sole organization of the ruling class into one of its organizations, its distinction being that it has the most general character of all such organizations. Finally, the third stage arrives, *in which the state swallows up these organizations and once more becomes the sole universal organization of the ruling class, with an internal, technical division of labor.* The once-independent organization groupings become the divisions of a gigantic state mechanism, which pounces upon the visible and internal enemy with crushing force. Thus emerges the finished type of contemporary imperialist robber state, the iron organization, which with its tenacious, raking claws embraces the living body of society. This is the New Leviathan, beside which the fantasy of Thomas Hobbes looks like a child's toy.

(Bukharin 1982[1920]:31, emphasis in the original)

State capitalism constituted a single world market in which the various national-state economies were increasingly politicized and competitive with one another because their "productive forces had developed beyond the point where they could be operated efficiently within the confines of any nation-state" (Howard and King 1989:246).

In *Imperialism and the World Economy*, Bukharin re-organized Hilferding's ideas. While the latter had focused on the concentration and centralization of capital and the fusion of economics and politics into a single nation-state, Bukharin argued that two contradictory processes were already occurring simultaneously on the eve of World War I (1914–1918). On the one hand, the various national economies constituting the world economy were becoming increasingly interdependent through international trade; on the other, national blocs of capital were emerging in the context of this world economy as the interests of the monopolies and the capitalist states in whose territories they were located intertwined. In a phrase, the finance capitalism of one nation-state was already participating in and financing the foreign enterprises in others (Bukharin 1973[1915]:17–62). Consequently, imperialism and crises were not a problem internal to one country but rather a problem of the world economy:[5]

Just as every individual enterprise is part of the 'national' economy, so every one of these 'national economies' is included in the system of world economy. This is why the struggle between modern 'national economic bodies' must be regarded first of all as the struggle of various competing parts of world economy—just as we consider the struggle of individual enterprises to be one of the phenomena of socio-economic life.

(Bukharin 1973[1915]:17)

Thus, "the relevant units of the world market ... came to coincide with the system of states, and competition was expressed in rivalry between different states" (Howard and King 1989:246).

For Bukharin, international trade had established the relations of production on a world scale; however, differences in the level of economic development and the different natural conditions in various parts of the world laid the foundations for a growing international division of labor:

> Important as the natural differences in the conditions of production may be, they recede more and more into the background compared with differences that are the result of the uneven development of productive forces in the various countries…. The cleavage between 'town' and 'country' as well as the 'development of this cleavage', formerly confined to one country alone, are now being reproduced on a tremendously enlarged basis. Viewed from this standpoint, entire countries appear today as 'towns', namely, the industrial countries, whereas entire agrarian territories appear to be 'country'.
>
> (Bukharin 1973[1915]:20–21)

While Hilferding argued that the concentration and centralization of capital typically occurred within the confines of a given country because of the linkages between its monopolies and state apparatus, Bukharin argued that these processes occasionally splashed over those boundaries and that the

> … various spheres of the concentration and organisation process stimulate each other, creating a very strong tendency toward transforming the entire national economy *into one gigantic combined enterprise under the tutelage of the financial kings and the capitalist state, an enterprise which monopolises the national market*…. It follows that world capitalism, the world system of production, assumes in our times the following aspect: a few consolidated, organised economic bodies ('the great civilised powers') on the one hand, and a periphery of underdeveloped countries with a semi-agrarian system on the other.
>
> (Bukharin 1973[1915]:73–74, emphasis in the original)

In Bukharin's view, "imperialist annexation is only a case of the general capitalist tendency towards centralisation of capital, a case of its centralisation at that maximum scale which corresponds to the competition of state capitalist trusts" (Bukharin's 1973[1915]:119–120).

The uneven development of the world system focused attention on the relations between capitalists and the state that emerged in the wake of the formation of finance capital—i.e. the creation of monopolies and the protective economic policies of the state. Uneven development meant that tendencies toward the formation of monopolies in one nation-state did not signal the end of competition but rather the emergence and intensification of a new form of competition that took place in the international arena as the smaller, less developed states were enmeshed in relations with their larger, more developed neighbors. Regarding the formation of this international division of labor, Bukharin (1973[1915]:74) continues,

The organisation process (which, parenthetically speaking, is by no means the aim or the motive power of the capitalist gentlemen, but is the objective result of their seeking to obtain a maximum of profit) tends to overstep 'national' boundaries. But it finds substantial obstacles on this road. First, it is much easier to overcome competition on a 'national' scale than on a world scale (international agreements usually arise on the basis of already existing 'national' monopolies); second, the existing differences of economic structure and consequently of production-costs make agreement disadvantageous for the advanced 'national' groups; third, the ties of unity with the state and its boundaries [such as tariffs] are in themselves an ever growing monopoly which guarantees additional profits.

In 1916, Vladimir I. Lenin (1870–1924)—Bolshevik political leader and critical Marxist theorist—wrote his widely read pamphlet, *Imperialism, The Highest Stage of Capitalism: A Popular Outline*, with the threat of tsarist censorship in mind; hence, he confined his analysis to "exclusively theoretical, specifically economic facts," with only a "few necessary observations on politics" (Lenin 1964[1917a]:187). However, the subject of imperialism was a major focus of his work between 1914 and 1917, and his then unpublished "Notebooks on Imperialism" and other writings from the period fill more than eight hundred pages in his *Collected Works* (e.g. Lenin 1968[1912–1917]). In other words, he engaged with other writers and with source materials for an extended period of time. He was familiar with their works and engaged in a critical dialog with their writings, but his views were not necessarily derived from them. He agreed with some points they made and disagreed with others.

Lenin—unlike Hilferding, Bukharin, and many Marxist theorists of the day—thought of social reality in terms of dialectical relations, transitions, crises, and contradictions within and between the multi-leveled totalities that constitute it. He did not view social reality as a mere aggregate of components, as unilinear sets of cause-and-effect relations, or as existing in some temporary stable equilibria. Kevin Anderson (1995:123–134) made this point most emphatically. For example, Lenin (1965[1919]:168) wrote that

In reality we have heterogeneous phenomena to deal with. In every agricultural gubernia [i.e. a territorial administrative unit in the Russian Empire] there is free competition side by side with monopoly industry. Nowhere in the world has monopoly capitalism existed in a whole series of branches without free competition nor will it exist. To write of such a system is to write of a system which is false and removed from reality. If Marx said of manufacture that it was a superstructure on mass small production, imperialism and finance capitalism are a superstructure on old capitalism. If its top is destroyed, the old capitalism is exposed. To maintain that there is such a thing as integral imperialism without the old imperialism is merely making the wish father to the thought. And if we had an altered capitalism, our task would have been a hundred thousand times easier. It would have resulted in a system in which everything would be subordinated to finance capital alone.

Lenin did indeed note that the transition between competitive and monopoly capitalism in the industrialized world occurred around 1900, when the colonizing countries divided up the whole world among themselves. It was a violent process that unleashed competition between whole industries, monopolies, and countries. But imperialism, the latest stage of capitalist development, did not yield some new equilibrium, it merely shifted and perpetuated the old struggles between small and big capital to new levels. The competition now took place on a world scale as imperialist states go to war with one another as they continually sought to re-apportion and enlarge their shares of a world that they have already divided among themselves (Anderson 1995:129–130). He wrote that

> Imperialism emerged as the development and direct continuation of the fundamental characteristics of capitalism in general. But capitalism only became capitalist imperialism at a definite and very high state of its development, when certain of its fundamental characteristics began to change into their opposites, when the features of the transition from capitalism to a higher social and economic system had taken shape and revealed themselves in all spheres. Economically, the main thing in this process is the displacement of capitalist free competition by capitalist monopoly. Free competition is the basic feature of capitalism, and of commodity production generally; *monopoly is the exact opposite of free competition, but we have seen the latter being transformed into monopoly before our eyes*, creating large-scale industry and forcing out small industry, replacing large-scale by still larger-scale industry, and carrying concentration of production and capital to the point where out of it has grown and is growing monopoly: cartels, syndicates, and trusts, and merging with them, the capital of a dozen or so banks which manipulate thousands of millions. At the same time, the monopolies, which have grown out of free competition, do not eliminate the latter, but exist above it and alongside it, and thereby give rise to a number of very acute antagonisms, frictions and conflicts.
>
> (Lenin 1964[1917a]:265–266, emphasis added)

This statement immediately preceded Lenin's list of what he saw as the basic features of imperialism:

> (1) the concentration of production and capital has developed to such a high stage that it has created monopolies which play a decisive role in economic life; (2) the merging of bank capital with industrial capital, and the creation, on the basis of 'finance capital', of a financial oligarchy; (3) the export of capital as distinguished from the export of commodities acquires exceptional importance; (4) the formation of international monopolist capitalist associations which share the world among themselves, and (5) the territorial division of the whole world among the biggest capitalist powers is completed.
>
> (Lenin 1964[1917a]:266)

Between 1910 and 1920, Marxist analysts constructed alternative theories of imperialism that examined the formation of monopolies and finance capital, the convergence of capitalist and state interests, the encapsulation of backward regions and underdeveloped countries into economic blocs that were part of a world economy, the existence of pre-capitalist social relations in the colonies, and the ongoing tensions and dynamics they engendered. These Marxists developed their views in the context of ongoing debates in which the participants brought different theoretical perspectives to the table.

Joseph Schumpeter (1883–1950)—historically-minded Austrian economist—responded and critiqued the arguments of Marxist scholars in his *The Sociology of Imperialism*, which appeared in 1919. Imperialism, in Schumpeter's (1951[1919]:7) view, was the "disposition on the part of a state to unlimited forcible expansion." While there may be an economic explanation for this phenomenon, he argued that the Marxist theorists had reduced imperialism to economic class interests, which given the "customary modes of political thought and feeling can never be mere 'reflexes' of, or counterparts to, the production of that age" (Schumpeter 1951[1919]:7).

Schumpeter's alternative was a restatement of liberal economic theory. He argued that imperialism did not represent the highest stage of capitalist development but was actually a transitional phenomenon resulting from the survival of residual political and social structures from the age of absolutist monarchies. While the monopoly capitalists had sought to control markets through protective tariffs and policies before 1914, the monopolies themselves emerged only after the protective tariffs imposed by various nation-states were already in place. In other words, the industrialists and bankers found reasons to support these measures and were ultimately able to profit from the export of goods and capital in that milieu (Schumpeter 1951[1919]:83–85, 110–118). Imperialism

does not *coincide* with nationalism and militarism, though it *fuses* with them by supporting them as it is supported by them. It too is—not only historically, but also sociologically—a heritage of the autocratic state, of its structural elements, organizational forms, interest alignments, human attitudes, the outcome of precapitalist forces which the autocratic state has re-organized, in part by the methods of early capitalism. It would never have been evolved by the 'inner logic' of capitalism itself. This is true even of mere export monopolism.... That it was able to develop to its present dimensions is owing to the momentum of a situation once created, which continued to engender ever new 'artificial' economic structures, that is, those which maintain themselves by political power alone....

The pre-capitalist elements in our social life may still have great vitality; special circumstances in national life may revive them from time to time; but in the end the climate of the modern world must destroy them.... Whatever opinion is held concerning the vitality of capitalism itself, whatever lifespan is predicted for it, it is bound to withstand the onslaughts of its enemies and its own irrationality much longer than essentially untenable export monopolism—untenable even from the capitalist point of view. Export monopolism may perish in revolution, or it may be peacefully relinquished; this may happen soon, or it may take some time and require desperate struggle; but one thing is certain—it *will* happen. This will immediately dispose of neither warlike instincts nor structural elements and organizational forms oriented toward war....

(Schumpeter 1951[1919]:128–130, emphasis in the original)

Schumpeter interpreted imperialism in the decades preceding World War I as a departure from the normal path of capitalist development, the internal logic of which was rooted in a competitive, laissez faire, free market economy. In his view, once the pre-capitalist survivals in modern society were replaced, imperialism would disappear.

The debates about imperialism raised other issues as well: The National Question focused on nations, subjugated national minorities, and rights of self-determination; the Agrarian Question was concerned with capitalist development in "backward" or "underdeveloped" areas and peasantries; and the Colonial Question broadly centered on issues of development and relations to colonial subjects and indigenous peoples and their rights. All of these debates were rekindled in the wake of World War II. In the remainder of the chapter, let us consider how they were initially formulated.

The National Question: Nations, Nationalism, and National Minorities

The National Question is the complex interplay of several interrelated issues. One is the concept of the *nation* itself as a form of collective identity that asserts a degree of unity and autonomy, and that often competes and merges with other forms of collective identity—such as class, race, region, religion, ethnicity, history, and gender. A second is the myriad manifestations of *nationalism*; for example, its complicated relation with the notion of the nation; its dispositions and sentiments; the beliefs, values, and habitual practices these engender; its capacity to mobilize people; its relations to imperialism, colonialism, and anti-colonial movements; its intersections with liberal, socialist, and conservative political thought and politics; the ways in which it emerged and is reproduced in nation-states; or its claims for autonomy and sovereignty (Calhoun 1997; Hutchinson and Smith 1994; Periwal 1995). A third is the presence of *national minorities* that have been or are enmeshed in modern nation-states.

Some analysts, like Anthony Smith (1986), argue that nations are primordial and have their origins in ethnic groups that link individuals to a community. Others suggest that they crystallized during The Enlightenment in the wake of the American, French, and other revolutions of the late eighteenth and early nineteenth centuries and in the tensions between romantics who viewed the nation in cultural terms and liberals who saw them as linking individuals to increasingly cosmopolitan, republican states (Ishay 1995). For example,

Johann G. Herder (1744–1803)—Prussian social critic and philosopher of history and mind—laid foundations for a cultural theory of the nation. The nation was a culturally, linguistically, and geographically bound group whose members shared the same language and patterns of thought in the course of everyday life. They were the farmers, artisans, traders, and intellectuals—not the aristocracy, the bureaucracy, or the poor—of remote, relatively un-stratified communities whose members retained close ties to their homelands (Barnard 1965, 2003; Beiser 1992:189–244). Herder challenged the republican theory of his teacher, Prussian philosopher Immanuel Kant (1724–1804), who argued,

> As native of a country, those who constitute a nation can be looked upon analogously to descendants of the same *ancestors* (*congeniti*) even though they are not. Yet in an intellectual sense and from the perspective of rights, since they are born of the same mother (the republic) they constitute as it were on family (*gens, natio*), whose members (citizens of the state) are of equally high status and do not mix with those who may live near them in a state of nature, whom they regard as inferior; the latter ... do not constitute states but only tribes.
>
> (Kant 1996[1797]:114)

In Kant's view, it was only in a properly organized state where both citizens and foreigners can find security and justice, and realize the natural rights to freedom, equality, and self-dependence. However, he distinguished between active and passive citizens (i.e. apprentices of artisans and merchants, domestic servants, minors, all women, teachers, and tenant farmers); the latter were dependent on the will of others and could not vote because they a lacked civic personality (Kant 1996[1797]:92).

Philosopher Georg W. F. Hegel (1770–1831) attempted to synthesize the tension between the cultural and republican views of the nation in the *Philosophy of Right* (1952[1821]:155–174) and the *Lectures on the Philosophy of World History* (1975[1830]:97–102). From his perspective, the nation was a political entity shaped by the state, and neither cultural nor linguistic unity was sufficient to weld a group into a nation. He further argued that in the network of governmental and political institutions of the state, the nation's constitution

> is typically a product of history and expresses the culture of a particular nation—its values, religious beliefs, views about the world, traditions and customs. That culture (or 'spirit') of the nation permeates also other human relations (least of all, however, those which have come under the relative sway of civil society) and gives the whole unity, and cohesion. The values of the national community and the operation of its central government are linked together through mediating institutions (such as corporations, estates and the representative system), which ensure that the activities of the government broadly express the basic ideals and interests of groups within the community or its individual members. If such mediating links do not

exist or cease to perform their proper function the nation or important sections become alienated from the government and the integrity or independence of the political community is jeopardized.

(Pelczynski 1984:266)

Marx and Engels were critical of cultural conceptions of the nation and of nationalism more generally. Initially, they did not develop a systematic view of either (Löwy 1971:371). Like Hegel, they conceptualized the nation in political rather than cultural and linguistic terms. In 1849, Engels adopted Hegel's distinction between "historic peoples" and "peoples without history." The former were national communities under the sway of civil society and the state—e.g. Austria, Hungary, or France; they were dynamic forces in history. The latter were national communities—like the Czechs, Slovaks, or Moravians—that had been oppressed, enslaved, and plundered by foreign powers for centuries and that, in Engels' (1977[1849]:367) view, lacked "the primary historical, geographical, political and industrial conditions for independence and viability." By this, he meant peoples who had been unable to forge a state in the past and who did not possess sufficient power to obtain national autonomy in the future or at least in the near future (Rosdolsky 1980[1964]:10). A year earlier, Marx and Engels (1976[1848]:519) had written that working men of the world have no country, only national differences, and urged that they lose the chains of nationalism and unite.

Marx and Engels shifted their views on national movements in the 1860s in the wake of the Irish resistance to British repression. In 1869, Marx (1987[1869]) pointed out that the nationalism of the English workers, which bound them to their rulers, was ultimately harmful to the workers themselves:

> The English working class... will never be able to do anything decisive here in England before they separate their attitude towards Ireland quite definitely from that of the ruling classes, and not only make common cause with the Irish, but even take the initiative in dissolving the Union established in 1801. And this must be done not out of sympathy with the Irish, but as a demand based on the interests of the English proletariat. If not the English proletariat will for ever remain bound to the leading strings of the ruling classes, because they will be forced to make a common front with them against Ireland....
>
> (Marx 1987[1869]:390)

Engels (1990[1884]) subsequently examined the material factors that gave rise to nation-states at the end of the Middle Ages. In his view, the disintegration of the feudal nobility was underwritten by the opposition of peasants and townsmen as well as by the growing importance of commodity production, commerce rather than the production of use values, and the use of money as a lubricant for exchange. The opponents of the nobility found allies in the monarchs whose interests were increasingly opposed to those of their vassals and who used gunpowder and artillery invented in the East to subordinate them. Language differences were often a basis of distinction within a given geographical region. Together with books printed in vernacular languages rather than Latin and the revival of classical literature, Marx and Engels promoted the formation of nations and nation-states.

By the end of the nineteenth century, nationalism was an increasingly pressing issue in many parts of the world. In the Austro-Hungarian Empire, for example, more than a dozen nations sought to assert their identities and independence. Most of them were peoples without history who had rallied under the banner of the Social Democratic Party (SDP) that promoted internationalism and the right of national self-determination. The debates that ensued in the 1890s and 1900s were contentious: There were ongoing struggles between socialists and anarchists; controversies between Marxist and non-Marxist socialists; and ongoing tensions between reformist, revisionist, and conservative tendencies within the international SDP that reflected real differences in the political structures of various countries represented in the party (Joll 1955). The debate over the National Question also articulated ongoing differences of opinion among those who were reviving Kantian thought—some sympathetic to socialism, some not. They discussed questions of whether or not the methodologies of the natural sciences were appropriate for the cultural or human sciences; critiques of materialism, positivism, scientism, reductionism, and teleology; and concerns about the nature of facts, truth, values, understanding, and explanation (Crowell 1998). This forced SDP leaders, like Otto Bauer (1881–1938), to confront the National Question head-on (Bottomore and Goode 1978:30–36; Nimni 1991:142–184).

Bauer rejected essentialist, voluntaristic, or empiricist theories of the nation—i.e. those claiming that the nation resides in the soul or the race of its members, that it expresses a will to form a state, or that it lists its characteristic features (Bauer 1979[1907]:23–39; Kolakowski 1981:285). He reframed the idea of the nation in the following way:

> *The nation is the totality of men bound together through a common destiny into a community of character.* Through a *common destiny*: this characteristic distinguishes the nation from other international groups, such as an occupation, a class, or the members of a state, which rest upon a similarity, not a community, of destiny. The *totality* of the associated characters: this distinguishes them from the narrower communities of character within the nation, that is determined by their own destiny, but only one that is closely associated with the whole nation, and consequently determined by the destiny of the latter. ... In a society which is based upon the private ownership of the means of labour, the ruling classes, once the knights and now the educated classes, constitute the nation as the totality of those in whom a similar upbringing resulting from the history of the nation, and a common language and national education, produces an affinity of character. But the popular masses do not constitute the nation: they do so no longer, because the age-old community of descent no longer binds them

closely enough together; and they do not yet do so, because they are not fully incorporated in the developing system of education. The difficulty of finding a satisfactory definition of the nation, upon which all earlier attempts came to grief, is therefore historically conditioned. People tried to discover the nation in our present class society, in which the old sharply defined community of descent has disintegrated into an immense number of local and descent groups, while the growth of a new community of education has not yet been able to unite these small groups in a national whole.

(Bauer 1978[1907]:107–108)

In Bauer's view, the nation is a complex historical phenomenon—the historical processes and stages of development by which the nation itself appeared. The processes involved *ethnocide*, the destruction of ways of life, and simultaneously constituted a milieu in which *ethnogenesis* could occur—i.e. people who occupied a particular position in a wider stratified society could recognize that they had a shared identity. This identity was rooted in their *national character*. Language was only a partial manifestation of this national character, merely one trait that was the product of the historical development of the nation itself. The diversity of traits meant that even when a people spoke the same language, like the Croats and the Serbians, they often forged distinctive national identities and considered themselves to be separate nations (Bauer 1979[1907]:5–168; Nimni 1991:146–160). Bauer wrote that

the living national character which operates in every one of its members is a residue of a historical development; in the nationality of the individual member there is reflected the history of society, whose produce is the individual. From the point of view of its formal structure it is a historical phenomenon, because diverse broad circles are bound together in a nation by different means and in different ways at the various stages of its development.... My conception of the nation dissolves the nation itself into a process. For me, history no longer reflects the struggles of nations; instead the nation itself appears as the reflection of historical struggles. For the nation is only manifested in the national character, in the nationality of the individual, and the nationality of the individual is only one aspect of his determination by the history of society, by the development of the conditions and techniques of labour.

(Bauer 1978[1907]:109)

Furthermore, as the nation crystallizes, the national culture becomes the common culture of the ruling classes that are politically powerful, control the forces of production, and participate fully in the culture and values of the nation. The highly fragmented and localized beliefs, values, and practices of the peasants, farmers, and workers are different from the national culture of the ruling classes that exploit them. The goods and labor power of the subordinated classes sustain the creation of the national cultures of the ruling classes from which they are excluded (Garcia Pelayo 1979:34–35; Nimni 1991:167). In multinational capitalist societies, like the Austro-Hungarian Empire, national education, which represents the common culture of the ruling classes, gradually overwhelms the particular national cultures of subordinated workers and peasants—i.e. those of the peoples without history:

> The working class section of the *nations without history* in Austria was nationalist: the state which enslaved them was German; the court which protected the property owners and threw the dispossessed in jail was also German; each death sentence was written in German, and German was used to issue the orders to the [multinational] armies which were sent to crush each strike by the hungry and defenseless workers.
>
> (Bauer 1979[1907]:296, emphasis in the original)

In Bauer's view, the educational systems sponsored by capitalist nation-states did not produce a homogeneous national working class but rather "a *nationally* conscious proletariat" (Munck 1986:40). Thus, his conclusion regarding the politics of practice was that the working-class sections of nations should subordinate the National Question to tactics that promoted the interests of the working class as a whole. While Bauer argued that they should not support separatist movements, he recognized that national oppression was a destructive force that the SDP had to confront.

His position regarding the National Question echoed sentiments expressed by other social critics, whose views about the intersections of the nation, social class structures, race, and the state reflected the influence of Neo-Kantian thought during the early 1900s. These included Durkheim, who wrestled with distinctions between nationalism, patriotism, and jingoism in France and Germany and their connections with the state (Llobera 1994). In the United States, where essentialist notions of nationality and race predominated, W. E. B. Du Bois (1898, 1963[1903]) and Franz Boas (1894, 1911a,b) were already pointing out that race, culture, language, and class position were distinct and that their interconnections were the result of complex historical processes. In Germany, Weber had a slightly different understanding of the interrelationships of class, nation, and state. For Weber,

> the nation-state rests on deep and elemental psychological foundations within the broad economically subordinate strata of the nation as well, that it is by no means a mere 'superstructure', the organization of the economically dominant classes. It is just that in normal times this political instinct sinks below the level of consciousness for the masses. In that case the specific function of the economically and politically leading strata is to be the repositories of political understanding.
>
> (Weber 1989[1895]:202)

Thus, a nation exists when the objective conditions shared by a group of people distinguish them from other groups. These conditions produce essentialist feelings of solidarity. Over time, Weber came to agree more fully with Bauer's view. Weber argued that the intensification of nationalism in his time was due to the economic conflicts of imperialism and to the spread of literacy and national literatures among the previously uneducated (culture-less) masses that lacked awareness of bourgeois culture (Weber 1978[1922]:395–398, 919–926).

Bauer's analysis of the National Question was not the only one brought up in the SDP in the years leading up to the outbreak of World War I in 1914. Opinion was split. At one point on the spectrum was Luxemburg's (1976[1908–1909]) argument that there really was no National Question because the nations themselves were already internally class-stratified, even as they were enmeshed in multination-states. Another point was represented by Marx and Engels, who wrote in 1882, with regard to Poland, that

> It is unimportant whether a reconstitution of Poland is possible before the next revolution. *We* have in no case the task to deter the Poles from their efforts to fight for the vital conditions of their future development, or to persuade them that national independence is a very secondary matter from the international point of view. On the contrary, independence is the basis of any common international action.
>
> (Engels 1952[1882]:117, quoted by Anderson 1995:136)

Karl Kautsky (1854–1938), a leading theoretician of the SDP, was also highly critical of Bauer's theory of the nation. In "The Modern Nationality" (1887), he argued that it was difficult to define nationality because the significance of the nation was continually being transformed and varied from one set of circumstances to another. In his view, the nation was best understood in relation to economic development and state structures:

> the classical form of the modern state is the nation state. But classical forms exist in general only as a tendency. It is rare that they are developed in a perfectly typical fashion... To the extent that economic antagonisms deepen, each economic region tries to develop its own urban and rural industry, but can do this less and less without hurting the industry of its neighbors. The different Austrian regions tend to separate, and the "reconciliation" of nations becomes more difficult.
>
> (Kautsky 1887 quoted in Haupt et al. 1974:114, 116)

In "Nationality and Internationality," Kautsky (1908) proposed an alternative to Bauer's theory. The nation-state emerged because capitalists desired to locate markets that were free from the interference of old state structures, and new state bureaucracies became increasingly important in the process. However, bureaucracies did not function very well without an official language and linguistic unification, which, of course, were also promoted by the commercialization of the society. However, when economic and political forces were powerful enough to foster a truly national language, the state's efforts to enforce linguistic uniformity actually promoted diversity as groups that suffered under these policies turned to national identities and languages that opposed those of the state. In Kautsky's view, Bauer did not truly appreciate the power of language in forging national sentiments that were opposed to those of the state (Harman 1992:21–23).

Luxemburg (1976[1908–1909]:176–177) combined elements of Bauer's and Kautsky's arguments concerning the National Question and challenged other claims, especially their views on the right of self-determination for nationalist movements. Using Italy and Germany as examples, Luxemburg located the rise of national movements in the economic activities of the big bourgeoisie who were driven to find domestic markets. However, this was not the case in her native Poland. There, nationalism was rooted in the nobility's view of its own social position; consequently, the bourgeoisie was an anti-nationalist factor, partly because it was foreign and partly because its industries engaged largely in the production of commodities that were exported to Russia. As a result, the Polish capitalist class leaned toward Russia and did not demand the creation of a unified nation-state. "In Poland there arose an opposition between the national idea and the bourgeois development, which gave the former not only a utopian but also a reactionary character" (Luxemburg 1976[1908–1909]:177).

Luxemburg (1976[1908–1909]:128–131) also disagreed with Kautsky's theory of convergence—his view that the spread of capitalism and the consequent rise of socialism would gradually remove all national distinctions—because

> The development of *world powers*, a characteristic feature of our times growing in importance along with the progress of capitalism, from the very outset condemns all small nations to political impotence. Apart from a few of the most powerful nations, the leaders in capitalist development, which possess the spiritual and material resources necessary to maintain their political and economic independence, 'self-determination', the independent existence of smaller and petty nations, is an illusion, and will become even more so. The return of all, or even the majority of the nations which are today oppressed, to independence would only be possible if the existence of small states in the era of capitalism had any chances or hopes for the future. Besides, the big-power economy and politics—a condition of survival for the capitalist states—turn the politically independent, formally equal, small European states into mutes on the European stage and more often into scapegoats....
>
> The very development of international trade in the capitalist period brings with it the inevitable, though at times slow ruin of all the more primitive societies, destroys their historically existing means of 'self-determination' and makes them dependent on the crushing wheel of capitalist development.... The destructive action of world trade is followed by outright partition or by the political dependence of colonial countries in various degrees and forms.
>
> (Luxemburg 1976[1908–1909]:129–130, emphasis in the original)

Lenin's views on nationalism and the right of national self-determination developed in tandem with his growing appreciation of imperialism and its place in world history. During the first decade of the twentieth century, there were nationalist revolutions in many countries; these were enmeshed in imperialist relations and in the newly created colonies: Cuba, the Philippines, China, Persia, Turkey, and Russia. Before 1905, Lenin had viewed the industrial capitalist countries of the West as the motor of change and the peoples of large parts of the world—Asia, Africa, the East, and the Americas—as passive recipients of changes introduced by foreigners. By 1908, he argued instead that "the world had entered 'a new and incomparably higher stage of proletarian struggle', and cited developments in Asia as factors contributing to, and characterizing, this new stage" (Seth 1992:112; Lenin 1963[1908a]). He recognized that the nationalist struggles in Asia and other parts of the world were products of and responses to the imperialist nature of capitalism in the late nineteenth and early twentieth centuries. He also recognized that there were linkages between the proletarian struggles taking place in Russia in 1905 and the struggles for independence taking place in Persia. This suggested that the National and Colonial Questions were connected. Six years later, Lenin argued that the spread of capitalist social relations across the globe unleashed new national movements and called for the formation of new nation-states, particularly in Asia. This implied that the "self-determination of nations ... *cannot*, from a historico-political point of view, have any other meaning than political self-determination, state independence, and the formation of a nation-state" (Lenin 1964[1914]:400, emphasis in the original).

The uneven development of capitalist imperialism on a world scale implied that "backwardness" was an integral feature of the highest stage of imperialism, that backward regions (colonies and semi-colonies, like China) were essential for its existence and reproduction, and that there were backward regions or peoples within the imperialist countries themselves—e.g. Russia and the United States.[6] In Lenin's view, the backward regions were no longer objects for the imperialist countries but active agents as a consequence of their incorporation into the capitalist world system in its imperialist stage (Anderson 1995:134–144; Seth 1992). In this way, he linked the National and Colonial Questions.

Given his dialectical-historical view of the development of capitalism, Lenin proceeded to argue in 1914 that it was essential to distinguish between two phases of capitalist development, which differ from one another with regard to national movements. The first was marked by the collapse of feudalism and absolutism, when national movements were mass movements calling for the formation of bourgeois-democratic states. The second phase occurred in fully developed capitalist states in which there were already marked antagonisms between the capitalist and working classes. In other words, one would expect to find different kinds of national movements in each phase. For Lenin, this implied that Marxists should take the general historical and concrete state conditions into account when assessing the revolutionary potential of any national movement's claim to self-determination:

The bourgeois nationalism of *any* oppressed nation has a general democratic content. This is directed *against* oppression, and it is this content
that we *unconditionally* support. At the same time we strictly distinguish it
from the tendency toward national exclusiveness....

(Lenin 1964[1914]:412, emphasis in the original)

From this, he concluded that the Russian working class was faced with

... a two-sided task: to combat nationalism of every kind, above all, Great
Russian nationalism; to recognise, not only fully equal rights for all nations in general, but also equality of rights as regards polity, i.e., the right of
nations to self- determination, to secession. And at the same time, it is their
task, in the interests of a successful struggle against all and every kind of
nationalism among nations, to preserve the unity of the proletarian struggle and the proletarian organisations, amalgamating these organisations
into a close-knit international association, despite bourgeois strivings for
national exclusiveness.

(Lenin 1964[1914]:453–454)

A second implication of Lenin's theory of imperialism for the National and Colonial Questions was his distinction between oppressor and oppressed nations.
From this perspective, the political significance of national struggles in the
colonies and semi-colonies (i.e. backward regions)—the right of national self-
determination—took on new meaning: oppressed peoples and ongoing resistance to the oppressor (imperialist) nations—sometimes armed, sometimes by
politics alone. Lenin wrote that

National wars waged by colonies and semi-colonies in the imperialist era
are not only probable but *inevitable*.... The national liberation movements
are already very strong, or are growing and maturing. Every war is the continuation of politics by other means. The continuation of national liberation politics in the colonies will inevitably take the form of national wars
against imperialism.

(Lenin 1964[1916a]:310, emphasis in the original)

By 1919, however, Lenin viewed the inchoate revolutions in the capitalist countries
of Europe as socialist in character and those in the colonies and semi-colonies
as bourgeois-democratic in nature, as efforts to rid themselves of corrupting
colonial and feudal overlords. He did not stress the difference between the two
forms of national liberation in large part because the Soviet Union was in the
throes of a civil war and had been invaded by nearly two dozen capitalist countries. Stressing the similarities of socialist and bourgeois-democratic revolution
was political, a way of forging alliances between nations that had a common
enemy, even though these allies may have conceptualized their struggles in different terms. Thus, Lenin never emphasized that colonial nationalism might be
anti-imperialist but not bourgeois-democratic in form.

Sanjay Seth (1992:124) observed that Lenin, who

> broke decisively with the rigidly determinist and evolutionist Marxism of
> the Second International [i.e. the SDP] ... continued to 'ground' politi-
> cal choices in an evolutionary (and teleological) interpretation of history,
> where what was politically desirable was also found to be consonant with
> historical progress, and was 'progressive' in this double sense, with each
> notion of progress (the political and the historical/evolutionary) under-
> writing the other.

The National Question generated heated debates, and the political issues raised
by the participants mentioned earlier, as well as by other writers who will be
discussed in subsequent chapters, remain unresolved, despite the fact that they
resurfaced repeatedly throughout the twentieth century.

The Colonial Question: Settlers, National Minorities, and Indigenous Peoples

During the last half of the nineteenth century, England, France, Germany, and
the United States staked out empires. This involved the conquest, annexation,
and settlement of adjacent lands or overseas territories; it entailed the dispossession of the inhabitants of those regions and frequently involved attempts to ex-
terminate them, especially in settler colonies, like Australia or the United States.
It typically entailed perceptions of indigenous people as different from the citizens of the colonizing nation state. Separated from the metropoles, the settlers
became colonial subjects; the residents, national minorities, or indigenous peoples ("backward" peoples), as a result of their subordinated status, were viewed
as ineligible for or incapable of full incorporation into the imperial state. For
liberal social evolutionists, national minorities and indigenous peoples occupied
the lower rungs of a ladder leading from savagery to civilization; they occupied
these positions as a consequence of nature or of manifest destiny. The evolutionists argued that settlers, companies, and agents from the colonizing states had a
mission to bring civilization, peace, progress, and prosperity to the colonies and
to remake the backward peoples to their own advantage or in their own image
(Mehta 1999). In the process, however, the colonists often shut their eyes to the
barbarism of the civilizing process and even of civilization itself.

Social analysts commented critically on the effects of liberal, imperial policies
on colonial subjects. For example, in the late eighteenth century, Edmund Burke
(1729–1797) had already remarked on the politics of exclusion resulting from
the subordination of Irish Catholics by the system of English Protestant political
control in Ireland; the abuses by colonial officials; the divisive distortions created in colonial societies by notions of hierarchy—different levels of civilization,
culture, or race; the cultural impoverishment resulting from territorial expansion and commercial avarice in India and elsewhere; the difficulties of exercising
power and authority at a distance; and the inevitability of the political independence of the American colonies (Mehta 1999:155; Pitts 2005:59–100). In the

wake of Napoleon's defeat at Waterloo in 1814, Benjamin Constant (1767–1830) railed against the militarism of his imperial policy. Constant argued that acquiring overseas possessions and property did nothing to improve the prosperity of France and that white colonial settlers threatened not only "basic justice for nonwhite colonial subjects" but also the very bases of French law and even the recently restored monarchy itself (Pitts 2005:183). In *The Condition of the Working Class in England*, Engels (1975[1845]:389–392, 557–561) referred repeatedly to the injustices faced by the Irish in the oldest of Europe's colonies: the misery of their everyday lives, abuse by colonial officials, racial and religious discrimination, dispossession from agricultural lands, and continual emigration to find wage labor in English factory towns where they were forced to live in the most squalid neighborhoods.

From the 1840s onward, Marx and Engels wrote extensively about colonies, especially Ireland and India; national minorities (the "peoples without history") in or on the margins of the Hapsburg Empire; and the "barbarian" societies of Asia and the Americas (a term commonly used to characterize the Irish, Germans, Austrians, and Slavs in the mid-nineteenth century). The theorists saw these communities in terms of their shared global history: They had both been born and raised in one of the thirty-nine largely rural, loosely affiliated absolutist states that would constitute Germany after their unification in 1870. Marx and Engels wrote about the colonization of Ireland in the twelfth century and the central roles it played in the early phase of capital accumulation in Europe and in the consolidation of the national state as the political form in which capitalism crystallized. They discussed the partition of Poland, an independent kingdom founded in the eleventh century, by Austria, Prussia, and Russia in the late 1700s and the repeated division and reapportionment of its people and lands. Thus, Marx and Engels did not see the European continent as free from the colonization, foreign domination, annexation, and national fragmentation that the capitalist nation states of Europe were launching in other parts of the world. Moreover, by the late 1850s, any reference to European "colonialism as a source of civilization or progress had largely disappeared" from their writings (Ahmad 2001:1; Anderson 2002:86). They recognized that there were different trajectories of historical development in Western Europe and in the precapitalist and non-capitalist societies of Eastern Europe, Asia, and the Americas (e.g. Engels 1990[1894]; Marx 1973[1857–1858]:471–514; 1983[1881]). They also recognized that colonialism—officials from the metropoles, their local surrogates, and settlers—provoked resistance among the colonized peoples, such as the Indian army mutiny or the opium wars in China. In a phrase, colonized peoples were enmeshed in social relations and struggles that were not entirely of their own making. Sometimes, they were able to make their own history; often, they were not.

Writers in the early 1900s treated the Colonial Question as a distinctly European problem. It was about nations subjugated and oppressed by capitalist imperial states and the tasks of ruling and managing them, and bending them to the needs of colonial powers. Lenin (1963[1908a]; 1963[1913]) suggested that this was not a useful way to conceptualize the problem. He noted that uprisings and rebellions often followed in the wake of colonial expansion and were, in fact, reactions to it; there had already been a number in the preceding decade—e.g. in the Philippines, China, Persia, Turkey, or the Balkans. He wrote,

> World capitalism and the 1905 movement in Russia have finally aroused Asia. Hundreds of millions of the downtrodden and benighted have awakened from mediaeval stagnation to a new life and are rising to fight for elementary human rights and democracy.
>
> (Lenin 1963[1913]:85–86)

Thus, Lenin re-asserted that colonial peoples were active historical subjects attempting to make their own histories rather than being passive objects in a global capitalist world and that events and forces in the East influenced developments in the capitalist metropoles of Europe and North America (Seth 1992:112). In so doing, Lenin merged the Colonial Question with the National Question and underscored the intimate relation of both with imperialism.

The colonies had become parts of a whole constituted by imperialism. They were essential for its reproduction. Lenin (1964[1914]:406) viewed them as "backward" areas, hinterlands with "bourgeois-democratic national movements which strive to create nationally independent and nationally uniform states" like those of the imperialist nation states. However, this was not possible because of uneven development. He explained that there were two stages of capitalism, each with its own distinctive form of national movement. The earlier stage occurred during the transition from feudal to absolutist states. Mass movements drawing elements from all classes, including the peasantry, were drawn into the struggles for political liberty and the rights of the nation. The conditions in which the second, current stage of nationalist movements formed in the late nineteenth and early twentieth centuries were different: There were already established nation states as well as class antagonisms within them. As a result, there were no mass bourgeois-democratic movements, even as nations had been brought in closer contact through commerce and the intermingling of peoples from different parts of the world (Lenin 1964[1914]:401).

While imperialism had erased the old distinctions between nations and colonies, it created new ones, dividing "the world into oppressor and oppressed nations. Here, the struggle for nationhood in oppressed countries was seen as a response to this—generated *by* and *against* imperialism" (Seth 1992:119). This was Lenin's stance in 1914 in an ongoing debate with Kautsky (1908) and Luxemburg (1976[1908–1909]) regarding the right of national self-determination. By 1916, Lenin was arguing that anti-imperialist politics and wars of national liberation were inevitable in the colonies (Lenin 1964[1916a]:310). He used this line of argumentation to support a political strategy based on cooperation between the communist parties of the capitalist world and the national liberation movements of the oppressed countries, even though the latter would typically have a bourgeois-democratic rather than socialist form (Lenin 1964[1916b]). This was an important premise underlying the formation of the Communist International (also known as the Comintern or the Third International) in 1919.

Writers from colonial and semi-colonial countries quickly pointed to practical difficulties with this strategy. For example, Ho Chi Minh (1890–1969)—Vietnamese social analyst and Communist political leader who had worked in Paris and New York during the 1910s—wrote about the absence of accurate understandings of the social-class structures, national and class consciousness, and the balance of force in the colonies. He lamented the indifference of Western workers toward colonial subjects and indigenous people. There was mutual suspicion: The French saw the Vietnamese as racially inferior, the latter saw the French as exploiters. In Ho's view, the Bolshevism of the Comintern could mean either destruction, which drives the fearful away, or emancipation, which serves nationalist tendencies. He continued, "Surrounded by all the refinements and courts martial and special courts, a native militant cannot educate his oppressed and ignorant brothers without the risk of falling into the clutches of his civilizers" (Ho 1922). The question he posed was how to overcome these difficulties.

Mao Zedong (1893–1976)—social theorist, founding member of the Communist Party of China (CPC) in 1921, political organizer and activist—was already analyzing the realities of China's semi-colonial society in the early 1920s (e.g. Mao 1994[1923]; 1994[1925]). Initially, the CPC drew its support from the small, urban working class and from an alliance, albeit a short-lived one, with the nationalist Kuomintang (Chinese National People's Party or KMT). While the Comintern saw the communist party and the urban working class in the vanguard of revolutionary change, Mao came to believe, by 1927, that the real center of gravity in Chinese society was the peasantry and "that the decisive blows against the existing reactionary order must be struck in the countryside by the peasants" (Schram 1994:xvii). Thus, his view on the revolutionary potential of the industrial proletariat versus that of the peasantry was diametrically opposed to the opinion of the Comintern. After the KMT slaughtered large numbers of the urban proletariat in 1927, Mao retreated to the countryside to organize an army that would launch a revolution based on land reform and guerrilla warfare tactics (Schram 1994:xvii–xviii). His analyses were resolutely anti-imperialist and linked the National and Colonial Questions to the other important issue of the day—the Agrarian Question.

José Mariátegui (1894–1930)—writer, journalist, union organizer, critical analyst, and founding member of the Socialist Party of Peru—also saw the semi-colonial society of that country through a lens that linked the National, Colonial, and Agrarian Questions with the Indian Problem (Löwy 1999[1980]). In his view, Peru was a society dominated by a semi-feudal *latifundia* system that involved landholding and servitude for the peasantry; this impeded the development of indigenous capitalism and underwrote grinding poverty in the coastal cities and rural Indian communities in the mountains. Capitalist development was limited to sugar mills located in close proximity to sugar-producing *latifundia* (i.e. large, privately-owned estates in rural areas that combine agricultural and industrial production) on the coast and to mining enclaves in the mountains. Two other economic forms coexisted with the *latifundia*: indigenous communal economies in the mountains and a backward-looking local bourgeoisie in some of the coastal areas. He called the political form that corresponded to the realities of the Peruvian economy bossism (*gamonalismo*); the bosses—the large landowners and their underlings in municipal and regional bureaucracies—colluded with the central government to preserve the existing structures of power. Hence, they had no reason to address either the Indian Problem or the Agrarian Question, which merged in the mountain communities. The struggle was over who possessed land and controlled the production and distribution of goods produced by the members of indigenous communities (Mariátegui 1971[1928]). Mariátegui (1999[1928]) organized unions of industrial and agricultural workers and rejected alliances with political forces or bodies that represented the interests of other social classes, except the landholding indigenous communities in the highlands who also resisted *gamonalismo*.

The Agrarian Question: Peasants and Rural Economic Change

The Agrarian Question was concerned with the impact of capitalism on agriculture (Alavi and Shanin 1988). In what ways does capitalism affect peasantries? How are peasants integrated into capitalist societies and economies? How are they marginalized? What distinguishes peasant production from petty commodity production in manufacturing? How does capitalism underwrite class differentiation and formation in rural society? How are goods and labor extracted from family farms and peasant communities by larger capitalist societies? What is the nature of agrarian change and the transition to capitalism? The agrarian transition, then, involved the "changes necessary in the countryside to the overall development of capitalism and ultimate dominance of that mode of production in a particular national social formation" (Byres 1991:3–4).

Writers on the Agrarian Question distinguished urban society from that of the countryside and associated the rise of industrial capitalism with processes unfolding in urban areas. Kautsky (1988[1899]:13), for example, assumed that

> With the exception of a few colonies, the capitalist mode of production begins its development in *towns*, in *industry*, leaving agriculture largely undisturbed initially. But the development of industry in itself soon begins to affect the character of agricultural production.
>
> (emphasis in the original)

Kautsky and the other writers viewed industrial towns and cities as centers of change and innovation; cities were magnets that drew people in search of wage-labor, better lives, and even the refinements of civilization itself from the hinterlands and beyond into the networks of the atomized and anonymous relationships that were characteristic features of urban life (e.g. Simmel 1997[1903]; Tönnies 1996[1887]:33–34).

These writers and many of their contemporaries viewed peasants as the inhabitants of backward, rural areas: They lived on family farms and provided for the subsistence needs of the family; land husbandry was their major means of production; they had few economic specialties; the economic relations of peasant families were tightly interwoven with social relations that derived from their membership in small, localized communities that provided the means for social living and for demographic, social, and cultural reproduction; and they were subjugated politically, economically, and culturally by outsiders who viewed them as backward and, hence, inferior (Shanin 2006).

Marx's first study of the relationship between rural agricultural populations and the development of capitalism focused on France in the early 1850s—the country that Engels (1990[1894]:487) would call "the classic land of the small peasant economy." Here, the peasants, especially those in the central and southern parts of the country, had waged a successful struggle against a landlord class and gained ownership of their property by allying themselves with the state in the wake of the Revolution of 1789 (Byres 1991:34–41). This alliance effectively isolated them from one another, from other social classes, and from what was taking place in the towns and cities. Moreover, it deprived them of political influence in either the Second Empire or the Provisional Government. When the latter decided to tax the wine produced by peasants, they rebelled; allied themselves with the industrialists, merchants, moneylenders, and army against the workers and aristocracy; and supported the *coup d'état* of Napoleon Bonaparte in 1850. Their loyalty to Bonaparte rested on his support of the Papacy and on their right to own the plots of land on which they worked.

Even though the peasants—most of whom owned their land—lived under conditions similar to those of the workers in the mid-nineteenth century, they opposed the workers:

> ... the identity of their interests begets no community, no national bond and no political organization among them, they do not form a class. They are consequently incapable of enforcing their class interest in their own name.... They cannot represent themselves... [and] their representative must at the same time appear as their mass, as an authority over them, as an unlimited government power that protects them against other classes and sends them rain and sunshine from above. The political influence of the small-holding peasants, therefore, finds its final expression in the executive power subordinating society itself.
>
> (Marx 1979[1852]:187–188)

As a result, their livelihoods grew steadily smaller and more precarious each year as they went further into debt and as they increasingly sent their impoverished sons into an imperialist army stationed in colonial outposts around the world (Marx 1978[1850]:79–88; 1979[1852]:185–195). This left the French peasants vulnerable to the desires and predations of the urban-dwelling capitalist classes. By the 1870s, the small peasants, especially those in the north, were beginning to feel the effects of modern capitalist agriculture—mortgages and debt, dispossession from their plots, the consolidation of landholdings by capitalist farmers who produced goods for sale rather than for use and the steady growth of a rural proletariat (Marx 1986[1871]:337–338). The fact that small peasants owned their land and instruments of production, and were allied with the state slowed what Marx and Engels saw as an inevitable agrarian transition and encapsulation of the peasantry into capitalist economic relations emanating from the urban areas.

In the mid-1890s, Engels (1990[1894]:483) noted the ongoing importance of the peasantry in Europe. Capitalism had effectively eliminated the peasantry as a significant economic and political force in only two regions of Europe—England and Prussia, east of the Elbe. What he and others also noticed was that the transition occurred in quite different ways in English and Prussian cases.

Marx (1977[1863–1867]:873–913; 1981[1864–1894]:931–936, 953) had already described the capitalist transformation of agriculture that occurred in England. The English peasantry began to lose access to their commons as early as the fourteenth century as a succession of Parliaments enacted Enclosure Acts that transformed common land and pasture owned by rural communities into privately held tracts of property. During the Civil War (1642–1651), the English governments seized the vast properties of the Catholic Church—the largest feudal landholder in the country—and redistributed them to the individuals favored by the state. The latter (a landlord class) soon expropriated (dispossessed) the serfs, tenants, and peasants from their lands, evicting them in some instances, simultaneously creating a class of individuals separated from the means of producing the goods they required for everyday life as well as a large underemployed or unemployed pool of potential wage laborers. The effect of this pool was to keep wages at low levels. The state subsequently enacted legislation that banned vagabondage, criminalized poverty, and laid the foundations for debtors' prisons. Thus, the English path of agrarian transition involved processes of social differentiation that involved the emergence of large landlords, tenant farmers, and rural proletarians as well as the disappearance of the peasantry. While Marx and Engels saw this transformation as largely completed in England by the end of the eighteenth century, they vacillated in their views about Ireland, Wales, and Scotland—the Celtic fringe inhabited by "peoples without history"—where peasantries persisted into the twentieth century (e.g. Davidson 2014:45–80).

Engels (1990[1885]; 1990[1894]) pointed out that agrarian transition in Prussia unfolded in a different manner. As feudalism had waned in other parts of Europe, a class of large landlords seized both peasant and Catholic Church lands in East Prussia (Byres 1991:22–23). He wrote that

> The peasants ... [were] suppressed without much difficulty. ... [They] were now made serfs without much ado, subjected to unlimited labour services and dues dependent solely on the arbitrary power of the landlord. Their free land was simply turned into seigneurial property, on which they only retained the usufruct [use rights] accorded to them by the landlord. ... In less than a hundred years the free peasants were turned into serfs, at first in fact, and then also in law.

In the meantime the feudal nobility became more and more bourgeois. To an ever increasing extent it became indebted to the urban money capitalists, and money thus came to be its pressing need. Yet there was no money to be had from the peasant.

(Engels 1990[1885]:342–343)

This structure began to change after an 1807 edict by the Prussian government that released the peasant serfs from their labor obligations in exchange for their land. Thus, the large estates grew in size as the peasants were dispossessed from their lands, and the peasants were transformed into rural wage-workers; the old system of mutual rights and obligations was replaced by a contractual one— wages in exchange for labor power. However, after 1870, the peasants were increasingly attracted to industrial urban centers in search of higher wages, and the aristocratic Junker landlords, who also controlled the political apparatus of the state, were forced to rely increasingly on seasonal migrant labor from Eastern Europe to harvest crops that would be sold in the market (Perkins 1984). In the 1890s, both Engels and Weber (1989[1894]) saw the waning influence of the large landlords; while Weber focused on the transformation of the rural class structure in East Elbe, Engels (1990[1894]) and the socialists were concerned with establishing connections between the rural and industrial proletarians and bringing the former into the fold of the SDP.

By the late 1890s, analysts recognized that successful agrarian transitions were taking diverse forms and occurring at different rates in the capitalist regions of Europe. Kautsky's (1988[1899]) *The Agrarian Question* was the first systematic study of the relationship between capitalism and agriculture (Alavi and Shanin 1988; Banaji 1990). His contemporaries saw it as an extension of Marx's third volume of *Capital* (e.g. Lenin 1960[1899a]:94). Kautsky also noted that subsistence agriculture, peasants, and peasant communities were not specific to any particular mode of production. They were instead both residues of "archaic" modes of production and persisted as integral parts of capitalist economies and society. Consequently, it was necessary to conceptualize the articulation between the urban industries of the capitalist mode of production and the family farms of the peasantry.

Kautsky made several observations. The first was that because arable land was a relatively fixed means of production, there was a contradiction between the capitalist farmers' desire to create larger farms, on the one hand, and the peasants' capacity to retain ownership or control of their lands, on the other; even with the benefits of the technical and scientific advances associated with economies of scale, it was difficult for capitalists to convert smallholdings into larger, more efficient units because the new lands they were able to acquire were not always contiguous. Kautsky's second observation was that the subsistence production of peasant family farms was not valorized in capitalist markets. As a result, peasant families were inextricably drawn into market relations, and the need for money increased; subsistence production slowly gave way to the production of commodities for the market, which were often not goods they chose to produce.

Kautsky's third observation was that class differentiation was occurring in rural societies. For various reasons, some peasants accumulated land and began to produce commodities to be sold in the markets; in effect, they became capitalist farmers. Other peasant households retained their lands and continued to engage largely but not exclusively in subsistence production. Still others lost their lands and became rural wage-workers or tenants. Kautsky's fourth observation was that peasant production involved the over-exploitation of peasant labor power by the cities, the state, capitalist farmers, and middle peasant family farmers themselves. One effect of this was that peasant families were typically large and supplied labor power for rural capitalists in the countryside and industrial capitalists in the towns and cities; they were also recruited by the state to become soldiers and policemen. These were incentives for states to ensure the continued existence of family farms in capitalist economic and social regimes.

A different process was unfolding in Russia in the late nineteenth century. Russia was largely an agricultural country; more than two-thirds of its population engaged in agriculture, and they contributed nearly half of the country's annual income on the eve of the Revolution of October 1917. Moreover, with some significant regional differences, most large factories were located either outside established urban centers or in newly founded factory towns often grafted onto existing rural settlements. Industry was attracted to these localities by the availability of cheap land, raw materials, power, small rural producers, and a labor force (Crisp 1976:44–52). The organization of the peasantry was complex. Some peasants were state serfs, defined as "free rural dwellers," who were able to buy land and change their place of residence; they were liable for taxes and military service. Other peasants were estate serfs who owed labor service and money payments to their aristocratic landlords as well as taxes and military service to the state. All peasants belonged to a *mir*, a rural commune or village community whose members owned arable land, pasture, and woods in common, and which was periodically redistributed; the *mir* was also an administrative unit for the state that ensured that tax and military service obligations were met. The Emancipation Act of 1861 freed the estate serfs; they were able to purchase land allotments, often marginal farm land, from the nobility using long-term loans from the government. The plan did not work smoothly. In the countryside, there was social differentiation between peasant households within the village communities. Some households were able to eke out bare subsistence from their land allotments. Others were not able to meet them because they had insufficient or marginal land. A few well-to-do households had livestock, agricultural implements, or draft animals; were able to purchase or rent additional land; hired neighbors as seasonal or permanent wage-workers; and could turn themselves into commodity-producing, capitalist farmers at the expense of other households in the *mir* (Hussain and Tribe 1981:1–15; Lenin 1960[1893]).

In *The Development of Capitalism in Russia*, Lenin (1960[1899b]) synthesized his views about what was happening in rural areas, specifically looking at the way in which two different home markets developed in the countryside—one for products and the other for labor power. Both the peasants and the rural bourgeoisie participated in the market for commodities; however, only the rural bourgeoisie was involved in the market in which the major means of production were exchanged. Lenin noted that the first stages of industrial development took place in peasant households, which laid the foundations for further industrial development in the countryside; he also noted that the urban proletariat was still peasant-based because of the control that the *mir* exerted over migrant labor. Two paths of capitalist development were taking place in rural areas: the transition of the peasant economy, on the one hand, and the landlords' economy, on the other. He pointed to the vulnerability of the middle peasants—those households that were least engaged with capitalist social relations. In good years, their harvests and the household goods they produced were sufficient to satisfy their needs; in poor years, they were driven to sell goods or labor power or to borrow money to purchase what they needed—i.e. they were ensnared in capitalist relations. In contrast, the landlords either used peasants who possessed their own means of production to produce agricultural commodities in return for various forms of payment, or they hired waged labor to produce agricultural commodities (Hussain and Tribe 1981:37–45).

Thus, two forms of capitalist development occurred in the Russian countryside. One involved the internal differentiation of the natural economy of the peasantry and rural class formation as capitalists and proletarians appeared. The other involved the transformation of estate farming into capitalist agriculture. Lenin argued that the former was revolutionary; the latter resulted in the kind of agrarian transformation that occurred in East Prussia and that was dominated by the Junkers. The former promoted unfettered capitalist development as the peasant became a free farmer; the latter impoverished and enslaved the peasantry, supported the private ownership of large tracts of land, and maintained the political and economic power of the landlords—all of which impeded capitalist development. Moreover, capitalist agriculture developed differently from industry in Russia. While industrial commodities were gradually being standardized, those produced by capitalist farmers were becoming more diverse as a result of regional specialization, the growth of dairy-farming, and the appearance of vegetable and fruit farming in suburban areas. From Lenin's perspective, the capitalist economy of Russia in the 1890s was dominated by rural production and markets that provided both consumer and capital goods (Lenin 1960[1899b]).

Lenin (1962[1907]:238–242) subsequently argued that there were two paths to the transition to capitalism in the countryside—the Prussian (Junker) path and what he called the American (revolutionary) path (Byres 1991; 1996:27–30). In the Prussian path, capitalism was imposed from above by a feudal landlord class that had transformed itself into agrarian capitalists; this stifled any development of the peasant economy and prevented the development of capitalist agriculture by segments of an increasingly differentiated peasantry. In the American path, he argued, capitalism emerged from the free development of the peasantry rather than from a pre-existing landlord class—i.e. the peasantry was the sole agent of agriculture, and some peasants evolved into capitalist farmers. Both contrasted with the English path, where the landlords survived as a landlord class rather than as a class of capitalist farmers. He argued that the American path represented capitalism from below as peasants evolved into capitalist farmers in circumstances shaped by the growth of an enormous home market. It involved "the free economy of the free farmer working the land" (Lenin 1963[1908b]:140). Lenin further argued that the uniqueness of the American path resulted from the availability of "free land" that was appropriated from the Indian tribes that were dispossessed (Lenin 1964[1915]:88).

Luxemburg (2003[1913]:309–398) addressed the Agrarian Question in more general terms in *The Accumulation of Capital*. In her view, industrial capitalism developed in a sea of non-capitalist societies; it required the continued existence of these non-capitalist or backward areas to ensure its own expanded reproduction. Rural and colonial areas inhabited by what others called "backward people" or "people without history" provided raw materials, reservoirs of labor power, and markets for commodities produced in capitalist factories. Commodity production and exchange disrupted the natural economies of self-sufficient household production in these areas. The disruption was exacerbated as new forms of transport—canals, railways, or new shipping routes—provided the infrastructure to spread the emerging commodity economy. An important step in the agrarian transition was the separation of agriculture from other productive activities in the household; as a result, rural industry was eradicated, and rural peoples increasingly specialized in the production of agricultural commodities.

Luxemburg also emphasized a different idea than Lenin's regarding the American path or "capitalism from below." She pointed out that states played an important role in the destruction of peasant economies. For example, she notes that in the United States, the federal government underwrote more than forty Indian wars, relocated indigenous communities, and condoned or initiated genocide in order to make room for white settler farmers. Within a generation or so, capitalist agriculture replaced subsistence and commodity-producing households east of the Mississippi River and drove them to frontier areas of the West in search of "free" land—free in the sense that the government and settlers removed native peoples from their homelands. However, land speculating companies and venture capitalists retained the best agricultural lands in the West and used the latest scientific methods and technological innovations to farm them efficiently and profitably. The "American farmer could not successfully compete with such capitalist enterprises" (Luxemburg 2003[1913]:385). Small farmers went into debt, and many lost their homes and lands. Those who emigrated to the wheatlands of Canada soon faced the same problem again once Canada began to export wheat to the world market. In Luxemburg's view, the Agrarian Question was not a uniquely European issue because similar processes were occurring in North America, Asia, and South Africa.

Unfortunately, the contributions of analysts of the Agrarian Question in other countries—such as Mexico or Peru, where it was typically linked with the National Question and called the Indian Question—were not more widely recognized at the time. For example, in 1909, Andrés Molina Enríquez (1868–1940)—anthropologist, critic of the positivist ideology of the state, and advocate of land reform—argued that government policies that allowed the formation of *latifundia* in the countryside destroyed communities that held lands in common, prevented the formation of a rural middle class, and slowed industrial development in urban areas. That the *latifundia* produced crops for export and did not pay their workers a living wage inhibited the development of a home market (Molina Enríquez 1978[1909]). In the years immediately preceding the Mexican Revolution, he condemned the reconstitution of feudal relations in the countryside and argued for the repeal of the federal legislation that underpinned those political-economic relations (Shadle 1994). In Peru, Luis Valcárcel (1891–1981)—anthropologist, *indigenista*, close friend of Mariátegui, and advocate for the formation of rural schools—was concerned with the rise of capitalist export agriculture on the coast and its impact on rural production, landownership, and everyday life in other parts of the country. He was particularly concerned with the struggles over land that existed between indigenous communities, whose members held land collectively, and neighboring *haciendas* (*latifundia*) in highland areas, like Cuzco. Like his contemporaries in Mexico, Valcárcel (1914; 1981:130–172) was critical of the rural class structures that were emerging in the wake of capitalist penetration into the countryside; consequently, he too was an advocate of land reform.

From Social Evolution to Uneven and Combined Development

In the preceding pages, we examined imperialism; the development of the National, Colonial, and Agrarian Questions; and their interconnections. Commentators in industrializing countries, such as England or the United States, often relied on ideas of societal evolution or stages of development to describe the history of human society in general and capitalist ones more particularly. On the one hand, their views typically involved notions about hierarchies of society—e.g. simple or complex—and the importance of free markets in economic development. On the other hand, they often incorporated justifications for scientific racism, eugenics, genocide, anti-immigration sentiments, and imperialism. In these perspectives, capitalism marked the highest stage of social and economic development; the inhabitants of backward regions and colonies would either be dragged into capitalist civilization as their ways of life were deformed and transformed, or they would be eliminated altogether as obstacles or impediments to the civilizing process.

What Marx, Engels, and their successors observed in the late nineteenth and early twentieth centuries was (1) that capitalism was developing in various ways in different places, (2) that the various manifestations of capitalist development were interrelated in complex ways, (3) that some capitalist states were more or less advanced or developed than others, (4) that there were complex linkages within capitalist states between their industrializing and non-industrial regions, economic sectors, and populations (i.e. backward) as well as between colonies and the nations they dominated. These overlapping processes were taking place simultaneously in the capitalist and non-capitalist worlds. There was uneven development among the capitalist nation states; there was combined development within capitalist states, their colonies, and subordinated countries on their peripheries. Marx recognized this in the 1870s. For example,

> But the basis of this whole [capitalist] development is the expropriation of the cultivators. So far, it has been carried out in a radical manner only in England: therefore this country will necessarily play the leading role in our sketch. But all the other countries of Western Europe are going through the same development, although in accordance with the particular environment it changes its local color, or confines itself to a narrower sphere, or shows a less pronounced character, or follows a different order of succession.
>
> (Marx 1985[1875]:169 quoted by Anderson 2010:179)

> ... Events with striking similarity, taking place in different historical contexts, led to totally disparate results.
>
> (Marx 1983[1877]:136)

> In Western Europe ... the process of primitive accumulation has more or less been accomplished. Here the capitalist regime has either directly subordinated to itself the whole of the nation's production, or, where economic relations are less developed, it has at least indirect control of those social layers, which, although they belong to antiquated modes of production, still continue to exist side by side with it in a state of decay.... It is otherwise in the colonies. There the capitalist regime constantly comes up against the obstacle presented by the producer, who, as the owner of his own conditions of labour, employs that labour to enrich himself instead of the capitalist. The contradiction between these two diametrically opposed economic systems has its practical manifestation here in the struggle between them. Where the capitalist has behind him the power of the mother country, he tries to use force to clear out of the way the modes of production and appropriation which rest on the personal labour of the independent producer.
>
> (Marx 1977[1863–1867]:931–932)

> The country that is more developed industrially only shows, to those which follow it on the industrial path [*échelle*], the image of its own future.
>
> (Marx 1963[1875]:549 quoted by Anderson 2002:88)

> The only possible answer to this question [i.e. the possibility of socialist revolution] at the present time is the following: If the Russian revolution becomes the signal for a proletarian revolution in the West, so that the two complement each other, the present Russian common ownership of land may serve as the starting point for communist development.
>
> (Marx and Engels 1989[1882]:426)

Marx spent the last decade of his life reading voraciously about how the processes of capitalist penetration were unfolding in both colonial settings and the rural or backward areas of European countries—most notably, Russia. In the latter, he thought that the actions of the tsarist regime combined with those of the urban-based capitalists might drive the Russian peasants toward political action, although it might take a different form from what happened in England or France. Subsequent writers, broadly sharing Marx's standpoint, pursued these issues and elaborated his inchoate notions of uneven and combined development.

Leon Trotsky (1879–1940)—Russian revolutionary, social theorist, and founder of the Red Army—crystallized the ideas of uneven and combined development (Trotsky 1969[1906]; 1973[1907–1909]; 1980[1932–1933]). He was the first of several writers—e.g. Gramsci (1977[1916]), Hilferding (1981[1910]), and Veblen (1939[1916])—who noted the important role of "backwardness" (Davidson 2006). Trotsky wrote that

> The privilege of historic backwardness—and such a privilege exists—permits, or rather compels, the adoption of whatever is ready in advance of any specified date, skipping a whole series of intermediate stages. ... The laws of history have nothing in common with a pedantic schematism. Unevenness, the most general law of the historic process, reveals itself most sharply and complexly in the destiny of the backward countries. Under the whip of external necessity their backward culture is compelled to make leaps. From the universal law of unevenness thus derives another law, which for the lack of a better name, we may call it the law of *combined development*—by which we mean a drawing together of the different stages of a journey, a combination of separate steps, an amalgam of archaic with more contemporary forms. Without this law, to be taken of course in its whole material content, it is impossible to understand the history of Russia, and indeed of any country of the second, third or tenth cultural class.
>
> (Trotsky 1980[1932–1933]:5–6)

Trotsky's theory was a breakthrough. It identified relative changes in the power relations between capitalist nation states and in the structural inequalities that existed between them and the colonies and countries they dominated. It explained what happened when the overleaping process or skipping of historical stages of development took place in the colonial or backward countries

> where it was impossible to 'catch up' with, let alone 'overtake' the developed West, but to do so instead in a fragmentary or partial way. But the resulting combined forms, because of their inbuilt social instability, paradoxically made revolutionary outbreaks more likely than in the developed world, with its greater levels of stability and reformist traditions. In other words, combined and uneven development made it possible for a strategy of permanent revolution to be pursued [on a global basis].
>
> (Davidson 2006:22)

Discussion

While late-eighteenth-century Romantic writers located the engine driving the development of national identities in the cultural realm, liberal analysts writing in the wake of the French and American revolutions located the motor in the political domain. Marxists pointed out that the formation of national identities was linked both politically and economically to the development of capitalism. In those countries in which industrial capitalism had developed, capitalists and wage-workers typically viewed themselves as sharing the same national identity—one that was opposed to those of capitalists and workers in other national states. Marx and Engels pointed this out in *The Communist Manifesto* when they urged the workers of the world to unite in opposition to the capitalist class. The problem of forging linkages and solidarity between the working classes of different countries was the single major concern of the labor and socialist movements from the mid-nineteenth-century onwards. World War I was partly a result of their inability to do so.

As Hobson and others indicated, the new form of imperialism that emerged in the late-nineteenth-century was based on the export of excess commodities and of capital to areas that promised high rates of profit. Millions of people from countries on the margins of capitalism emigrated to find work. When they came to the United States, for example, they found themselves enmeshed in labor markets stratified by nationality, with native-born U.S. workers at the top, Eastern and Southern European immigrants in the middle, and blacks either at the bottom of the class or outside it altogether. In the 1890s, liberal nationalists, like Weber, expressed concern about the effects of immigration at the same time that they upheld imperial expansion because it benefited the German state and its citizens, and had the ability to bring civilization to those overseas peoples that were becoming enmeshed in the social relations of the imperialist state.

Various analysts were aware that imperialism—the spread of capitalist social relations—fostered the creation of nationalist movements across the globe, most especially in Asia. As you will recall, Lenin argued that the national movements emerging along the capitalist periphery were often mass movements calling for the formation of bourgeois-democratic states. In his view, the working classes of the capitalist states should support these movements for self-determination and the formation of bourgeois-democratic states at the same time that they combated nationalism in all its guises in their own countries. Like Marx, Lenin was aware that this was not happening to any significant degree. Luxemburg posed the problem of imperialism in different terms when she argued that it could exist only if there were non-capitalist societies that afforded opportunities for the sale of surplus goods. The accumulation of capital occurred because of markets in non-capitalist areas rather than the exploitation of wage-workers. As a result, the proletariats of the various capitalist countries benefited from the economic penetration and exploitation of the non-capitalist peoples residing on the periphery—a view that Bukharin rejected because he saw capitalist relations developing on a world scale.

Imperialism created conditions that fueled the growth of nationalist sentiments and promoted both ethnocide and ethnogenesis. Questions about national identity and character flourished in multinational states, like Austria, and in colonial areas, like the Indian subcontinent, where some groups were already beginning to forge national identities in opposition to that of the imperial state and to lay the foundations for nationalist movements that would eventually challenge both the policies and the legitimacy of the state. In other areas, like the Americas, the lifeways of indigenous peoples were destroyed, along with the resources they used and too often with the people themselves.

The socialists, of course, were not the only writers deploying arguments about capitalist development. Notions of progress and civilization; colonial expansion and the civilizing mission of capitalist societies; the intersection of presupposed racial, social, and cultural hierarchies; or the inferiority of non-capitalist peoples and modes of production abounded in the late nineteenth and early twentieth centuries. Anthropologists, among others, exposed how these and other standpoints structured social relations, beliefs, and practices on the margins of capitalist economies and societies as well as understandings in the core capitalist countries. Some bore witness to the savagery and barbarism of capitalist civilization.

For example, the social evolutionists assumed that human cultures and societies developed from simple to more complex forms. They believed they could portray the passage from savagery to civilization by arranging contemporary objects, like house types or pottery from the same region, in terms of a simple-to-complex continuum that purportedly represented change and development through time. Boas—German-born, American anthropologist and socialist—argued that contemporary tribal societies on the peripheries of capitalism were the end-product of complex, historically contingent sociohistorical processes and relations; their members occupied particular places in sets of power relations and were bound together by the cultures that shaped the historically transmitted ideas, behaviors, and objects that gave them a sense of shared identity and history (Boas 1887a,b).

Besides arguing that different tribal peoples had their own cultures that reflected their unique historical experiences, Boas, along with Du Bois (1868–1963)—American-born civil rights advocate and writer—and others, challenged the Social Darwinist claims about the existence of racial hierarchies, which was a pervasive view in the United States at the time. The Social Darwinists asserted that the various races were distinguished from one another by various hereditary differences—head form, intelligence, or the propensity to engage in criminal activity—and used them to legitimate oppressive and exploitative social relations. The Anti-Immigration League also used these arguments to force the U.S. Congress to stem the flow of immigrants from Eastern and Southern Europe and Asia. Boas (1940[1922]) was not particularly interested in the static racial classifications of the day but rather in the processes by which human populations came to have particular features and in the historical and environmental conditions that shaped and constrained those processes. He used anthropometric data and statistical arguments to show that there was greater variability within racial groups than between them and that the human form was exceedingly plastic because of its sensitivity to various historical and environmental factors. By doing so, he effectively called into question the validity of the claims of the racist Anti-Immigration League and the scientific publications that supported them.

Beginning in the mid-1880s, James E. Mooney (1861–1921)—American anthropologist, son of Irish-Catholic immigrants, and supporter of Irish Home Rule—focused his attention on peoples, mostly but not exclusively Indian tribes, in the Southeast and Midwest who had been displaced, murdered, sold into slavery, and generally abused in myriad ways by the spread of civilization and its agents. His first studies took him to the mountainous region of North Carolina, where he interviewed both poor white and Eastern Cherokee informants. In 1890, Mooney traveled to the West, shortly after the U.S. Army massacred more than two hundred men, women, and children at the Pine Ridge reservation in South Dakota. The Army had mistakenly believed that dancing associated with the Ghost Dance religion signaled an imminent uprising among the Sioux. Over the next three years, Mooney would record the accounts of numerous individuals— Paiute, Arapaho, Sioux, and Kiowa—who had first-hand knowledge of the movement. The Ghost Dance was a religious movement adopted by various American Indian tribes in the West and the Great Plains whose members were witnessing the dissolution of their own tribal cultures in the wake of the deliberate destruction of the great buffalo herds a decade or so earlier and the influx of settlers into their tribal homelands. Mooney (1896:657) wrote,

> And when the race lies crushed and groaning beneath an alien yoke, how natural is the dream of a redeemer, an Arthur, who shall return from exile or awake from some long sleep to drive out the usurper and win back for his people what they have lost. The hope becomes a faith and the faith becomes the creed of priests and prophets, until the hero is a god and the dream a religion, looking to some great miracle of nature for its culmination and accomplishment. The doctrines of the Hindu avatar, the Hebrew Messiah, the Christian God, and the Hesûnanin of the Indian Ghost dance are essentially the same, and have their origin in a hope and longing common to all humanity.

The Ghost Dance was a pan-tribal movement that linked together peoples who had formerly seen themselves as distinct. It was an entirely new religion that spread rapidly. Individuals from the various tribes that participated in the movement saw themselves as sharing a common fate and a destiny revealed in its rituals and prophecies. They dreamed that the old ways and the buffalo would be restored, that the Indians would be reunited with ancestors and old friends, and that the ways of the white man would be cast aside. Mooney compared the Ghost Dance with other religious movements that erupted suddenly in circumstances of rapid social and cultural change, when people were forced to seek solace from the wretchedness of their lives in a heartless world. One of these was the Peyote Religion that appeared around 1900. His sympathies for the participants of the Ghost Dance and other American Indians conflicted with those of his employer—the U.S. government. They did, however, lay the foundations for subsequent analyses of other resistance movements based on religions of the oppressed, especially those that appeared when indigenous peoples were forced, by circumstances that were often beyond their control, to confront civilization and capitalism.

William H. R. Rivers (1864–1923)—English anthropologist, psychiatrist, and socialist—in an essay on imperial policies toward colonial subjects, noted that

> Whenever one people assumes the management of another, three lines of action are possible. One is to wipe out the indigenous culture as completely as possible and govern the people in accordance with the ideas and institutions of their new rulers. The second is to preserve the indigenous culture in its entirety and to attempt to govern the people in accordance with the ideas which have come down to them from their fathers. The third and intermediate course is to uphold the indigenous culture except where it conflicts with the moral and social ideals of the governing people.
>
> (Rivers 1917:303)

Because most states pursued the third course, at least when it was convenient for them to do so, anthropologists did have something to contribute to understanding the consequences of culture change in these circumstances. Besides correcting errors of fact, their knowledge might prevent colonial administrators from making mistakes.

Colonial officials often made mistakes, Rivers argued, because they did not understand the culture and practices of their subjects—for example, the role of chieftains. He pointed out that, after establishing control over a region, the administrator's first order of business was usually to find or to create intermediaries who would link the colonial state with the indigenous peoples it ruled. The official

> ... will either treat as chief one of those whom the people regard in this light and impose on him functions to which he is wholly strange, for which perhaps he is quite unfitted. Or, and this is the more frequent case, he treats as a chief one whom the people do not regard, and never have regarded in this light, some man of superior address or intelligence who may combine these qualities with others which lead to the unscrupulous use of his new position to exploit his fellows for his own ends.
>
> (Rivers 1917:315–316)

Fifteen years earlier, Rivers (1906) had documented the contradictions that appear among peoples experiencing the effects of class and state formation in colonial settings in the Nilgiri Hills of southern India. He described the struggles and alliances between a Toda headman appointed by the colonial government to collect taxes from his neighbors, and kin and the traditional lineage and clan headmen of the Todas. Rivers showed how the social organization of traditional Toda society was simultaneously distorted, disassembled, and reconstituted as class interests were increasingly given precedence over those of kin and neighbor.

Anthropologists were particularly aware of the ways in which imperialism and capitalist penetration into rural and colonial areas promoted class and state formation at home and abroad. Social relations were overturned as yeoman farmers became proletarians, as rural folk emigrated to the cities, and as the new bourgeoisies attempted to emulate the opulent lifestyles of European royalty and aristocracy. In the undeveloped areas, traditional social relations were also overturned as the colonial states, the capitalist enterprises, and their agents forged new and varied kinds of relations with some segments of the colonial populations and not with others. The members of these segments became agents of the colonial state, representatives of the capitalist enterprises, or the operators of businesses that served or satisfied their needs. Away from the centers of power, individuals from particular regions were often recruited as agents of the colonial state to collect taxes or to oversee the activities of their less acculturated kin and neighbors. This promoted the formation of class structures as well as the dissolution of pre-capitalist communal and tributary relations centered in the rural areas.

In Chapter 4, we will examine how social commentators explained the crises of capitalism as they were manifest in the interwar years: social reform, socialist revolution, rural class structures and alternative pathways of agrarian development, the National Question, and psychological accounts of social change. These commentators dealt with the dialectic of the desire for social change, on the one hand, and the search for the maintenance of social order, on the other.

Notes

1 In the first half of the nineteenth century, empires were aggregates of territories, states, or colonies under the authority of a single sovereign state—e.g. Great Britain. British writers began to use the word "imperialism" to unfavorably compare the domestic policies of Napoleon III, who ruled France from 1852 to 1870, with their own (Koebner and Schmidt 1965). Napoleon seized all executive power after the *coup d'état* of 1851; he also claimed absolute sovereignty in the name of defending the republican aims of the French Revolution, disbanded parliament, censored the press, repressed and jailed opponents, proclaimed that he was the source of all public benevolence, and forged an overseas empire with troops recruited largely from the peasantry that he had fragmented and marginalized politically and that nonetheless supported his claim that he was freeing the masses of the French nation. His policies were the basis for Marx's (1979[1852]:98) famous quip comparing the First Empire of Napoleon I with that of his nephew: "Hegel remarks somewhere that all facts and personages of great historical importance in world history occur, as it were, twice. He forgot to add: the first time as tragedy, the second as farce."

2 Wakefield (1796–1862) employed "underconsumption" and "free trade" arguments to justify colonial land and emigration schemes: British industries were producing more than could be consumed in the mother country, and the formation of settler colonies—like Australia or New Zealand, where he had been an administrator—provided an outlet for surplus industrial production, emigration, and further colonial expansion (Semmel 1970:76–125).

3 Conant's and Hobson's contemporaries—Durkheim and Weber—did not elaborate on theories of imperialism. On the one hand, Durkheim was appalled by the relations between colonial powers and their colonies, but his notions of society, equilibrium, civilization, and social order made it impossible for him to problematize unequal power relations (Durkheim 1961[1925]:193, 196; Pearce 1989:71–75). On the other hand, Weber viewed imperialism as a mix of political and economic elements, as part of German world policy, and, hence, ultimately, as a political phenomenon (Mommsen 1984:68–90; Swedberg 2005:122–123; Weber 1978[1922]:913–921).

4 Briefly, *monopolies* occur when only a single firm produces a given commodity. *Cartels* are associations of firms that produce a particular commodity and collude to set prices artificially and to prevent competition from other firms that might want to produce that good. *Trusts* involve a relationship between two or more firms whereby the property held by one benefits the others. *Mergers* involve buying, selling, dividing, or combining different firms.

5 Bukharin agreed with Luxemburg regarding the interconnections of imperialism, world economic systems, ongoing crises, and wars; they were inextricably linked. He saw the barbarism of capitalism and viewed socialism as the only alternative. However, he was also critical of her work. He argued that she viewed imperialism and the collapse of capitalism largely in voluntaristic, political terms rather than in ones that acknowledged the transformative effects of monopolies and finance capital. A second point of disagreement was her thesis that capitalism could not survive in the absence of non-capitalist societies (Bukharin 1973[1915]).

6 Semi-colonial countries are those in which (1) imperialist states lack the capacity to limit the sovereignty of the indigenous societies and thus advance their own interests, and (2) the indigenous elite has some power over the local productive classes (Walker 1999:15).

4

Capitalism in Crisis and the Search for Social Order, 1918–1945

An explosive mixture of social relations emerged in the late nineteenth and early twentieth centuries. One was that the economic and political spheres of imperialist states fused; John D. Rockefeller, the founder of Standard Oil and its more than one hundred subsidiaries worldwide, remarked in the early 1900s that "What's good for Standard Oil is good for America." A second was the competition between imperialist states and their corporations for access to and control of raw materials, labor, markets, and profits, and their consequent struggle for world domination. A third was the claim by imperialist states that they were, in fact, nation states, despite the diverse ethnic and national origins, and assertions of their residents to the contrary. Xenophobia, anti-immigrant sentiment, racism, and jingoistic patriotism flourished and intensified in these milieux. A fourth was the civil unrest and economic crises that wracked the industrial world—often violent strikes; police brutality; assassinations; revolutions in Russia, China, and Mexico; movements for colonial liberation; and widespread perceptions of social inequality in imperialist states as well as between them and their colonies (Hobsbawm 1987).

This powder keg finally exploded with the outbreak of World War I (1914–1918)—the first truly world war, even though most of the battles were waged in Europe and the Middle East. Initially, it was a European war, pitting France, England, and Russia against Germany and Austria-Hungary; however, other countries—like the United States and Japan—eventually joined the fray. The war, whose brutality scarred its survivors and non-combatants in different ways, had other consequences as well. From the viewpoint of the victorious capitalist states, these included the emergence in Russia of a revolutionary Bolshevik regime that had to be contained, if not crushed altogether; a Germany that had to remain weakened; and the appearance of new (multinational) nation-states in areas controlled only a few years earlier by the Russian, Austro-Hungarian, and Ottoman empires, whose continued existence would be sustained as long as they remained sufficiently anti-Bolshevik (Hobsbawm 1996:24–31, 65–70). In addition, the capitalist states still had to confront the transformation of the agrarian sectors of their own economies, the rise of nationalism at home and abroad, and the policies concerning the assimilation or further marginalization of indigenous and minority communities. The new socialist government of the Soviet Union also had to confront these and other issues—e.g. how to promote non-capitalist industrialization.

In the years following the Paris Peace Conference in 1918–1919, the United States emerged as the world's dominant political power and major exporter. While employment was relatively high in the United States, unemployment topped twenty percent across Europe, labor unions were weakened worldwide, wages stagnated, agricultural prices collapsed, and income inequality increased dramatically during the "Roaring '20s." Virtually no efforts were made to integrate the world's capitalist economies as one country after another erected protective tariffs to protect their struggling economies. Many recognized this potentially explosive situation. However, almost no one recognized what was going to happen in 1929—the collapse of the world capitalist economy and the great economic depression that lasted for a decade or more (Hobsbawm 1996:85–100). It was truly a worldwide depression, not only in the industrial countries but also in those on the margins of the capitalist world that relied on exports of one or a few commodities for their revenues. It added fuel to the fire for social change or, alternatively, for the maintenance of social order. This petri dish fed the growth of fascist and ultra-nationalist political parties, on the one hand, and leftist parties, on the other. World War II erupted in the mid- to late-1930s, depending on what date and place one chooses to mark its beginning, and lasted until 1945. More than thirty nation-states, arrayed in two opposing alliances, waged this global conflict and fought battles in Europe, Africa, Asia, and the Pacific Islands. The brutality of World War I paled by comparison.

In this chapter, let us consider the issues raised in the preceding paragraphs, keeping in mind that uneven development was an important theoretical and practical problem during the first half of the twentieth century. Our goal is to examine how scholars have conceptualized change and development in those colonial societies and countries, including the Soviet Union, on the periphery of the capitalist world, in which large segments of the population were not involved in any obvious way in capitalist production relations.

Economic Crises, Cycles, or Evolution?

Late-nineteenth-century businessmen recognized that there were times when business was good and times when it was not (Benkemoune 2009). Economists at the turn of the twentieth century explained these fluctuations (boom and slump cycles) in two different ways. The differences were significant. The first started from the behavior of autonomous individuals who were aggregated into a society; it was a unilinear, non-dialectical concept of historical progress akin to that of late-nineteenth-century social evolutionists and positivists. The second was a dialectical view of the dynamics and contradictions of capitalist social relations.

Neoclassical (liberal) economists, who advocated the first view, saw crises as a consequence of exogenous factors—such as wars or shifts in governmental policies—that originated outside of the economic system and impinged on it. Each downward fluctuation was a single event because the economic sphere was more or less in an equilibrium resulting from the supply of and demand for commodities; firms attempting to maximize profits; individuals trying to optimize utility, given limited incomes; and both acting rationally on the basis of complete, relevant information. Their view was synchronic in the sense that they compared snapshots of the economy in equilibrium at different moments in time in order to determine whether the rate of economic growth was increasing or decreasing.

Conservative economic and political theorist Joseph Schumpeter (1983[1911]) broke with the equilibrium models of his neoclassical contemporaries. His aim was "to construct a theory of economic development ... [in which] the economic system itself generated (and did not merely respond to) change" (Medearis 2001, 2013[2009]:40). He argued that fluctuations in the numbers and rates of technological innovations disrupted economic equilibrium, promoted instability, and caused fluctuations in investment—i.e. business cycles. Moreover, he suggested that innovations tended to cluster in time creating "neighborhoods of change," which underwrote long cycles of growth; these neighborhoods resulted from the actions of entrepreneurs—rational individuals who acted and thought in unconventional rather than traditional ways. Credit, which was the creation of bankers, allowed entrepreneurs to redirect their existing productive resources in new, innovative ways. Thus, in Schumpeter's view, business cycles with their periodic upturns and downturns were an integral feature of capitalist economies. He also saw democratic social movements as erosive and potentially disruptive of capitalism, even though he had an aristocrat's disdain, like Weber, for the competence of the masses.

Marx (1978[1884]:153–156; 1981[1864–1894]:606–625) had already laid the foundations for alternative, dialectical view of crises in *Capital*. He had argued that business cycles were integral to the dynamics of capitalist accumulation because of ever-present structural contradictions within the capitalist mode of production. Crises were thus an inherent, necessary part of capitalist economies rather than the result of accidents or outside forces:

> An economic crisis occurs when capitalists are unable to sell their commodities without incurring substantial losses, reverberating through the system in a chain of defaults and curtailing production in a cumulative downward spiral. ...The abstract possibility of crisis is already contained in the separation of purchase and sale. If a significant number of sellers withdraw their money from circulation, rather than using it to buy further commodities, then the latter commodities will remain unsold. ... For Marx, the "sole end and purpose" of capitalist production is not consumption but the production and appropriation of surplus value. The sale of commodities represents the reconversion of the capitalist's expanded capital into the form of money with which to renew the process of capital accumulation. The capitalist will devote some of the money realized to [his] own consumption, but the remainder will be reinvested, provided only that there are opportunities for profitable investment.
>
> (Clarke 2012:90)

While Marx never fully developed a theory of economic crisis that took account of competition and credit, his successors in the German Social Democratic Party, the largest and most influential party in the Second International, sought to fill the void. As a result, four Marxist theories of crisis competed with the explanations of neoclassical economists in the first decades of the twentieth century (Clarke 1994, 2012:90–92).

The first was a *theory of overproduction*. In this view, capitalist firms producing the same commodity compete with one another in the market. Those that produce the commodity more cheaply, as a result of adopting technological innovations or coercing workers to work longer hours for the same wage, ultimately drive out their competitors and increase their control over the market. This leads to the concentration and centralization of capital in that branch of production, the over-accumulation of the money form of capital, and the formation of credit systems. In order to continue realizing their profit rates, the firms either have to create new markets or invest their accumulated capital in other industrial or commercial sectors (Kautsky 1971[1892]:81–97; Marx 1977[1863–1867]: 762–870; 1981[1864–1894]:525–574).

The second was a *theory of under-consumption* (Bleaney 1976; Sweezy 1970[1942]). Engels (1987[1877]:254–271) and Luxemburg (2003[1913]:328–347) advocated this view. They argued that capitalist firms have an inherent tendency to produce more commodities than the demand for those goods because production and consumption are governed by different laws. Without finding or creating new markets, the firms cannot realize profits from their excess production. As Engels (1987[1877]:263) put it,

Commerce is at a standstill, the markets are glutted, products accumulate, as multitudinous as they are unsaleable, hard cash disappears, credit vanishes, factories are closed, the mass of the workers are in want of the means of subsistence; bankruptcy follows upon bankruptcy, execution upon execution. The stagnation lasts for years; productive forces and products are wasted and destroyed wholesale, until the accumulated mass of commodities finally filters off, more or less depreciated in value, until production and exchange gradually begin to move again.

The third was Hilferding's (1981[1910]:266–296) *disproportionality theory of crisis*, which focused attention on investment cycles and the role of fixed capital (i.e. assets, such as land, buildings, or equipment that are not used up in the production process). He pointed out that there is diversity among firms producing the same commodity. Some rely more heavily than others on the use of fixed capital rather than waged-workers (variable capital in Marx's terms). As a result, they typically respond more slowly to new market demands or to technological innovations. Thus, those that rely more heavily on variable capital possess greater flexibility with regard to change. In order to maximize profits, capitalists redeploy their investments into those firms or sectors of the economy that yield the highest or rising rates of profit. The downside of this is that they tend to over-invest in those sectors that rely most heavily on fixed capital and are less likely to respond quickly to new demands, innovations, or changes in the price structure of the commodity. In order to shift capital from one sector to another, investors frequently need access to credit because their accumulated capital may be tied up in fixed capital. This, in Hilferding's view, significantly increased the importance of financial institutions whose profits derive ultimately from interest on medium- and long-term loans.

Thus, the evolutionary socialists of the Second International (Kautsky, Bernstein, Hilfering, and Bauer) argued (1) that the general tendency of capitalist development was upward, (2) that the differences between the highs and lows of business cycles were diminishing, (3) that the period of time separating the highs and lows of the cycles was also getting shorter, and (4) that the development of cartels, the expansion of domestic and overseas markets, and the new forms of credit and democracy gave capitalism a new lease on life (e.g. Bernstein 1909, 1961[1898]:79–80, 164–165). In brief, depressions were getting milder and the fluctuations more frequent (Gay 1962:191–194). Even though under-consumption, overproduction, and disproportionality still existed, the effects were ameliorated by the internal development of the capitalist mode of production itself and could be further ameliorated by centralized, capitalist-state economic planning.

However, there was also a fourth Marxian explanation of capitalist economic crises and breakdown. It was socialist activist and economist Henryk Grossmann's (1881–1950) *theory of the tendency of the rate of profit to fall* (Grossmann 1992[1929], 2000[1919]). He argued that capitalism is inherently crisis-prone because of its myriad contradictions. Revolutions, he suggested, occur when contingent circumstances weaken the power and ability of the capitalist class to rule. Economic crises undermine that ability. The tendency toward economic crises develops in the sphere of production. The disproportion between the scale of their production of commodities and their profit rates is a constant feature that is reproduced from one economic cycle to the next. In his view, cyclical crises judge past investments and destroy those they deem redundant. While this momentarily restores the proportionality within and between production of the means of production and the production of commodities, this is only a temporary condition. The process of over-accumulation and the tendency of the rate of profit to fall are renewed, laying the foundations for the next breakdown as firms begin once again to invest profits in speculative ventures that have less and less to do with either the production of the means of production or the production of commodities. Unlike the proponents of the under-consumption and disproportionality theses, Grossmann's argument focused on the sphere of production rather than those of distribution or exchange (Kennedy 1992; Kuhn 2004, 2005).

It is worth noting that Grossmann's book, *The Law of Accumulation and Breakdown of the Capitalist System*, was published two months before the start of the Great Depression in 1929. Two other Soviet economists had already written about capitalist cycles and breakdowns before the Great Depression. During the 1920s, economist Nikolai Kondratieff (1892–1938) proposed that the capitalist world economy was characterized by long waves of expansion and contraction. These long waves had a duration of fifty to sixty years; cycles of shorter duration were superimposed on them. In Kondratieff's view, long-wave cycles begin when there is high investment in new technologies (new means of production) and infrastructure. This creates new employment, income, and demand for consumer goods. After a few decades, the rates of profit fall below the interest rates; investment in the affected economic sectors declines; overproduction leads to layoffs; and the demand for consumer goods diminishes. A new cycle of investment begins about fifty years later. A technological explanation of Kondratieff's argument resembles Schumpeter's claim that innovations cluster in neighborhoods of technological change.

Pavel Maksakovsky (1900–1928) was the other Soviet economist to write about the Marxist theory of capitalist cycle during the 1920s (Day 2004; Maksakovsky 2004[1928]). He recognized the cyclical and uneven nature of capitalist development—rapid growth during phases of expansion, contraction during phases of crisis, as well as stagnation or depression. He was particularly concerned with the problem of conjuncture. That is

> the problem of the specific form and movement of capitalism's dynamic; ... at how the 'capitalist' physiology works as a whole and how its functions are coordinated—not in the hidden depths of internal processes, but within the real dimensions of space and time, that is, those on capitalism's surface....
>
> When things are viewed in these terms, each category ... acquires an emphatically dynamic expression. Each is to be regarded as a constituent moment of capitalist reproduction as it emerges in real-historical form, beginning with its depths in production and ending with the dancing shadows at the ghostly heights of the money market....
>
> *The conjuncture is the form in which the action of all the categories of the capitalist economy is expressed through their interaction and interpenetration—a movement that is objectified in the cyclical dynamic of the capitalist whole.* ... It is precisely the activity of the particular categories that imparts to the conjuncture its empirical 'corporality'.
>
> (Maksakovsky 2004[1928]:19–21)

Like Grossman and Krondratieff, Maksakovsky too saw a crisis looming on the horizon of the industrial capitalist countries.

Capitalism in Crisis: Social Reform or Socialist Revolution?

The theorists and activists of the socialist parties constituting the Second International (1889–1914) believed that capitalism was in crisis at the turn of the twentieth century. They also had different perspectives about the transition from capitalism to socialism (Coates 1991a,b). Could it be achieved without violence? Was it going to be a smooth, continuous process of incremental change, or would it involve further crises and struggles? Could it be attained within existing political institutions, or would it require the replacement of those structures by new forms of popular administration? For example, Kautsky separated theory from practice rather than seeing them as interdependent, did not participate actively in grass-roots politics, and saw Marxism through the lens of scientific materialism as the unfolding of an inevitable process of evolutionary change leading to the breakdown of capitalism; his was the reformist perspective of a revolutionary party rather than that of a revolution-making party (Geary 1987; Steenson 1978).

Bernstein, from the political Right, challenged Kautsky's construction of a Marxist orthodoxy as well as Marx's and Engels's views about the breakdown of capitalism. He argued that the recent changes in capitalism and democracy had given capitalism a new lease on life and that it would continue to develop under these new conditions in the future. Hence, the socialist parties should strive not for revolutionary changes in the relations of production but rather for alliances with the liberal middle class and the peasantry as well as legislative reforms that would gradually alter political-economic relations and yield equality for all members of society. Bernstein's Neo-Kantian, revisionist views made socialism more palatable instead of inevitable. Moreover, the party should abandon the idea that the state should take over the production and distribution of goods.

Representatives of the revolutionary left among the Social Democrats responded quickly to Bernstein's proposal. In Germany, Luxemburg argued that by removing the concept of an economic breakdown from the historical development of capitalism as Marx and Engels saw it, Bernstein got "a nice comfy notion of evolution" that overlooked the history of class struggle:

> Comrades who think they can lead society into socialism peacefully, without a cataclysm, have no historical basis in fact. By revolution we do not have to mean pitchforks and bloodshed. A revolution can also take place on a cultural level, and if ever there were any prospect of that, it would be in the proletarian revolution, since we are the last to take up violent means, the last to wish violent revolution on ourselves. But such matters do not depend on us, they depend on our opponents.
>
> (Luxemburg 1971[1899]:48–49)

In Luxemburg's view, Bernstein did not wish to establish a new kind of society but rather to modify or reform the surface of capitalist society. His goal was to subdue the exploitation and excesses of capitalism instead of suppressing capitalism itself (Luxemburg 1970[1900]:78).

Lenin was also critical of Bernstein and his defenders in the Union of Russian Social Democrats Abroad. They not only deprived socialists of the opportunity to show workers that their interests were opposed to those of the capitalist class but also demoralized socialist consciousness by vulgarizing Marxist thought

> …by reducing the working-class movement and the class struggle to narrow trade-unionism, and to a 'realistic' struggle for petty, gradual reforms.

This was synonymous with the bourgeois democracy's denial of socialism's right to independence and, consequently, of its right to existence; in practice it meant a striving to convert the nascent working-class movement into an appendage of the liberals.

(Lenin 1961[1902]:362–363)

Luxemburg and Lenin sought tactics and organizational forms that would promote socialist revolution. She (1970[1906]:198–199) focused on tactics— mass actions (strikes and demonstrations) that involved the participation, cooperation, and support of the widest possible group (Geras 1976:111–132). Recognizing that different conditions existed in Germany and Russia, Lenin was concerned not with mass parties or parliamentary activity but rather with developing a stable organization of full-time activists who were aware of the threat posed by the police and other agents of the state. The aim of this vanguard was to educate, to strengthen local party committees in the cities and rural districts, and to increase participation in trade unions (Lenin 1961[1902]:464–509). Thus, there were intense debates within the various Social Democratic parties over the relative merits and liabilities of particular proposals. Some members sought to reform the worst excesses of capitalism, while others supported revolutionary tactics and organizational forms in order to dissolve capitalism and forge a socialist alternative. Moreover, the Social Democrats were never the only political party in a country.

The world was in shambles in 1918 as World War I came to a close. Massive anti-war demonstrations, strikes, and riots had swept across Europe. Civil wars raged from Mexico through Central Europe and Russia to the Middle East. The Russian, Austro-Hungarian, and Ottoman empires collapsed. The nationalist successor states that took their place in the Balkans, North Africa, and the Middle East often waged genocidal (ethnic cleansing) campaigns to ensure the purity of their residents. Their citizens desired land and harbored suspicions of cities, strangers, and governments. Workers' councils (soviets) appeared in Russia, Germany, Italy, Hungary, and later China.[1] Socialist republics rose in Russia, Bavaria, and Hungary. Lenin, hoping that the Russian experience might serve as a beacon, formed the Third or Communist International in 1919 to provide support for workers' movements in other countries, whose members were disciplined activists committed to "casting off the yoke of capitalism." Moreover, there were rumblings in the colonies and many of the countries on the periphery of the capitalist world. From a different perspective, most of the capitalist economies were also in shambles, with high unemployment and growing income inequalities.

Russia has traditionally been the model for understanding the formation of a socialist state. Briefly, in 1917, the Russian tsar abdicated and was replaced by a provisional government that shared power with the workers councils, which had widespread popular support, partly because of their opposition to the war and to the imperialist views of the Russian nationalists and aristocracy. The workers councils overthrew the provisional government and appointed their members to lead the various ministries; civil war erupted between the socialists (the Reds) and the anti-socialist White Russians; more than a dozen capitalist countries— including the United States, Great Britain, France, and Japan—sent soldiers to aid the White Russians and to prevent the Bolsheviks (i.e. communists) and their socialist allies from gaining power. Anti-capitalist socialist and communist parties crystallized in more than fifty countries. Short-lived socialist republics were formed in Germany and Hungary in 1918 and 1919, and, after their collapse, battles raged between nationalist and leftist groups well into the 1920s. The Soviet Union was established in 1922 as the Bolsheviks consolidated power.

Let us consider the background to these events, the political debates and the processes that unleashed them, in more detail. In the 1890s, the tsarist government spent enormous sums on railroads, subsidies for private industrialists, protective tariffs, and promoting foreign investment. These investments occurred largely in the two main cities and in the mining regions, and the peasants bore the costs. However, capitalism was also emerging in the countryside with the appearance of domestic and foreign markets for grain. Rural class formation accompanied the development of agrarian capitalism as poor peasants (those without land) were compelled to work for their commodity-producing neighbors or were forced to migrate in search of work. In 1900, more than eighty percent of the state's 126 million residents and 140 nations still lived in the countryside or in the backward (non-industrial) regions. The economic downturn of 1902 fueled further urban migration, urban squalor, unemployment, rising social and economic disparities, and the proliferation of crime. The failure of imperial policies and the military weakness of the state, revealed by its humiliating defeat in the Russo-Japanese War, set the stage on which these social and political problems unfolded. Various forms of resistance—hunger revolts, peasant land grabs, strikes, the creation of soviets, an armed workers' uprising, and military mutinies—followed as the crises deepened.

The tensions and contradictions in Russian society were already evident when a revolution broke out in 1905. The tsar's power was weakened; he responded by granting limited civil liberties and voting rights to some and by establishing a two-chamber parliament (Duma), one of which he appointed. At the same time, he retained absolute veto power over any legislation and complete control over the executive, foreign policy, the church, and the army. The new government led by Pyotr Stolypin (1862–1911) sought to strengthen the throne, promote capitalist development, privatize agricultural lands, and repress strikers and peasants—more than 4,000 of whom were executed between 1906 and 1911. His efforts to expand the rights of ethno-religious minorities—i.e. Jews and Armenians—were thwarted by the conservative nobles and monarchists who viewed them as threats to their authority and to that of the tsar (Shanin 1986:236–251). There was a right-wing alliance of conservative elements in the bourgeoisie and large-landowning aristocrats that supported the hegemony of the tsar. The non-revolutionary, centrist Octobrists (right-wing liberals) preferred a constitutional monarchy, supported the privatization of farmland, and were unwilling to grant autonomy to ethnic minorities. Conservative intellectuals—influenced by Neo-Kantian concerns about personal freedom, morality, and religious mysticism—sought to continue capitalist development and linked it with the hegemony of the tsar, the state, and the Russian Orthodox Church. Ultra-nationalist Russians (the Black Hundreds) focused on the past glories of a mythical golden age; they were xenophobic, anti-Semitic, and prone to violence (assassinations and pogroms). They sought to organize the masses in support of the tsar and to eliminate social democracy. The Socialist Revolutionaries proposed to socialize agricultural land in order to prevent capitalist penetration into the countryside and rural class formation; while they advocated increased benefits and privileges for industrial workers, they refused to socialize factories, arguing instead that the land on which factories stood might be socialized by the towns in which they were located (Radkey 1958:25–46). The liberal Kadet party drew its support from the urban intellectuals and professionals (lawyers and professors) who advocated a constitutional democracy, the eight-hour workday, and full citizenship for minorities.

There were also several discernible factions of Russian Social Democrats, the most prominent of which were the reformist Mensheviks and the revolutionary Bolsheviks. Stolypin viewed both as threats to the tsar. The Mensheviks argued that a socialist revolution was not possible in Russia because the country was too backward, because it was not sufficiently capitalist, and because the working class lacked the class consciousness necessary for a successful socialist revolution. The Bolsheviks, led by Lenin, sought to gain state power and recognized that they had to seek representation in any provisional government that formed in the future; this meant becoming a public rather than a clandestine party and seeking alliances with peasants (the agrarian Socialist Revolutionaries and the Peasant Union) as well as non-Russian nationalists like Riga workers and Georgian peasants.

Both Lenin (1960[1899b]:193–198) and Trotsky (1969[1906]) commented on the peculiarities of Russia's social historical development; at the same time, they pointed to its underlying similarity with the trajectory of the Western capitalist countries. They were both convinced that a socialist revolution was possible in Russia. Lenin had long pointed to the articulation of different modes of production in the country, and Trotsky breathed new life into Marx and Engels's (1989[1882]) preface to the Russian edition of the *Communist Manifesto* when characterizing Russia as an underdeveloped, semi-feudal, largely pre-industrial country—a backward country—on the margins of the capitalist world. In Trotsky's view, the prerequisites for a socialist revolution had "already been created by the economic development of the advanced capitalist countries" (Trotsky 1969[1906]:100). However, because bourgeois democracy was poorly developed in Russia, the Russian workers supported by the peasants would be able to gain power before the liberal bourgeoisie could assert their political skills in a revolutionary situation (Trotsky 1969[1906]:63). Unlike the conditions in the Western capitalist countries where socialist revolution had not yet occurred, there would be an uninterrupted movement through the democratic and the socialist revolutions in Russia (Löwy 1981:30–69; Trotsky 1969[1930]:158–177, 239–243).

Russia was ripe for revolution in 1917. The war was going badly. The army was suffering heavy losses, and food and other goods were scarce because the military soaked up most of the production. The tsar's regime collapsed, and he abdicated in February when Russian women and workers confronted the government and demanded food, better wages, and shorter hours (they were working nearly seventy hours a week). The first Provisional Government, formed in February, included the Bolsheviks who had opposed Russia's entry into World War I three years earlier. It fell apart in July over the question of Ukrainian independence. Alexander Kerensky (1881–1970)—the Minister of Justice in the coalition—formed a second Provisional Government and named himself Minister of War, Prime Minister, and then Supreme Commander-in-Chief. Shortages of food and necessities grew more intense; the military suffered more losses; and the number of desertions, incidents of sabotage, and mutinies soared. Kerensky responded by undercutting the authority of the officers and replacing it with soviets (councils). Meanwhile, the Bolsheviks, who were in the Provisional Government, used the slogan "Bread, Peace, and Land" to organize in the industrial towns and among the military and poor peasants. The government collapsed on October 25. The Bolsheviks, widely viewed as the party best-suited to lead the country, took control of the state apparatus. Their political support came from industrial workers, sectors of the military, and a few of the poor peasants who were seizing farmlands from the nobility. This was their strength. It was also one of their weaknesses, which would ultimately constrain the kinds of changes they would be able to implement.

On October 26, the Bolsheviks withdrew the Russian army from combat with Germany and its allies, and demobilized the army. Twelve days later, a civil war erupted between the Red Army (the Bolsheviks) and the White Army (the monarchists, deposed nobles, capitalists, ultra-nationalists, and several anti-Bolshevik socialist groups). It lasted until 1922, fueled in no small part by the Western capitalist countries that invaded Russia in 1918 and provided materiel and support to the White Army. The Bolsheviks finally got the peace they desired; however, they had to simultaneously confront the civil war; the secession of various regions; international isolation; foreign invasions; widespread terror, violence, assassinations, and disappearances; economic collapse; intolerable hardships; famine; no fuel to heat homes in the winter; and continual criticism from both the Mensheviks and Kautsky, who believed that they were attempting to take a shortcut to communism by precipitating a socialist revolution in an economically backward country (Hobsbawm 1996:60–66). As the Bolsheviks were confronting these issues, they also had to deal with the political and economic structures of the country.[2] The institutions and practices they put in place between 1918 and 1921 were known as "war communism," the goals of which were to keep the army supplied with weapons and materiel, and to ensure that the industrial towns had food.

The Bolsheviks actually had little power in the countryside where grains and other foods were produced. In May 1918, they organized "food detachments" of poor peasants to appropriate grain from rich farmers (*kulaks* or capitalist farmers) and speculators suspected of hoarding crops and waiting for prices to increase in the market. This effort was difficult to enforce and did little to increase food production beyond the subsistence needs of the peasants themselves, who had long been suspicious of the intentions of the state. A second effort, in June, involved nationalizing industries and placing them under the control of soviets. However, most of the factory workers lacked the experience to run the industries effectively, and the state had to hire experienced factory managers from the old regime. A third effort was concerned with commerce. Rationing and price stabilization were not effective in an economy in which money was rapidly losing its value, and the black market was rampant. The state proposed to accumulate commodities produced in the industrial towns in order to exchange them for food, thereby shifting from a market economy to one rooted in a state-controlled redistribution system. A fourth effort angered the industrial unions, which saw the state as trying to transform the workers' collectives into organs of the state. Ill-will was further exacerbated as the Red Army, and the White Army, for that matter, requisitioned what they needed from the peasants by claiming that it was a military necessity (Bettelheim 1976[1974]:143–394; Carr 1979:20–29).

In March 1921, the All-Russian Communist Party (i.e. the Bolsheviks) replaced war communism in order to deal with the havoc and destruction created by the civil war. Their New Economic Policy (NEP) (1921–1924) rejected the central elements of war communism: the concentration of economic power with centralized control and management; the substitution of large-scale for small units of production, unified planning; the movement away from market forms of distribution; rationing; and the substitution of a "natural" for a "market" economy.

> The policies of concentration and centralization were applied almost exclusively in industry; attempts to transfer them to agriculture met with no success. ...The policies of the flight from money and the substitution of a "natural" economy arose not from a preconceived plan but from inability to solve the problems of a backward peasant economy which occupied more than 80 percent of the population... The policies of requisition, which had worked after a fashion during the civil war, was bankrupt. The peasant had retreated into a subsistence economy, and had no incentive to produce surpluses which would be seized by authorities. ...It was imperative, if the rest of the country was not to starve, to provide the peasant with the incentives which were denied him under a system of requisition.
>
> (Carr 1979:30–31)

The NEP relaxed the government's control over the economy and permitted private enterprise to flourish among the peasants, which changed the conditions of everyday life in the countryside as well as the circumstances under which the government operated.

The essential features of the new policy were that the state would (1) encourage the development of small rural artisanal industries that produced the kinds of consumer goods the peasants desired and (2) collect a portion of the peasants' production (a tax in kind). The NEP had a negative impact on the development of the large-scale, nationalized industries; management and administration devolved as factories were free to sell products on the market. Thus, the exchange mechanisms of the war communism period were replaced by buying and selling. This provoked a financial crisis as prices and the value of the currency fluctuated wildly in the market. The prices and value of agricultural products soared relative to the value of the declining currency. Industries, which lacked both working capital and credit, were forced to sell their products at a loss. This led to discontent among the industrial workers, many of whom were being paid with agricultural produce rather than money. It also led to unemployment and the return of many industrial workers to their natal communities in the countryside (Carr 1979:50–60). Moreover, the terms of trade were unfavorable to the peasants who were reluctant to sell their produce.

The NEP provoked intense debate. The focus was the relationship between the small, relatively weak, socialized industrial sector and the private sector. Lenin (1965[1921a]:61) viewed the NEP as a strategic retreat—a concession to both the peasants and the capitalists—because the "...direct transition from the old Russian economy to state production on communist lines" had not, in fact, occurred. Bukharin (1971[1920]) and other Right Bolsheviks (e.g. Stalin and Zinoviev) supported the NEP and its alliance with the rich peasants who controlled a large portion of the food supply and with the emerging urban commercial bourgeoisie who sold their goods. They wanted to implement the policy slowly so that the economy would be gradually transformed. The Left Opposition—led by Evgeny Preobrazhensky (1886–1937) and Trotsky—wanted to abandon the policy as soon as possible in order to industrialize the economy and reactivate damaged and unused factories at relatively low costs. They argued that the socialist sector could not bear the whole burden of the investment required for rapid industrialization. In their view, under the NEP, Russia (renamed the Union of Soviet Socialist Republics in 1922) would continue to be dependent on the Western capitalist countries for many industrial goods—a dependence complicated by the fact that it was isolated in the international community, and many of the capitalist countries had imposed trade sanctions on it (Nove 1965).

The NEP spawned a growing bureaucracy as former officials and administrators were drawn back into the service of the state and as new individuals were recruited (Carr 1953:273). At the same time that the Bolsheviks eased their control over the Soviet economy, they also banned the participation of organized oppositional groups in the soviets as well as in the Communist Party itself. They feared that the urban bourgeoisie, which had re-emerged and flourished under the NEP, would form an alliance with rich peasants and the intelligentsia to challenge the power of the proletarian state. While Lenin and Trotsky, for example, viewed the ban as a temporary measure that would be lifted when the social and economic conditions of the country had become more stable, others in the party, given the conditions provoked by the NEP, viewed it as a more permanent arrangement.

In December 1927, Joseph Stalin (1879–1953), who had consolidated his power base in the country and in the communist party during the preceding four years, re-initiated the drive to industrialize the Soviet economy under the control of the state (Erlich 1960). He called for investments in certain sectors of the economy, price controls on basic materials, and subsidies for the production of particular goods. In the process, the guided market economy of the NEP would be replaced both financially and physically by direct planning. Stalin and the state planners realized that there were contradictions between their industrial development plan and the existing structure of peasant agriculture. The only way to resolve them in Stalin's view was

> ...to turn the small and scattered peasant farms into large united farms based on cultivation of the land in common, to go over to collective cultivation of the land on the basis of a new higher technique.... There is no other way out.

> (quoted by Nove 1969:148)

Thus, the first Five-Year Plan, launched in the spring of 1929, involved the collectivization of agriculture in spite of peasant resistance, massive financial investment in industry, and food subsidies to sustain industrial development as well as the defeat of the Left Opposition, whose members challenged these policies and who had earlier contested the NEP reforms (Lewin 1974:3–124). The human costs of Stalin's Five-Year plans were high—including six to eight million people who died of famine—as the state attacked existing social structures and created chaotic conditions. This led to even more state intervention and to the rapid expansion and growing importance of its bureaucratic apparatus (Lewin 1968, 1985). In effect, Stalin implemented a theory he had criticized: Preobrazhensky's (1965[1926]:77–146) theory of "primitive socialist accumulation" in which the rural population would bear the brunt and costs of industrial development. In spite of the human costs and the inefficiencies that resulted from the consolidation and centralization of power and decision making, the Soviet Union did achieve high rates of industrial growth and succeeded in becoming an industrialized country during the 1930s, even as the specter of fascism was rising from the ashes of World War I in Central Europe.

For complicated reasons, socialist revolutions failed to materialize in other countries after World War I (e.g. Broué 2006[1971]). While this led the Communist International to promote "United Front" organizations in various countries, it led Stalin to promote the idea of "Socialism in One Country" in 1924 (Carr 1982). He de-emphasized the central place of world revolution in the agenda of the Communist International but did not eliminate the Comintern altogether. Trotsky, Zinoviev, and others in the Left Opposition vigorously opposed his policy; they were marginalized, expelled from the party, exiled, imprisoned, or executed.

A central issue was that while the industrial sector of the economy was state-owned and -controlled, the agricultural sector remained largely capitalist. By the end of the decade, the Soviet Union was still dependent economically on the capitalist countries for commodities to fuel its industrial economy and the needs of the state. At the same time that the country was grappling with the problems of industrialization, it also had to confront the collection of grain and the collectivization of the agricultural sector. It regularized its relations with the West in order to acquire the manufactured goods it needed but did not yet produce. It experienced rapid industrialization and economic development in the 1930s. As early as 1926, Preobrazhenky saw the coming crisis of the capitalist economic and political order that had been established in the West after World War I. The collapse of the world financial markets in 1929 and the Great Depression of the 1930s validated this perspective. The prospect of revolution on a world scale provided hope for millions around the world, many of whom came to see their own aspirations as dependent on the security and prosperity of the Soviet state.

Many have viewed the Russian Revolution and its aftermath as the model of socialist revolution—the only way this process could take place. They understood transition to socialism in teleological terms: the law-like unfolding of progressive stages. What they did not always consider more carefully was the interplay of historical contingency, options that were pursued, and alternatives that were either not recognized or not followed for one reason or another. The historical trajectory of the Soviet Revolution raised and continues to raise questions about what was done, what should not have been done, what could have been done, and what a socialist society looks like anyways. The answers to these questions often depended on one's theoretical and political standpoints. For others, especially in the capitalist states that attempted to thwart socialist revolutions, the Russian Revolution and the Soviet Union was a recipe for what should not happen.

Rural Class Structures and Alternative Paths of Agrarian Development

During the inter-war years, social scientists were concerned with analyzing peasant economies, rural class structures, and the processes underlying their development. The debates were particularly intense in Russia where rapid, dramatic changes were taking place and where more than eighty percent of the country's population continued to earn its livelihood from agricultural pursuits after the Revolution. As you will recall from the preceding chapter, a range of social commentators debated the Agrarian Question in the late nineteenth century. This question captured the attention of political activists and scholars in Russia as well as in other countries—China, France, Italy, Peru, and Mexico. In this section, let us consider the debates that took place in the Soviet Union and China in more detail.

Russian analysts of the Agrarian Question held diverse views about the peasantry and its relation to capitalist development. Their theoretical analyses had real and immediate practical implications for the kinds of policies that Stolypin, the two provisional governments, and the Bolsheviks would pursue. At one extreme was Lenin's view that there were close linkages between rural transformation and capitalist development, on the one hand, and the urban and rural proletariats, on the other. At the other extreme were Alexander V. Chayanov's (1888–1939) arguments that the peasant economy was autonomous and that peasant farms were not capitalist enterprises. While Lenin believed that capitalist social relations were already predominant in the countryside, Chayanov argued that more than eighty percent of the farms in Russia did not employ hired labor. As a result, they had different solutions with regard to issues like food shortages, organization, and the integration of the peasant and socialist economies (Hussain and Tribe 1981; Kerblay 1986[1966]; Shanin 1986a; Thorner 1986[1966]).

In *The Development of Capitalism in Russia*, Lenin (1960[1899b]) relied on agricultural statistics collected by local governments in the Central Black Earth and Middle Volga regions southeast of Moscow to examine the transformation of rural society after the emancipation of serfs in 1864. The data he examined spanned more than three decades. He recognized that the redistribution of agricultural land and resources had not been equitable. He used them to describe (1) the growing number of poor peasants (rural proletarians) without sufficient land to sustain themselves, who were landless or forced to sell their labor power, and (2) rich peasants (the capitalist farmers of the rural bourgeoisie) who had excess land, possessed draft animals and farming machines, and employed labor power. These two groups engaged in capitalist social relations and, together, produced an increasingly diverse array of cash crops, first for the local markets and then for the national one that was being created—i.e. the factory towns and mining regions. There was a dwindling third group: (3) the middle peasant households of southern Russia that were fighting a losing battle to retain their self-sufficiency; consequently, they were the least engaged in commodity production and capitalist relations. Lenin further identified two processes in the formation of capitalist agriculture: the internal differentiation of the peasantry and the transition from feudal estate farming to capitalist production. In 1906, he modified his views in two significant ways. "Taken as a whole," he wrote, "the landed estate in Russia today rests on a system of feudal bondage rather than on the capitalist system. Those who deny this cannot explain the present breadth and depth of the revolutionary peasant movement in Russia" (Lenin 1962[1906]:177). This further opened the door for examining the articulation of different modes of production as well as the transition from a tributary feudal mode of production to something else.

After the civil war, Lenin (1966[1920]) elaborated on his classification of Russia's rural population. He recognized the following classes: (1) an agricultural proletariat that derives its livelihood from working on capitalist enterprises; (2) semi-proletarians or peasants who work small plots of land that they own or rent and derive the remainder of their livelihood from working as wage laborers in agricultural or industrial capitalist enterprises; and (3) small peasants who derive their livelihood from the plots they work and do not employ outside workers. In his view, the three groups constituted the majority of the rural population. He proceeded to distinguish them from (4) middle peasants (small farmers) who provide for their family's subsistence and frequently employ hired labor, selling their surplus in local markets, and (5) the big peasants or "capitalist en-trepreneurs in agriculture" who hired peasant workers to produce food com-modities and were connected with them "only in their low cultural level, habits of life, and the manual labour they themselves perform on the farms" (Lenin 1966[1920]:157). Lenin's policy recommendations to the Second Congress of the Communist International were the electrification of rural areas and urging the small farmers to adopt large-scale collective and mechanized agriculture.

While the war communism policies of 1918 to 1920 enabled the Soviet gov-ernment to re-establish itself over virtually all of the territory of the Russian Empire, the grain requisitioning policy was not viable under conditions of peace. The economy was ruined, and there were widespread peasant disturbances in the rural areas. By 1921, there was a severe food crisis. In 1921, the Bolsheviks launched the NEP, which replaced requisitioning with an agricultural tax in kind and allowed peasants to dispose of any surplus through local barter or exchanges for consumer goods produced and distributed by state agencies. It marked a new relationship between the urban workers and the peasantry, the re-creation of state capitalism, the resurrection of a monetary market economy, the devel-opment of commercial enterprises, and capitulation to the country's agricul-tural entrepreneurs (Bettelheim 1976[1974]:395–505; 1978[1977]). For Lenin (1965[1921b]):95–96), the Communists had incorrectly assessed the conditions as well as the balance of forces.

Marxist and Populist social scientists carried out studies of the Russian peas-antry during the 1910s and 1920s. L. N. Kritsman (1890–1937) and Alexander V. Chayanov (1888–1939) had profound understandings of their circumstances and of what was happening to the Soviet peasantry. Kritsman used the categories that Lenin had discerned in the countryside during the transition: self-sufficient peasant farmers, small commodity producers, private capitalists who used wage labor and sought to maximize profits, state-capitalist enterprises guided by the proletarian state, and socialist economic enterprises planned by the state. He added that there were also feudal structures in parts of Central Asia. This meant that class stratification took different forms in different regions and that these differences in part reflected whether production was primarily for commod-ities or for domestic consumption. This was especially true after the NEP re-introduced the market in 1921 and breathed life into the possibility of developing capitalist agriculture (Cox 1984:55–56). Kritsman and his associates launched a series of regional studies in the Soviet Union in order to acquire the kinds of statistical data required to produce an accurate picture of the development of rural socio-economic structures (Cox 1984). Their studies focused on peasant households as the basic units of analysis and explored the contradictory develop-mental tendencies found in them, especially the ones that engaged in small-scale commodity production.

They drew a series of tentative conclusions about capitalist agriculture in dif-ferent regions (Kritsman 1984[1926]:139–141). These included the ideas that (1) in many areas, the basic form of capitalist agriculture was not the ownership of land but rather the possession of animals and farm equipment that were rented out to peasant farmers, and in this form, the possessors of these indispensable means of production were disguised as the workers of farmers who hired them; (2) a second form of capitalist agriculture involved hiring wage laborers; (3) moneylenders (usurers' capitalists) flourished in rural areas because of annual variations in the size of harvests; (4) merchant capitalists also prospered because of monopoly connections to the market; (5) the possession of draft animals and farming equipment was the most important driver for rural class formation; and (6) there were important contrasts between peasant households that produced for consumption and those that produced grain as a commodity.

Chayanov was also concerned with the fate of the Russian peasants, given the potential for capitalist development created by the NEP during the 1920s (Banaji 1976; Littlejohn 1977; Thorner 1986[1966]). Unlike Kritsman, Chayanov viewed peasant economy and society as independent of the of wider economic and social structures of Soviet society. While he agreed with Kritsman that the peasant household was a basic economic unit, his analysis followed a different path and focused instead on the organization and nature of peasant production processes. Thus,

> on the family labor farm, the family, equipped with means of production, uses its labor power to cultivate the soil and receives as the result of a year's work a certain amount of goods.... The size of the labor product was determined mainly by the size and composition of the working family, the number of its members capable of work, then by the productivity of the labor unit, and—this is especially important—by the degree of the labor effort—the degree of self-exploitation through which the working members effect a certain quantity of labor units in the course of the year.
> (Chayanov 1986[1924]:5–6)

What distinguished the autonomous peasant household from capitalist entrepreneurs and/or waged workers was that its members determined the time and intensity of the work required to produce the goods they would consume. The balance between labor and consumption was established by the consumption needs of the family and the degree of effort or drudgery its working members were willing to expend during the year to produce the amount of goods they needed for consumption.

The labor-consumption balance was the main regulator of the farm's economic activity. It also reflected the demographic cycle of the peasant family. Both the quantity of goods produced and the number of working members were small immediately after the household was established; both grew as the family had children who would soon become workers; and both began to decline as the children left to establish their own households or as the farmstead was partitioned. This implied that the economic activity of the peasant farm was largely a result of its family size and composition and that any differentiation within the peasantry was caused by demographic rather than social factors (Littlejohn 1977:131).

Chayanov (1986[1926]:90–94) conceptualized the organization of the peasant farm in terms of a combination of three traditional factors of production—land, labor, and capital. If there were a shortage in any one factor, then there would be a proportional decline in the other two from the optimal level of the combination. Unless there were some increase in labor intensity and productivity, this would lead either to a reduction in the size of the peasant family farm or to members of the family supplementing their earnings with non-agricultural pursuits in order to maintain the labor-consumption balance in instances when in which family demands could not be satisfied by income derived from the farm itself. This implied, however, that there was a market. It further implied that the market affected the labor-consumption balance of the household and that the farm's products would ultimately be divided into commodities for sale and goods for family consumption.

The peasant farm, in Chayanov's view, was an autonomous economic unit until it hired workers from the outside. At that moment, it became a capitalist enterprise. Thus, his understanding of the emergence of capitalist relations in the countryside contrasted with Kritsman's, which emphasized the importance of peasants who rented farm animals and equipment. For Chayanov, who presumed that the earnings of a family farm were proportional to the labor effort expended by its members, any peasant household that employed workers was making an entirely new capitalist set of economic calculations. Because of the market, the peasant household no longer had to produce everything it consumed; items its members needed but no longer produced could be purchased in the market with the income gained by selling excess amounts of the goods they continued to produce. This meant that the peasant household could begin to specialize in the production and sale of certain goods—ones that required lower levels of labor effort than it would take to produce the goods they were purchasing in the market.

Chayanov (1986[1926]:255–269) believed that capitalist farms were not widespread in the Soviet Union and that the social differentiation of the peasantry was still in its early stages. Capitalist social relations initially penetrated the countryside when trade transformed the isolated peasant farm into a small commodity producer that was linked through the market to other farmsteads, to traders, and to artisans and factories whose workers transformed the raw materials into commodities that were consumed in the city—e.g. the transformation of hides into shoes or gelatin. In Chayanov's view, a system of wholesale and retail cooperatives, organized vertically, would strengthen these linkages. The cooperatives would also protect the family farm from the menace of large capitalist farms and insure that the continued existence of the rural market did not promote rural proletarianization, oppressive forms of credit, and sweatshop systems of capitalist exploitation as it forced the reorganization of the family farm economy. In his view, cooperatives subordinated to state control provided the best path for the development of Soviet agriculture.

Preobrazhensky (1965[1926]:79–145) pointed out the significance of Kritsman's and Chayanov's studies of social differentiation among the Soviet peasantry under the economic policies of the NEP. In his view, the fundamental economic problem of the Soviet Union was: How the revolutionary state could promote the growth of state-owned industry in a country where much of the capital was held by wealthy peasants who had acquired the means of capital accumulation only a few years earlier when the large productive estates had been seized and divided among them? Another way of saying this is that two contradictory forms of accumulation co-existed in the Soviet Union during the NEP: socialist accumulation in the state-owned, urban-based industrial sector and capitalist accumulation, the law of value, in the rural agricultural sector. The question for Preobrazhensky (1965[1926]:79–145), then, was how to ensure that the socialist sector expanded more rapidly than the capitalist one.

In Preobrazhensky's view, the government had to acquire material resources from outside the economic system it controlled in order to finance desperately-needed industrialization. In the absence of significant foreign investment because of the embargoes by the capitalist countries, there were two ways to get private owners to invest in the state-owned industrial sector: direct taxation of the private sector and state control of the market exchanges between the state and private sectors. Preobrazhensky favored the latter because of the high probability that the peasants would attempt to evade paying taxes. In his view, control of the market exchanges meant increasing off-farm sales to the state in order to feed the towns and the state-controlled export sector, increasing the efficiency and productivity of Soviet industry and controlling the prices of goods sold to the peasants so that socialist accumulation could proceed (Dobb 1966:183–191; Nove 1965:xi–xvii).

Stalin ended the NEP policies in 1927 before the government had any clear idea about how to replace them. The reason for abandoning them was the "weakness of industrial growth, especially in the *delay* in implementing measures of planned industrialization" (Lewin 1985[1965]:91). Agricultural production had stagnated and declined below pre-war levels; however, the demand was greater. The prices paid by the state for grain were not favorable to the farmers, many of whom hid or hoarded grain to sell it in the market. Briefly, the goal of Stalin's top-down policy of the collectivization of the farms—the Great Leap Forward (1929–1934)—was to transfer surplus from the capitalist agricultural sector to finance the expansion of the state-owned industrial sector. The difficulty was that the government did not talk with farmers or agronomists in their own research institutions. The state all but ignored the wide range of cooperatives that already existed in the rural areas as well as the experiences and knowledge of the people who participated in them. Inexperienced Young Communists from the towns were sent into rural communities to re-organize agricultural production. The drive for rapid industrialization succeeded in the 1930s. It should not be surprising that Kritsman, Chayanov, and Preobrazhenky were critical of the collectivization plan and the impact it would have on rural farming communities (Cox 1984; Littlejohn 1984:68; Solomon 1977).

Social relations in China during the first decades of the turn of the century were different from those in Russia. Consequently, the transition to socialism followed a different path from that of the Soviet Union. Its center of gravity was not in the actions and organization of an urban proletariat but rather in the peasant movements and struggles in the countryside. In 1911, only a million of China's 400 million people were urban proletarian factory workers. The overwhelming majority of the population lived and worked in the countryside. A few international merchant and financial capitalists in the port cities served as intermediaries between Chinese local markets and the Western capitalist countries. The local landlord-gentry had close ties with the old imperial state. While the capitalist countries undermined the power and authority of the old empire, the landlord-gentry established new ties with the capitalists at the same time they continued to exploit the peasantry. However, imperialism had also weakened the old social order of the empire, which, in turn, eroded the authority of the landlord-gentry and accelerated its decay. Distinctive features of China during this period were (1) the separation of political power from socioeconomic changes, (2) the consolidation of regional warlords whose power was rooted in their armies, (3) the growing demands of the landlord-gentry, warlords, and local capitalists on peasant households, (4) the steadily mounting resistance of peasant households and communities from the late nineteenth century onwards against the exactions of both landlords and capitalists, and (5) the formation (ethnogenesis) of a peasant popular culture—rooted simultaneously in autonomist, nationalist, and anti-imperialist sentiments—that expressed the shared interests of its constituent classes and historic blocs (Meisner 1986:3–51; Walker 1999:238–252).

Mao Zedong (1893–1976)—one of the founders of the Chinese Communist Party in 1921—recognized the importance of peasant associations. This was especially true after the nationalist Kuomintang party massacred more than a fifth of the fifty thousand or so members of the Communist party in 1925. This completely disrupted Communist organizing efforts among the small urban proletariat. Mao led the remnants into a remote, old bandit stronghold in Hunan Province in 1927 and reported on the formation of peasant associations in the region. They had 300–400 thousand members in 1926, more than two million in 1927, and ten million a year later. The peasant organizations brought about fundamental changes in the power relations that existed in the countryside. Mao wrote that

> The main targets of attack by the peasants are the local tyrants, the evil gentry and the lawless landlords, but in passing they also hit out against patriarchal ideas and institutions, against corrupt officials in the cities and against bad practices and customs in the rural areas. In force and momentum the attack is tempestuous; those who bow before it survive and those who resist perish. As a result, the privileges which the feudal landlords enjoyed for thousands of years are being shattered to pieces. Every bit of the dignity and prestige built up by the landlords is being swept into dust. With the collapse of the power of the landlords, the peasant associations have now become the sole organs of authority and the popular slogan 'All power to the peasant associations' has become a reality.
> (Mao 1965[1927]:25)

The goals of the peasant associations included banning gambling, opium-smoking, the distilling of spirits, and the use of sedan-chairs; limiting the number of pigs and ducks that could be owned by a family because they destroyed grain; curbing the aggressive behavior of certain tramps and vagabonds; eliminating banditry; abolishing levies imposed on peasants by the landlords and gentry that controlled the rural state apparatus; increasing education; forming consumers' marketing and credit cooperatives; and constructing and repairing roads and embankments (Mao 1965[1927]:49–56).

Mao also focused on class formation and the changing relationships between men and women in the countryside. His initial survey modified earlier categories used by Marx and Lenin; he recognized seven classes that included both the urban and rural segments of the population: (1) the *landlord* class and the *comprador* class—i.e. the Chinese managers of foreign commercial establishments—were linked with the international bourgeoisie; (2) the national or *middle bourgeoisie* represented capitalist social relations in both town and country; (3) the *petit bourgeoisie* included owner-peasants, master craftsmen, traders, schoolteachers, and low-level government officials; (4) the *semi-proletariat* included small craftsmen, shop assistants, small traders, semi-owner peasants who worked partly on their own land and partly on landed rented from others, and poor peasants or tenants who had no land of their own; (5) *poor peasants* owned tools and had access to funds, and those that did not were forced to sell their labor power; (6) the urban *proletariat* was employed in the textile, mining, railroad, maritime transport, and shipbuilding industries; and (7) the large *lumpen-proletariat* was composed of peasants who had lost their land and craftsmen who were unable to find work (Mao 1965[1926]).

In subsequent surveys, Mao (1965[1933], 1990[1930]:148–158) focused exclusively on rural class structures and social relations. He discerned five classes in the countryside: (1) *landlords* who were divided into three layers based on income and whether they worked, derived most of their income from land rent, or supplemented their primary income through moneylending or extracting surplus value from workers hired to toil in their commercial or industrial activities; (2) *rich peasants* who owned their own lands, possessed implements of production, had access to capital, and sometimes hired workers or rented land; (3) *middle peasants* who owned some land, rented other plots, and derived their income from their own labor; (4) *poor peasants* who rented the land they worked and sold their labor power; and (5) *farm workers* who typically had neither land nor implements and made their living by selling their labor power.

Mao (1965[1927]:44–46) also observed the changing relations between men and women and how these changes intersected with the rural class structure. Here are a few examples: One was that the authority of husbands was always weakest among the poor peasant families, in which women toiled alongside their husbands and had an important voice in family decisions. A second was that women from rich peasant households, in which the men were engaged elsewhere in wage labor, had considerable authority and power over both male and female poor peasant farm workers. A third was that peasant women from different villages were forming women's groups to protect themselves from harassment and violence at the hands of men. These groups challenged and weakened the three traditional systems of authority in the Hunan countryside—i.e. the patriarchal clan, the religious shrines, and their fathers and husbands—as they struggled for more egalitarian gender relations.

Mao, of course, was not the only commentator to write about the Agrarian Question in China. In the mid-1930s, anthropologist Fei Xiaotong (1910–2005)—at the time, a self-described functionalist interested in equilibrium models—described the interrelations of the economic system and social structure of a rural community in the Yangtze Valley about five hundred miles northeast of the area that Mao had written about a few years earlier. Fei (1939:120, 192) argued that there were no real social differences among the villagers, even though a few of them owned land, and some were wealthier than others; the wealth differentials that existed were due to differences in the amounts of rent paid to the absentee landlords. Thus, the economic circumstances of the villagers, including the decline of the local silk industry, were a consequence of outsiders charging exorbitant rents, practicing usury, and collecting onerous taxes—all of which upset the well-adapted social system of the village. Fei also indicated that the international capitalist economy and the Nationalist government created problems for the villagers.

Given his structural-functionalist assumptions, Fei made little reference to the chaos that existed in the countryside, although he was completely aware of it. In his view, while land reform would ease the economic problems of the village, the real solution ultimately rested on rebuilding rural industry. The real problems, however, were that the Nationalist government was spending too much of its revenues trying to defeat the Communists and that the Kuomintang did not understand peasant villages or the problems they faced (Fei 1939:110–116, 282–285). The political subdivisions imposed by the state on the countryside were artificial and had no foundation in the traditional economy and society; the schools it established paid no attention to the tempo of rural life and taught skills the peasants did not find useful (Arkush 1981:74–79, 1988).

It is important to keep in mind that the socialist revolutions in Russia and China had different centers of gravity. The Russians viewed the party and the urban factory workers as the leading edge of revolutionary change, whereas the Chinese quickly recognized the importance of the peasant associations. This produced different trajectories of change in the two countries, which would play out over the next fifty years. Both states industrialized; however, the Soviets located their factories in urban factory cities, while Chinese industry was dispersed, and the agricultural and industrial sectors were seemingly more tightly articulated with peasant associations. Writers in both countries viewed the questions of class formation in the countryside and rural transformation in starkly different terms. Lenin and Mao emphasized the intimate connections between class formation and the penetration of capitalist relations into the countryside; Chayanov saw economic differences in the wealth of peasant households largely in terms of demographic processes—changes in the numbers and ages of the participants in the production force; Fei understood changes in the peasant economy and society as consequences of disruptive forces emanating from outside—the Nationalist state, capitalism, and imperialism.

Articulation, Integration, and the Constitution of Multi-Nation Nation-States

The Agrarian Question merged almost imperceptibly with the National Question in countries like Italy, Peru, Indonesia, and Mexico: How were peasants, national minorities, or tribal peoples living in rural regions integrated into nation-states with multiple nationalities? The "Southern Question," the "Indian Question," "dual economies," and "the folk-urban continuum" were only a few of the concepts that emerged around this issue.

Antonio Gramsci (1891–1937)—a communist activist and linguist imprisoned by the Italian fascist government in 1924—wrote extensively about political-economic, social, and cultural developments in Italy during and after the period of national unification. He was concerned with developing a revolutionary political strategy that would be applicable in a particular, advanced capitalist country (Italy). He was reacting to economistic arguments, imperialism, the defeat of revolutionary movements in the 1920s, the rise of fascism, the economic collapse of 1929, and the growth of the corporatist-interventionist state in the 1930s. He focused on the exercise of state power and the role that coercion, fraud-corruption, and persuasion-consent played in maintaining and reproducing existing class relations. He was concerned less with the coercive apparatuses of the state than with the roles that different kinds of intellectuals played in securing the consent of the populace and in organizing the hegemony of the dominant class, whose political power ultimately derived from the economic base but could not be reduced in any simple way to it (Jessop 1982:142–152).

Because the complex relationship between town and countryside was the motor driving Italian history, any examination had to consider the interconnections of the Northern urban force, the Southern rural force, the North-Central rural force, and the rural forces of Sicily and Sardinia. The complexity of this relationship resulted from the fact that industrial capitalism was thinly and unevenly developed on the Italian peninsula; it was concentrated almost entirely in the cities of the Northern Piedmont where the bourgeoisie and the factory workers were tied to the capitalist mode of production and shared a worldview, ultimately rooted in the economy, that united them against the tempo and mode of everyday life in the countryside. The rest of the peninsula was dominated by a semi-feudal agrarian bloc composed of peasants, landowners, and traditional intellectuals whose activities cemented relations between the two rural classes (Gramsci 1967[1926]; 1971[1931]:90–102; 1992[1929]:133).

The political unification of Italy in 1870 brought together regions with different histories, economic foundations, and cultural practices under a single state apparatus. In Gramsci's view, political unification did not create the conditions for further capitalist development and expansion into the South, it merely compounded the old social and regional divisions that already existed. From an economic standpoint, the North colonized the South and drained it of both capital and labor, which fueled further capitalist growth in the Piedmont. From a political standpoint, the Northern bourgeoisie was unable to rally other groups, to constitute itself as the dominant economic class, or to establish clear programs of its own. As a result, it had to share state power with the semi-feudal landowners who always promoted their own economic interests.

Gramsci (1967[1926]:45–47, 1971[1933]:14–15) observed that Southern intellectuals constituted sixty percent of the state bureaucracy. This meant that the Southern agrarian bloc as a whole was the overseer for Northern capital and the large banks. In the South, the traditional intellectuals of the rural towns—the lawyers, notaries, priests, and teachers—were the intermediaries between the peasant masses and the state. As a result, Gramsci was especially interested in the cultural characteristics of that group. They came mainly from a stratum of small and middle landowners who derived their income from renting land to peasants rather than from working it themselves and whose standard of living was higher than that of the average peasant. The members of this class also viewed peasants as little more than machines to be despised and feared because of their penchant for violence. The Southern priests, unlike the clergy in the North, which had artisan or peasant roots, also came from the layer of small and middle landowning families and shared the views of their class toward the peasants.

Gramsci pointed out that the peasants held contradictory views about the traditional intellectuals. On the one hand, they respected them, and many hoped that at least one son could become an intellectual, especially a priest, and thereby raise the family's social and economic position through connections they would acquire by interacting more closely with the landowning class. On the other, their admiration for the intellectuals was mixed with envy and anger. Because the priests were mainly from the landowning class, the peasants viewed them as bailiffs and usurers whose womanizing and money dealings inspired little confidence in either their discretion or their impartiality.

The role of the Southern intellectuals, including the priests, was to block any efforts by the peasants to organize mass movements and to prevent splits from developing in the agrarian bloc. In effect, those who held positions in the liberal democratic government before the rise of fascism in the mid-1920s muted the desires and needs voiced by the peasantry and shunted them to the margins of the political arena by portraying the characteristics and interests of the peasants as oppositional to those of the state. For example, they saw peasant culture as simple and fragmentary, while that of the state was complex and unitary (Cirese 1982).

In order to overcome the weaknesses of the political programs of the democratic liberals, Gramsci stressed the need for genuine worker-peasant alliances. By contrast, the programs of the democratic liberals perpetuated the traditional forms of corruption and extortion in the rural areas. In the name of creating unity, the democratic liberals had built a bloc of urban industrialists and workers in the Northern cities that reinforced the economy and hegemony of the North and reduced the rest of the peninsula to a colony. The South was disciplined by police repression; by the periodic massacres of peasants; by political measures, such as personal favors and jobs for Southern intellectuals; and by not enforcing ecclesiastical laws in the rural areas.

José M. Mariátegui (1894–1930)—a journalist, social analyst, and communist who once attended a conference with Gramsci in Livorno, Italy—used a similar lens to analyze the circumstances that prevailed in Peru—a country that was still dominated economically by a semi-feudal *latifundia* system that involved land-holding and servitude for the peasantry. This impeded the development of an indigenous capitalism and underwrote the stagnation and grinding poverty of urban life on the coast and of rural Indian communities in the mountains. The owners of the *latifundia*, who grew sugar and cotton for export, served as intermediaries between the native population and foreign firms engaged in mining, commerce, and transportation. As a result, industrial development on the coast in the early decades of the twentieth century was confined largely to sugar mills located in close proximity to clusters of sugar-producing *latifundia*. Two other economic forms co-existed with the *latifundia*. One was the indigenous communal economies found in the mountainous regions, and the other was the small, backward-looking bourgeois economy found in some coastal areas (Mariátegui 1971[1928]:16).

Mariátegui (1971[1928]:18, 30, 158–170) called the political form that corresponded with the realities of the Peruvian economy *gamonalismo* (bossism). That is, the big bosses in various parts of the country, many of whom were large landowners, and their underlings in the state bureaucracy controlled education, law enforcement, and the administration of justice in the regions where they lived. The control they exerted over regional government ensured that the feudal estates were regularly exempted from the taxes and other regulations imposed by the central government on the indigenous communities and the cities and that the rural folks linked to the estates could be disciplined. In short, the regional bosses who held power did not oppose the central government; they colluded with it to ensure that the existing structures of power were preserved and reproduced. Consequently, they had no reason to address either the Indian Problem or the Agrarian Question, which often merged and focused mainly on the indigenous communities in the mountains.

For Mariátegui and his contemporaries, like Luis Valcárcel (mentioned in the last chapter), the indigenous communities were not a residue of the ancient, pre-Colombian society that survived mainly in the mountains after they had been eradicated on the coast. Instead, they were a communal form of production based on cooperation and association that defended the rural populations from the *latifundistas'* demand for labor service. The communities preserved the rural population, protecting it, on the one hand, from the threats of the bosses and, on the other, from the individualism promoted by liberal reformers, who argued fervently that the problems the Indian communities confronted could be overcome through education, assimilation, and private ownership of the land. The liberals, from Mariátegui's perspective, failed to grasp the political and economic forces that threatened the highland Indian communities in the decades following the War of the Pacific (1879–1883). For him, the Agrarian and Indian Questions were intimately linked. Solutions to the problems required that the *latifundia* as well as Indian servitude be abolished. The problems are socio-economic and political ones that have "to be dealt with by men who move in this sphere of acts and ideas. And it is useless to try to convert it, for example, into a technical-agricultural problem for agronomists" (Mariátegui 1971[1928]:32). Thus, the integration of Indian communities into the nation-state was a political problem whose solution had to also be political.

In the early 1930s, Julius H. Boeke (1884–1953)—Dutch economist and analyst of colonial societies—developed an alternative analysis of the kind of articulation and social relations described by Gramsci and Mariátegui. In his view, colonial societies, like the Dutch East Indies, had *dual economies*; as a result, they were more complicated than those of Western capitalist countries because they had two distinct socio-economic systems. One occurred in the towns and cities; the other in self-sufficient, rural village communities that were held together by shared religious beliefs and traditions. The Westernized residents of the towns participated in capitalist world markets, while the social relations of the villages were pre-capitalist (Boeke 1953:27). The communal bonds of the villagers were weakened by the capitalist policies promoted by the government and private interests. As a result, the villagers struggled to adapt to the changing circumstances that impinged on their lives, to retain rights to their means of production, to meet the duties and obligations of membership in the community, and to ensure the solidarity of their communities. In some areas, the population of the rural villages had grown to the point where able-bodied young men were, in fact, superfluous to the village economy. As capitalist labor markets penetrated into such areas, these men were employed as unskilled, casual workers who could be paid well below the wage required to sustain them because their needs and those of their families were still actually being met by their kin and neighbors in the villages (Boeke 1953:33, 81, 138–141).

The growth of capitalist export agriculture created a steadily increasing demand for land. Agrarian capitalist firms gained access to land because native landowners needed money to pay debts or taxes and to purchase goods that were no longer produced locally in the villages. The villagers acquired the cash they needed by renting and/or selling both arable fields and waste land they did not farm (Boeke 1953:130–136). Boeke (1953:227, emphasis in the original) pointed out

> ...*that Indonesia today is further removed from self-sufficiency than it was a century ago*; and that its national small industries, its rural and communal self-provisioning with manufactured products, has for the most part been ruined in the course of modern development.... [T]he economic development of the country has increased its economic dependence—the dependence, that is, of the rural population, of those born and bred in the villages.

In a word, Indonesia had become more dependent on capital that came less and less from Asia. While the state should intervene in the economy and control of capitalist development, it should do so in ways that would benefit the whole of Indonesian society, including the rural villages. To accomplish this, Boeke recommended that the government adopt economic policies that addressed equally the issues of both the capitalist and the traditional sectors of the society (Boeke 1953:226–229). However, most of his recommendations were for policies that dealt with the capitalist economy of the towns—the control of production, wage and price controls, the regulation of imports and exports, or the promotion of certain national industries. He briefly addressed the circumstances that produced unemployment in the rural areas:

> The rapid growth of the plants in the tropics; the small holdings; the deficient markets; the unprofitable transport; the inevitable intermediaries; all these are factors that cannot be altered and make the problem of rural unemployment unsolvable. One can only try to fill the spare time of the peasant with non-economic interests and occupations (village restoration).
>
> (Boeke 1953:318)

While those villagers that engaged in casual work in the capitalist sector could be supported, at least in part, by their villages, the rural proletariat employed by agrarian capitalist estates or the migrants to the cities were increasingly separated from their natal communities. As a result, they had no fund of foodstuffs and resources to fall back on. Thus, Boeke concluded, people from the traditional villages would be supported by their natal communities only during the early stages of their incorporation into the capitalist economic sector; once they were separated from their natal communities, unemployment would become an increasingly serious problem.

Crisis, Conflict, and the Quest for Social Order

The capitalist classes faced growing crises in the 1880s and 1890s: the runaway corruption of officials and business leaders, the threat posed to their privileged status by labor unrest at home and abroad, the specter of socialism or worse, and their dawning awareness that explanations rooted in utilitarianism and free-trade liberalism were not adequately accounting for the emerging complexities of the world they lived in—a world increasingly shaped by the consolidation of modern industrial capitalism. Social reformers, both from the capitalist classes and the governments, argued that it was essential to restore the states' social, cultural, and political authority, and "to replace corrupt politicians with the disinterested leadership of the 'best men,' namely themselves" (Ross 1991:61). Their goal was nothing less than the reshaping and reorienting of social thought (Alchon 1985).

Initially, social reformers created social science associations that built on their reputations as authorities on the human condition and the problems they perceived as challenging the established social order. These early efforts were soon replaced in the 1890s by organizations whose members were professionals (i.e. they were paid for their services) and whose employers were universities, museums, or government bureaucracies. In the early 1900s, a few members of the capitalist class in the United States—John D. Rockefeller, Andrew Carnegie, and Russell Sage—established philanthropic foundations that promoted the social sciences and would serve as buffers between civil society and the state. The goals of these foundations were to shape public opinion, influence policy, and "prevent the collapse of liberal democratic capitalism" (Fisher 1993:232). Their trustees and officers supported the hegemony and interests of the capitalist class: the resolution of social conflict, the expansion of markets, social control, the maintenance of social order, as well as the professionalization and specialization of academic researchers.

The foundations minimized advocacy while simultaneously emphasizing the importance of empirical observation, experimentation, and "objective" (value-free) scientific research stripped from the cultural and sociohistorical matrices in which it was being carried out. The orientations of the research were generally empiricist, modernist, and scientistic in that they minimized the relevance of history while stressing the importance of present-day conditions and laboratory sciences, like physics, as appropriate modes of explanation and interpretation (e.g. Arnove 1982; Fisher 1983, 1993; Richardson and Fisher 1999). While advocating interdisciplinary research, the agendas supported by the foundations were often reductionist in the sense that they sought to explain the complexities and problems of modern society in terms of personality formation or the behavior of individuals. Their focus was the social problems of the day—e.g. colonial administration, scientific management, race relations, immigration, urban migration, hygiene, eugenics, mental illness, the prevention of disease, the curbing of crime and delinquency, population, and economic cycles.

The Rockefellers created a network of foundations in the early twentieth century that invested the equivalent of several billion of today's dollars in research centers and universities—e.g. the University of Chicago, Harvard, Yale, and the London School of Economics as well as universities in several British colonies— Canada, South Africa, and Australia. The Rockefeller foundations stressed the centrality of some social science disciplines—notably, psychology, economics, sociology, geography, and political science—in some instances. Others, like the Social Science Research Council and the Laura Spelman Rockefeller Memorial Foundation, supported interdisciplinary research in colonial settings. For example, Polish-born anthropologist Bronislaw Malinowski (1884–1942) was the conduit for most of the five million dollars awarded in the 1930s to support the social sciences in Great Britain. Malinowski was at the London School of Economics and also had close ties with the Institute for African and Oriental Studies and the British Colonial Office. He dispersed Rockefeller funds to support the dissertation research of more than ninety individuals on the interrelations of indigenous peoples and colonial administrations in Africa and the Pacific. This effectively created and established the field of functionalist anthropology in the British Empire (Stocking 1995:391–406).

In his introduction to the African Institute's *Methods of Study of Culture Contact in Africa*, Malinowski commented on the power relations between the colonial metropolis and the colony, and the profound shaping effects they had on culture contact and change in Africa:

> The whole concept of European culture as a cornucopia from which things are freely given is misleading. It does not take a specialist in anthropology to see that the European 'give' is always highly selective. We never give any native people under our control—and we never shall, for it would be sheer folly as long as we stand on the basis of our present Realpolitik—the following elements of our culture:
>
> 1. The instruments of physical power: fire-arms, bombing planes, poison gas, and all that makes effective defence or aggression possible.
> 2. We do not give out instruments of political mastery [i.e. sovereignty or voting rights]...
> 3. We do not share with them the substance of economic wealth and advantages.... Even when under indirect economic exploitation, as in West Africa or Uganda, we allow the native a share of the profits, the full control of economic organization remains in the hands of Western enterprise.
> 4. We do not admit them as equals to Church Assembly, school, or drawing room.... [F]ull political, social and even religious equality is nowhere granted.
>
> (Malinowski 1938:xxii–xxiii)

Malinowski (1938:xxiv–xxv) believed that studies of culture change had to take into account not only the impact of the "higher" Western culture on the substance of the native culture against which it was directed but also the unintended consequences of the autonomous changes that resulted from their interaction. The impact the two cultures had on one another was more than the mechanical mixture of elements; it disrupted the equilibrium of the tribal group, producing maladjustment, deterioration, confusion, strain, and conflict, on the one hand, and cooperation and even compromise, on the other. Setting aside his observations about power relations, he stressed the give-and-take nature of culture contact situations and the mutual dependence of the colonial and tribal cultures as the old cultural forms were dissolved, and new cultural realities emerged in their place.

Malinowski and his associates, like anthropologist Monica Hunter (1908–1982), also stressed the places and institutional contexts in which culture contact occurred—churches, schools, markets, foreign-owned mines, or the capitalist economic system. These contexts were usually regulated by legal codes that combined customary and British law, and were supervised by European magistrates who may not have been familiar with the customary legal practices of the natives. Thus, anthropologists had to be alert to how and in what ways the sanctions that regulated social behavior under traditional conditions were modified by contact. This led them to examine the roles played by the various agents involved in culture contact—teachers, students, administrators, and district commissioners as well as the native men, women, and children who left their natal communities and went to the towns and mines to engage in wage labor (Hunter 1936, 1938:23–24).

Meyer Fortes (1906–1983)—a South African anthropologist and one of Malinowski's students—saw the contact agents as integral parts of native communities that were being rapidly but unevenly transformed as a result of the infiltration of foreign practices. In his view, change was taking place in the communities rather than in customs themselves. Consequently, the communities should be the objects of investigation. He focused his attention on migrant workers who left their communities to gain a livelihood and raised a series of questions about the migrant workers: What were the circumstances that led or forced them to leave their communities? What was their reaction to these conditions? How did other members of their communities react to immigration? What influence did immigration ultimately have on the institutional life, practices, habits, and beliefs of the tribal community? Fortes (1938:72–91) compared the effects of migrant labor on tribal communities in the Northern Territories of the Gold Coast and in Bechuanaland. He noted that while migrant workers were rapidly reabsorbed into their natal communities on the Gold Coast, this was not the case in South Africa, where the migrants flouted traditional authority, grew lazy and dissolute, and were perceived as a problem by the elders. The differences were due, in his view, to the fact that they reflected different stages of contact. The Gold Coast communities were only marginally involved with the outside. Those of Bechuanaland had been completely drawn into the capitalist economic system as sources of labor; as a result, the morality of the towns was transferred to the reserve as the income derived from the migrants' work eroded the "...traditional closed system of tribal economics" (Fortes 1938:88).

In *The Analysis of Social Change*, Godfrey B. Wilson (1908–1944) and Monica Hunter Wilson summarized much of the research on social and cultural change carried out in Africa during the 1930s and early 1940s (Wilson and Wilson 1954[1945]). They argued that the economy of Northern Rhodesia was already an integral part of the world economy and that the tribal peoples in the area were no longer economically self-sufficient (Brown 1973). The area and its inhabitants had been pulled into the world economy by virtue of the mineral wealth coming from the mines at Broken Hill and in the Copperbelt. For several decades, the mines had attracted workers from the neighboring areas, incorporating them slowly but inexorably into the capitalist economy of the mining towns and beyond. At the same time, they broke down the natal communities of the workers by stripping them of the human resources they needed to ensure their demographic and social reproduction and by eroding the foundations of the traditional systems of political authority in the villages. One of the concerns of the colonial state, given the transformations taking place, was whether the tribal communities would continue to reproduce the labor force for the mines and provide for the extended kin of those members who had been incorporated into the capitalist economy and society of the mining towns (Wilson and Wilson 1954[1945]:3–22).

The labor demands of the mines combined with the policies of the colonial state had created uneven and unequal development on a massive scale. The emerging society of Northern Rhodesia, especially in the mining towns, was characterized by opposition and maladjustment. One opposition was the race problem, which pitted the large, subject African population and the European colonists against one another and left the small Indian community poised uneasily between them. This opposition spilled over into the workplace, where there were conflicts between African workers and European employers over wages and between African and European industrial workers over the admission of Africans to skilled jobs. These conflicts underwrote the 1935 and 1940 strikes and riots in the Copperbelt, which led to the death of a score of African workers. There was further competition between African and European farmers for land and between African and European men for African women. There was also conflict between various tribal communities whose members struggled to retain control over their lives and colonial authorities who sought to constrain practices and activities they deemed illegal, immoral, or threatening to the authority and well-being of the colonial state.

The Wilsons (1954[1945]:15–16) described the social relations and sentiments produced by this opposition in the following terms:

> Courtesy very markedly fails to govern the relations of the races in town, and less markedly in the country also. In Northern Rhodesia post offices and shops commonly provide separate entrances and a lower standard of courtesy for their African clients, who resent the differentiation, and sometimes push and clamour for attention. The increasing assumption by Africans of European dress and manners, though it symbolizes an increasing civilization, is accompanied by more rather than less discourtesy from many Europeans, who sense in it a bid for conventional equality.
>
> To describe the character of this situation as a prevalent discourtesy is inadequate; it is rather an opposition of courtesies. Africans resent being passed over, but a shopman who should attend to an African in his turn when a European was waiting would be felt by the latter to have insulted him. To slight Africans is, in the European group, itself a convention, whose breach leads to embarrassment.
>
> This opposition of the races is complicated by the fact that there is opposition within the European group itself over 'Native policy'; and within the African group between conservatives who would maintain traditional ways, and radicals who seek to approximate to Europeans in all things....

The Wilsons recognized the destructive and potentially explosive consequences of culture contact. These were conditions that ignited and fueled the growth of movements for decolonization, national liberation, and political independence before and after World War II. In their analyses, the Wilsons employed the notions of anomie and alienation to explain the revivals and creations of the cultural nationalists; they employed the arguments for autonomy that were promulgated by political nationalists, such as Mohandas Gandhi, Ho Chi Minh, or Jomo Kenyatta.

U.S. anthropologists also re-conceptualized the processes of culture contact during the inter-war years. Their views derived from investigations carried out among Native American tribes at a time when the policies of the federal government were shifting from ethnocide and genocide to assimilation and finally to the re-creation of native cultures (Herskovits 1938; Linton 1940; Steward 1977:335–336). They focused their attention on *acculturation*—"...those phenomena which result when groups of individuals having different cultures come into continuous first-hand contact, with subsequent changes in the original cultural patterns of either or both groups" (Redfield, Linton and Herskovits 1936:149).

In their influential 1936 memorandum, prepared for the Rockefeller-funded Social Science Research Council (SSRC), Robert Redfield (1897–1958), Ralph Linton (1893–1953), and Melville J. Herskovits (1895–1963) raised a series of questions that they believed should be considered in studies of acculturation. What was the nature of the contact—e.g. was it friendly between entire groups or between certain kinds of individuals? What were the circumstances surrounding the contact and subsequent acculturative processes—e.g. were there inequalities between the groups, or was force involved? What processes of acculturation were involved—i.e. how were traits selected by the donor and recipient groups, and how were they integrated into the patterns of the recipient culture? What psychological mechanisms underpinned the acceptance, rejection, and integration of the new elements? What were the results of acculturation—i.e. were large numbers of new traits accepted; were original traits from both cultures combined to produce a new, smoothly functioning whole; or was the acceptance of new traits resisted? The authors were particularly concerned with the psychology of acculturation—i.e. with determining the covert, core value orientations of the recipient cultures as well as the psychological characteristics of individuals from those cultures who might accept or reject elements from the donor culture under the particular circumstances of contact. They wanted to determine why some societies adopted new elements, and others did not or why some individuals in a particular society adopted foreign traits, while others rejected them. This perspective was applied to examine early occurrences of the Ghost Dance and religious revivals among the Indian tribes of the Western United States (Gayton 1932; Nash 1937). A few years later, Harvard anthropologist Clyde Kluckhohn (1905–1960) would point out how important it was for administrators in the U.S. Indian Service to understand the covert culture—the unconscious value orientations—of a society in situations in which acculturation was taking place or in which the adoption of new traits was being resisted (Kluckhohn 1943).

From the late 1920s onward, Redfield (1897–1958)—an anthropologist who spent his student days and his entire career at the University of Chicago, which had been heavily funded by the Rockefeller foundations—elaborated on an alternative explanation of the process of national integration based on investigations that he and others carried out in southern Mexico in the wake of the Mexican Revolution. He developed an argument that incorporated significant elements of Durkheim's functionalist theoretical framework—e.g. a society and its culture were functionally integrated wholes, and culture functioned to maintain existing social relations and changed slowly through time because of social differentiation. He believed that the assimilation and integration of the rural communities into the Mexican state were inevitable, that these influences emanated from the cities, and that the task of applied anthropologists and development workers was to ensure that the transition experienced by the folk communities found in the peasant villages was as painless as possible.

In Redfield's view (1962[1930]), the development of culture in the tribal communities and peasant villages of rural Mexico resulted from contact and communication with cities, which were the source of modern Western ideas and practices. The tribal communities of Quintana Roo, for example, were relatively immobile and isolated from urban society; consequently, their cultures were quite homogeneous because communication was still based largely on face-to-face encounters between their members. This contrasted with the peasant villages where at least some members of the community—the teachers, artisans, or shopkeepers—wore shoes, read newspapers, and visited Mexico City. Their peasant neighbors lived on the edges of towns and gained their livelihood primarily or exclusively by farming while retaining their traditional beliefs and practices. At the same time and place, the more cosmopolitan residents of the towns had undergone a twofold process of change. They were deculturated in the sense that they gave up part of their cultural heritage; they were acculturated in the sense that they adopted ideas and practices emanating from the modern cities. One of the attitudes they adopted was that the peasants were despicable, mentally inferior, and driven by tradition. In Redfield's view, the peasants were increasingly puzzled by the behavior of their more acculturated neighbors.

While Redfield (1962[1934], 1962[1942]) recognized that the incorporation and integration of tribal peoples and peasant villages into the national state was a historical process, he focused attention on its spatial dimensions. In his view, the remote tribal peoples were more isolated from urban influences than the peasant communities, and both were more traditional or backward than city-dwellers. He called this acculturation process the folk-urban continuum. The cultural homogeneity of primitive tribal groups crumbled as they moved to the peasant villages and from those spaces to the modern cities with their cosmopolitan, outward-looking inhabitants (Redfield 1962[1935]). What distinguished communities at different points along the folk-urban continuum was "their degree of isolation from urban centers of modifying influence" (Redfield 1962[1942]:250).

Redfield was also struck by the mobility of merchants from peasant villages in the Guatemalan highlands. As many as thirty percent of the men from one community were traders who spent about seventy percent of their time on the road, peddling cash crops or commodities or acting as middlemen who participated in daily or weekly markets in other communities. While the traveling merchants were not isolated from the communities where they bought and sold commodities, their interactions with the inhabitants of those villages was limited to the market. They viewed themselves as strangers and, at the same time, retained a strong sense of identity with their natal community, even though they were rarely there:

> Each town center with its dependent countryside ... is conscious of its own individuality. The people of a given community do not marry with outsiders, and they have their own government—subject only to the authority of the Guatemalan nation.
>
> (Redfield 1962[1939]:203)

Redfield interpreted the particular combination of commercial activity and primitive practices as a stable cultural configuration that probably emerged before the Spanish Conquest rather than as evidence of capitalist penetration into the countryside in the nineteenth and early twentieth centuries. These investigations reinforced the view that, left to themselves, folk society and culture were relatively stable. What Redfield missed with his relatively static notions of folk culture and society was the impact that capitalist social relations had on the peoples of the Yucatán Peninsula. The inhabitants of many folk communities had, in fact, been rural proletarians engaged in wage labor on *henequin* plantations since the late nineteenth century, and the tribal peoples of Quintana Roo were actively resisting the incursions of the Mexican state in the twentieth century (Mintz 1953; Sullivan 1989).

A second focus of the foundation-sponsored research agenda was the scientific management of industry in order to increase productivity. Elton Mayo (1880–1949), an Australian psychiatrist employed by the Harvard Business School and a close friend of Malinowski's, founded Harvard's Committee on Industrial Physiology. In the 1920s and 1930s, Mayo's research on the effects of fatigue among workers at Western Electric's Hawthorne plant was entirely funded by the Laura Spelman Rockefeller Memorial. Mayo discovered that the workers' productivity linked in important ways to their participation in groups, to interpersonal relations, and to cultural factors (Spicer 1977:120–124). He brought a young anthropologist—W. Lloyd Warner (1898–1942), who received his doctorate from the University of Sydney—to investigate the cultural factors involved, including the relationship of the industry to the community in which the workers lived. For comparison, Warner focused his attention on Newburyport, Massachusetts, which he called Yankee City to disguise its identity. With support from the Committee and hence the Rockefeller philanthropies, Warner and his students launched a series of community studies there between 1933 and 1936; industrial relations in the city's shoe factory and the relations of the workers with each other outside of the factory were merely two facets of their studies (Chapple 1953; Whyte 1987). This was also a launching pad for studies of race relations in Natchez, Mississippi (aka Old City) and on the South Side neighborhoods (aka Black Metropolis) where the University of Chicago is located (Davis, Gardner, and Gardner 1941; Drake and Cayton 1945).

The foundations and the U.S. government—e.g. the Department of Commerce or the National Bureau of Economic Research—were less successful in their analyses of the ebbs and flows of economic activity during the interwar years. They established various offices and bureaus to plan, oversee, and manage the mobilization leading up to the country's entry into World War I in 1917. In the decade following the war, there was seemingly growing economic prosperity and expanding investment. However, few, if any, planners and technocrats in the government or the foundations foresaw what loomed on the horizon. The whole edifice collapsed with the Crash of 1929. The Great Depression would last a decade until the outbreak of World War II in the late 1930s (Alchon 1985:152–171).

John Maynard Keynes (1883–1946)—British civil servant and economist—was one analyst who had a glimmer of what would happen after World War I. He rejected the static equilibrium models of the neoclassical economists, took cognizance of existing sociohistorical conditions, and advocated the use of monetary policies to ameliorate the effects of the crises they provoked. For example, the British government financed World War I by borrowing from the Bank of England. The money earned by capitalist firms profiting from the war quickly found its way back to the banks, which, in turn, increased their ability to extend credit with low-interest loans. There was a short-lived economic boom immediately after the war, followed by a severe slump in 1921, with double-digit unemployment and falling prices. A year earlier, Keynes had advised the Chancellor of the Exchequer to raise interest rates in order to slow borrowing and imports, and to depreciate the value of the currency to maintain employment levels. However, his proposals were never fully implemented. Keynes was also appointed by the Prime Minister to participate in the Versailles peace talks that marked the end of the war; he resigned after the first day because of American demands to impose reparations and indemnities on Germany. He believed that these would produce hyper-inflation and instability, and impoverish large segments of the population because Germany would be forced to borrow money from the victors to pay for its war debts (Keynes 1919). His predictions would come true. While the war shattered the bases of the pre-war social and economic order, the capitalist economies also proved to be resilient. After the Great Crash of 1929, Keynes (1933, 1936) broke with the laissez faire, free-trade economic liberals and argued that (1) governments should increase spending in order to ameliorate unemployment; (2) governments should devalue the currency; (3) governments should erect protectionist tariffs on imports; and (4) the state should intervene in their national economies in order to restore social order, regulate economic activity, and promote economic growth. Early in World War II, Keynes (1940) argued that the capitalist governments should institute higher rates of taxation and compulsory savings to avoid deficit spending and inflation.

Discussion

Commentators writing during the inter-war years realized that they were witnessing unprecedented social changes occurring on a world scale and that peoples with diverse cultures in all parts of the world were being brought into closer proximity with one another than ever before. Commentators attempted to explain the complex interconnections between economic crises and the political crises they precipitated in capitalist societies, their colonial possessions, and non-industrialized countries on their margins. The crises were not derived from the business cycles that were already an integral feature of capitalist society— they were more general and threatened the breakdown and even the collapse of the operating principles undergirding capitalist nation states. They provided conditions for the transformation of those organizing principles in the Soviet Union as well as significant modifications in the capitalist countries themselves as one capitalist state after another, especially those in Scandinavia, heeded Keynes's arguments and advice.

The forces unleashed by capitalist expansion and penetration were apparent not only in the industrial cities—whose populations swelled as men, women, and children came in search of work in their factories—but also in the rural and colonial homelands of the immigrants. By the 1890s, Weber and Lenin were already describing and analyzing, at least in a preliminary manner, the processes set in motion in East Elbe and Russia. They portrayed these in terms of rural class formation or social differentiation and the appearance of alternative paths of agrarian capitalist development. In the 1920s, the new Soviet state directed Chayanov, Kritsman, and their associates to investigate the structure and organization of peasant agriculture and the changes that were occurring in it as a result of capitalist development in the rural areas. Fei and Mao undertook similar investigations in China, even though they reached quite different conclusions from their Russian counterparts about the nature of rural society. This research would subsequently lay important foundations for the development of peasant studies after World War II.

Investigations of rural class formation and structures were, by definition, also studies of the interconnections between urban centers and their hinterlands, and of how the uneven development of capitalism in towns and the countryside fueled their reproduction. The question of how capitalist enclaves located in cities articulated with the pre- or non-capitalist economies of rural areas became increasingly pressing. Gramsci and Boeke explored the economic and political underpinnings of uneven development in terms of the Southern Question in Italy and the formation of dual economies in Dutch Indonesia. Redfield discussed the cultural dimensions of the linkages in terms of a folk-urban continuum that emphasized differences in the intensity of communication among Westernized cities, peasant villages, and remote tribal communities, and largely ignored the political-economic relations forged by capitalist enterprises in the Yucatán Peninsula.

Marxist theorists—notably Mao, Gramsci, and Mariátegui—believed that peasantries were capable of developing an understanding of the conditions that were impinging on their lives and, given a historically contingent balance of force, of making their own history. Liberal commentators—Redfield, Boeke, and Fortes—argued that the lives of peasants and tribal peoples would ultimately be shaped in fundamental ways by relations, practices, habits, and ideas that originated in capitalist civilization and emanated from the Westernized culture of the cities, whose residents were already enmeshed in the social relations of the capitalist world economy.

Chapter 5 will build on the materials discussed in this chapter. We will examine how, when writing after World War II, social theorists from capitalist countries explained imperialism as economic growth and modernization, and how their contemporaries from Latin America or colonial states—who championed decolonization and political independence—described imperialism in terms of dependency, underdevelopment, or neo-colonialism.

Notes

1 Workers' councils are based on the principle of workers' control over an enterprise and production and occasionally over everyday life in working-class districts or communities. They are expressions of citizens' movements to run the affairs of local communities; they have often been constituted in opposition to management, political parties, and unions (Széll 2006). The most famous worker's councils in the early twentieth century were the soviets in Russia; however, they have also existed and continue to exist in a number of capitalist countries—for example, the cooperative villages in China (Hou 2013; Ratner 2015).

2 Lenin (1964[1917c]) outlined his views in *State and Revolution* as the second Provisional Government was crumbling. He grounded his views on Marx's and Engels's analyses of the Revolutions of 1848–1851 and the Paris Commune as well as his own observations about the conditions that prevailed in Russia. The state, in his view, was the product of the irreconcilability of class antagonisms in a class-stratified society; more specifically, it was the means by which the capitalist class retained and reproduced its absolute grasp on power—a hold that was, of course, constantly threatened by the struggle of subordinated classes. Lenin's alternative to the dictatorship of the bourgeoisie was the dictatorship of the proletariat, which would occur when the working class succeeded in seizing state power. The development and success of the class struggle that underpinned such a transition was historically contingent and could not be programmed in advance. In Lenin's words, "the transition from capitalism to communism is certainly bound to yield a tremendous abundance and variety of political forms..." (Balibar 1977:58–60; Lenin 1964[1917c]:418).

5

The Cold War, Decolonization, and the Third World, 1945–1970

European capitalist countries were in disarray at the end of World War II. The United States was one of only a few (Canada, Australia, and New Zealand) whose industrial base had emerged unscathed from the war; the economies of the others—England, France, Germany, and Japan—were severely damaged and would require nearly a decade to rebuild. The goals of U.S. policies at home and abroad were (1) to assert political and economic hegemony in the postwar world, (2) to preserve and expand business opportunities and overseas markets for U.S. corporations, and (3) to suppress the spread of communism. The policies were arguably less concerned with political democracy, equitable economic development, and containing communism than with preserving political stability and ensuring that nationalist leaders would not restrict U.S. business opportunities (Kolko 1968, 1972). The United States had lent or supplied the Allies with food, oil, and war material after 1941 and 1945; it canceled the Lend Lease Program in 1945. The British government finally repaid their last installment on the loan in 2006. Equally important was the Marshall Plan (the European Recovery Program) that lent $13 billion to the European countries between 1948 and 1952 to rebuild and modernize their economies, to remove interstate trade barriers, to drop regulations constraining business, and to reduce the influence of the communists. The loans allowed capitalist countries in Europe, which had exhausted their foreign reserves during the war, to purchase goods they could not produce, to rebuild their industries, and, in the case of France and the Netherlands, to wage wars against nationalist movements in their North African and Southeast Asian colonies. While the popular image of these loan programs is one of American generosity, it is also important to recognize that they virtually guaranteed a market for goods produced by U.S. firms in the years immediately following the war.

The industrial base of the Soviet Union was also relatively intact after the war because the factory towns it built during the Five-Year Plans in the 1930s were located mainly beyond the range of German bombers. In 1947, the United States and its capitalist, liberal democratic allies precipitated the Cold War, which pitted them against the Soviet Union and the Eastern European countries it occupied as the war came to a close. The Cold War revived earlier efforts by the capitalist countries to halt the advance of communism. It was an uneven balance of power maintained by enormous expenditures on weapons by both sides (Walker 1993). As historian Eric Hobsbawm (1996:226) put it, "Entire generations grew up under the shadow of global nuclear battles which, it was widely believed, could break out at any moment and devastate humanity.... It did not happen, but for some forty years it looked a daily possibility." From the late 1940s forward, the Cold War was a dominant feature of world history.

Decolonization was another prominent feature of the postwar years. Colonial subjects of the United States, England, France, and the Netherlands seized opportunities afforded by the weaknesses of the imperial states after the war to proclaim political independence or to launch popular movements, both armed and otherwise, to gain their sovereignty. By 1960, nearly 1.3 billion people—more than a third of the world's population at the time—had gained independence as a result of successful national liberation movements. Furthermore, the number of independent countries in Asia and Africa increased from a mere handful to more than fifty (Hobsbawm 1996: 208–222). If the Cold War intensified the conditions for the separation of the capitalist First World from the communist Second World, then decolonization precipitated the formation of a Third World by the early 1950s. This was composed largely of former colonies and the independent but poor countries of Asia, Africa, Latin America, and the Pacific (Pletsch 1981; Worsley 1964, 1984). The non-aligned countries constituting the Third World generally did not subscribe to the political projects of either the capitalist or socialist blocs; however, they did accept funds from both, sometimes simultaneously, to underwrite their own cultural, social, and economic projects. As a result, they were often the arenas or battlegrounds where disputes between the First and Second Worlds erupted, were waged, and occasionally resolved.

American foreign policy, the Cold War, and decolonization had a profound impact on the ways in which scholars in capitalist countries conflated communism and socialism, and how they conceptualized theories of change and development in a world where capitalism was alive; the communist counties and socialist parties provided an alternative; and the issues raised by imperialism, nationalism, and the Agrarian Question remained unresolved. Keynes, as you will recall, had argued in the 1930s that governments should increase spending in order to reduce unemployment and promote economic development. What development meant was contested. For devotees of neoclassical economics, it was a technical question of how to rebuild the capitalist economies of Europe and ensure that Third World countries acquired the consumption levels and patterns of the capitalist world. They underpinned their theories with ideas of progress, modernity, equilibrium, societal evolution, and economic determinism. At the same time, many ignored the ethical and political questions of development.

The perspectives of theorists of change and development in the United States provoked a series of richly textured responses from Third World and Marxist commentators. The latter typically rejected their conceptual categories and evolutionary or transhistorical arguments, which posited that development would occur through the same sequence of stages that had occurred in the West, provided that certain initial conditions prevailed. Instead, critics analyzed change in terms of underdevelopment, uneven development, and unequal exchange between the capitalist world and its periphery; the similarities they saw between these circumstances and ones that existed during the transition from feudalism to capitalism in the West; or the articulation of different modes of production. In a milieu shaped by the struggles for political independence, they investigated the participation of national minorities, peasants, and tribal peoples in national liberation movements and their integration into the newly independent states. They resurrected imperialism, colonialism, and the National and Agrarian Questions instead of obscuring their significance for most of the world's population.

In this chapter, let us examine some of the more influential theories that have been proposed to explain or direct social change between the end of World War II and the mid-1970s.

Theories of Economic Growth and Modernization

Concerns with full employment, the reconstruction of capitalist economies in Europe (1948–1952), and the extension of foreign aid to the "underdeveloped" countries of Asia and Africa after 1952 once again brought issues of economic growth and development to the fore. Growth and development appeared as a potent panacea. This "growth mania" had its immediate roots in Keynes's recommendation during the Great Depression that governments should intervene in their economies to resolve the pressing issue of unemployment. His *General Theory of Employment, Interest and Money* (1936) focused on the insufficient demand for commodities as the main cause of unemployment; it deployed "explicitly static assumptions of *constant* technology, population and capital" (Kurihara 1968:131, emphasis in the original). In 1939, British economist Roy Harrod (1900–1978) examined longer-term situations in which certain forces operated steadily to increase or decrease certain magnitudes in the system (Harrod 1939:14). His dynamic economics relied on the interplay of a limited number of economic variables to explain sustained growth over a period of time. The accelerator for growth in the long run was increased investment in more efficient capital and more productive technologies that would absorb a steadily growing number of workers. Two implications of his theory were that growth might potentially be continuous and, hence, that equilibrium might not be achieved. In contrast, U.S. economist Robert Solow's (1924–) neoclassical account argued that, in the short run, growth is determined by movement toward a new steady-state equilibrium (Solow 1956).[1]

Development economist Paul Streeten (1917–) described the economic growth theories of the late 1940s and early 1950s in the following way:

> Deeply embedded in current thought on development is the view that each country passes, at different times, through a series of comparable stages of development; that there are basic similarities in this process; and that we can therefore learn from the pre-industrial phase of now industrialised societies lessons which are applicable to underdeveloped societies today.
>
> (Streeten 1972:5)

The economic growth theorists couched their analyses in structural-functionalist terms, using fixed conceptual categories. The growth theorists argued that change was directional; that it proceeded gradually though a fixed succession of stages; that the engine and accelerator were located in the economic base; and, occasionally, that all aspects of society and culture were interconnected but secondary to the economy. They recycled the growth and evolution analogies of earlier generations, adopted a modernist perspective that eschewed history, and implicitly or explicitly asserted that there were few significant differences between one pre-modern or traditional society and another (Bock 1963). In effect, they framed their arguments in terms of the kinds of positivist and structural-functionalist arguments favored by an array of foundations and government agencies that supported social science research on the current problems of society. They criticized the "stage theory" found in the more reductive, economistic versions of Marxist thought at the same time that they advocated their own ethnocentric visions of economic and technological determinism.

U.S. anthropologist Julian Steward (1902–1972) made use of an evolutionary analogy. In his view, change was inevitable. Every culture has a core, "a basic economy which produces a configuration that [functionally] interrelates a large number of elements" closely related to subsistence activities and economic arrangements (Steward and Setzler 1938:7). This core, which involved historically determined technologies and productive arrangements developed through a progression of increasingly complex stages, had potent shaping effects on the less fixed, secondary aspects of social organization (Steward 1955[1950], 1977[1941]). After describing a base-superstructure model of society a la Lewis H. Morgan, Steward elaborated on an evolutionary analogy in a cross-cultural study of the cause-and-effect regularities associated with the development of early civilizations in semi-arid areas (Steward 1949).[2] By 1950, he had conceptualized world history in terms of a succession of stages that unfolded gradually as hunting and foraging bands developed into agricultural villages and then state-based political organizations; the succession culminated in contemporary Euro-American societies characterized by free enterprise and competition between business institutions:

> At first there were small communities of incipient farmers. Later the communities cooperated in the construction of irrigation works and the populations became larger and more settled. Villages amalgamated into states under theocratic rulers.... Finally culture ceased to develop, and the states of each area entered into competition with one another.... One or another state succeeded in dominating the others, that is, in building an empire, but such empires ran their course and collapsed after some... years only to be succeeded by another empire not very different from the first.
>
> (Steward 1950: 103–104)

For the historian this era of cyclical conquests is filled with great men, wars and battle strategy, shifting power centers, and other social events. For the culture historian the changes are much less significant than those of the previous eras when the basic civilizations developed in the Near East, or those of the subsequent Iron Age when the cultural patterns changed again and the centers of civilization shifted to new areas [i.e. Europe].

(Steward 1950:104)

...The industrial revolution brought profound cultural change to Western Europe and caused competition for colonies and for areas of exploitation. Japan entered the competition as soon as she acquired the general pattern. The realignments of power caused by Germany's losses in the first world war and by Italy's and Japan's in the second are of a social order. What new cultural patterns will result from these remains to be seen.

(Steward 1950:104–105)

The general assumption today seems to be that we are in danger of basic cultural changes caused by the spread of communism. Russia acquired drastically new cultural patterns as a result of her revolution. Whether communism has the same meaning in other nations has still to be determined.

(Steward 1950:105)

Steward recognized one limitation of this conception of world history. It was too general, and certain areas, like colonial possessions, did not fit neatly into it. In the late 1940s, he initiated a project in Puerto Rico to study the impact of U.S. capitalism on a largely rural agrarian colony that depended on an export crop and imported "...nearly all of its manufactured goods and about half of its food" (Steward 1950:129). The cultural heterogeneity of Puerto Rican society was due to the differential penetration of "...the processes by which production, social patterns, and related modes of life are selectively borrowed from the outside and adapted to local needs..." (Steward 1950:133–134).[3]

Steward saw the social structure of the island as composed of two interdependent features: (1) a series of distinctive, localized sociocultural subgroups crosscut by class, ethnic, and other social categories that were arranged hierarchically throughout the island; and (2) extra-insular institutions—i.e. economic relationships and the legal and government system—that regulated the society and had be understood apart from the behavior of the individuals connected with them. In his view, "the most important factors in Puerto Rico's cultural change... appeared to penetrate the Island along the axes of these basic institutions" (Steward 1950:145). The folk cultures of the island were not disappearing as this more complex stage of development was being reached—they were being modified instead and becoming specialized, dependent parts of a new configuration—a multi-faceted national culture (Steward 1955[1950]:51–53). Harold Brookfield (1926–) remarked that "from this point forward the theory of culture change began to rub shoulders with the theory of economic growth, though it remained empirically based" (Brookfield 1973:78). Unlike the growth theories and modernization theories that appeared in the late 1950s and 1960s,

Steward's multilinear evolution arguments specifically recognized that multiple paths of historical development had and were taking place.

The limitations of economic growth theories became more apparent after 1955 as colonial empires collapsed, decolonization intensified, diverse indigenous regimes replaced colonial governments, the new Third World countries emerged as significant actors in world politics, and the Soviet Union began extending foreign aid to the Third World. Robert McNamara—U.S. Secretary of Defense during the 1960s—saw these countries as "seething cauldrons of change," fueled by the "threat of Communist subversion" (quoted by Magdoff 1969:116–117). While the problem of economic development remained, the inability of economic growth theorists to account for issues of political, social, and cultural change, on one hand, and stability and disintegration, on the other, became more apparent. Theorists could not adequately address crucial questions resulting from organized opposition to capitalist development in Third World countries.

Modernization theory crystallized in the wake of the 1955 conference of non-aligned nations in Bandung, Indonesia, and the beginning of Soviet foreign aid; it reached its high point in the early 1960s. Clark Kerr (1911–2003)—industrial relations economist and President of the University of California from 1958 to 1967—described modernization clearly:

> The world is currently undergoing a great economic and social transformation. In essence, this transformation is the commitment of man to a new way of life. Throughout history most of mankind has been committed to a constant way of life. ...The current period in history is distinguished from all others, however, by the immensity of the process of destroying old commitments, no matter how constant they may have been, and by the world-wide uniformity of the new commitment. Men everywhere are transferring themselves fully and finally into the industrial way of life. ... Viewed from the end result, the transformation is one great process of such overwhelming impact that the current and local variations are almost unimportant. Viewed from points in between, there are roads and alleys and even dead ends; some societies choose one of these and some choose another. The great questions are: Why was one choice made rather than another, which choice is best, and may the choice be influenced?
>
> (Kerr 1960:348)

Kerr's claim implies that (1) there is sharp division between traditional and modern societies; (2) social change is uni-directional; (3) social change involves movement from rural, non-industrial traditional societies to an increasingly homogenous, urban-industrial modern capitalist society; and (4) the impetus for change is external to traditional society.

Walt W. Rostow's (1916–2003) *The Stages of Economic Growth: A Non-Communist Manifesto* was a bridge between the economic growth and modernization theorists (Rostow 1971[1960]). Rostow—a member of the Office of Strategic Services (OSS) during World War II, economic historian at the MIT Center for

International Studies, and presidential advisor in the 1950s and 1960s—sought to explain world history and account for why a dynamic social type oriented to economic progress appeared in the West and the transition from traditional to modern society was impeded elsewhere. He claimed that all societies, at least in terms of their economic dimensions, belonged to one of five universal types. He outlined the conditions and processes that promoted the transition from traditional society to the era of high mass-consumption that appeared in capitalist countries during the 1950s.

Traditional society was a diverse catch-all category composed of societies that employed non-industrial technologies and devoted a high proportion of their resources to agriculture. These hierarchically organized societies had regional political structures dominated by landlords. They could not improve per capita output because "...the potentialities which flow from modern science and technology were either not available or not regularly and systematically applied" (Rostow 1971[1960]:4). The preconditions for economic take-off, which first developed in England around 1700, occurred when the insights of modern science were harnessed to increase agricultural and industrial production in a context shaped by overseas expansion. As the idea of progress became a more pervasive aspect of everyday life, resistance to the idea of continuous growth was overcome, and the institutions of traditional society were ultimately dissolved (Rostow 1971[1960]:4–7, 1971:26–97). While the era of take-off was achieved in England and its colonies because of this technological motor, political regimes favorable to modernization were needed elsewhere.

During economic take-off, societies increased investment to ten percent or more of their national income in order to enlarge agricultural and industrial production, to promote a new but relatively narrow complex of industry and technology, to expand urban-industrial employment, and to support the emergence of a new class of entrepreneurs. After a decade or two, the social and political structures of these societies were transformed in ways that would sustain steady economic growth (Rostow 1971[1960]:17–36, 1971:98–183). The drive to maturity over the next fifty or sixty years was characterized by the spread of modern technology throughout the entire economy; by regular increases in output that outstripped population growth; and by continuous changes in the make-up of the economy as new industries appeared, import-substitution occurred, and new exports were created. At this stage,

> The society makes such terms as it will with the requirements of modern efficient production, balancing of the new against the older values and institutions, or revising the latter in such ways as to support rather than retard the growth process.
>
> (Rostow 1971[1960]:9)

Mature societies had the technological and entrepreneurial skills to produce virtually anything they wanted. This underpinned the age of high mass-consumption that appeared in capitalist countries during the 1950s when the leading economic sectors shifted toward the production of durable consumer goods. Real per capita income increased, and the structure of the labor force changed as a larger proportion of the total population worked in urban settings in office or skilled factory jobs. Thus, the Western societies were also able to allocate additional resources to social welfare and security. While the Soviet Union was technically ready for this stage, its leaders, in Rostow's view, had not yet faced the difficult political and social problems of adjustment that would occur if it were launched (Rostow 1971[1960]: 10–11, 73–92).

Modernization theorists came from a variety of academic specializations— anthropology, economics, sociology, and social psychology. While the growth theorists located the engines of change in the economy, the modernization theorists, depending on their training, situated these engines variously in the psychological, cultural, social, political, and economic realms of a nation as well as in the social system as a whole. Growth theorists viewed modernization as a complex phenomenon. They saw it as a disruptive process that ultimately dissolved the political, economic, social, cultural, and psychological commitments of traditional societies. The members of these "backward" or "underdeveloped" nations were exposed through the media, literacy, and foreign aid to various aspects of modern capitalist cultures, such as industrialization, rationalization, the affirmation of empirical science, the scientific method, individualism, bureaucracies, political parties, and the ideology of democracy. Modernization was the one-way passage from the past to an imagined future. Ultimately, the growth theorists built on Harvard sociologist Talcott Parson's (1902–1979) interpretation of Weber's views about ideal types, rationality, bureaucracy, and political parties (Parsons 1949[1937]).

Modernization, from the perspectives of its advocates, consisted of a number of functionally interrelated processes of change in the new nations. Economically, it meant developing technologies based on capitalist conceptions of scientific knowledge, replacing human and animal power with machines, moving from subsistence to commercial agriculture, establishing markets, creating urban-based industries, and consolidating an ever-increasing proportion of an increasingly skilled and differentiated labor force into cities. Politically, it involved a shift from tribal forms of authority to suffrage, political parties, elected representatives, and democratization as a result of external forces of social mobilization (Apter 1965; Deutsch 1963:6). Socially, it meant the diminishing importance of various kin and neighborhood institutions that provided emotional supports and safety nets for the members of traditional communities and granting greater roles to nuclear families (Eisenstadt 1973:21–22; Smelser 1961). Culturally, it reflected fundamental changes in the value orientations of society (Geertz 1956, 1963). Psychologically, it implied the formation of acquisitive, entrepreneurial personalities, which resulted from new forms of self-reliance, new ways of thinking, new desires, and new ways of satisfying them (Lerner 1958; McClelland 1961, 1964[1962]).

Using the idiom of systems theory, which was popularized in the late 1940s and early 1950s, Talcott Parsons described modernization in terms of movement from one stable equilibrium to another through simultaneous processes of alteration and differentiation, an argument reminiscent of those made earlier by Spencer and Durkheim:

> Theoretical analysis of change should distinguish between processes which maintain the equilibrium of a system and structural changes wherein a system moves from one equilibrium to another. Structural change occurs when disturbances in or around a system are sufficient to overcome the forces of equilibrium. ... For social systems one source of disturbance is alterations in the relation of the system to its environment which produces deficits in the input of goal attainment to acting units. When such units are performing multiple functions there is pressure toward structural differentiation, an important category of structural change. Differentiation can not occur, however, unless concomitant processes of social reorganization provide facilities for performance of the functions in the new differentiated context and patterns of normative legitimation and support.
>
> (Parsons 1961a:219)

Modernization theorists believed that Third World countries would have to confront a series of political questions (Shils 1960a, 1960b, 1963). They had to establish effective governments, which meant (1) organizing and maintaining a rational political apparatus that was viewed as legitimate by the masses; (2) staffing it with indigenous personnel schooled in or receptive to modern Western culture; (3) integrating the mass of the population, steeped in traditional culture, into the new national society; (4) developing new economic institutions and techniques to move the nation from traditional subsistence farming to commercial agriculture or industry; and (5) persuading the traditional masses to accept these innovations. Consequently, it was necessary for the theorists to determine how various institutions, practices, and beliefs "...function in the articulation of the society, in attaching or detaching or fixing each sector [of the population] in its relationship to the central institutional and value systems of the society" (Shils 1963:23–24).

Modernization theorists also made extensive use of Parsons's views about society and change as well as his interpretations of Durkheim and Weber in order to explain precisely how the processes they discerned took place and how they were reproduced. Parsons distinguished the changes that continually occur within society—e.g. when a new conjugal family was formed or when the personalities of children were shaped—from structural changes of society. He saw change in terms of shifts in the culturally determined motivations by which individuals or groups optimized gratification. Individuals and groups with vested interests blocked or attempted to prevent changes in motivation and need gratification in order to maintain the existing cultural system. When competing kinds of motivation and need gratification appeared, strains appeared in the interactions defining the social system, in the values of the cultural system, and in the ways in which the personalities of individuals allowed them to cope with the new situation. For the changes to be reproduced rather than to remain isolated instances of deviance, the consequences of the new motivations had to become an integral part of the belief and value component of the newly re-organized cultural system (Parsons 1951:480–503).

What fascinated Parsons (1961b:37, 1961c) was a category of change intermediate between those changes in society in which the patterns of the institutionalized culture remained constant and those changes in which the structure of the action system was transformed. He called this *structural differentiation*. It was initiated when a force originating from any number of sources—economic, political, or cultural—disrupted the existing boundary relationships between a society and its sociohistorical milieu. Differentiation produced strains that shifted value commitments away from specific role performances; these, in turn, produced social conflicts as vested interests affected by the strains simultaneously attempted to combat them and to reassert their legitimacy and control over any breakaway units. If they failed, further differentiation occurred, and

> The institutions associated with the different dimensions of society—with the functional demands of adaptation, goal attainment, integration, and pattern maintenance—become separated from one another. In the process, each develops the capacity to mobilize the resources of the other systems and to assert an independent, though partial regulation of them.
>
> (Alexander 1983:128)

The newly differentiated structures continued to develop, like a biological organism, until the equilibrium of the system was re-established, and the patterns of social integration and solidarity were transformed as the system was re-organized.

During the mid-1960s, Parsons attempted to account for certain universals he saw in the process of modernization. One involved the "break out" from the primitive stage of societal evolution caused by the appearance of social stratification and the cultural legitimation of differentiated societal functions, especially the political function, that were independent of kinship. Their appearance led to the formation of intermediate societies—the ancient Mesopotamian empires, China, the Islamic empires, or Rome—that were neither primitive nor modern. Once literacy was institutionalized in those intermediate societies, two additional changes occurred: the development of administrative bureaucracies, especially in government, and money and markets (Parsons 1967[1964], 1971).

Parsons (1966:24–27) was also concerned with how and why these intermediate societies were different from modern ones. From his perspective, the breakthrough they failed to achieve was the development of a generalized legal system—the kind that was instituted by English common law. While the antecedents for this breakthrough were found in the legal order established in ancient Greece and ancient Israel, neither was able to institutionalize its inventions under the prevailing circumstances. However, the legacy of these "seed bed" societies was capitalized on more than a thousand years later by the English, who successfully made the breakthrough to modernity.

Economic growth and modernization theorists set forth arguments to account for the changes that had taken place in the postwar world. Many agreed with Steward and Rostow, who argued that changes in the economic base had profound shaping effects on the political, social, and cultural realms of society. Others agreed with Parsons's Durkheimian claim that the determinants of change were ultimately located in the cultural system. Unfortunately, proponents of the two positions never confronted this discrepancy. Implicit in the views of both the economic and cultural determinists was the idea of convergence, which implied that the social and political-economic systems of the capitalist West and the Soviet Union would ultimately converge because the logic of industrialism promotes uniformity:

> As industrialism advances and becomes increasingly a world-wide phenomenon ... the range of viable institutional structures and of viable systems of value and belief is necessarily reduced. All societies, whatever path by which they entered the industrial world, will tend to approximate, even if asymptotically, [the ideal type of] the pure industrial form.
>
> (Goldthorpe 1971:263)

Modernization theory was largely the postwar creation of American social scientists used to legitimate U.S. business, political, and military expansion, and intervention in the internal affairs of Third World countries—i.e. imperialism by another name. Some critics of modernization theory thought that it needed to be revised and refined; others denied the utility of abstract schema altogether. The criticisms of modernization theory included the ideas that (1) it was based on dichotomous thinking—i.e. two mutually exclusive categories: traditional and modern; (2) the two categories were Weberian ideal types, not generalizations about historical process; (3) it viewed modernization as a totalizing process that affected all aspects of society; (4) it assumed that industrialization had the same effects everywhere; (5) it was evolutionist and viewed change as the interaction between fixed sets of pre-conditions and fixed sets of interrelated variables; (6) it was ethnocentric, and Social Darwinist, in that all societies would eventually progress toward the end-product of the industrial capitalist societies of Western Europe and North America; (7) its underlying commitment to the idea of progress made it difficult to consider political instability or political decay; and (8) it was reductionist (e.g. Bendix 1967; Bernstein 1971; Brookfield 1973:53–85; Huntington 1965; Tipps 1973). Marxist and structuralist critiques originating in Third World countries took a different tack: Both rejected the neoclassical and stagist models that underpinned economic growth and modernization theories.

Underdevelopment, Dependency, and the Modern World System

By 1950, two economists at the United Nations—Raúl Prebisch (1901–1986), Director of the Economic Commission for Latin America (ECLA) and former President of the Central Bank of Argentina, and Hans Singer (1910–2006), a 1932 refugee from Nazi Germany—had argued against the conventional wisdom of mainstream economics (Prebisch 1949; Singer 1949). Their critique has been called the Prebisch-Singer Theory. Instead of assuming that industrialization would absorb increasingly larger portions of the agricultural workforces of underdeveloped countries, they suggested that unequal exchange between countries in the global market underpinned persistent inequality between capitalist and underdeveloped nations. Moreover, the magnitude of the disparity between countries exporting primary products (e.g. raw materials, like food or minerals) and those exporting consumer (e.g. textiles) or capital (e.g. iron, steel, coal, or railroads) goods would increase rather than decrease with the growth of trade. Prebisch and his associates at ECLA pointed to the social and economic structures of Argentina, Mexico, and Brazil—all of which had attempted to lessen their dependence on and vulnerability to world markets after the crash of 1929 through political alliances and state policies that controlled foreign investment and commerce. In spite of their efforts, industrialization had not occurred, and they were more dependent on the capitalist countries than they had been four decades earlier. In a phrase, convergence had not occurred as the mainstream economic growth theorists predicted. As Prebisch (1950:1) put it,

> In Latin America, reality is undermining the out-dated schema of the international division of labour, which achieved great importance in the nineteenth century and, as a theoretical concept, continued to exert considerable influence until very recently. Under that schema, the specific task that fell to Latin America, as part of the periphery of the world economic system, was that of producing food and raw materials for the great industrial centres. There was no place within it for the industrialization of those countries.

What had changed in those decades, however, were the agents of dependency. The new agents were not the extractive mining and capitalist export agricultural companies of earlier times but rather transnational corporations that integrated diverse activities into single firms, which operated in a number of countries. The world economy was structured in terms of a dominant center and a dependent periphery, which were linked together by exchange relations that were not equally beneficial to both. The patterns of economic development that occurred in the dependent countries were consequences of decisions made in the industrial capitalist countries—the United States; Great Britain; Germany; and, to a lesser extent, Japan.

The power of the transnational corporations was their control over commercial technology. In order to gain access to their technology, local industrialists had to enter into joint ventures with them. This set in motion processes that simultaneously de-nationalized industry in the Latin American countries, opened up their internal markets to foreign commodities, and altered the balance of force within the ruling classes. This economic restructuring had devastating consequences. Local capital was used to finance the joint ventures with transnational firms; the amount of locally generated capital exported from Latin America in the form of profits, royalties, and commissions to the dominant economies increased significantly; and, consequently, less local capital was available for investment in the various national economies (O'Brien 1975:16–19).

Critiques based on the Prebisch-Singer Theory developed along two interrelated lines in the 1950s and 1960s: the American Marxist and Latin American structuralist traditions (Love 1990; Toye and Toye 2003). Collectively, these were called *dependency theory*. While there were differences within and between the two traditions, their proponents agreed that

> at the core of the dependency relation between [industrial] center and periphery lies the inability of the periphery to develop an autonomous and dynamic process of technological innovation. ... The center countries controlled technology and the systems for generating technology. Foreign capital could not solve the problem because it only led to limited transmission of technology, but not the process of innovation itself.
>
> (Vernengo 2006:552–553)

Stanford economist Paul Baran (1910–1964) began to develop the Marxist critique of the growth theorists in the early 1950s (Baran 1969[1952], 1969[1953], 1957). He indicated that the "pure" economic models of the growth theorists, built on notions of static equilibrium and perfect competition, were ill-equipped to deal with the social and economic dynamics emphasized in their research and policy agendas. He (1969[1952]) began with the political economy of backwardness: Why did countries on the margins of the capitalist world not benefit from the influx of foreign capital during the late nineteenth and early twentieth centuries? In his view, these investments were geared toward the production of commodities for export. The wealth of the "backward" country was its raw materials and the growth potential of its reserve army of labor, whose members were increasingly less able to be employed efficiently in the agricultural or small local manufacturing sectors. Profits flowed largely to the metropoles and foreign investors rather than being retained in the country. As a result, little capital was available locally for investment. The investments that were made were geared toward making profits in the short run—e.g. selling goods that were not produced locally and were desired by the small classes that could afford them; local investment was rarely made in enterprises—like infrastructure—in which profits would only be realized in the long run. Moreover, the political power bases in these countries were typically coalitions of local businessmen, large landowners, and agents representing foreign firms, all of whom had little incentive to change the existing social conditions.

Baran (1969[1953], 1956) also focused on the concepts of economic progress and economic surplus. Economic growth or progress was an increase through time in the per capita output of goods and services, resulting from one or more of the following: (1) the incorporation of previously unutilized resources (raw materials or labor power) in the productive process without changes in the organization of labor or technological innovations; (2) increasing productivity through organizational measures, such as lengthening the work day, moving workers from less productive to more productive occupations, or improving their nutrition; and (3) using more efficient technologies or adding them to the already existing stock (Baran (1969[1953]:272). The first two do not entail net investment; the third one does. Baran continued,

> Net investment can only take place, however, if society's total output *exceeds* what is used for its current consumption and for replacement of the wear and tear of its productive facilities during the period in question. The volume and the nature of net investment taking place in a society at any given time depends, therefore, on the *size* and the *mode of utilization* of the currently generated *economic surplus*.
>
> (Baran 1969[1953]:273, italics in the original)

He described two kinds of economic surplus and elaborated what he meant by the term. First, *actual* economic surplus is the difference between a society's actual current output and its actual current consumption; it includes factories and other productive facilities, inventories, foreign balances, and savings. Second, *potential* economic surplus is the difference between what could be produced and what is actually being produced under the given conditions of the actually employed workforce and what is deemed essential consumption; its realization implies drastic reorganization of the production and distribution of output (Baran 1969[1953]:273–274). Baran's conclusion was that while the potential economic surplus was high in underdeveloped countries, the actual economic surplus was low. The reason for this was the ways in which the social and political structures distributed and utilized the actual surplus. Thus, the lack of economic development or slow development were consequences of political decisions.

In *The Political Economy of Growth*, Baran (1957) observed that many underdeveloped Latin American states had small, highly productive industrial sectors combined with large, relatively unproductive agricultural sectors. While the potential for growth and employment lay in the industrial sector, the small size of the domestic market and the small amount of surplus available for investment and capital formation constrained expansion. He noted that various forms of surplus extraction coexisted in the underdeveloped countries: Landlords extracted land-rents from the peasants; moneylenders charged interest on credit; merchants made profit on trade; and the capitalists, mostly foreign, extracted surplus value from industrial workers. He proceeded to argue that none of these classes had any real interest in promoting industrialization. The traditional classes of the agricultural sector—the landlords, moneylenders, and merchants—opposed industrialization because it threatened their access to surplus. The capitalists, both foreign and national, also opposed further industrialization because it would promote competition that would ultimately challenge their monopoly control over domestic markets and threaten the high profit rates that they were already extracting from them (Martinussen 1997:85–88).

Chicago-trained economist André Gunder Frank (1929–2005)—who taught in Mexico City, Brazil, and the University of Chile between 1963 and 1973—did much to popularize the Marxist strand of dependency theory in the United States through his critiques of mainstream development and modernization theory (Frank 1967, 1969[1966], 1972). Frank agreed with Baran that monopoly capital in industrialized countries created the underdevelopment of the periphery. However, his analysis differed from Baran's in two important ways: (1) capitalism was defined in terms of unequal market relations rather than production, and (2) there were no pre-capitalist social relations in countries on the periphery once they and their ruling classes were linked by exchange relations to the industrial countries and their ruling classes. In Frank's view, "development and underdevelopment each cause and are caused by the other in the total development of capitalism" (Frank 1969:240). In other words,

> The now developed countries were never *under*developed, though they may have been *un*developed. It is also widely believed that the contemporary underdevelopment of a country can be understood as the product or reflection solely of its own economic, political, social, and cultural characteristics or structure. Yet historical research demonstrates that contemporary underdevelopment is in large part the historical product of past and continuing economic and other relations between the satellite underdeveloped and the now developed metropolitan countries. Furthermore, these relations are an essential part of the structure and development of the capitalist system on a world scale as a whole.
>
> ...[T]he expansion of the capitalist system over the past centuries effectively and entirely penetrated even the apparently most isolated sectors of the underdeveloped world. Therefore the economic, political, social, and cultural institutions and relations we now observe there are the products of the historical development of the capitalist system no less than are the seemingly more modern or capitalist features of the national metropoles of these underdeveloped countries.
>
> (Frank 1969[1966]:4–5, emphasis in the original)

Moreover, he argued, the Latin American countries had been part of a world capitalist system since the early days of the colonial period. Consequently, it made no sense to describe their economic structures as feudal; semi-feudal; or archaic, dual, or plural societies because they had been forged by the same historical processes of capitalist development and underdevelopment that affected the industrialized countries of Europe and North America.

Thus, underdevelopment was reproduced by the inherent contradictions in capitalism. Only a small portion of the economic surplus generated by their economic development was actually saved and invested in the underdeveloped countries themselves; the remaining, larger portion was either appropriated by another part of the world capitalist system or was wasted on the consumption of luxury goods:

> ...[T]his exploitative relation ... in chain-like fashion extends the capitalist link between the capitalist world and national metropolises to the regional centers (part of whose surplus they appropriate), and from these to local centers, and so on to the large landowners or merchants who expropriate surplus from small peasants and tenants, and sometimes even from these latter to landless laborers exploited by them in return.
>
> (Frank 1967:7–8)

Capitalist development and expansion were facets of the same historical process. It simultaneously produced economic development in the metropolitan countries and structural underdevelopment in those on the periphery. It also polarized the metropole and the satellite countries as well as different regions within the countries on the periphery. Polarization occurred because

> For the generation of structural underdevelopment, more important still than the drain of economic surplus from the satellite after its incorporation into the world capitalist system, is the impregnation of the satellite's domestic economy with the same capitalist structure and its fundamental contradictions.
>
> (Frank 1967:10)

This meant that the conditions required to maintain underdevelopment were manifested in the class structures of underdeveloped countries (Frank 1972:1–12). It also implied that the "...satellites experience their greatest economic development and especially their most classically capitalist industrial development when the ties to the metropole are weakest" (Frank 1969[1966]:9–10).

Celso Furtado (1920–2003)—a Brazilian economist associated with ECLA—laid important foundations for the Latin American structuralist critique. In his view, development and underdevelopment were two aspects of the same dialectical process. The interrelations could only be understood by examining the historical development of the whole. Development meant industrialization. It occurred earlier in the capitalist countries of Europe and North America than it did in the colonies and underdeveloped countries that produced primary products. The industrial capitalist countries produced both consumer and capital goods that either were not manufactured in the peripheral countries or whose production was insufficient to meet demand. Efforts to promote industrialization on the periphery during times of crisis—the Great Depression and World War II—usually involved *import substitution*. In these instances, the state enacted policies favoring local investment in domestic firms to produce consumer goods to re-place imported ones; these firms were often inefficient, produced inferior goods, and were protected by high tariffs. In other words, there were few incentives to produce capital goods, whose production and distribution remained under the control of firms in the developed, industrial countries (Furtado 1963[1959], 1964[1955], 1965[1964]).

This led to a critique of the theory of dual economies employed by the growth and modernization theorists who built on Boeke's earlier work (see Chapter 4). In that argument, as you will recall, when capitalist structures and practices, like production for export, were introduced into a country with a largely sub-sistence economy, only a small number of local workers were incorporated into the capitalist enterprise, and the archaic economic structures were not changed dramatically. For change to occur, many more individuals had to be employed in the capitalist sector and receive income that could be spent on consumption or invested. However, the income generated by the capitalist sector in a depen-dent country was only partially linked to that country because the larger portion of it was exported and invested to promote a dynamic capitalist sector in the metropole. As a result, hybrid economies that linked a capitalist core to archaic structures on the periphery were forged repeatedly as the frontiers of Western capitalism were steadily extended during the nineteenth and twentieth centu-ries. What emerged in the dependent countries were three-sector economies composed of a remnant subsistence economy, a capitalist export economy, and a small capitalist manufacturing economy concerned with local consumption. The only dynamic elements in the dependent countries were external demand and the wages generated in the export sector. However, if more of the population engaged in subsistence production (i.e. the reserve army of labor for the other two sectors) were employed, then there might be further investment in the do-mestic manufacturing sector, depending on the political decisions of the power bloc controlling the state (Furtado 1964[1958]). Furtado (1970:107–108) elabo-rated on this argument a few years later. In describing the interrelations of the accumulation of power, social stratification, the shared interests of social classes across the developed-underdeveloped divide, and class struggle, he wrote that

> substitutive industrialization has been aggravating the disequilibrium at the factor level, and amplifying the gap between the modern sector and the precapitalist economy, without opening any prospect of reducing the importance of the latter as a main source of employment for a rapidly in-creasing labor force. In the urban sector the aggravation of this structural equilibrium is manifested by the rapid growth of underemployment....
>
> The institutional framework that prevails in Latin America produces patterns of income distribution responsible for ways which are incompat-ible with the most rational utilization of the available resources, that is, with the maximization of total output within a time horizon. There exists an inconsistency between the interests of those groups that control the pro-cess of capital formation and the interests of the community as a whole. As

these economic groups also occupy all the strategic positions in the power system, it is not surprising that the political signals become inadequate to register the structural tensions, and that the instruments for political decision are not fit to promote the removal of the obstacles to development in a timely fashion. ...The core of the problem resides in the structural relations that determine the field within which the relevant decisions are made.

Two of Furtado's associates at ECLA, Fernando H. Cardoso (1931–), who would become President of Brazil (1995–2003), and Chilean economist Enzo Faletto (1935–2003) pointed out that certain important features of the capitalist system—notably the technological and financial sectors—were almost the exclusive possessions of developed states. Because they were crucial for further development, the dependency of the underdeveloped countries, as well as the domination of the developed ones, was reinforced as the former attempted to expand their economies. For Cardoso and Faletto (1979[1969]:xxi–xxii), the dependent countries were like borrowers approaching a bank president. Moreover, this relationship underwrote the growing debt incurred by the underdeveloped countries after World War II.

U.S. political sociologist Immanuel Wallerstein (1931–) elaborated on the underdevelopment and dependency perspectives, especially those of Frank, that crystallized in the late 1960s. In *The Origins of the Modern World System*, Wallerstein argued that states never existed in isolation and were instead parts of systems of varying sizes in which each polity was linked to its contemporaries by exchange relations (Wallerstein 1974). Economic development was largely impossible in the world economies that existed before the sixteenth century because the bureaucracies of the constituent states effectively absorbed virtually all surplus production, thereby precluding the accumulation and productive investment of capital. The crisis of the medieval world economy was resolved with its dissolution and the emergence of the modern capitalist world system centered in northwestern Europe around 1500. This coincided with the

...expansion of the geographical size of the world in question, the development of variegated methods of labor control for different products and different zones of the world-economy, and the creation of relatively strong state machineries in what would become the core-states of this capitalist world-economy.

(Wallerstein 1974:38)

In his view, this industrial core formed

By a series of accidents—historical, ecological, geographic—northwest Europe was better situated in the sixteenth century to diversify its agricultural production and add to it certain industries (such as textiles, shipbuilding, and metal wares) than were other parts of Europe. Northwest Europe emerged as the core area of this world-economy, specializing in agricultural production of higher skill levels, which favored ... tenancy and wage labor as the modes of labor control.

(Wallerstein 1979[1976]:18)

As a result, these countries were able to impose regional specialization on production—e.g. sugar in the Caribbean, bullion in the Andes, and cereals in Eastern Europe. The increasingly powerful state machines of the core countries that controlled the division of labor were able to consolidate the accumulation of surplus and to ensure that it ultimately flowed into the core region. They were also able to enforce backwardness on the peripheries of Latin America and Eastern Europe and on the semi-periphery of Southern Europe, which had once been a core area but had turned in the direction of the periphery. While wage labor was the predominant form of labor control in Northwestern Europe, forced or coerced labor prevailed in the periphery, and sharecropping was dominant in the semi-periphery.

Semi-peripheries were geographical areas or states that fell between the core and the periphery because of their in-between forms of labor control (Wallerstein 1974:101–108). They played a different role from the core and periphery because

In part they act as a peripheral zone for core countries and in part they act as a core country for some peripheral areas. Both their internal politics and their social structure are distinctive, and it turns out that their ability to take advantage of the flexibilities offered by the downturns of economic activity is in general greater than that of either the core or the peripheral countries.

(Wallerstein 1979[1976]:97)

In a phrase, the semi-periphery is "both exploiter and exploited" (Wallerstein 2000[1974]:91).

The semi-periphery of the postwar era consisted of states—like Canada, Mexico, Norway, Yugoslavia, the Soviet Union (USSR), Saudi Arabia, Israel, Indonesia, and the People's Republic of China—that have diverse economic and political regimes. Socialist states—like the USSR or China—had nationalized the means of production, while in others, like Canada, the major means of production were controlled by capitalists. In Wallerstein's (1979[1976]:117) view, neither the socialist countries nor those of the Third World constituted distinct world systems governed by non-capitalist economic relations. They occupied spaces in a single, hierarchically organized system driven by unequal exchange. The countries of the semi-periphery, both socialist and non-socialist, belonged to the sub-system in which significant change would occur. Thus, the defining feature of the modern world system was its globality.

For Wallerstein (2000[1975]), the capitalist world system was composed of three elements: a single capitalist market, a series of state structures that impeded and distorted the working of the free capitalist market, and three tiers or levels of exploitation that underpin the dialectical formation of both class structures and ethno-nationalism. The dynamic feature of the modern world system was the system itself rather than its constituent parts—the core, the periphery, and the semi-periphery; it was the appropriate level of analysis. This had a number of implications: for example, (1) the states in the three tiers were not independent but tied together by unequal exchange relations; (2) therefore, the social-class structure of capitalism exists at the level of the world system itself; (3) the relative positions of the three tiers were not fixed but could change through time; (4) what happened in the semi-periphery and periphery resulted from contradictions in the world system as a whole; (5) thus, changes in the periphery and semi-periphery were determined by forces that were external to both; (6) independent states and struggles for national independence were anti-systemic movements operating at different levels against the capitalist world system; and (7) for social transformation to occur, anti-systemic movements against capitalism had to be worldwide rather than confined to different zones or subordinate levels of the system as a whole.

The importance of the underdevelopment and dependency debates in the 1950s and 1960s might be summarized as follows: (1) they were broadly anti-imperialist, a view that found resonance in the underdeveloped, non-aligned nations of the world after World War II (Girvan 1973; Oxaal, Barnett, and Booth 1975; Rodney 1974[1972]; (2) they demonstrated the short- and long-term consequences of dependent development; (3) they laid bare the devastating effects of the core-periphery relationship in both developed and underdeveloped countries; (4) they focused on the growing importance of transnational corporations as agents of change; and (5) they shifted attention from development in particular states to development in an increasingly capitalist world system. Moreover, they brought attention to (6) the changing balance of force within the ruling power structures of dependent states; (7) the new emergent relations between social-class and state structures; (8) the shared interests of classes on both sides of the developed-underdeveloped divide; (9) the imperialism of trade or unequal exchange in a world economy dominated by capitalism; and (10) the contradictions and social transformations that appeared in the wake of the penetration of capitalist social relations into underdeveloped societies.

Unequal Exchange, the Imperialism of International Trade, and the Political Economy of Multinational Corporate Capital

The dependency and underdevelopment theorists never questioned the central role that the forces of production played in explanations of the process of industrialization through capital accumulation (Chakrabarti and Cullenberg 2003:24). As you will recall, commentators in the late nineteenth century viewed imperialism in terms of the monopolies of overseas investment exercised by capitalist states over particular colonies and regions. Firms in a given industrial state invested capital in its colonies in order to extract raw materials or primary products and to export them to factories in the home country for further processing into commodities. These circumstances began to change dramatically after World War II due to the destruction of capitalist industrial economies during the war and the success of the decolonization movements that erupted when it was over. The ideology of free trade once again came to the fore as the protective barriers of the pre-war era were stripped away. Many theorists viewed the emerging world economy largely in terms of the "sucking out of surplus" from the periphery.

The international trade emerging after the war was not equally beneficial to all of the participants (Emmanuel 1972[1969]). A few benefited, but many did not. International trade, from the perspective of Greek Marxist economist Arghiri Emmanuel (1911–2001), was unequal exchange between countries with high wages and those with low wages. Those with high-wage levels were industrialized; those with low-wage levels were underdeveloped. The wage disparities explained why goods produced in the West were expensive, and goods produced in the Third World were cheap. Emmanuel also observed that the ideology of free trade in the modern world economy was a myth because international trade in this milieu was actually competitive, exploitative, and laden with protectionist barriers. In his view, capital in search of profits from the sale of commodities was quite mobile in the modern world, and labor was not.

Exchanges between high- and low-wage countries were unequal and exploitative. What determines the price of a commodity is whether it comes from a high- or low-wage country. Over time, the terms of trade have deteriorated in the low-wage countries because of hidden transfers of resources (Emmanuel 1972[1969]:xxx). The extent of the unequal exchange (i.e. the rate of exploitation) is proportional to the wage disparity, on the one hand, and the volume of trade, on the other. Purchasing a given commodity produced in a high-wage country costs the low-wage country a greater percentage of its total national income than it does in the former. The rate of exploitation increases with the passage of time or as the level of trade increases. These processes cause a continual drain on the monetary resources of poor countries—a hidden transfer that is reproduced on an ever-expanding scale. It provides a fuller explanation of how the "sucking out of surplus" process occurred.

Emmanuel's theory of unequal exchange provoked a number of responses in the 1970s. Some criticized his premises: the unity of a world economy shaped exclusively by the laws and values of the capitalist mode of production; the relative mobility of capital and commodity and the immobility of labor; higher rates of exploitation in low-wage countries because of wage disparities; the tendency of profit rates to equalize internationally; wage differentials as an independent variable; or imperialism ultimately as mercantile—capital driven in search of markets rather than overseas investment (e.g. Bettelheim 1972[1969]; Mandel 1978[1972]; Shaikh 1979, 1980).

Emmanuel also raised a number of difficult questions: Why do truck drivers performing the same work in high- and low-wage countries receive different wages and have different standards of living? Why have wage differentials not been eliminated between countries? Are workers performing the same task exploited at different rates when they receive different wages? Are consumers in industrial countries the major beneficiaries of international wage disparities? Is there an aristocracy of labor on a global scale that benefits from wage differentials? If so, does this account for the difficulty of organizing labor across international borders and getting the workers of the world to unite? Are multinational corporations free from competition on a world scale? How should we understand the protective barriers that impede international trade? How do these barriers affect the repatriation of profits to developed countries (Howard and King 1992:189–200)?

Egyptian Marxist economist Samir Amin (1931–) built on Emmanuel's theory of unequal exchange; however, he rejected the central premise developed by Emmanuel and others that the modern world capitalist system is shaped by a single mode of production. While the process of capital accumulation occurs on a world scale, it does so in a world divided into a multitude of national societies in which the capitalist mode of production is combined with various pre-capitalist modes of production (Amin 1974[1970], 1976[1973]); it has resulted in the formation of two distinct categories of national societies—the center and periphery. Economic development in the social formations of the center, which manifest exclusively the capitalist mode of production, has involved the satisfaction of mass consumer needs. Economic activity in the peripheral social formations has involved the extraction or production of primary products for export and the importation or production of a few luxury items. This means that the processes of accumulation have proceeded along different trajectories in the center and periphery. It is *autocentric* in the center—i.e. self-centered and governed by the laws of motions of the capitalist mode of production described by Marx. It is *extraverted* in the periphery—i.e. simultaneously dependent on the relations between the center and periphery at one level of the global system and constrained by the capitalist production relations that provide coherence and dominate at another level of the world economy.

The differences between Amin's autocentric and extraverted nations appeared because the industrial capitalist mode of production was manifested earlier in the center. Initially, wages were held close to subsistence levels in both the center and periphery; however, the center gained a lead when wages began to rise in certain economic sectors, and the remnants of pre-capitalist social relations were eliminated. This established a pattern of unequal regional specialization. Unemployment and the persistence of pre-capitalist social relations, which held wages down on the periphery, fueled further unequal specialization and development. While the center was increasingly dominated by the capitalist relations of production and reproduction, the societies on the periphery, with their disarticulated economic sectors, were based on combinations of capitalist and pre-capitalist modes of production. The capitalist export sectors, which were often foreign-owned, coexisted with various pre-capitalist social relations—i.e. they were similar to Boeke's theory of a dual society.

What this meant is that the modern world economy could not simply be reduced to the laws of motion of capitalism. For Amin, the expanded reproduction of capitalist social relations in the periphery was a new form of primitive accumulation by the center against the periphery. Thus, there was a potential dynamism or historical contingency found in the periphery regions that was not so apparent in the center. Moreover, the contradictions were petri dishes for crises, especially around public finances and external payments, which have the potential to block the expanded reproduction of capitalist social relations on both a local and world scale (Amin 1974[1970]:299–302).

Belgian Marxist economist Ernest Mandel (1923–1995) took a different tack (Mandel 1978[1972]:343–376). He argued that important structural transformations took place in the world economy after 1953. Unequal exchange, not foreign investment, became the major form of colonial exploitation. The main flows of commodities were no longer between the center and the periphery but now occurred among the capitalist metropoles themselves. Foreign direct investment in the underdeveloped countries shifted from the extraction of primary products to the manufacture of durable goods—machines, equipment, and vehicles. Multinational corporations, mainly those in Europe and Japan, produced these goods and increasingly challenged the worldwide economic dominance of the United States that had prevailed for nearly a decade after World War II. Anti-imperialist groups in the underdeveloped countries responded by promoting measures that would impede the transfer of profits and dividends to the metropoles. This, of course, focused attention on the international operations of multinational corporations.

Like Mandel, Stephen Hymer (1934–1974)—Canadian Marxist economist— saw a new pattern of foreign direct investment developing in the wake of World War II. He described the multinational corporations as

typically large firms operating in imperfect markets and the question of their efficiency is a question of the efficiency of the oligopolistic decision making, an area where much of welfare economics breaks down, especially the proposition that competition allocates resources efficiently and that there is a harmony between private profit maximization and the general interest. Moreover, multinational corporations bring into high definition such social and political problems as want creation, alienation, domination, and the relationship or interface between corporations and national states including the question of imperialism, which cannot be analyzed in purely 'economic' terms.

(Hymer 1970:441)

Between 1960 and 1972, Hymer published path-breaking studies on the international operations of national firms operating in international environments as well as their political economy and their impact on less developed countries (Hymer 1968, 1970, 1972a,b, 1976[1960]). There were several interrelated strands to the argument he developed. First, international firms—e.g. the mercantilist British East India Company—have existed since the fifteenth century; their impact on local societies was complex, reflecting the social and political structures of those societies and the proportion of the population engaged in food production as opposed to non-agricultural or state-sponsored pursuits. The shape of international firms has changed. As you will recall, international firms engaged in mining or plantation activities emerged from the late 1870s onward. After World War II, however, innovative multinational corporations—mostly European and Japanese—invested in the production of manufactured goods in the less-developed countries on the periphery (Hymer and Resnick 1971).

Second, during the twentieth century, capitalist firms made decisions to eschew the mass production of commodities that would benefit large numbers of people in favor of capital-deepening activities that involved continual innovations for a small number of consumers. In the developed countries, such decisions created a small class of relatively high-wage earners—the emerging white-collar managers in the regional and head offices—and a much larger class of low-wage earners who could not afford the commodities that were being produced. In the less-developed countries, they created large, low-wage sectors. Once the initial development and production costs of the commodities were covered, there was a "trickle-down effect" as their purchase prices declined—as with personal computers in the late twentieth century; as a result, larger numbers of consumers in the higher wage sectors were able to purchase these goods, reinforcing ideologies or illusions of social mobility as manifested in consumption patterns (Hymer 1972a).

Third, the multinational corporations that appeared in the 1950s were complex enterprises that coordinated the division of labor in both the factory and the market. They were divided horizontally into specialized departments—e.g. production, purchasing, sales, or maintenance—and vertically into field offices that were overseen by regional offices, which, in turn, followed the lead of executive head offices that were the administrative, planning, innovative, and investment hubs of the firms. Because the market for their commodities was imperfect, there was a continuous interplay between the structure of the market, on the one hand, and the number of firms participating in the industrial sector and their efficiency relative to their competitors, on the other. Multinational enterprises carefully weighed the advantages of entering markets in less-developed countries with the disadvantages of being foreigners in those countries. One way in which they entered overseas markets was by forming alliances with local capitalists to manufacture goods—like machinery or vehicles; these import substitution activities often experienced high growth rates until the domestic markets were saturated. The enterprises took various forms—mergers, licenses, direct investment in smaller firms that supplied materials or distributed final products, and tacit collusion with both local capitalists and state officials (Hymer 1968; Hymer and Resnick 1971). The multinational corporations, through their foreign direct investments, reproduced uneven development. This raised political questions. While the multinational corporations were dependent for their development on both nationalism and the underdeveloped Third World states, they were simultaneously eroding the political institutions that brought them into existence.

Modes of Production in Third World Societies

The Third World crystallized in the wake of the political independence and anti-imperialist movements in the 1950s and 1960s. It consisted of former colonies in Africa and Asia and semi-colonies—like China and Cuba—whose economic, political, and social relations were dominated by the capitalist metropoles. The unity of the newly independent, but generally poor, states was a negative one: They were neither capitalist nor socialist, and they were aligned politically with neither the capitalist countries of the First World nor the communist states of the Second World (Worsley 1984:296–345). Discussions of underdevelopment, unequal exchange, and peripheral capitalism in the Third World were interwoven into a new fabric with familiar threads from earlier and ongoing controversies: imperialism, the Agrarian Question, and the National Question. A number of Marxist and Third World analysts were critical of the teleological (stagist) arguments of economic growth and modernization theorists, on the one hand, and the emphasis on exchange in the arguments of dependency, underdevelopment, and world systems theorists, on the other. They were concerned, instead, with (1) the historical specificity of the structures and processes of change in particular countries or regions, (2) how to conceptualize colonial forms of society that were in between feudalism and capitalism, (3) how to understand the articulations (linkages) between the modern industrial (capitalist) and traditional agrarian (non-capitalist) sectors of Third World societies, and (4) how to explain how those structures and processes came to be the way they are (e.g. Banerjee 1985; Foster-Carter 1978a,b; Raatgever 1985).

From the late 1960s onward, Third World analysts, many of whom described themselves broadly as Marxists, critiqued theories of development, dependency, underdevelopment, and unequal exchange. They argued over whether the regions where they worked were best described as capitalist, as transitions between feudalism and capitalism, as distinctive colonial or plantation societies, or as societies manifesting various combinations of different modes of production. Let us consider these debates in more detail.

The controversy that appeared in India was concerned with whether or not there was a break in the nature of agricultural production and capitalist accumulation before and after independence (McEachern 1976; Patnaik 1990; Thorner 1982). One impetus for the debate was the Green Revolution of the 1960s when the Indian government and the Ford Foundation introduced high-yielding varieties of wheat and rice—along with pesticides, seeds, fertilizers, efficient irrigation systems, and failed land reform programs—to increase food production in the wake of the 1961 famine. Indian economist Utsa Patnaik (c. 1940–), for one, argued that there was a difference between the colonial and post-independence economies of India and that the country's trajectory of development had not been like that of Western Europe. An important distinction was that the colonial state converted a substantial portion of the rents and taxes collected from direct producers into commodities that were exported to Britain or shipped to other countries for foreign exchange. The limited capital that circulated was controlled by landlords, merchants, or moneylenders. Thus, domestic investment in agriculture and in consumption, especially of foodstuffs, suffered under the colonial regime. The process of capital accumulation did not lead to the proletarianization of the rural workers as it did in Western Europe but rather to their pauperization.[4]

Jairus Banaji (1947–)—Indian agrarian historian—referred to this condition, at least briefly, as the *colonial mode of production*:

> The colonial modes of production were precisely the circuits through which capital was drained out of the colonies in the form of bullion, consumption goods, raw materials, and so on. The financing of the primary accumulation outside the colonial world was their chief historical function and it was this fact which determined their peculiar retrograde logic. We can describe this in the following terms: the colonial modes of production transmitted to the colonies the pressures of the accumulation process in the metropolis without releasing any corresponding expansion of the forces of production.
>
> (Banaji 1972:2500)

Banaji argued that the distinctive features of colonial modes of production were their subordination to metropolitan accumulation, the form of exploitation, and the predominance of non-wage-workers in the agricultural sector. He showed the kinds of features that many colonial countries had in common (McEachern 1976:431). However, a few years later, he referred to them as instances of backward capitalism or combined and uneven development: "In the epoch of colonial imperialism the formation of a unified international market transfigured the world economy as the old systems of scattered national modes of production disintegrated under its impulse" (Banaji 1973:393–394).

The mode of production controversy took a different turn in Latin America. While the economic system described by the dependency and underdevelopment theorists, notably Frank, characterized Colonial Period in Latin America as capitalist in the sense that capital was the appropriated surplus from the region, many analysts of Latin American societies did not rely on these exchange models. They employed Marx's concept of a mode of production; however, they did not mean by this a linear progression of stages from primitive communism to socialism and beyond. Argentine political theorist Ernesto Laclau (1935–2014) described a mode of production as "an integrated complex of social productive forces and relations of a determinate type of ownership of the means of production," and distinguished this abstraction from the concrete reality of a structured and differentiated whole, an 'economic system' ... [that] designates the mutual relations between different sectors of the economy, or between different productive units, whether on a regional, national or world scale. ... An economic system can include, as constitutive elements, different modes of production—provided always that we define it as a whole, that is, by proceeding from the element or law of motion that establishes the unity of its different manifestations.

(Laclau 1971:33)

The focus of Laclau's inquiries and that of many of his Latin Americanist colleagues was the articulation of modes of production during the colonial period.

Argentine historian Carlos Sempat Assadourian (1937–) provided an important example of economic systems forged by the articulation of different modes of production. He agreed with some colleagues that the expansion of the Spanish Crown into the Americas was a mercantile venture and not a sign of the transition from feudalism to capitalism in Europe. However, he also argued that the motor for change did not reside in unequal exchange between the center and periphery but rather in the formation of internal markets in the colony around two growth poles: the silver mines of Potosí and the viceregal capital and port-city of Lima. The internal markets generated by the mining pole spread into an extensive economic space stretching from the Mato Grosso to Ecuador, which produced everything from human labor to mules and *yerbe mate* (tea). The economic space and internal markets enmeshed both local and regional communities, transforming their economies and histories as they were incorporated into the commercial life of the region; however, they did not encapsulate all of the communities in the same way. Thus, capitalism in the Andes was not the result of the transition from feudalism to capitalism in Europe or of the low volume of European goods making their way across the ocean; it was, however, a consequence of the formation of a proletarianized workforce and home market in the Andean region (Assadourian 1973; Stern 1985).

French anthropologist Pierre-Philippe Rey (c. 1940–) formulated a third approach to understanding the impact of colonialism and capitalism on local societies in West Africa during decolonization and the transitions to independence in the 1950s and 1960s (Rey 1971, 1979, 1982[1973]). Influenced by the Algerian War of Independence (1954–1962), he had first-hand association with the struggles of peasants and workers in Congo-Brazzaville and Togo and, later, with their struggles as migrants in France. He saw the confrontations and class alliances as processes associated with the *articulation of modes of production* during the transition period in colonial and post-colonial societies. Simply put, articulation occurred as capitalism encroached on and grafted itself onto the dominant pre-capitalist system—first, in the sphere of exchange, which reinforced the existing class structure, and then in its distortion, dissolution, reconstitution, and reintegration into an emergent class structure increasingly dominated by the expansion of capitalist relations. Thus, articulation was a collision between pre-capitalist or non-capitalist and capitalist modes of production—both a

process and relation of transformation that specified the underlying contradictions as well as the nature of the class struggle itself (Foster-Carter 1978a,b; Raatgever 1985; Wolpe 1980, 1985). The question was how does this happen?

Rey distinguished between modes of production and social formations.
Modes of production are abstractions best understood as processes with their
own distinctive logics and dynamics rather than as static architectural structures. What distinguishes one mode of production from another are the forms of
exploitation, relations of distribution, and class structures associated with them.
Social formations, by contrast, are real societies that often manifest articulations
of different modes of production. Rey (1979) argued that the contradictions and
social structures in pre-capitalist West Africa during the colonial period were not
determined by control of one class over the means of production but rather by
control it had over the means of reproduction. The social (not biological) elders
controlled the labor of socially younger men because they seemingly allocated
the productive and reproductive capacities of their social daughters through
bridewealth payments. While the younger men provided labor to the elders in
order to make those payments, dependent women were, in fact, exploited more
permanently. Exploitation took place in a sequence:

> (a) production by the dependants [*sic.*]; (b) conveyance of products and
> services to the elders; (c) circulation on the basis of reciprocity among the
> elders; (d) accumulation in the sphere of circulation, and/or destruction. ...
> Bridewealth is the specific form through which exploitation is accom-
> plished: dependants provide the wherewithal for the acquisition of prestige
> goods which then circulate among the elders as marriage payments.
>
> (Raatgever 1985:308)

Rey pointed out that the elders of the local agricultural communities in
Congo-Brazzaville and Togo appropriated the labor time of the younger men
and women. This determined the structure of distribution and the organization of production. Rey calls this formal subordination and distinguishes it from
real subordination, which means that technical aspects of the labor process and
innovation—such as new crop varieties—were also determined by subordination. He proceeded to locate the contradiction underlying one confrontation and
provide an answer to the question of how the transition was taking place in the
1950s and 1960s. The point of contestation was, on the one hand, that the elders
tolerated agricultural innovations only to the extent that they do not diminish
their control and, on the other, that the subordinated groups were constantly attempting to adopt new crops that did not fall under the traditional control of the
elders (Raatgever 1985:315–316). Capitalist encroachment potentially reinforced
the dominant pre-capitalist mode of production in Congo-Brazzaville and Togo
when it was limited to the sphere of exchange. However, colonial settlement
weakened the traditional structure as the settlers created demands for both labor
and commodities that competed with those of the elders and opened possibilities for establishing new alliances. In these instances, the process of articulation

linked forms of exploitation and social reproduction associated with different modes of production.

In sum, Rey argues that articulation is an ongoing battle between modes of production manifest in the confrontations and alliances between the classes they define. He emphasizes (1) that capitalism never immediately or completely eliminates elements of the pre-capitalist modes of production it seeks to replace; (2) that it may not always be the dominant mode of production in a social formation; and (3) that forms associated with non-capitalist modes of production may reappear, or forms associated with new modes of production may appear. What was important about the mode of production debates in the 1970s were the kinds of questions raised.

For example, South African anthropologist Harold Wolpe (1926–1996) used the concept of articulated modes of production to explain the development of South African society after c. 1870 (Wolpe 1980[1972], 1988). This meant simultaneously addressing the racialization of the colony's population, class structures and alliances, and social transformation during the colonial period. He argued that the redistributive economies of the country were dominant systems before the advent of British mining in the late nineteenth century. The capitalist mining companies paid lower than subsistence wages to workers, the balance of whose needs were provided by kin on family farms or on the Reserves, where land was held communally and goods circulated according to established norms of distribution. By the 1920s, there were three modes of production: the capitalist, the non-capitalist traditional forms, and the sharecropping and tenancy relations associated with family farms and market exchange. The state reproduced and strengthened the hold of capitalist social relations in the twentieth century by creating state enterprises, a domestic market, agencies and policies that benefited white settlers, and a repressive apparatus that coerced both black and white workers. It also enacted legislation that naturalized race as a category, regulated relationships between people assigned to these categories, and masked the expanding reproduction of capitalist social relations. Extended families in the Reserves provided "social security" for cheap migrant labor that was incorporated in the urban and rural sectors of the capitalist system and paid less than the cost of reproduction.

The quasi-equilibrium (balance of force) between capitalist and traditional forms of reproduction was disrupted in the 1940s by World War II. Distinctions between landowners, landless individuals without cattle, and landless individuals who grazed their cattle on communal lands increased. Rapid industrialization during the war swelled the urban working class, weakening the ties between African workers and their kin on the Reserves. While the growth of industry in the cities underwrote the expansion of commercial enterprises and service-sector jobs, it also helped to underwrite the declining productivity of the Reserves. The Reserves provided steadily smaller portions of the subsistence needed by their migrants. At the same time, the number of strikes and other conflicts over wages and the structure of the society itself increased dramatically after the war. The Apartheid practices and policies implemented in 1948 were intended to maintain a cheap labor force. The repression that ensued was a response by the nationalist government to the challenges raised by a coalition of workers from urban and rural areas.

The Transition Question from Feudalism to Capitalism

The debates discussed earlier were enmeshed in a broader question: What is involved in the transition from one mode of production to another? Three debates concerned with the transition question reappeared during the tumultuous years following World War II. The preceding question was concerned with the transformations taking form and gaining momentum in the former colonies, the second with the transition from feudalism to capitalism, and the third with the transition from capitalism to socialism. They were not unrelated because it was a time of turmoil and change. Transition was the important question at the time. Recall that between 1945 and 1952, roughly a third of the world's population proclaimed itself to be socialist, and another third had either proclaimed political independence from the imperialist states or were in the process of doing so. Many had economic and social structures that were not quite capitalist or whose development had either been blocked or deformed by the spread of capitalism. Theorists trying to conceptualize social transformation in the underdeveloped Third World; the Colonial, Agrarian, and National Questions that refused to go away; and the road to socialism frequently described the social and economic structures of those countries as "feudal," "semi-feudal," or "feudal-like." As one commentator put it, "We live in the period of transition from capitalism to socialism; and this fact lends particular interest to studies of earlier transitions from one social system to another" (Sweezy 1976[1950]:33).

English economist Maurice Dobb (1900–1976) laid the foundations for the transition from feudalism to capitalism debate in his *Studies in the Development of Capitalism* (Despain 2011:50–110; Dobb 1946). He viewed feudalism, or serfdom, in terms of (1) a particular form of surplus extraction in which the direct producers are obliged to perform service for their immediate rulers, who lived on the labor of the producers and (2) the relations between the producers and technology they employed. He criticized mainstream economic and historical accounts of the dissolution of feudal society, which he characterized in the following manner:

> We are often presented with the picture of a more or less stable [feudal] economy that was disintegrated by the impact of commerce acting as an external force developing outside the system that it finally overwhelmed. We are given an interpretation of the transition from the old order to the new that finds the dominant causal sequences within the sphere of exchange between the manorial economy and the outside world. 'Natural economy' [based on the production of goods for use] and 'exchange economy' are two economic orders that cannot mix, and the presence of the latter, we are told, is sufficient to cause the former to go into dissolution.
>
> (Dobb 1946:38)[5]

Dobb criticized this explanation: (1) it did not deal with the dynamism of technological change, (2) it underplayed the ongoing role of markets during the feudal epoch of Western Europe, and (3) it misrepresented the internal contradictions between direct producers and social rulers as well as the mutually beneficial interdependency of the latter and the merchant class. While he acknowledged that the rise of commerce had a "disruptive effect on the feudal" order of Europe, he questioned whether "the widening of the market can be held to have been a *sufficient* condition for the decline of Feudalism—whether an explanation is possible in terms of this as the sole or decisive factor" (Dobb 1946:37, emphasis in the original). He argued that the commercialization model did not pay sufficient attention to the internal crises of feudalism: exploitation, persistent attempts to avoid exploitation, and the absence of social and cultural structures that would impede social-class differentiation in the face of the "growing needs of the ruling class for revenues" and its frequent attempts to intensify exploitation (Dobb 1946:42). Depending on the historically contingent conditions, these crises were sometimes accompanied by a strengthening of extra-economic forms of compulsion and subordination, sometimes by their diminution, and occasionally even by the appearance of wealthy peasants who were able to exploit their more desperate neighbors. Thus, without relying on the external motor of market exchange, Dobb spelled out the internal dynamics of the feudal mode of production, a pathway by means of which direct producers become merchants, as well as the mechanisms by means of which the feudal mode of production was not merely reproduced but also transformed.

Furthermore, he rejected claims of the commercialization model that economic transformation was best understood in terms of transhistorical, economic, or social evolutionary laws. Taking Marx's lead, Dobb argued instead that economic development—the growth of labor productivity—had to be understood in terms of the possibilities and constraints offered by the historically contingent sets of production relations that were characteristic of a given era and mode of production. He brought into focus the structural similarities that existed in the West during the early stages of capitalist development and those that still prevailed in most of the world.

U.S. socialist Paul Sweezy (1910–2004) sparked the debate in 1950 after the mainstream history journals had largely ignored Dobb's work. Sweezy found Dobb's work thought-provoking but had a number reservations about it: (1) his mode of production concept was too general because it was an abstraction manifested in a number of distinct societies, and his main interest was really the feudal societies of Western Europe; (2) he neglected the inherently conservative nature of feudal societies and their inherent resistance to processes of change; (3) he viewed the decline of feudal societies as a consequence of internal contradictions—inefficient methods of production, on the one hand, and over-exploitation, on the other; and (4) his explanation of the crisis and decline of feudalism did not preclude the growth of trade as an important engine of change. Therefore, his account was incomplete.

Sweezy's (1976[1950]:41–46) alternative to Dobb was that there were actually two potentially contradictory systems of production in feudal society: one geared for use and the other for market exchange. There were itinerant peddlers of the ninth and early tenth centuries who propped up the existing social relations in feudal society; however, the revival of long-distance exchange fueled the growth of the "production for the market" economy, ultimately at the expense of the "production for use" system. This underwrote the concentration of artisans, merchants, and people escaping the bonds of serfdom around the old, non-agricultural settlements. It generated new tastes and preferences, especially within the ruling classes. It created new kinds of production that were not constrained by the social relations of serfdom—i.e. wage labor. This pre-capitalist commodity production led slowly to the dissolution of feudalism and the rise of capitalist enterprises.

This established the terrain of the debate. Dobb (1976[1950]) replied to the critique, indicating that there was agreement in many areas, differences in emphasis in others, and disagreement in a few. One area of disagreement concerned his definition of feudalism, which he viewed in terms of the relation of production between direct producers and overlords rather than the access of direct producers to the market. He emphasized the conflict between the two classes and gave agency to the subject serfs. In his view, class struggle was the internal dynamic of feudalism rather than the secondary tensions between feudal lords and petty commodity-producing merchants. The latter only became important at a later stage in the transition. A second disagreement was that Dobb thought the feudal mode of production was more dynamic, unstable, and fragile than Sweezy, who rejected the idea of a crisis of feudalism. Thus, a third disagreement was Sweezy's implicit view that class struggle had no revolutionary or transformative tendencies and that transformation occurred only after the petty commodity producers shook free from feudal exploitation. From Dobb's perspective, Sweezy overestimated the role of market exchange in the dissolution of feudalism and the rise of capitalism; he put too much emphasis for the transformation on external forces of changes and neglected internal ones.

Japanese historian Kohachiro Takahashi (1912–1985) observed that the Sweezy-Dobb debate provided a basis for comparative studies of capitalist structures and processes of historical transition outside of Western Europe (Takahashi 1976[1952]:68). He made a number of important observations worth re-emphasizing. First, he pointed out that Dobb and Sweezy conceptualized serfdom in different terms: the former as the production relations specific to the feudal mode of production, the latter as a transhistorical relation found in societies manifesting different modes of production. Second, Dobb sought the decline of feudalism and the emergence of industrial capitalism in class conflict as well as the rise of petty commodity-producing peasants, and Sweezy conceptualized it in terms of the local rulers' need for cash and their growing alliance with peddlers engaged in long-distance trade and presumably moneylending. Takahashi made the point that the important element in these dual processes was not the appearance per se of market exchange but rather how it was integrated into the internal organization of the production system. This brought to the fore Marx's comments on revolutionary and conservative routes of capitalist development. In the revolutionary route, the producers became merchants; in the conservative path, the merchants sought to control production by putting-out work to rural producers and through putting-out systems and their alliances with the ruling class. He pointed out that both routes occurred during the transition, and, depending on local historical circumstances, one or the other predominated.

English medieval historian Rodney Hilton (1916–2002) took a slightly different tack, emphasizing the importance of class struggle and the differentiation of the peasantry in feudal society. Episodic demands on the peasantry for increased feudal rent (i.e. labor service, products, or money) were resisted and provided both agriculturalists and artisans with incentives to keep as much of their product as possible. They did this by attempting to reduce the demands of the ruling class, by increasing the productivity of their labor, or by increasing the amount of land they cultivated or goods they produced. Thus, town life and the development of the productive forces—new tools and the labor skills of the agriculturalists and artisans—were consequences of economic and social development within feudal society rather than the effects of itinerant traders. Furthermore, petty commodity production did not destroy the solidity and internal articulation of the feudal mode of production, even as the character of production changed through different phases of feudal development (Hilton 1976[1953]).

In summarizing the debate through 1962, historian Eric Hobsbawm (1917–2012) noted that the transition from feudalism had been a highly uneven development when viewed on a world scale. From his perspective, the rise of industrial capitalism occurred in Western Europe alone because of a long, complex process that did not operate uniformly in every area or in each of the five or six historical phases that extended from the break-up of the Western Roman Empire to the triumph of capitalism during the Industrial Revolution. This thousand-year span of European history was marked time and again by major crises. During each crisis, the most advanced sections of bourgeois development in Europe—like the Italian and Flemish textile industries, with their capitalist employers and workers in the fourteenth century—collapsed or were overtaken by backward areas—like England.

In Hobsbawm's view, feudalism was not replaced as a result of some steady unfolding or progression of stages that inevitably led to capitalism. Such a characterization was applicable only to a limited extent outside Europe, where there were

> ...certain signs of comparable development under the impetus of the development of the world market after the 16th century, perhaps in the encouragement of textile manufactures in India. But these are more than offset by the *opposite* tendency, namely that which turned the other areas that came into contact with and under the influence of the European powers into dependent economies and colonies of the west. In fact, large parts of the Americas were turned into slave economies to serve the needs of

European capitalism, and large parts of Africa were pushed back economically through the slave-trade; large areas of eastern Europe were turned into neo-feudal economies for similar reasons.... The net effect of the rise of European capitalism was therefore to intensify uneven development, and to divide the world ever more sharply into two sectors; the 'developed' and the 'under-developed' countries, in other words the exploiting and the exploited.

(Hobsbawm 1976[1962]:163–164)

Robert Brenner (1943–) launched a second round of the debate about the transition between feudal and capitalist social formations in the mid-1970s (Brenner 1985[1976]). By the mid-1980s, it was called the Brenner Debate (Aston and Philpin 1985). Although the subject matter was similar to the Sweezy-Dobb controversy in the 1950s, the participants in this debate embraced a wider range of perspectives on historical development. Neo-Malthusian demographic determinist theories as well as the growth of trade-centered theories of economic transformation were added to the Marxist views that shaped the earlier debate. Not surprisingly, the discussion of the 1950s, rooted in Marxist thought, was not frequently cited. Brenner (1977, 1985[1976]:13–29) was critical of both demographic and commercialization models as well as the arguments discussed earlier by Sweezy, Frank, and Wallerstein.

Brenner's question was what caused the emergence of industrial capitalism in Western Europe. He argued that class struggle was the primary cause of movement and transformation. The conflicts underpinned class formation and social differentiation in the countryside—i.e. new property relations, new forms of exploitation (surplus extraction), and new dynamics of class struggle. In fourteenth-century England, the conflict between landlords and serfs was over the level or intensity of surplus extraction. The serfs won their freedom; serfdom was eroded—slowly in some areas, more rapidly in others; and social differentiation occurred in the emergent peasant class. Peasants without land drifted toward wage labor, those with small plots farmed their own lands, and those with larger holdings leased additional land from the lords and hired laborers in order to produce commodities and accumulate capital. Thus, the new forms of exploitation in the emergent class structure were those between employer and employee (the extraction of surplus value) and between lord and capitalist tenant farmer (the appropriation of surplus in the form of rent). While the lords retained their dominance in the political sphere, the larger, capitalist tenants improved agricultural production methods and crop selection to reduce costs and increase accumulation; in effect, they became small businessmen producing for domestic markets. The trajectory of development was different in France because of the persistence of peasant resistance and organization in that country (Brenner 1985[1976]).

French medieval historian Guy Bois (c. 1940–) was appreciative of Brenner's thesis that the decisive part of the transition from feudalism to capitalism occurred in the countryside and was also sympathetic to his critique of Neo-Malthusian demographic arguments (Bois 1984[1976], 1985). However, Bois was also a critic of Brenner's "political Marxism" and his proclivities toward separating the political and economic realms of the feudal mode of production to pass over the effects of the long- and short-term dynamics of that mode of production, and to begin with theoretical models and cherry-pick evidence to fit the argument. Bois saw Brenner's question differently. First, the tendency of the rate of the levies exacted by feudal lords to fall originated in structural contradictions between small-scale production and large-scale property. The dominant class was unable to maintain its hegemony, which strengthened the position of the middle peasantry and facilitated the excessive growth of the state apparatus, adding a whole new layer of levies. Second, the secular movements of the feudal economy resulting in alternating periods of growth and crisis, and the social and economic phenomena associated with them, also originate in the structure of feudalism—small-scale production and estates whose numbers seem almost infinitely expandable. These movements—the rise and fall of prices during periods of growth and decline—create economic conditions that are essential for understanding the origins of agrarian capitalism; they are the petri dishes in which the size of production units, the number of wage laborers, and the laborers' standards of living increase or decline (cf. Kula 1976[1962]). Third, the upsurge in agrarian capitalism in Western Europe during the sixteenth century was a consequence of decisions made by the feudal lords who found that the revenues produced by the serfs on their estates were insufficient to maintain standards of living to which they aspired. They released the serfs, expanded the size of their estates, and turned to wage-workers to produce commodities for sale in local and regional markets.

The transition from feudal to capitalism debate persists (e.g. Aston and Philpin 1985; Brenner 1997, 2001; Byres 1996, 2006; Habib 1995[1983]; Hilton 1985[1976]; Hoppensbrouwers and van Zanden 2001). The reason for this is that there is no single process of transition. Transitions are complicated processes that occur at multiple levels of social formations constituted by the articulation of multiple modes of production. As French economist Charles Bettelheim (1913–2006) put it,

> Transitions are never simple or brief processes. On the contrary, they typically occupy and even define whole historical epochs. One aspect of their complexity is what might be called multi-directionality: movement in one direction may turn back on itself and resume in a forward direction from a new basis. In some places the reversal may be prolonged or conceivably even permanent.
>
> (Sweezy and Bettelheim 1971:107–108)

That is, social formations manifesting articulated modes of production are bundles of the contradictions associated with each and the new ones forged by linkages. They are fragile. New balances of power and class alliances have their beginning in these arrays of contradictions, relations, and circumstances. Gramsci (1971[1930–1932]) referred to the struggles taking place in these moments of change as "wars of maneuver" and contrasted them with the "wars of position" or "underground wars" occurring in those historical epochs of seeming stasis in which the dominance of the ruling classes prevailed, while contradictions accumulated and festered.

Precipitants of Transitions

World War II weakened capitalism on a world scale. The decade and a half following the war can be characterized as time of maneuver, when new balances of power were forged by colonial states and anti-colonial movements. Tensions arising from imperialism, colonialism, nationalism, and the Agrarian Question erupted in the 1940s. Let us consider their impact.

Anti-Colonialism, National Liberation Movements, and New Nations

Colonial administrators believed that tribes were the traditional units of political authority and that colonial administrations were structures imposed from the outside. In this view, tribal authorities were intermediaries between their kin and neighbors and the colonial state. As such, they belonged to the lower rungs of colonial administrations; their purpose was to maintain social order (Worsley 1961). Nationalist leaders in the colonies believed that the colonies themselves, rather than their constituent societies and cultures, were the basic units to which the idea of self-determination should be applied. In their view, the colonies were race- and class-stratified power structures dominated by Europeans, who were usually citizens of the metropolitan country or their descendants (Wallerstein 1966). Because tribal societies constituted only a layer of colonial society, it was essential to understand their relationship with the metropolitan power and the larger global society as well as with circumstances that were created within and by the colony.

Nationalist writers were acutely aware of the power of nationalism after World War II. Jawaharlal Nehru (1889–1964), the Prime Minister of India, wrote that it was "one of the most powerful urges that move a people, and round it cluster sentiments and traditions and a sense of living and common purpose" (Nehru 1946:41). While culture and tradition were arenas in which the struggle for national liberation would be waged, not every class would participate because the

> ...[Indian] middle class felt caged and circumscribed and wanted to grow and develop itself. Unable to do so within the framework of British rule, a spirit of revolt grew against this rule, and yet this spirit was not directed against the structure that crushed us. It sought to retain it and control it by displacing the British. These middle classes were too much the product of that structure to challenge it and seek to uproot it.
>
> (Nehru 1946:45)

Nehru recognized three strands of thought critical of colonial regimes that fueled nationalist sentiments in the postwar years: cultural nationalism, the psychopathologies of the colonial experience, and socialism.

Cultural nationalists argued that identities were based on shared personal experiences, suffering, and struggles. The most fully developed cultural nationalist viewpoint after the war was Negritude, which originated in the writings of diasporic Africans, mostly from French West Africa and the French Caribbean. Cultural nationalists described their experiences of racism and the subordinate relationships they had with whites in their quest for freedom and personal identity (Irele 1973a,b). They saw colonialism in terms of the relations between individuals or races rather than class structures, imperialism, and exploitation. Certain themes—exile, racial consciousness, alienation, African cultural heritage, and African personality—played prominent roles in the formation of these identities. Exile and the alienation of the colonial situation were oppressive, denying blacks the capacity to achieve their full self-development and distorting or erasing altogether their true cultural heritage. Cultural nationalist thought appealed largely to the colonial middle classes and provided a powerful but incomplete explanation for the oppression they felt. Many of the new elites that emerged after independence used cultural nationalist arguments to justify not developing the productive forces or altering the distribution of wealth (McCulloch 1983a:5–9).[6]

French psychoanalyst Octave Mannoni (1899–1989) described the psychological effects of the colonial experience on both settlers and indigenous peoples in the wake of the unsuccessful Malagasy rebellion for political independence in 1948 (Mannoni 1964[1950]). He argued that not all people can be colonized, and not all people become colonizers. What was required, in his view, was that the personality type of the subject population be shaped by a dependency complex while that of the settlers be based on individualism and self-dependency. The combination made European colonialism possible in Madagascar. Mannoni portrayed the situation in terms of the two personality types deployed in Shakespeare's *The Tempest*: Prospero, the omnipotent settler who became touchy whenever his authority was even remotely threatened, and Caliban, the slave whom Prospero ruthlessly exploited as well as the unruly and incorrigible son whom he disowned. For Prospero, Caliban was the scapegoat on whom he projected his own evil intentions. Caliban responded by plotting against Prospero—not to gain his own freedom but to become the "foot-licker" of a new master (Mannoni 1964[1950]:105–106).

Mannoni's thesis had several implications. The settler mentalities were shaped in Europe rather than in the colonial experience, and the Europeans were drawn to the colony to resolve their own feelings of inferiority by expressing them in a desire for perfection, aggression, and escapism, and by projecting them onto the native peoples whom they dominated and controlled. The mentalities of the Malagasy were manifested in their dependence on the authority of the dead and already existed when the French colonizers arrived. In this view, culture was a function of personality, and

the other characteristic features of a colonial situation—domination of a mass by a minority, economic exploitation, paternalism, racialism, etc.— are either the direct outcome of the relationship between the two peoples, as, for instance, paternalism, or they are distinctly 'colonial' as a result of that relationship.

(Mannoni 1964[1950]:27)

Mannoni further argued that cultural change and acculturation could occur only if

...the personality of the native is first destroyed through uprooting, enslavement, and the collapse of social structure, and this is in fact what happened—with debatable success—in the older colonies [like the French Antilles, which had been a slave-based society].

(Mannoni 1964[1950]:27)

This meant isolating individuals from their natal communities and raising them in ways that allowed them to acquire a European personality or to superimpose one onto their Malagasy personality. If they repressed their Malagasy personality, they sought out the company of Europeans but were not accepted as their equals. These individuals were uncomfortable in both societies, and this only heightened their awareness of racial differences. Europeanized Malagasy who failed to integrate the European traits into their own personality grew increasingly resentful and hostile and were the ones who fomented and led the revolt (Mannoni 1964[1950]:74–80).

In the 1950s, the Martiniquan psychiatrist Frantz Fanon (1925–1961), whose views were shaped by the Algerian struggles for independence (1954–1962), also examined the psychopathological underpinnings and consequences of the colonial situation. He was influenced by and critical of Mannoni's work. In his view, there was "a connection between colonialism as a pathogenic social system and the incidence of mental disorders found among colonized peoples" (McCulloch 1983a:90). When the colonizers seized the productive forces and subordinated the indigenous population, conditions appeared that led to the distortion and deformation of the personality and culture of both the colonized community and the settlers (Fanon 1967[1952]:18; McCulloch 1983a:125). Fanon linked these conditions to the form racism took during different stages of colonial domination. When the colonists had just established their presence by force, they dehumanized native peoples and claimed that their subordination was rooted in some physiological or racial inferiority. After skilled indigenous peoples were incorporated into the lower levels of the state apparatus, the colonizers claimed that the subordination of the natives was due to the inferiority of their culture. In contrast to Mannoni, Fanon believed that racism, exploitation, personality, and other features of the colonial experience were forged in the colonial situation.

The colonial condition involved the suppression of the indigenous culture—the denigration of traditional foods, dress, music, practices, and beliefs that gave meaning to everyday life. This affected the indigenous middle classes; the peasants; and the beggars, prostitutes, and unemployed people, who in different ways constituted the *lumpenproletariat*. The members of the native middle class—the schoolteachers, policemen, government workers, and shopkeepers—accepted the devaluation of the indigenous culture in order to acquire and maintain their position in the colonial society. Tragically, they came to see themselves and their kin and neighbors through the eyes of the colonizer; the result was despair and self-loathing among the colonized middle classes. Alienated from the colonial society and mistrustful of its authority, the peasants and the *lumpenproletariat* withdrew into traditionalism in order to preserve some of the originality of their native culture; however, in the process, they were often unable to distinguish between the harmful aspects of the imperialist culture and those that might be beneficial—such as Western medicine—or they lacked the opportunity to make use of them. The cultural withdrawal of the peasants and the *lumpenproletariat* (criminals, vagrants, and unemployed people assumed not to know their collective interests) and the oppositional national cultural identity they maintained made them not the educated middle classes, as Mannoni claimed, but the potentially revolutionary classes in colonial situations (Fanon 1965[1959]:51, 1967[1961]:101).

In *The Wretched of the Earth*, Fanon described the role national culture played in colonized societies and, more importantly, in struggles for national liberation. While colonialism actively distorted and destroyed the cultural traditions of colonized peoples, nationalism rehabilitated the idea of a national consciousness, promoted social unity, and provided hope for the creation of a national culture in the future. Nationalism could trigger anti-colonial struggles; however, if national consciousness did not acquire a social dimension after liberation, there was a very real danger that the history of repression and poverty of the colonial era would be repeated, especially if the national middle classes seized power. In Fanon's (1967[1961]:122) view, they would act as a "...transmission line between the nation and a capitalism, rampant though camouflaged, which today puts on the mask of neo-colonialism."

Marxism in various forms also shaped postwar discussions of national liberation. Guinean agronomist Amílcar Cabral (1924–1973) was one of its most articulate, influential spokespersons (Chabal 1983; Chilcote 1991; McCulloch 1983b). In his view, people had a right to their own history. But imperialism, colonialism, and neo-colonialism interrupted the history of Third World peoples and impeded the formation of national consciousness and independence.[7] National liberation was the way these peoples could recover their interrupted history. Once they regained control over their mode of production, they could overcome the condition of being a people without history (Cabral 1979:143).

Cabral (1969:56–75) argued that class structures expressed the relation of various groups to the dominant pattern of ownership of productive wealth. The class structure of Guinea-Bissau was complex. There were four classes in the urban areas: a small class composed of high-ranking state officials and professionals; the petite bourgeoisie made up of low-level officials, shopkeepers, and wage-workers; workers without contracts—e.g. domestic servants or people employed in workshops; and *déclassés*—individuals from the petite bourgeoisie who did not work, peasants who had recently been uprooted from the countryside, and the *lumpenproletariat*. The class structures were different among the twenty tribal groups in the countryside, ranging from the semi-feudal, class-stratified Fula to the primitive communism of Balanta society, in which social stratification and ranking based on differences of wealth and privilege were absent, land was owned by the village, and day-to-day decisions were made by a council of elders.

Culture was the vital element in the process of national liberation because colonial systems repressed the cultural life of colonized peoples. Culture was a product of the relationship between people and nature, on the one hand, and among people, on the other. It was a result of the tensions within economic and political activities. It provided individuals with a sense of identity that told them who they were in their own social milieu and how they were similar to and different from other people. While culture could not be deduced solely from class relations, any change in those relations would alter not only an individual's sense of himself but also the whole system of identities that had been forged and reproduced (Cabral 1973: 40–45; McCulloch 1983b:84–86).

The colonial system had different effects on the cultures of the various urban classes and tribal societies. The peasants retained a vibrant cultural life because the colonizers had been unable to inhibit the cultural activity of the rural populations. As a result, their culture could serve as a basis for new forms of resistance to colonial domination. However, the tribal divisions in the countryside were a problem that could be overcome by proper political mobilization and organization. On the one hand, Fula chieftains resisted the idea of national liberation because it would undermine their authority in the cultural realm, but Fula peasants who were exploited by their chiefs cooperated with the nationalists. On the other hand, the peasants of the stateless ethnic groups, like the Balanta, readily joined the nationalists because they were acutely aware of how the colonial economy had already disrupted their own agricultural practices.

But the impetus for national liberation in Guinea-Bissau would come from the urban petite bourgeoisie because its members were most acutely aware of the limitations on their privileges in the colonial system:

> The *petite bourgeoisie* is a new class created by foreign domination and indispensable to the operation of colonial exploitation. It is located between the working masses of the countryside and of the cities on the one hand, and on the other the local representatives of the foreign ruling classes.... The *petite bourgeoisie* usually aspires to emulate the life of the foreign minority while at the same time reducing its links with the masses.... But it can never integrate itself into the foreign minority however successful it might have been at overcoming the colonial hurdles. It is a prisoner of the cultural and social contradictions imposed on it by the colonial reality, which defines it as a marginal or marginalised class.
>
> (Cabral quoted by Chabal 1983:174)

The weakness of the colonial system was that it engendered nationalism among the class it created to serve as collaborators. Thus, the major contradiction was between the colonized people as a nation-class and the colonial state. Nationalist movements required unity, and their leaders came from the urban petite bourgeoisie. The reason for this was the poorly developed, embryonic character of the native working class in Portuguese Guinea. For the revolution to succeed, the petite bourgeoisie had to be capable of committing suicide as a class in order to be reborn as revolutionary workers (Cabral 1969:89).

Peasant men and women who had emigrated to the cities and who had ties with the petite bourgeoisie were an important group in national liberation movements. They carried political mobilization into the rural areas from which they came—areas where cultural traditions remained strong, and the colonizers had been unable to inhibit the activity of the subject population (Chabal 1983:174–175). While the cultural traditions of the rural areas would be models for new economic, social, and political forms of resistance meant to challenge foreign domination, they would ultimately be crafted and implemented by the petite bourgeoisie (Chilcote 1991:28–31).

Nationalist writers realized the importance of national cultures. Fanon and Cabral, for instance, recognized that peasants had important roles to play in national liberation movements. In Fanon's view, peasants played a leading role; in Cabral's, they provided linkages, and their cultures provided models to the urban petite bourgeoisie; however, the latter was the leading class in revolutionary nationalist movements because its members were the most aware of how limited their privileges were in the colonial system. The creative capacities and revolutionary potential of peasants in national liberation movements will be examined further in the next section.

Once nationalist movements succeeded, they had to confront the effects of primordial attachments on the constitution of the new civic or national identity (Geertz 1963). These were the culturally assumed "givens" of social existence—ethnicity, tribe, race, language, region, culture, or religion—that shaped the search for identity and the demands that those identities be acknowledged publicly in the new states. These identities were forged by the same forces that buttressed movements for political independence. They could be a motor for progress, rising standards of living, and a more effective political order; at the same time, they could impede or block the creation of new civic identities and values. As a result, school systems, social statistics, dress, official histories, and the official symbols of public authority often became sites of contestation between the traditional givens of social existence and the newly constituted civic values of the state.

It is difficult to dissolve the tensions between primordial identities and civic politics. Nevertheless, some new states attempted to domesticate culturally prescribed identities instead of denigrating or denying them. Others sought to aggregate these "primordial" groups into larger, more diffuse units so that their governments could proceed without threatening the cultural frameworks that underpinned the issue of personal identity and without seriously distorting the political functioning of the state bureaucracy.

Rural Development, Social Revolution, and Peasant Communities

Rural communities were center stage in the postwar years. Historically, they had played key roles in underwriting industrial development in both capitalist and socialist countries. Policy makers recognized this centrality, especially after the Chinese Communists took power in 1949. The peasants were increasingly seen as potential forces of revolutionary change (Wolf 1969). This led the ruling classes and progressive forces in a number of countries—e.g. Guatemala, Bolivia, and South Korea—to recognize the importance of land reform and a more equitable distribution of income and wealth as necessary conditions for maintaining or transforming the existing balance of power in those states. It also meant that policy makers and social scientists had to pay renewed attention to peasant communities and how they were integrated into national structures.

Peasantries perplexed theorists of change, particularly those who predicted that they would eventually disappear as industrialization progressed. What perplexed the theorists was that peasant communities, the majority of the world's population, were not disappearing and that they remained a potent political force. In this context, the Agrarian Question became not merely an economic question but also

> a political question that was given a primarily economic answer. To know who the peasants were and how they would act in a political upheaval, or how they could be incorporated within an urban-directed socialist movement, one had to analyze their class position, their role and fate in capitalist development, their relation to the state.
>
> (Roseberry 1993:336)

In the process of analyzing rural class structures and their relation to national structures, both policy makers and social scientists realized that their analyses of rural life were deficient. Broadly speaking, there were four perspectives with varying degrees of compatibility. The dominant one was the "folk-urban continuum" that distinguished traditional from modern societies and viewed change in terms of increasing complexity resulting from the one-way transmission of culture from modern city-dwellers to the countryside. A second was U.S. anthropologist George Foster's (1913–2006) argument that peasants were the rural representatives of earlier national traditions whose inertia prevented them from industrializing, modernizing, and adopting the capitalist economic rationality of city-dwellers, which would ultimately lead to their dissolution (Foster 1967). A third built on Chayanov's ahistorical notions of peasant farm organization and non-capitalist economic structures, and sought to show how autonomous family farms generated peasant social structures at the local level and dual economies at the national level (Shanin 1971; Silverman 1979). A fourth focused on processes of rural class formation and social differentiation.

For example, U.S. anthropologist Robert Redfield (1956), who had studied rural communities in Mexico during the 1930s, did not use the concept of peasant until the mid-1950s. Up to that time, he referred to non-literate farming communities and tribal peoples in rural areas of Yucatán as "folk;" contrasted their lives and cultures with the values, beliefs, and social relations of city-dwellers; and placed them on what he described as the "folk-urban continuum" (Redfield 1962[1935]:176). He ignored the notion of rural class structures altogether. Sidney Mintz, a U.S. anthropologist schooled after World War II, agreed that typological distinctions were useful; however, he also observed that the rural proletarians working on the henequen plantations that formed the backbone of the Yucatecan economy were not a social type discussed by Redfield. In fact, they stood outside the folk-urban continuum altogether, even though they constituted more than half of the labor force. They constituted a form of industrial organization that was an integral feature of modern, industrial society. They were a social class whose existence was "predicated on the existence of other classes who own the instruments of production, provide work opportunities, pay the wages, and sell the commodities to be bought" (Mintz 1953:141). They were molded by the same social forces that shaped urban industrial societies, and their connections with wider structures needed to be investigated empirically, comparatively, and historically (Mintz 1973, 1974; Rubin 1959; Wolf and Mintz 1957).

U.S. anthropologist Eric Wolf noted that there were diverse types of peasant communities in Latin America (Wolf 1955, 1956, 1957). There were closed corporate communities whose members were agricultural producers who retained effective control over their lands and were concerned with subsistence rather than agriculture as a business requiring continual reinvestment. They were often characterized as "Indian." The persistence of Indian cultural forms both shaped and depended on the maintenance and reproduction of the structural identity of those communities. Their members defended the traditional rights and customs that perpetuated those subsistence imperatives and usages that protected them from memories of famine, risk, and the market. A second type consisted of the open communities whose members engaged in the production of coffee, cocoa, and other cash crops for the market. Fifty to seventy-five percent of their produce was sold in the market. As a result, their livelihoods were subject to fluctuations in market demand for the crops they grew, and they continually needed capital to invest in their businesses. The landowning middle peasants of the open communities had continuous interactions with the outside through the capitalist market. Their fortunes were tied to the larger market-based structures of which they were a part.

Wolf recognized other types of peasant communities: those that produced entirely for the market; those that sold their goods in local markets; those whose holdings were residual bits of earlier large-scale organizations; foreign colonists; and those that lived on the margins of capitalist markets and sold portions of their crops to obtain goods they could not produce for themselves. He viewed peasants as rural cultivators whose surplus production was transferred to a politically dominant group as tribute or rent. He distinguished peasants from farmers, for whom agriculture was a business enterprise, and from tribal peoples, for whom agriculture was about subsistence and surplus to be exchanged with other groups (Wolf 1966:2–10; Mintz 1973).

Wolf and Mintz built on the Marxist tradition of class analysis. They did not view all peasantries as exploited producers left over from some pre-capitalist system of production nor see them as a class that was disappearing in the wake of the expansion of capitalist social relations. They argued instead that the class structures and social relations of the more open-ended types of peasantries and rural proletarian communities were forged in the context of the expansion of capitalist market relations. They distinguished the theoretical underpinnings of their work from other approaches to understanding peasant societies. Their work can also be seen as a critique of the other approaches.

The social upheavals in Africa, Asia, and Latin America sparked renewed interest in the relationships between peasants and social revolution. These efforts were important because they paid close attention to the historical specificity and particularities of different cases at the same time that they attempted to provide empirically grounded generalizations about peasant wars.

An early analysis was the Pakistani sociologist Hamsa Alavi's (1921–2003) comparative study of "the respective rôles of the so-called *middle peasants* and *poor peasants* and the pre-conditions that ... are necessary for the revolutionary mobilization of the *poor peasant*" (Alavi 1965:243, emphasis in the original). Alavi argued that the peasantries in Russia, China, and India were internally differentiated and that rich, middle, and poor peasants did not stand in a single hierarchical order but rather belonged to three different sectors of the rural economy. In the first sector, the land owned by landlords was worked by sharecroppers—i.e. poor peasants. In the second, middle peasants owned the land they cultivated and did not rely on the labor of others. The third sector was constituted by capitalist farmers—i.e. rich peasants—who owned substantial amounts of land and relied on the waged work of a rural proletariat rather than sharecroppers or tenants (Alavi 1965:243–244).

Alavi concluded that the poor peasants were initially the least militant of the peasant classes because they and their families were totally dependent on particular landlords for their livelihood and were often enmeshed in paternalistic patron-client relations with them. However,

> this backwardness of the [poor] peasantry, rooted as it is in objective dependence, is only a relative and not an absolute condition. In a revolutionary situation, when anti-landlord and anti-rich-peasant sentiment is built up by, say, the militancy of the middle peasants, his morale is raised and he is ready to respond to calls to action....
> The middle peasants, on the other hand, are initially the most militant element of the peasantry, and they can be a powerful ally of the proletarian movement in the countryside, especially in generating the initial impetus

of peasant revolution. But their social perspective is limited by their class position. When the movement in the countryside advances to a revolutionary stage they may move away from the revolutionary movement unless their fears are allayed and they are drawn into a process of co-operative endeavor.

(Alavi 1965:275)

Alavi argued that the middle peasants were initially the leading force and then the main force of revolutionary change in the countryside and further that once the success of the revolution was no longer in doubt, their position was taken over by the poor peasants, whose revolutionary energies were set in motion by the militancy of the landowning middle peasants.

In *Peasant Wars of the Twentieth Century*, Wolf (1969:295) remarked that the "peasant rebellions of the twentieth century are no longer simple responses to local problems.... They are ... parochial reactions to major social dislocations, set in motion by major societal changes" associated with the spread of Western capitalism, markets, and capitalist economic rationality. The intrusion of capitalism upset traditional social relations and ways of making a living as well as the balance of force. As peasants lost control over their lands and were transformed into "economic actors, independent of prior social commitments to kin and neighbors," a crisis in the exercise of power emerged (Wolf 1969:279). Peasant revolutions were one possible response to crises provoked by social change and sometimes crystallized in these circumstances.

These revolutions, in Wolf's view, were launched by landholding peasants who had material and organizational advantages that sharecropping poor peasants and rural proletarians lacked. Because they controlled the disposal of their crops and were outside the direct control of landlords, they were neither as poor nor as vulnerable to repression as the poor peasants and rural waged workers. It was the middle peasants and tenants in villages outside the direct control of landlords, as well as the free peasants in frontier areas where landlords and state authorities exercised indirect and/or intermittent control at best, who possessed tactical advantages during these transitional phases. Furthermore, the middle peasant who remained on the land while he sent his children to town to work was also more exposed to the influences of the urban proletariat. As a result, he became the transmitter of urban unrest and political ideas. It was his attempt "...to remain traditional which makes him revolutionary" (Wolf 1969:292).

For Wolf, the battlefield of peasant revolutions in the twentieth century was society itself:

Where the peasantry has successfully rebelled against the established order--under its own banner and with its own leaders--it was sometimes able to reshape the social structure of the countryside closer to its heart's desires; but it did not lay hold of the state, of the cities which house the centers of control, of the strategic nonagricultural resources of the society....

Thus a peasant rebellion which takes place in a complex society already caught up in commercialization and industrialization tends to be self-limiting, and, hence, anachronistic.

(Wolf 1969: 294)

The peasant's role in these revolutions is both tragic and hopeful: tragic in the sense that "his efforts to undo a grievous present only usher in a vaster, more uncertain future" and hopeful to the extent that "theirs is the party of humanity" (Wolf 1969:301–302).

U.S. political sociologist Barrington Moore (1913–2005) focused on the patterns of social relations that facilitated or suppressed peasant rebellion during the transformation from agrarian to industrial society. His thesis was that "the ways in which the landed upper classes and the peasants reacted to the challenge of commercial agriculture were decisive factors in determining the political outcome" (Moore 1966:xvii). He saw three possible trajectories of change. Parliamentary democracies—England, France, and the United States—had their beginnings in circumstances in which the peasants were unable to resist the efforts of the landed upper classes to promote commercialized agriculture and to benefit along with capitalist merchants and industrialists from the operation of markets in the towns and countryside. Fascism had its roots in societies—Germany and Japan—in which capitalist groups were unable to challenge the landlord class that held state power, and the social structure of the peasantry prevented tenants, sharecroppers, and smallholders from mounting effective opposition. Communism—Russia and China—began in countries where the capitalist merchant and industrial classes were weak, and their repression and exploitation of the peasants could not stem the growth of peasant movements and rebellions. In Moore's (1966:477–479) view,

> The most important causes of peasant revolutions have been the absence of a commercial revolution in agriculture led by the landed upper classes and the concomitant survival of peasant social institutions into the modern era when they are subject to new stresses and strains. Where the peasant community survives, as in Japan, it must remain closely linked to the dominant class in the countryside if revolution is to be avoided. Hence an important contributing cause of peasant revolution has been the weakness of the institutional links binding peasant society to the upper classes, together with the exploitative character of this relationship. Part of the general syndrome has been the regime's loss of the support of an upper class of wealthy peasants because these have begun to go over to more capitalist modes of cultivation and to establish their independence against an aristocracy seeking to maintain its position through the intensification of traditional obligations, as in eighteenth-century France. When these conditions have been absent or reversed, peasant revolts have failed to break out or have been easily suppressed.

The great agrarian bureaucracies of royal absolutism including China, have been especially liable to the combination of factors favoring peasant revolution. Their very strength enables them to inhibit the growth of an independent commercial and manufacturing class.... By taming the bourgeoisie, the crown reduces the impetus toward further modernization.... Furthermore, an agrarian bureaucracy, through its heavy demands for taxes, risks driving the peasants into an alliance with local élites in the towns.... Finally, to the extent that it takes over the protective and judicial functions of the locally residing overlord, royal absolutism weakens the crucial links that the peasants have to the upper classes.

Like Wolf and Alavi, Moore examined the shifting relations within the entire class structure rather than those that affected mainly the rural classes. He argued that peasant social structures did not always underpin effective forms of resistance. However, in the route leading to communism, he asserted that the forces promoting the development of commercial agriculture and labor-repressive forms of agricultural exploitation were weak and that peasants were able to mobilize and collaborate to varying degrees in affecting structural change.

Transitions between Capitalism and Socialism and Vice Versa

Events after World War II showed that there was no single road to socialism and that structurally different forms of society referred to themselves as socialist or on the road to socialism. They also clarified what was involved in the transitions to socialism. French commentators Étienne Balibar (1942–) and Charles Bettelheim (1913–2006) conceptualized transitions in terms of social formations manifesting the co-existence and interaction of several modes of production (Balibar 1970[1965]; Bettelheim 1975[1968]). While the social relations associated with each mode of production contributed to the constitution of the whole, the production relations and forms of appropriation and distribution of the dominant one structured the totality. Besides the dominant mode, some were residual with relations that were dissolving, and others were emergent with social relations that were crystallizing.

Bettelheim coined the term "economy of transition" to conceptualize those moments in social formation when there is a relative balance of force among the modes of production or when they exist in some quasi-equilibrium. In his view, these circumstances provide the conditions for the emergence or beginning of a new mode of production and the erosion of the others. The dissolution of the dominant mode of production merely creates the conditions for the appearance or beginnings of a new mode; it does not guarantee that a new social formation will emerge. The conditions for transformation and transition are determined by the totality of economic, social, political, and ideological relations as well as the forms of social and cultural consciousness associated with the society. The economy of transition, for Balibar, involved the difficult problem of periodization. In his view, history and the dynamics of social formations were opposite sides of the same coin. We understand the former from the flow of events conceived as a linear progression and changing balances of force; we understand the latter by analyzing what is happening beneath the surface in order to comprehend the whole. The totality of these economies or moments of transition are historically contingent, multi-leveled unities of contradictions characterized by the interaction and interpenetration of forces and relations from different levels, the co-existence of opposing principles that shape interaction, positive and negative feedback, and spontaneous activity. The various elements of the totality as well as the totality itself are continually changing, though they are doing so at different rates. At any given moment, one element might appear fixed in relation to the others, and new elements appear, while others wither. The effect is that the economies of transition are unstable and fragile as various class blocs struggle for hegemony.

Bettelheim distinguished two forms of transition. One involved the radical transformation of the capitalist mode of production to socialism through upheavals in production and class relations, and the replacement of one status apparatus by another. The other was more limited and occurred in the former colonies and countries on the periphery of the industrial capitalist states. Here, the transitions were more limited in the sense that they had to deal with various forms of capitalism, neo-imperialism, neo-colonialism, and socialism. Thus, it was already clear empirically that some Third World states were following paths of development that were neither capitalist nor communist and that the social changes taking place within them did not mirror the economy of transition in the wake of the Russian Revolution or in China and Yugoslavia. In a phrase, there was no general theory of transition.

Discussion

The late 1940s to the late 1960s was a time of crisis. It was also a time of sustained economic growth in the capitalist countries. In the years immediately following the war, the United States made loans to the capitalist countries of Europe and Japan to rebuild their economies; to provide markets for the commodities produced in American factories; and to provide full employment as long as the rates of accumulation, profits, and investment remained high. U.S. corporations produced steadily growing arrays of mass-produced goods on assembly lines in factories that combined expensive machinery with workers who specialized in completing single steps or tasks in complicated production processes. There were more than 600 strikes in 1946; the number declined to a handful after the anti-labor Taft-Hartley Act (1947) was passed, overriding a presidential veto, and multi-year contracts were introduced. Significant differences remained between the income levels of union and non-union workers, and pockets of grinding poverty persisted across the country. Cracks were already appearing in the system by the mid-1950s as (1) U.S. corporations intensified their confrontation with unions over wages, mechanization, and workplace conditions; and (2) corporations in Western Europe and Japan began to produce commodities for export—cameras, automobiles, or telecommunications equipment—that competed for markets in the United States and Third World countries. Factories in

Third World countries were often newer and had more efficient equipment than the ones built ten to forty years earlier in the United States. Competition increased during the late 1950s and 1960s, and, concomitantly, the market share of U.S. corporations slowly declined, as did rates of accumulation, profit, and investment in updating new facilities.

These events, of course, were closely tied to the Cold War, decolonization, and the emergence of Third World countries that aligned with neither the capitalist West nor the communist Soviet Union. The amount of foreign aid the United States provided to countries in Africa, Latin America, and South Asia was miniscule in comparison to the aid packages provided to Western Europe and Japan after the war. What U.S. policy makers advocated, following the advice of both modernization and dependency theorists, was that Third World countries should industrialize; they should launch industries, like textiles, that produced for national markets and reduced their reliance on imports. These were called import substitution industries. While they attracted migrants from rural areas to cities in search of work, they did not create many jobs. The markets for their goods, often inefficiently or poorly produced, were limited, and the benefits and costs of this kind of industrialization were unevenly distributed across the society. A few countries in East Asia—South Korea, Taiwan, and Singapore—successfully broke into the export market in the 1960s.

This international system was breaking down by the late 1960s with the rise of economic competition; the declining role of U.S. hegemony in the world political economy; the end of fixed exchange rates and the growing importance of finance capital; the devaluation of U.S. currency in the 1970s; massive increases in the cost of raw materials, like oil; de-industrialization in the industrial states of the Northeast and Great Lakes region of the United States; the slowdown in accumulation and investment; large differences in wages and standards of living between capitalist and non-capitalist countries; and the ongoing resistance of Third World countries to capitalist expansion and influence. We will examine the development of this crisis further in the next chapter.

Notes

1 For a more detailed and mathematical discussion of the historical development of economic growth theory, see Michio Morishima's (1969) *Theory of Economic Growth*.

2 Steward's was not the only evolutionary theory of economic growth that flourished after World War II (Leacock 1982). Australian archaeologist and socialist V. Gordon Childe (1892–1957) and U.S. anthropologists Alexander Lesser (1902–1982) and Leslie White (1900–1975) had already elaborated on evolutionary theories of social development before or during the war. Childe (1951[1936], 1942) explained change in terms of social, political, and economic institutions, and the role they played in underwriting technological innovations (Trigger 1989:250–263). Lesser (1985[1939]:90) argued that

> the difficulty involved [in explaining them] should not blind us to the actual existence of sequences of precondition and subsequent condition, however limited the character of the determining relation of one to the other, on the basis of present knowledge.

White (1943) argued that culture was the extrasomatic ways and means that humanity employed in the struggle for survival; it was the way in which its members captured and harnessed energy. Agriculture and stock raising, which greatly increased the amount of energy that could be harnessed, provide an impetus for the further development of property relations and the rise of private property (Carneiro 1981; Peace 1993).

3 Anthropologists focused their criticism on three aspects of cultural evolutionary theory. First, they questioned the functionalist assumptions related to the integrity of the economic core and the presumed associations of given technologies with particular forms of social and political organization. Second, they demanded greater specificity in relation to the economic and political spheres of particular culture types. Third, they challenged Steward's separation of cultural process from history and advocated, instead, studies that synthesized and explained the historical specificity of cultural and social forms in particular areas.

4 The chronic under- and unemployment of the colonial era spilled over into the post-independence period. For Patnaik, the private and state investments in agriculture during the Green Revolution of the 1960s fueled commodity production for an internal market, proletarianizing a portion of the reserve army of labor in some regions and not in others.

5 Belgian historian Henri Pirenne (1862–1935) crystallized the mainstream account of the decline of feudalism and the rise of capitalism in Western Europe during and after World War II (Havighurst 1958; Pirenne 1914, 1939, 1952[1925]). His thesis was unchallenged during the inter-war years. Briefly, he argued that (1) the unity of the world was broken by the Arab conquest of the Eastern Mediterranean, North Africa, and Spain in the seventh and early eighth centuries; (2) this conquest ruptured the ties of Western Europe to the Mediterranean world and turned it into an economic backwater as foreign trade collapsed by the end of the eighth century; (3) fortresses, abbeys, monasteries, and noble residences were the only non-agricultural settlements in Western Europe during the ninth century; (4) the re-establishment of commercial ties toward the end of the tenth century led to the formation of towns as artisans and peasants fleeing from the countryside—i.e. escaping the existing social structures— established suburbs near the non-agricultural settlements; (5) the towns relied increasingly on manufacturing and export for their revenues; and (6) the towns become increasingly more specialized—those in Flanders produced fine cloth, while those in Northern Italy engaged in moneylending and banking activities.

6 During the civil rights struggles of the 1960s in the United States, various groups— black separatists, some Puerto Rican *independentistas*, Native Americans, and Chicanos of La Raza Unida—made cultural nationalist claims, which also appealed largely to the more class-conscious petite bourgeoisie, which was constituted in part because of those struggles (Marable 1995:194–195).

7 Neo-colonialism in Cabral's (1969:73) view was the strategy of a post-World War II phase of imperialism characterized by monopoly capital and multinational corporations:

> Neocolonialism is at work on two fronts—in Europe as well as in the underdeveloped countries. Its current framework in the underdeveloped countries is the policy of aid, and one of the essential aims of this policy is to create a false bourgeoisie to put a brake on the revolution and to enlarge the possibility of the petty bourgeoisie as a neutralizer of the revolution: at the same time it invests capital in France, Italy, Belgium, England, and so on. In our opinion, the aim of this is to stimulate the growth of a workers' aristocracy, to enlarge the field of action of the petty bourgeoisie so as to block the revolution.

6

The World in Crisis, 1970–2017

Crises are decisive moments, turning points, in the flow of history. Severe crises have racked the world's population for more than a hundred years. The economic crashes of the last fifty years have been as deep and widespread as the Great Depression of the 1930s. Economic growth has yet to reappear in much of Africa, Latin America, and large swaths of Asia. In North America and Europe, the motors have been repeatedly started, have sputtered at much lower rates than before, and have stopped only to be re-ignited, sputter, and stop again. What distinguishes these crises from previous ones is that they appear continuous rather than cyclical, global rather than limited to particular countries, and both longer and more intense (Mészáros 1995:680–681). Crises occur at different levels and have manifested themselves in various ways in the last seventy years: more than two hundred and fifty wars; decolonization and neo-colonialism; hundreds of banking problems; disruptions of credit and markets, and financial recessions; levels of income inequality unseen for a century; and environmental degradation. Today, several billion people are destitute; several billion more have been driven to the brink of abject poverty; and tens of millions more have been dispossessed or have fled from their native lands seeking survival, refuge, and uncertain futures elsewhere. Crises have shaped their life experiences; they shaped those of earlier generations and will continue to do so in the future.

Crises at one level of society—such as political or economic—have ramifications as they impinge on and interact with other levels. They disrupt the existing social order and any illusions of social stability they create. Their effects are internalized and hence affect other aspects of a person's daily life, although they do so differently in different times and places. In other words, a war is not just a war, and losing a home to foreclosure is not just a financial or legal action. Crises are felt profoundly in myriad ways. They provoke strong emotions about how people view themselves, experience those around them, and understand their circumstances. These turning points can promote feelings of despair, helplessness, or acquiescence; at the same time, they can clarify and enhance accurate understanding of that world or empower the rise of social movements protesting its wretchedness. Thus, crises can simultaneously be experienced as breakdowns or potential breakthroughs (O'Connor 1985).

The question is why are there crises? The short answer for mainstream commentators is that crises are consequences of external events or processes that are beyond the control of society. These commentators also believe that, given enough time and experience, technocrats and policy makers will gain control over the uncontrollable through growing understanding, new technologies, or some combination of both. Economist Anwar Shaikh wrote succinctly about what some highly regarded economists have said about crises, business cycles, and depressions since 1970:

> ... just before the start of the Stagflation Crisis of 1970, the enormously influential MIT economist and Nobel Laureate Paul Samuelson famously said that the business cycle was a thing of the past.... In 2003, only a few years before the 2007 Global Crisis, [Robert Lucas, another Nobel laureate in economics] ... declared that the 'central problem of depression prevention has been solved'.... In 2004, Ben Bernanke, Chairman of the Federal Reserve from 2006 to 2014 but at the time only a member of [its] Board of Governors, 'said ... that prosperity would be everlasting because the state and its central banking branch had perfected the art of modulating the business cycle and smoothing the natural bumps and grinds of free market capitalism'.
>
> (Shaikh 2016:728)

For those who do not subscribe to mainstream views, crises are inherent in the formation of global capitalism. The processes involved are not only contingent and tendential but also rife with contradictions. Many years ago, Mao Zedong (1965[1937]) distinguished between the primary and secondary contradictions of any social formation; the complex articulation of the contradictions; and their overdetermination in the sense that their outcomes, consequences, or resolutions are not simply shaped by the primary contradiction. He recognized differences between the primary and secondary aspects of contradictions and asked: Given the balance of force at these crucial turning points in social formation, which contradictions are more or less likely to be reproduced on an expanded scale? He also pointed out that the contradictions in a given social formation at a particular moment are unevenly developed.

Ngai-Ling Sum and Bob Jessop (2013:249–251) have argued that the inherent contradictions of capitalist social formations have been reproduced and mediated through institutional and spatio-temporal fixes and policies.

The contradictions and their associated dilemmas may be handled through

- *hierarchization* (treating some contradictions as more important than others);
- *prioritization* of one aspect of a contradiction or dilemma over the other aspect;
- *spatialization* (relying on different scales and sites of action to address one or another contradiction or aspect, or displacing the problems associated with the neglected aspect to a marginal or liminal space, place or scale); and
- *temporalization* (alternating regularly between treatment of different aspects or focusing one-sidedly on a subset of contradictions, dilemmas, or aspects until it becomes urgent to address what has hitherto been neglected).

(Sum and Jessop 2013:249–250)

Thus, there is variation between the configurations of different capitalist social formations at any given moment. These reflect differences in (1) the balance of force and (2) the weights attributed to the fixes and policies being employed.

A second question is how have the inherent crises and contradictions of capitalist social formations been "managed"? By the mid-1970s, European commentators were conceptualizing this issue in terms of regimes of capital accumulation in the international economy (Aglietta 1979[1976]). They portrayed a regime of capital accumulation as a relatively stable relation that was reproduced for a limited period of time at the level of the internal economy. The form of regulation was a historically contingent network of institutions and practices that ensured the reproduction of the capitalist property relations that guided the regime of accumulation in particular national economies. Each national economy had its own distinctive mode of development, depending on how it was inserted into the international division of labor. They

> … decomposed the capital relation into a series of structural forms, each of which has its own characteristics and dilemmas, requiring specific forms of regulation. These are conventionally described as [1] the *wage relation* (individual and social wage, wage form, and lifestyle); [2] the *enterprise form and competition* (internal organization, source of profits, forms of competition, ties among enterprises and/or banks); [3] *money and credit* (form and emission, banking and credit systems, allocation of capital to production, national currencies and world monies, and monetary regimes); [4] the *state* (institutionalized compromise between capital and labour, forms of state intervention); and [5] *international regimes* (trade, investment, monetary and political arrangements that link national economies, national states, and the world system). The choice of these forms probably reflects the institutional configuration of Atlantic Fordism in a specific world-historical context rather than a generic set of forms applicable to all accumulation regimes.
>
> (Sum and Jessop 2013:251, italics added)[1]

The hierarchization, prioritization, spatialization, and temporalization of fixes for the inherent contradictions in capitalist social formations "secur[e] the conditions for [the] dominance [of particular historic blocs or class fractions]… and giv[e] the appearance that contradictions had been harmonized, social conflict moderated, and the conditions for permanent prosperity established" (Sum and Jessop 2013:253).

While none of the contradictions or fixes are particularly novel, what is new since the 1990s is (1) the intensification and extension of the linkages between them, (2) the ways in which they have become and are becoming articulated, (3) the ways in which they and other circumstances and conditions push and pull each other in all directions, and (4) the strategies they engender and their consequences—e.g. the quest for high incomes, increasing inequality, accumulating trade deficits, exploding levels of indebtedness, and overproduction (Bello 2010; Duménil and Lévy 2011:34). In this view, contradictions operating unevenly at multiple levels and different temporal and spatial scales are becoming synchronous, more frequent, more widespread, and more deeply felt (Albo 2003).

From a slightly different perspective, the current crises have fueled nationalist, sexist, homophobic, racist, misogynistic, xenophobic, genocidal (ethnic cleansing), and anti-immigrant sentiments around the world. They have also empowered the rise of fundamentalist and fascist movements in Africa, Europe, Latin America, Asia, the Middle East, and the United States.

For critics of mainstream thinking about current conditions in the world, the questions are not whether there will be another crisis but rather when and where it will occur and how severe it will be. While the current crises have some new features, they are rooted in old, familiar ones, such as imperialism, the accumulation of capital, the National Question, or the role of the state as an agent of change.

An Overview of Social Formation in an Age of Continual Crises

The United States emerged from World War II with unprecedented structural dominance in the global political economy: Its industries and financial institutions were the only ones intact. The political goals of its governing class after the war were (1) to rebuild the capitalist economies of Europe and Japan, (2) to eliminate their overseas empires, (3) to minimize the consequences of decolonization and assert or reinforce its influence in those areas, (4) to open or secure new markets and sources of raw materials, (5) to contain or curtail the influence and expansion of communism at home and abroad, (6) to construct domestic and overseas markets for consumer goods, (7) to create a favorable climate for investment and capital accumulation, (8) to preserve its hegemonic position in the international financial system, and (9) to prevent domestic civil unrest by criminalizing leftist political parties and radical union leaders.

Through the Marshall Plan and other aid programs from 1948 to 1953, the U.S. government gave $20 billion (roughly $400 billion today) to the capitalist countries of Western Europe and Japan, and to strategic countries (e.g. the Philippines, South Korea, Taiwan, India, Turkey, and Yugoslavia) to rebuild their industrial economies, remove trade barriers, restore prosperity, and prevent the spread of communism. The recipients used most of the total to purchase raw materials, semi-manufactured goods, food, fertilizer, machines, vehicles, equipment, and fuel from U.S. firms; they spent the remainder on rebuilding their industries and infrastructures. Many of their industries were effectively rebuilt by the mid-1950s; their populations had jobs and money to purchase goods manufactured by U.S. firms, and, at the same time, their exports were beginning to compete with U.S. firms in domestic and overseas markets (Brenner 2006:453–483; Kolko and Kolko 1972).

Large sectors of the U.S. economy shifted from wartime production to the manufacture of consumer goods that had been in short supply for nearly a decade. The pent-up demand for motor vehicles, housing, foodstuffs, and other essentials as well as for new, mass-produced electronic innovations, like television sets, sustained high levels of production, investment, and rates of profit. This supported *full employment*, with high wages in many sectors. At the same time, wartime levels of production continued in some economic sectors (weapons, warships, and aircraft—what President Eisenhower called the military-industrial complex) to protect American overseas interests and investments, to contain the spread of communism, and to influence the kinds of political regimes appearing in the wake of decolonization. The federal government contributed to this era of rapid growth: It was a major investor; a consumer of construction materials (e.g. the interstate highway system and racially segregated suburbs and inner cities); and the underwriter of social welfare and educational programs, such as the GI Bill, which provided honorably discharged veterans with tuition and living expenses to complete their education, low-interest loans, and one year of unemployment benefits while they transitioned to civilian life. These provided consumers with the cash or credit to purchase the commodities they required (credit cards first appeared in 1951). The federal and many state governments also curtailed the rights of unions to strike; this created a labor-capital "peace" involving relatively few strikes for the next two decades in exchange for regular cost-of-living wage increases. This strategy reinforced the dominant position of capital in the labor-capital relation and provided a secure environment for investment and capital accumulation.

All of these measures taken together is the background of modernization theory. Modernization theory would provide the ideological and theoretical underpinnings of U.S. aid policies toward former colonies and the politically independent but "backward" or "traditional" countries of Latin America, Asia, Africa, and the Middle East (Gerschenkron 1962[1952]). In this view, modern countries exhibited the liberal ideals of egalitarianism, secularism, rationality, and progressivism. They promoted democratic ideals, scientific knowledge, technological innovation, and the welfare and well-being of their citizens. They were economically advanced; were industrialized; had high rates of literacy; were open to change; and would pursue new goals set and promoted by a centralized, interventionist state (e.g. the Kennedy administration's goal of sending a man to moon by the end of the 1960s). Moreover, they were not communist, and they were different from their polar opposites: those traditional or economically backward societies that would come to be known as the Third World in the mid-1950s. In a phrase, the modernization theorists were advocates of Enlightenment.

The advocates of modernization theory, both in and outside of the government, drew sharp distinctions between modern societies, on the one hand, and those that were not industrialized, on the other. Modernization theorists also homogenized the vast differences that existed among the less-industrialized countries. They were concerned with remaking the world in the image of the United States, and the question was how to accomplish this goal. Was the driver of change industrializing; creating a consumer society; Westernizing; or working with local political-economic elites who, for their own reasons, were willing to cooperate with U.S. political and economic interests? For the modernization theorists, the processes of economic growth, political development, and becoming modern became virtually synonymous. The evolution of traditional society into modern society, the progression from one stage of social development to the next, was uni-directional and linear. As the processes unfolded, the societies of the world would converge, becoming increasingly similar to one another (and the United States) as they pursued the open-ended modernity that marked Hegel's "end of history."

Modernization theory had its greatest impact in the early and mid-1960s. Its influence waned in the late 1960s largely because of mounting political and economic crises in the United States and stubbornly effective military and political opponents abroad (Gilman 2003; Hudson 2003; Saad-Filho 2005). Symptoms of the contradictions and emerging crises included various counterculture movements; the resurgence of eugenics and culture of poverty arguments; growing inflation and unemployment; increased competition from foreign capitalist firms; overproduction and falling rates of profit; the financial shocks of the late 1960s and early 1970s; the devaluation of the U.S. dollar and falling standards of living; the scarcity and high cost of living; the failure of import-substitution industrialization projects, especially in Latin America; and soaring rates of debt in those socialist and Third World countries that imported oil. Modernization theorists of the 1950s and 1960s advocated state-sponsored programs aimed at creating the conditions for economic growth—such as infrastructure or urban renewal in the United States or import-substitution industrialization in Latin America. Their proposals and policies were rooted in Keynesian theory. The implementation of monetarist and neoclassical economic policies in the 1970s ended state support for such programs. The states, both in the United States and abroad, implemented austerity and structural adjustment; privatized infrastructural, social welfare, and educational programs; supported direct foreign investment; reduced government spending and debt levels; tightened the money supply and limited the availability of credit; and deregulated the economy. In other words, the policies implemented by various state and local governments in the United States as well as by the World Bank and International Monetary Fund in the late 1960s and early 1970s were in direct opposition to the ones that prevailed during the preceding two or three decades.

The breakdown of Keynesian-influenced policies in the United States coincided with the end of developmental states in the Third World and the waning influence of modernization theory. While the latter withered, it would not die. Questions posed by policy makers with increasing frequency in the 1970s and 1980s were: Were growth and development desirable policy goals in a world with diminished expectations, a growing population, and environmental destruction? Might no-growth policies be more realistic? Did the gains conferred by modernization and modernity offset the loss of community? Nils Gilman (2003:251–252) described this as the postmodern turn and

> ... the return of an old dialectic in Western thought, which might be concisely described as a back and forth between Enlightenment and romanticism. Indeed, the quarrel that the romantics had with the

Enlightenment bears uncanny resemblance to the quarrel that many critics during the 1970s and 1980s would have with the liberal modernists. For both the romantics of the early nineteenth century and for the neo-romantic critics of the late 1960s through the 1980s, the problem was that their opponents had too much fondness for uniformity, and too little appreciation for the losses entailed by the capitalist demolition of traditional lifeways. This explains claims that by the mid-1970s, modernization theory resembled warmed-over nineteenth-century social evolutionism, bereft of any of the nineteenth century's skepticism about progress.

Many modernization theorists changed their views about growth and development in the 1980s. Conceptually, it is possible to discern half a dozen or more successor currents in mainstream thought. These are some of the more common currents:

- *Neoliberalism* (the Washington Consensus) is concerned with trade liberalization, competitive exchange rates, deregulation of the financial sector, privatizing state enterprises, cutting marginal tax rates, avoiding large fiscal deficits, the liberalization of foreign direct investment, weakening trade unions, individuation, and individual responsibility.
- *Globalization* focuses on innovations in transportation and communications (space-time compression); the circulation, movement, or flow of people, culture, and goods; the presumed erosion of the power of national states by transnational forms of governance; and denials of the convergence of industrialized and industrializing states. It is the transition from traditional and modern forms of social life, conceptualized in terms of society or nation-states, to postmodern forms, viewed in terms of the hybridization created by flows between different spaces.
- *Postmodernism* rejects structural-functionalism and the totalizing theoretical narratives of the 1960s and 1970s, like the ones modernization theorists promoted a few years earlier; it embraces culture, thick description, the resurgence of area studies, and the meticulous details of the particular, which had previously been scorned as mindless empiricism or historicism. As a result, many commentators on the postmodern condition accept the idea of hybridity.
- *Post-Socialism and the End of History.* In this view, the dissolution of the socialist states in Eastern Europe in 1989–1991 marked the end of communism, the end of the Cold War, the passing of a particular period of postwar history, and "the endpoint of mankind's ideological evolution and the universalization of Western liberal democracy as the final form of human government" (Fukuyama 1989). It also witnesses the reappearance of *convergence theory*, in which the end of history is viewed as unimpeded global capitalism in which the whole world is industrializing and differences in the political, social, and cultural realms are being erased.

- *Neoconservativism* remains committed to the values of modernity—rationality, the authority of science, and the maintenance of social order but not necessarily social welfare. Its advocates increasingly saw the modernization process as the problem because they deem that developmental states will not be able to contain cultural contradictions and, simultaneously, to maintain social and political order.
- *Communitarianism* questions whether individualism and rationality are the most important features of modernity and the modernization process. Its proponents argue that modernization has eroded the social fabric of communities and, hence, weakened their traditional ability to provide the goods and services needed by their members.

Commentators—whose views are rooted in Marxian thought about crises, competition, and cycles—have different explanations of what happened and why, and what will happen next. One current looks at the interrelations of profit, investment, and debt (Roberts 2009, 2016). Many firms accumulated capital during World War II. Some of this was invested in new equipment and plants during the conversion from war-time to peace-time production. Technological innovations were numerous and profitable in the wake of the war. With nearly full employment (a deceptive term), pent-up demand, and readily available credit, an enormous market emerged. The rise in profit rates was squeezed initially by the demands of organized labor and then increasingly by competition from the re-industrialized capitalist economies for shares in both domestic and foreign markets. Profit rates began to fall in the late 1950s and bottomed in the early 1980s. They rose again, but not to the previous levels, and then bottomed again with the Dot.Com bust of 2000–2002. After a brief resurgence, they fell to even greater depths during the Great Recession of 2007–2012.

The profits of capitalist firms are based on the things their employees make and the services they provide during a specified period of time (usually quarterly or annually) minus the costs of doing business—e.g. maintaining factories, buying raw materials, and paying workers. The workers create the surplus value. The aim of these companies is always to make the largest profits and to extract the greatest amount of surplus value possible given the historical circumstances in which they operate. They have relatively few ways to do this: (1) introduce more productive machinery and efficient forms of work organization while employing the same or fewer numbers of workers—i.e. increasing what Marx called the "organic composition" of capital; (2) increase production through longer work weeks with no compensating increase in wages; (3) relocate production facilities to places where the costs of labor are cheaper—de-industrialization, outsourcing, and the formation of a new international division of labor based on flexible production and replaceable or disposable workforces; or (4) invest accumulated capital in economic sectors and ventures, usually the financial sectors, that promise higher rates of return. All of the options were implemented as early as the 1950s, and all of them can and have had devastating consequences for the working classes (e.g. Curry 1993:100–101; Fröbel, Heinrichs, and Kreye 1977;

Harvey 1989:189–197; Herold and Kozlov 1987; Jenkins 1984, 1987; Piore and Sabel 1984; Pollert 1988).

There is an inverse relationship between the rate of profit and the organic composition of capital. In the United States, for example, the rate of profit fell steadily from the "cost plus twenty-five percent" contracts of the defense industries (the nascent military-industrial complex) and profit rates of World War II until 1960. It rose until 1965 but did not reach the wartime levels. It declined steadily until 1982 when it reached its nadir. It rose more slowly until the late 1990s when it began to level off. It fell again in 2008. In contrast, the organic composition of capital rose from c. 1946 to 1958 because of investments in mass-produced motor vehicles and electronics. It declined steadily between the late 1950s and 1970. It rose almost continuously again from 1970 and 1982 due to investment in computers and communications networks. It declined slowly in the 1980s and 1990s, bottoming out around 2000. It began to rise again because of investment in climate change industries, health care, nanotechnology, pharmaceuticals, genomics, information communication, and big data. Marxian theorists have argued for more than a century that

> … capitalists try to boost their profits by investing in new technology to save labour costs. Schumpeter reckoned that when capitalism went into a crisis or slump, it made obsolete much of the old equipment and plant. Other capitalists then began to turn to new technology to gain advantage. So capitalist slumps eventually lead to new innovations. Schumpeter called this process 'creative destruction.'
>
> … a cycle of new technology would start after a major slump, but the new technology would not be developed until the profit cycle moved into an upwave. Then there would be a take-off of the new technology. The next downwave would mean a setback to the new technology and an even worse situation for capitalists depending on the old technology.
>
> (Roberts 2009:59)

When capitalist firms invest in new machines or purchase other companies to increase their productivity and profit rates, they often borrow much of the capital they need. They raise money in four ways. First, and most frequently, they borrow it from a bank, which accumulates capital from companies and individuals in order to lend it at a profitable rate. Second, the firms issue bonds, whose holders loan the company a given amount of capital for a specified period of time for which they receive a given annual rate of interest for the term of the loan; when the loan expires, the firm buys back the bonds for the original investment. Third, the firms issue stocks that entitle their holders to a share of the company; the stockholders hope either that the company will pay an annual dividend (share of the profit) and/or that the value of their shares will increase over time. Bank loans and bonds are different from stocks. Fourth, when the share prices of stocks increase, as they did in the 1990s and again in the mid-2000s, shareholders can speculate in the stock market. If the share price of a company increases, shareholders can make money by buying and selling shares, and the company can borrow more money at a lower interest rate (Roberts 2016:49–50).

Since 1995, capitalist investment has occurred increasingly in the financial, insurance, and real estate development sectors. Today, c. 2017, roughly forty percent of all investment is in speculative ventures—the creation of fictitious capital that does not produce anything new but does support the expansion of the unproductive labor (e.g. managers, lawyers, merchants, brokers, or techno-crats) that is necessary for the reproduction of capitalist social relations. When fictitious capital is created, a firm's share prices become more important than its profits. "Therein lies the seeds of the stock market [and real estate] crash" (Roberts 2016:50). For example, many start-up internet companies in the late 1990s had ideas that attracted speculators. Their stock prices soared, but they were merely promising to deliver something new rather than actually doing it; their price to earnings ratios (P/E) soared as well. However, they were not mak-ing profits. The edifice collapsed in 2000. During the next two years, many of the companies went bankrupt and disappeared; others, like Cisco and Amazon, saw their market capitalization decline by eighty five–ninety five percent. Share-holders lost six trillion dollars of their investments (fictitious capital) as the stock market plunged. Thousands lost their homes and savings; many thousands more lost their jobs (Brenner 2006:266–344). This was repeated again—a mere five years later—during the global recession of 2007–2012.

On January 28, 2016, a headline in the *Los Angeles Times* proclaimed, "Fears of U.S. recession are growing." For Marxians, the question is not whether there will be another crisis. There will. The questions are when and where it will occur, how severe it will be, and what will happen. A more fundamental question, the one asked by Lenin a hundred years ago, remains: "What is to be done?"

In the remainder of the chapter, we will examine the explanations of social change that have been elaborated on or recycled during the last four decades.

Neoliberalism and the Current Crisis

Neoliberalism is a difficult term to define concisely because its meaning and ref-erents have changed over time (Mirowski and Plehwe 2009). It consists of three mutually reinforcing sets of meaning that continually interact with one another. They are (1) a theory of the relation between the individual and society, (2) an ideology, and (3) political and economic policies reinforcing and promoting the ideology. Let us consider each of these in more detail.

Neoliberalism as a Theory of Society

Neoliberal theory of the relation between the individual and society ultimately derives from Adam Smith's (1976[1776]:17) claim that society is an aggregate of individuals who possess an innate, natural propensity to "truck, barter, and exchange one thing for another" in order to secure goods and services that are mutually beneficial and that can be used or consumed (Clarke 2003). From the late-eighteenth-century onward, romantic critics of Smith's portrayal of commercial society said that it ignored the fact that human beings lived in communities and were social animals. Conservative critics claimed that individuals were subordinated to the values of the community, society, or the state (Nisbet 1978). Utilitarians, like John Stuart Mill (1806–1873), believed that societies were actually agglomerations of individuals, each pursuing his or her own self-interest, and that their decisions and actions cannot be analyzed in terms of super-individual categories—like society or culture—that do not exist in reality and are merely the creations of analysts (Schumpeter 1981:887–889).

Toward the end of the nineteenth century, political economists in a number of countries transitioning rapidly to industrial capitalism began to focus their attention on market exchange: the relationships between supply and demand, prices, trade, income distribution, and recurring business cycles. They laid the foundations of neoclassical economics. Building on the utilitarian notion that society was merely an aggregate of autonomous individuals, economists assumed (1) that individuals seek to maximize utility, and firms seek to maximize profits; and (2) that they act independently on the basis of complete knowledge to make rational choices between alternative courses of action in order to achieve, maximize, or optimize their goals. The economists also sought to explain how the market operated under more or less equilibrium conditions; however, the values they presupposed—optimization, maximization, or rationality—were actually created outside of the market and were assumed to be part of some unchanging human nature found in all human beings. Furthermore, the economists argued that the best way for these agglomerations to maximize their desires was through minimal, if any, interference by the state—in other words, a laissez faire or free market economy. Thus, this theory of society emphasizes the autonomy of rational individuals who are free to enter contracts in which they buy and sell commodities in the market in order to optimize or maximize their choices among alternative courses of action.

Neoliberalism as an Ideology

For our purposes, ideology is the political consciousness linked with the interests of dominant social class. It is "a conception of the world that is implicitly manifest in art, in law, in economic activity and in all manifestations of individual and collective life" (Gramsci 1971[1933–1937]:328). The purpose of an ideology is to promote the cohesion and stability of society, to advance particular explanations and understandings of why society is the way it is, and to obscure or cover up its contradictions. It is reproduced in most social institutions—e.g. political and legal systems, schools, the media, churches, literature and the arts, and even sports. It is critiqued by those who either occupy different class positions or belong to different fractions of the ruling class (Larrain 1983). In this perspective, different classes in capitalist societies may advocate different ideologies.

The theory of society described in the preceding section did not adequately account for the Great Depression of the 1930s nor did its celebration of free market economics provide an answer for resolving the crisis and threat of "social revolution posed by the unemployed, the poverty stricken, and the many disillusioned with capitalism as an economic system" (Wolff and Resnick 2012:54). Economist John Maynard Keynes (1933, 1936) did propose one: Increase the federal government's spending and involvement in the market, and use centralized state planning to stimulate job growth and social services. His views became policy from the 1930s until the end of postwar reconstruction that persisted into the late 1960s.

The term "neoliberalism" was coined in the mid-1930s to describe an economic policy that occupied a space midway between the failed free market liberalism of the 1920s and the socialist economic policies of the Soviet Union—one that advocated state intervention in the economy. However, the free market ideology did not disappear but survived as a critique of Keynesian policies, especially among academic economists. It began to gain traction again in the early 1960s, most notably in the writings of two University of Chicago economists— Friedrich A. Hayek (1899–1992) and Milton Friedman (1912–2006) (Friedman 1962; Hayek 1960). Free market fundamentalism—the belief that unregulated markets are the best way to ensure equity and prosperity—quickly became hegemonic during the crises of capitalist welfare states, following the postwar reconstruction boom in the late 1960s and early 1970s (Duménil and Lévy 2004, 2005, 2011; Lapavitsas 2005). Today, the central tenets of neoliberal ideology are (1) the completely autonomous individual (firm); (2) a market completely free of government intervention, central planning, or regulation; and (3) fiscal policies that assert the primacy of the money supply over investment and government spending and that target the growth of the money supply.

Neoliberalism and its Political Agenda

The ideological framework advocated by Hayek, Friedman, and others in the 1960s was a petri dish for the policies that U.S. and Latin American technocrats forged to deal with economic crises in their countries. They worked closely with the International Monetary Fund, the World Bank, and other financial institutions in Washington, D.C. The specific policies came to be known as the Washington Consensus. A brief list includes de-regulating the market; minimizing state intervention in the market; privatizing state-owned enterprises; stabilizing the money supply to prevent inflation; lowering income rates; liberalizing trade and inward flows of foreign investment; protecting property rights; implementing austerity budget cuts in education, social services, and public health programs; and holding individuals responsible for their own well-being. Economic policies like these have profound political, social, and cultural consequences. They use state power to impose financial market incentives to change existing social relations in those places where the policies are put in place; it is a particular form of capitalist organization designed to weaken the power of both democracy and labor. In a phrase, the implementation of neoliberal policies creates dissent and arenas of conflict (Saad-Filho and Johnston 2005:3). The first two neoliberal shock treatments were performed in New York City and Chile in the mid-1970s. Many others followed in their wake.

A fiscal crisis loomed in New York City in 1975. The city had already been spending beyond its means for several years. There were a number of reasons for this: declining tax revenues, de-industrialization, white flight to the suburbs, inflation, and rising prices. The city had already been borrowing money from the large banks for several years in order to pay its debts. In the spring, the city ran out of money to pay for its operating expenses; it could not borrow more money because its credit ratings had fallen, and it was threatening to default on its loan payments and perhaps even declare bankruptcy. The state legislature stepped in with a short-term loan on the condition that the city turn over the management of its finances to a blue-ribbon advisory committee (Municipal Assistance Corporation) headed by an investment banker. The federal government made additional short-term loans to the city in November, with the proviso that it increase the cost of city services, cancel negotiated wage increases for city employees, and cut the size of the city's workforce. These demands translated immediately into higher taxes, an increased cost of living, layoffs of forty thousand city workers, cutbacks in hospitals, closures of day care centers and single-room occupancy hotels, tuition imposed for the first time on students attending college at any of the City University of New York campuses, and an explosion of homelessness from near zero to more than 14,000 in the first year (by 2016, that number increased to more than 80,000). For example, on New York's Upper West—which had the widest range of incomes in the city and large numbers of welfare (single-room occupancy) hotels and rent-controlled apartments in 1970—hotels were closed, landlords fought to have rent control eased, rents quadrupled, and the cost of food increased by more than fifty percent in the decade that followed (Tabb 1982).

The New York City crisis announced what was already happening in the old industrial states of the Northeast and the Great Lakes, and foreshadowed what would soon unfold elsewhere: the re-entry of women into jobs previously held by men, with the women being paid less than three-quarters of what their male counterparts earned; the steady decline in the size of the middle class; the steady erosion of jobs with security of employment and benefits; the increasing number of individuals working two or more jobs merely to survive as the rate of underemployment soared; an increase in the number of small businesses and simultaneous exploding number of their failures and bankruptcies; and the sharp decline in public spending for health and welfare services. At the same time, budgets for military and police expenditures increased to ensure safe investment climates at home and abroad (and larger profits for defense-related firms). For neoliberals and their conservative allies, the fiscal crisis of New York City was a symbol for everything that was wrong in the United States: Governments were too large, their spending was too lavish, the unions were too powerful, public sector employees were paid too much, the poor who relied on government services for their health and well-being were too irresponsible, and all of the demonstrations of dissent in the city during the late 1960s and 1970s were hotbeds for the moral decadence and decay that neoliberals saw in the city specifically and the country more broadly.

The second neoliberal shock treatment was applied in Chile in 1976. The background to this includes the election of Salvador Allende's socialist Popular Unity government in 1971; the government's nationalization and transfer of many enterprises controlled by global corporations or members of the national bourgeoisie from the private to the public sector; the growing number of Popular Unity legislators following the 1973 elections; and, a few months later, in September, a military coup supported by landowners, sectors of the middle class, the owners of companies that had been nationalized, global companies operating in Chile, a group of Chilean economists trained at the University of Chicago—the "Chicago Boys"—and the U.S. government. The coup was quick: Brutality was institutionalized; every form of dissent and opposition to the junta was violently suppressed. More than three thousand were killed by the military government, thousands were imprisoned, and an even larger number fled the country.

Before the coup, the Chicago Boys provided Chilean military leaders with a blueprint or prescription for curing the country's "economic ills." During the first year, the government implemented a series of neoliberal prescriptions as the only possible cures: that the private sector should operate freely;

> that private enterprise is the most efficient form of economic organization and that, therefore, the private sector should be the predominant factor in the economy. Prices should fluctuate freely in accordance with the laws of competition. Inflation, the worst enemy of economic progress, is the direct result of monetary expansion and can be eliminated only by drastic reduction in government spending.
>
> (Letelier 1976)

Here are a few of the results of implementing those policies: By 1976, more than half of the roughly five hundred firms nationalized by the Popular Unity had been returned to private ownership. The economy was deregulated: The cost of milk increased by forty percent, while the price paid to producers fell by twenty two percent. Unemployment soared from three percent in 1973 to more than a quarter of the country's population three years later. Foreign enterprises refused to send goods to Chile, especially goods that their subsidiaries already produced. The economic group controlling industrial production also controlled the financial sector and invested millions of dollars on speculative ventures in the country and abroad. By the end of 1975, the annual inflation rate was three hundred and seventy five percent, the highest in the world, and consumer prices had risen more than four hundred and forty percent. Ironically, the classes that supported the junta were the same ones that bore the brunt of inflation and rising prices. The most dramatic result, however, was dire effects on the mass of the population: malnutrition, rising infant mortality rates, and homelessness (Letelier 1976). These continue to the present day.

The tragedy is that neoliberal policies and those of the Washington Consensus have been implemented thousands of times in other countries, states, counties, and cities since New York City and Chile. The devastation caused by their implementation is even greater in countries on the margins of the capitalist world

(Byres 2005). The results have always been the same. Ideologues never learn from their errors in the past; they merely repeat them again and again.

Globalization and the New Imperialism

While the movement of people, goods, and knowledge has a long history, the burst of activity in the 1990s resulted from the conjuncture of a particular set of forces, conditions, and events, and the crisis produced by this combination. These included the end of the Cold War, dissolution of socialist states, expansion of the capitalist economy, increased international investment, globalization of capitalist production, reduced cost and speed of transporting goods and people, rapid development of computer and information technologies, virtually instantaneous dissemination of information, and formation of new supranational institutions of governance (e.g. the European Union). Harbingers of the changes were already evident in the early 1970s—e.g. George Modelski's (1972) *Principles of World Politics* and Richard Barnet and Ronald Muller's (1974) *Global Reach: The Power of Multinational Corporations*. By 1990, commentators were suggesting that the changes unfolding were so profound that existing social theories did not adequately account for either their breadth or their rapidity. The globalization theorists focused on the emergence of social relations that transcended the spatial boundaries of nation-states (e.g. Appadurai 1990; Featherstone 1990; Giddens 1990). Theorists of the new imperialism see the same relations in terms of either the formation of an informal empire dominated by the United States or the appearance of new configurations of economic and geopolitical competition that build on existing asymmetries of power and inequality (e.g. Harvey 2003; Panitch and Gindin 2012).

Globalization Theory

The idea of globalization began to crystallize in the late 1980s and became a "buzzword" in the 1990s, spawning hundreds, if not thousands, of books and many more articles and chapters (Bisley 2007:13–31; Held and McGrew 2003). It indicated a process of becoming world-wide; however, it has proven difficult to define and led the authors of a highly regarded synthesis to write that "there ... is no cogent theory of globalization nor even a systematic analysis of its primary features" (Held et al. 1999:1). Compare three efforts to clarify the meaning of the term. The first argues that "globalization can be defined as the intensification of worldwide social relations which link distinct localities in such a way that local happenings are shaped by events occurring many miles away and vice versa" (Giddens 1990:64). The second sees it as

> a process (or set of processes) which embodies a transformation in the spatial organization of social relations and transactions—assessed in terms of their extensity, velocity, and impact—generating transcontinental or interregional flows and networks of activity, interaction, and the exercise of power.
> (Held et al. 1999:16)

The third says that "globalization ... refers to the flows (people, capital, goods), networks (information, production), institutions (UN, WTO, etc.), and challenges (environment, terrorism, poverty), that (supposedly) transcend territory, particularly the nation-state" (Kiely 2007:78).

Globalization theorists were concerned with the material realities of the world economy and how it functioned rather than with models of the free market. They saw the global political economy as a system of power, competition, cooperation, and conflict rather than as systems of signs or semiotics. They simultaneously rejected postmodernism (see the following); resurrected the influence of Parsons (and Durkheim); engaged in a dialog with multiple currents of liberal and neoliberal thought; and marginalized Marxian discussions of capitalism and imperialism, thereby ensuring that Marxist thought would also be refined outside mainstream academic outlets (Fine 2004).

Two questions raised by these definitions are: What are the processes producing this growing interconnectivity, and how profound are the changes? The globalization theorists make two claims: The intensification is transforming human society globally, and it is replacing the system of territorially-based, sovereign states (nation-states) that prevailed in the post-colonial era with a new, multi-layered system of global governance. The assertions are both historical and empirical (Rosenberg 2005:3–10).

The basic theses of globalization theory are (1) that capital has broken loose from its geographical moorings, and direct foreign investment is flattening wealth disparities around the world; (2) that the world economy has become increasingly dominated by transnational corporations (TNCs); (3) that the TNCs are erasing the boundaries and eroding the power of nation-states, which are "too small [to solve] ... the big problems of life, and too big [to solve] ... the small problems of life," and they are dysfunctional and no longer play a central role in the expansion of capitalism (Bell 1987:14; Jameson 1991:319, 412; Ohmae 1990); and (4) that globalization, like its modernization precursor, has been overwhelming. It is a teleological but not necessarily unilineal process, which has already happened so that linkages with the past are irreversibility severed; hence, our focus should be on the essence of globalization and its implications rather than on the processes that underpinned its formation (Giddens 1990:64). Globalization theorists claim that the processes producing growing interconnectivity are transforming human society globally and that they are underwriting the formation of a system of global governance (Rosenberg 2005:3–10).

Mainstream globalization theory has a significant ideological component. It is rooted in the neoliberalism of the 1980s and "depoliticizes highly contentious, and therefore highly political issues" (Kiely 2007:12). Briefly, it asserts that every country can benefit from globalization provided that it adopts the correct policies. This means that countries should specialize in those forms of production that allow them to maximize their comparative advantage in the international economy—an idea first proposed by David Ricardo (1772–1823) in 1817. This means that capital can flow from countries where the cost of producing these commodities is high to those where the costs are lower. Political economist Ray Kiely (2007:15) describes how this supposedly works:

Provided the correct (open) policies are pursued, developing countries can exercise their (comparative) advantage because they have lower costs. This is reinforced by the return of smaller-scale businesses, which are both 'leaner' and more efficient than large and cumbersome companies. Although this will initially mean that they concentrate in labour-intensive sectors, the increase in investment will provide the funds to allow them to upgrade into more capital-intensive sectors (Balassa 1989). This is sometimes associated with the 'flying geese' model, in which Japan and first-tier newly industrializing countries (NICs) in East Asia upgrade to higher-value production, shedding their lower-value, labour-intensive sectors, and thus allowing the next tier of NICs to concentrate production in these sectors.

In this perspective, globalization provides the foundations for the economic development of poorer countries and the eventual convergence of less-developed and developed countries. To ensure this, the less-developed countries need to promote specialization and the liberalization of investment, financial, and trade regulations in order to maximize their comparative advantage.

The other claim of mainstream globalization theory is that these increasingly global networks are either weakening or transforming the sovereignty of national governments (Held et al. 1999:3, 7–10). Michael Hardt and Antonio Negri (2000:xi–xii) wrote that

Empire is materializing before our very eyes. Over the past several decades, as colonial regimes were overthrown and then precipitously after the Soviet barriers to the capitalist world market finally collapsed, we have witnessed an irresistible and irreversible globalization of economic and cultural changes. Along with the global market and global circuits of production has emerged a new global order, a new logic and structure of rule—in short, a new form of sovereignty. ...

Even the most dominant nation-states should no longer be thought of as supreme and sovereign authorities, either outside or even within their own borders. The decline in sovereignty of nation-states, however, does not mean that sovereignty as such has declined. Throughout the contemporary transformations, political controls, state functions and regulatory mechanisms have continued to rule the realm of economic and social production and exchange....[S]overeignty has taken a new form, composed of a series of national and supranational organisms united under a single logic of rule. This new global form of sovereignty is what we call Empire.

(Hardt and Negri 2000:xi–xii)

Empire is neither a function of the world market nor a social order dictated by a single power or bloc (e.g. the United States or the European Union).[2] It is, instead, a new world order based on the existence of permanent crisis—the product of the ongoing relationship and struggle between sovereign authority that seeks to pacify and to impose its order, on the one hand, and the multitude (a proletariat in the broadest sense) that "creates social relationships and forms through collaborative forms of labor," on the other (Hardt and Negri 2004:95, 332). "The crisis is a continual process of the generation of Empire, its corruption, and its reappropriation by the multitude as it creates its mode of production and its being" (Hardt and Negri 2000:408). Hardt and Negri actually have little to say about the political economy. They are concerned, instead, with the legitimation of Empire, which rests on "the capacity to present force as being in the service of right and peace to enlarge the realm of consensus that supports its own power" (Hardt and Negri 2000:15; Panitch and Gindin 2002:29).

The critics of mainstream globalization theory are particularly skeptical of its exaggeration of the transnationality of capital, lack of explanatory power, and historical amnesia (Kiely 2005, 2007; Rosenberg 2000, 2005). Let us briefly consider five major points:

First, not everyone agrees that globalization is an already established reality in the modern world or that it is, indeed, all that different from earlier phases of capitalist development, especially the one from the 1870s to 1929. In this view, the formation of global capital began in the eighteenth century, if not earlier. Did globalization in the 1990s constitute a new, unprecedented form of capitalist accumulation that was qualitatively and quantitatively different from earlier forms, or was it merely a manifestation of earlier processes dressed up in new clothes? Sweezy (1997), for example, pointed out that monopolization, the financialization of capital accumulation, and uneven development were the dominant features of the capitalist world economy from the 1890s to the collapse of 1929 and that they reappeared as motor forces of capital accumulation on an increasingly world scale in the 1970s.

Second, while the critics do not dispute claims about the movement of goods, people, capital, and money across national borders at the present time, they ask instead whether the current volume is without historical precedent, whether it is truly worldwide in scope, and whether it retains significant national and regional dimensions. Critics use the same kind of statistical arguments as the globalization theorists to buttress their arguments. For example, (1) in 1913, the ratios of export trade to gross domestic product (GDP) and the ratios of capital flows to outputs for the industrialized countries exceeded those of the interwar years, 1919–1939, and resembled those of the 1980s; (2) the ratio of world trade to output, which grew in the 1960s and 1970s, weakened in the 1980s and 1990s; (3) while the underdeveloped countries' share of total global manufacturing increased from 1964 to 1984, it was actually less than it had been in the 1940s; (4) employment in the export processing zones of underdeveloped countries rarely constituted more than 5 percent of the countries' industrial employment; (5) the importance of direct foreign investment varied from country to country;

(6) much direct foreign investment goes toward existing ventures—often non-productive ones, like real estate, golf courses, or mergers and acquisitions; (7) inter-regional trade—which now accounts for about two-thirds of the total exports in North America, Europe, and Asia—has been growing more rapidly than trade with the rest of the world; and (8) production, trade, and investment are still concentrated in the old industrialized countries (e.g. Kiely 1994; Weiss 1997).

Third, contrary to assertions that the power of nation-states is being eroded and transformed as new international organizations—like the European Union or the World Trade Organization (WTO)—become more influential, critics argue that nation-states have always been political and economic instruments of capitalism. In their view, states have a significant degree of autonomy. They are objective structures in the capitalist international economy that underwrite capitalist production and capital accumulation, on the one hand, and the re-production of the system, on the other. States guarantee property rights, the standardization of weights and measures, and the free movement of goods; they ensure the availability of low-cost inputs, like land and labor, so that economic infrastructures are available; they assure the existence and training of workers, control their wages, and ameliorate the effects of their exploitation; they regulate business cycles, provide aid to ailing firms, and absorb surplus; they collect taxes to support their activities; they enact and enforce laws; and they manage external relations through military power, foreign aid, and commercial and financial sanctions. During periods of capitalist expansion, states act as the political agents of capitalist firms, especially dominant ones (e.g. Standard Oil or Apple). They cooperate with other states to protect property, exploit resources, and coordinate economic functions through their participation in private international relations councils and intergovernmental organizations (Panitch 1994; Weiss 1998).

Fourth, critics argue that the term "globalization" masks the uneven and regional development of capital accumulation taking place today (e.g. Arrighi, Silver, and Brewer 2003; Smith 2016). The world is becoming more unevenly developed than it was in the 1950s, with even greater wealth disparities. Capital accumulation is concentrated in certain regions and not in others. For example, a significant concentration of capital did occur in the newly industrialized countries of East Asia in the 1980s and 1990s; however, it was local rather than foreign capital, and it occurred because of strong state intervention rather than because of its absence or its market forces. The governments of Japan, South Korea, and Taiwan intervened repeatedly to promote economic development. They (1) implemented land reform policies and income redistribution policies that created classes of small landowners allied with the state; (2) promoted savings; (3) enacted tariffs to protect domestic markets; (4) provided subsidies to promote technology, exports, and technical linkages among industries; and (5) supported companies through inexpensive public education and legislation that disciplined and subordinated labor to capital (e.g. Amsden 1990, 1991; Appelbaum and Henderson 1992; Bello 1998; Deyo 1987).

Fifth, critics point out that there is a historical amnesia in globalization theory. On the one hand, it flattens out the historical development of nation-states by viewing them as if they are all being transformed in the same way or even transcended. It does not sufficiently recognize the diversity of the nation-states' structures and their differential capacities to pursue domestic economic policies nor the significance of the differences between strong states that can promote new conditions and relations or make use of them once they appear and weaker states that have only limited or no capacity to do so. On the other hand, it has a tendency to obfuscate the fact that the conditions created by the adoption of neoliberal policies in the 1980s actually facilitated globalization in the 1990s. Thus, far from breaking with history or existing forms of social theory, explanations of the processes of globalization cannot be separated from them (e.g. Kiely 2007:4, 86; Rosenberg 2005).

Signs of the waning influence of globalization theory were beginning to appear by the end of the 1990s: massive demonstrations against the WTO, first in Seattle (1999) and then elsewhere over the next few years; the looming financial crisis of 2000–2002; growing evidence of global inequality; and the emergence of the post-Washington Consensus, which pointed to the all-too-frequent failures of policies rooted in neoliberal market fundamentalism (Halliday 2002). In a phrase, critics recognized that globalization was actually further entrenching uneven development on a world scale. The critiques have led some theorists to reconsider earlier explanations of development and to consider globalization as uneven development or a new form of imperialism.

The New Imperialism and Global Capitalism

Globalization theorists rarely mention the word imperialism (or, for that matter, capitalism), even though there have been substantive debates about the concept in general for nearly a century and about American imperialism in particular since at least the 1960s. Critical discussions of imperialism resurfaced in the early 2000s (e.g. Bacevich 2003; Chomsky 2003; Harvey 2003; Mann 2003). There were several reasons for this: (1) protests against neoliberal arguments that markets are the most efficient way to reallocate resources in the global economy; (2) complex changes in global power and economic relations, the emergence of new conditions, and the crystallization of new contradictions in the 1990s; (3) the resurgence of neo-conservative militarism and unilateralism in the United States during the Bush II presidency; (4) acknowledgement by both liberal and right commentators that imperialism exists; and (5) mainstream media attention to Hardt and Negri's *Empire*, with its postmodernist overtones and challenge to rethink what imperialism is today (Chibber 2004; Harvey 2003:7).

There are certainly historical parallels between the imperialism and colonial domination of pre-1945 and the new imperialism of today. More importantly, there are also significant differences. From 1900 to the 1920s, the first generation of Marxist commentators—e.g. Lenin, Hilferding, Luxemburg, and Trotsky—viewed imperialism as a new stage of capitalist development structured by monopoly capital, the relation of capital to particular nation-states, and the mutually beneficial policies that were promoted. They characterized imperialism in terms of aggression and destruction; emphasized inter-imperialist rivalries between industrial capitalist states; and the expansion of the capitalist mode of production (primitive accumulation) in a world that was not yet fully capitalist. The second generation of Marxist commentators—the dependency and world systems theorists of the 1970s, who did not confuse the ideology of Eurocentrism with historical reality—viewed imperialism as the polarization of the world between a Western European center and a periphery located in the rest of the world—a polarization which emerged in the seventeenth century. They also pointed to the multiple sources of international inequality, economic exploitation, and political domination (Sutcliffe 2002:45–46, 50). Today's commentators have to consider circumstances in which there is greater international and transnational integration and cooperation than before; state sovereignty has been universalized; and inequality and uneven development persist, both within and among these sovereign states, and especially among the main capitalist ones (Kiely 2007:261).

Commentators across the political spectrum have written about (1) the contradictions that underpin the unfolding events of the period from c. 1990 to the present (2017) in terms of the interaction of geopolitical and economic competition in a world of sovereign states, glaring inequalities, and uneven development; and (2) the emergence of global capitalism and an informal American empire.

THE NEW IMPERIALISM

In a book of the same name, David Harvey (1935–) examines the dialectical interaction of the systemic pressures of capitalism and the politics behind U.S. imperial ambitions after the Cold War. He writes,

> 'capitalist imperialism' is a contradictory fusion of 'the politics of state and empire' (imperialism as a distinctively political project on the part of actors and a capacity to mobilize its human and natural resources towards political, economic, and military ends) and 'the molecular processes of capital accumulation in space and time' (imperialism as a diffuse political-economic process in space and time in which command over and use of capital takes primacy). With the former, I want to stress the political, diplomatic, and military strategies invoked and used by a state (or some collection of states operating as a political power bloc) as it struggles to assert its interests and achieve its goals in the world at large. With the latter, I focus on the ways in which economic power flows across and through continuous space, towards or away from territorial entities (such as states or regional power blocs) through the daily practices of production, trade, commerce, capital flows, money transfers, labour migration, technology transfer, currency speculation, flows of information, cultural impulses, and the like.

What Arrighi [1994] refers to as the 'territorial' and the 'capitalist' logics of power are rather different from each other. To begin with, the motivations and interests of agents differ. The capitalist holding money capital will wish to put it wherever profits can be had, and typically seeks to accumulate more capital. Politicians and statesmen typically seek outcomes that sustain or augment the power of their own state vis-à-vis other states. The capitalist seeks individual advantage and (though usually constrained by law) is responsible to no one other than his or her immediate social circle, while the statesman seeks a collective advantage and is constrained by the political and military situation of the state and is in some sense or other responsible to a citizenry or, more often, to an elite group, a class, a kinship structure, or some other group.

The relation between these two logics should be seen, therefore, as problematic and often contradictory (that is, dialectical) rather than as functional or one-sided. This dialectical relation sets the stage for an analysis of capitalist imperialism in terms of the intersection of these two distinctive but intertwined logics of power. The difficulty for concrete analyses of actual situations is to keep the two sides of this dialectic simultaneously in motion and not to lapse into either a solely political or a predominantly economic mode of argumentation.

(Harvey 2003:26–27)

That is, while the territorial logic of the state is fixed in space, the logic of capitalism is not confined to particular spaces but rather free to roam into other spaces in order to maximize capital accumulation. The two logics intersect, sometimes reinforcing one another, sometimes weakening one another, and sometimes canceling one another out. They are internal relations of one another.

Harvey situates the new imperialism within the historically contingent conditions caused by the chronic tendency of the rate of profit to fall and the recurring crises of over-accumulation that it has created since the mid-1970s (Harvey 2011). As you recall, the logic of a capitalist firm in competition with other firms producing the same commodity is to maximize profits. The spatial arrangement of its production facilities at any given moment is a solution to conditions and problems that existed in the recent past. It involved investment in a particular built environment—i.e. physical infrastructures fixed on the land, such as factories, roads, or power plants. Over-accumulation emerges in a territorial system as it begins to experience

surpluses of labour (rising unemployment) and surpluses of capital (registered as a glut of commodities on the market that cannot be disposed of without a loss, as idle productive capacity and/or as surpluses of money capital lacking outlets for productive and profitable investment). Such surpluses can be potentially absorbed by (a) temporal displacement through investment in long-term capital projects or social expenditures (such as education and research) that defer the re-entry of capital values into circulation into the future, (*b*) spatial displacements through opening up new markets, new production capacities, and new resource, social, and labour possibilities elsewhere, or (*c*) some combination of (*a*) and (*b*).

(Harvey 2003:109)

Harvey refers to these responses to capitalist crises as "spatio-temporal fixes." They are temporary and enable the capitalists' never-ending quest for comparative advantages and higher profits, at least in the short term.

Harvey examines the critical role that state power has played and continues to play in the processes of capital accumulation, which Marx called *primitive or original accumulation*. States have provided the conditions in which it can take place. They have underwritten the seizure, privatization, and commodification of land, water, and other resources; the forceful expulsion of people from their homes and means of production; the suppression of alternative forms of production and consumption; the appropriation, co-optation, and supersession of traditional lifeways; the criminalization of vagabonds, the unemployed, and the homeless; legislation that drives down wages, sets the minimum length of the workday, and prevents workers from organizing collectively to improve their lot; the conversion of various forms of common property into exclusively private property; the monopolization of the means of force and violence; the colonization of new lands and the imperial appropriation of their peoples, assets, and resources; taxation; and the creation of national debt. The original forms of accumulation laid the foundations for the continuous reproduction of both capital and labor power on an expanded scale. They are recurring features of capitalist accumulation that persist to the present day in every country on earth, including the United States (Harvey 2003:145–146).

Harvey is particularly concerned with the processes of accumulation that have become important after the 1973–1974 reorganization of the world financial system—what he terms *accumulation by dispossession*. These include fine-tuning the credit and financial systems to sustain new levels of corporate fraud, theft, and predation—e.g. raiding pension funds, speculating on hedge funds, or devaluating assets; emphasizing intellectual property rights, such as patenting genetic material or seeds and licensing their use; depleting global common property (such as land, water, and air) and replacing traditional forms of food production with capital-intensive forms; degrading habitats; commodifying cultural forms; corporatizing and privatizing public assets, like water, land, or utilities; turning over community-owned property—such as public housing, education, transportation, or telecommunications—to private companies; and rolling back regulatory legislation and frameworks designed to protect people and the environments in which they live. He points out that the collapse of Enron in the early 2000s dispossessed many people from their livelihoods and pensions. He further notes that "the collapse of the Soviet Union and then the opening up of China entailed a massive release of hitherto unavailable assets into the mainstream of capital accumulation" (Harvey 2003:149). States, of course, have played and continue to play primary roles in devaluing productive public assets and then selling them to private companies for pennies on the dollar (Harvey 2003:145–182).

In Harvey's (2011:32–33) view, the current crisis in the global economy began to crystallize in the late 1960s in the United States. Its tax revenues were simply not sufficient to pay for both its war in Vietnam and Lyndon Johnson's "Great Society" anti-poverty program. At about the same time, U.S. corporations began to invest surplus capital overseas; thus,

> surplus dollars, outside of US control, were accumulating within the European banking system. Belief in the fixed exchange rate of the dollar against gold began to erode. But what was to replace it?
>
> Keynes' idea of a neutral global currency in the form of 'special drawing rights,' based on the value of five major currencies and managed by the IMF, was revived in 1969. But this threatened US hegemony. A more acceptable solution to the US, worked out in a series of complicated international accords between 1968 and 1973, was for the fixed exchange with gold to be abandoned. All the major currencies of the world would then float against the dollar. While this introduced both flexibility and volatility into the international trading system, the global reserve currency remained under US control.
>
> The effect was to displace one challenge to US hegemony by another. If the US dollar was to remain strong, the US productive economy had to perform as well as, if not better than, its rivals. By the 1980s, it was clear that the economies of Japan and West Germany were way ahead of the US in terms of productivity and efficiency. ... Finance capital had to move to the fore to allocate surplus capital to wherever the profit rate was highest.
>
> In many industries that turned out not to be in the United States, and especially not in the traditional centres of production in the north-east and the mid-west, but in the west and the south. The result was the wrenching and relentless reorganization and relocation of production throughout the world. Deindustrialisation of older production centres occurred everywhere. ... This was paralleled by an astonishing spurt in the industrialisation of entirely new spaces of the global economy, particularly those with specific resource or organizational advantages—Taiwan, South Korea, Bangladesh, and the special production zones such as Mexico's maquiladores (tax-free assembly plants) or the export platforms created in China's Pearl River delta. Global shifts in production capacity accompanied by highly competitive technological innovations, many of which were labour-saving, contributed further to the disciplining of global labour.
>
> The United States still retained immense financial power, even as it lost its earlier dominance (though not significance) in the realm of production. Increasingly, the US relied upon the extraction of rents, either on the basis of its technological and financial innovation or intellectual property rights. But this meant that finance should not be burdened by excessive regulation.
>
> (Harvey 2011:32–34)

AMERICAN EMPIRE

In *The Making of Global Capitalism*, Leo Panitch and Sam Gindin (2012) focus on the emergence, formation, and expanded reproduction of the new imperialism and on the circumstances in which this occurred. They pursue these and two closely related, historically contingent issues: the making of global capitalism and the strengthening of the informal American empire after World War II. They agree with Harvey that the new imperialism crystallized around 1980 and that its formation was fueled by efforts to contain contradictions that developed in the wake of World War II; however, they disagree with him about how and why this happened. Panitch and Gindin place states, especially the United States, and historical contingency rather than developmental tendencies or crises of over-accumulation at the center of their analysis and explanation of global capitalism. As they put it,

> the American state has played an exceptional role in the creation of a fully global capitalism and in coordinating its management as well as restructuring other states to these ends. ... It was the immense strength of US capitalism [at the end of World War II] which made globalization possible, and what continued to make the American state distinctive was its vital role in managing and superintending capitalism on a worldwide plane.
> (Panitch and Gindin 2012:1)

Thus, their thesis contrasts with that of Hardt and Negri (2000), who argue that the nation-state has been transcended by the spread of global capitalism, and with that of Harvey (2003) and others, who argue that "globalization represents the decline of American hegemony and the return of inter-imperialist conflict" (Garrod 2015:38). Let us look at Panitch and Gindin's argument in more detail.

Panitch and Gindin agree with the early Marxist theorists of imperialism who recognized that the export of capital transformed the role of the state in both the capital-exporting and importing countries. The weaknesses of the early theorists' accounts were that (1) they associated imperialism with the export of capital and with the territorial extension of political rule through military conquest, (2) they attempted to explain the export of capital in terms of saturated domesticated markets without paying adequate attention to the implications of the long-term growth of working-class organizations on the dynamic of capital, (3) they did not pay sufficient attention to the impact of the pre-capitalist ruling classes in the inter-imperialist rivalries of the time, (4) they extrapolated the concept of finance capital too far when describing the loose connections between production and finance that were emerging in the United States, and (5) they did not appreciate the potential long-term significance of the kind of informal empire that the United States was forging in the Americas and the Far East in the late nineteenth and early twentieth centuries. In short, they did not adequately disentangle or differentiate the economic and political spheres, and their dynamic interrelations (Panitch and Gindin 2012:5).

For Pantich and Gindin (2012:53–66), the years immediately following World War II marked a critical moment in the separation of the economic and political spheres. The United States occupied a unique position among the advanced industrial capitalist states at the end of the war because its economy was the only one intact and because it was the only one capable of and willing to relaunch the project of global capitalism. However, the foundations for its circumstances were actually laid in mid-1930s, when the U.S. government, under the guise of the "New Deal," enacted financial and regulatory reforms that diminished the power of the capitalist class. The legislation allowed union organization, contained labor militancy, and created an uneasy truce between labor and capital. In the late 1930s, the government also laid the foundations for a permanent military-industrial complex that linked state funding and corporate profits. Collectively, the state and capitalist corporations supported research and development that underwrote technological innovation and more efficient forms of industrial management and restructured production to increase productivity. The United States created a central bank that strengthened the relationship between the Treasury Department, staffed by well-trained civil servants, and Wall Street banking and financial interests.

After the war, the U.S. state internationalized many of the domestic reforms of the New Deal. Through lend lease and reconstruction policies, it established dense linkages with the old imperial states and weakened their connections with their colonies by supporting, at least rhetorically, the nationalist sentiments of the postwar de-colonization movements. It built on the weakened positions and influence of the old ruling classes in the war-torn countries of Europe and simultaneously opposed, isolated, and suppressed communist insurgencies abroad and promoted centrist political coalitions and parties. With the Bretton Woods agreement, worked out jointly between U.S. Treasury Department officials and representatives from forty-three countries in 1944, it effectively established fixed exchange rates between the U.S. dollar and other currencies; the dollar, in effect, replaced the British pound sterling as the world currency. Internationally, U.S. support for rebuilding the industrial economies of Western Europe and Japan created an enormous market for oil, food, and other commodities produced in the United States; this support was also a harbinger of the fact that European and Japanese firms would soon be competing with U.S. firms in both their domestic and international markets. At home, the pent-up savings unleashed after the war intensified the commodification of everyday life. At the same time, in the late 1940s, the U.S. government significantly weakened labor militancy and radical unions and negotiations between automobile companies, and unions set a framework for relative labor peace (i.e. the "class compromise") that would last for more than a decade—no strike contracts in exchange for regular cost-of-living wage increases, health care, and pension benefits (Panitch and Gindin 2012:67–107).

Contradictions emerged and intensified in the United States, Europe, and Japan during the 1960s and 1970s. On the one hand, U.S. multinational corporations as well as management, legal, banking, and investment firms operating in Western Europe and Japan spread and deepened the country's hegemony. The industrial capitalist countries were increasingly tied to one another through expanded financial markets, the shift from the British sterling to the U.S. dollar as the world's store of value, and the formation of mutual defense pacts (NATO and SEATO). The World Bank laid the state and legal foundations for settling international economic disputes—e.g. the expropriation of property. In the United States, economic policy passed from Treasury Department officials to Wall Street when private investment bankers were appointed to head that department as well as the Federal Reserve. On the other hand, there was renewed labor militancy; the formation of new social movements, such as those concerned with civil rights and women, anti-war, anti-nuclear, and environmental issues; urban uprisings; and surveillance and repression by the state. Moreover, there were growing conflicts with Third World countries—e.g. Vietnam, Cuba, Indonesia, and Chile. The U.S. government's efforts to contain them involved cuts in the highest personal income and corporate tax rates in the early 1960s and the creation of the Great Society programs in the mid-1960s. These short-term fixes were unsustainable, especially when the Vietnam War was not funded by Congress. As its balance-of-trade deficits soared, the U.S. government established controls to limit the outflow of capital and to attract foreign investment to cover its mounting debt. By 1971, the country was racked by falling rates of profit, financial instability, inflation, and rising unemployment at home because it had no consistent fiscal or monetary policy at the time. The world crisis of the early 1970s marked the end of the Bretton Woods agreements over the convertibility of the U.S. dollar and fixed exchange rates (Panitch and Gindin 2012:14, 111–159).

Confidence in the U.S. financial system was restored in 1979 when the Federal Reserve raised interest rates to fight inflation at a time of double-digit unemployment. The imposition of this monetarist policy restored confidence in the ability of the United States to provide stability, a safe haven for direct foreign investment, and a reliable anchor for international finance. This meant that the U.S. Treasury, Federal Reserve, and Wall Street investment banks now played indispensable roles in managing the global financial system. Labor unions and the Left suffered crushing defeats in the 1980s—for example, unions (such as those of the air-traffic controllers and miners) were de-certified in the United States and Britain. Neoliberal reforms to maximize profitability were instituted; these included outsourcing, the relocation of facilities, the restructuring of production processes, and the adoption of new technologies to improve productivity and efficiency while reducing the number of workers. The new financial system underwrote free trade and capital movements between countries. One effect was massive foreign investment by the Japanese and others in the United States, much of it in real estate, speculative capital, and derivatives. This allowed the United States to continue running massive budget deficits, cut taxes for the wealthy and corporations, increase military spending, and de-regulate financial institutions. At the same time, the European Economic Community, the precursor of the European Union, was awash with U.S. dollars; however, it was also unable to develop ways of transferring capital from member states with surpluses to those running deficits. This further reinforced its dependence on the United States (Panitch and Gindin 2012:14–17, 163–220).

Thus, the primary concerns of the U.S. government were increasingly (1) to consolidate and extend global capitalism and (2) to manage and prevent the spread of financial crises because of the global mobility and volatility of capital. They were connected with legislative and administrative measures promulgated jointly by the U.S. Treasury, Federal Reserve, and Wall Street financial firms, whose officials moved with increasing numbers and frequency back and forth between them as well as into the International Monetary Fund, the World Bank, the newly created North American Free Trade Agreement (NAFTA), the WTO, and the Bank of International Settlements. These measures promoted free trade, extended the proliferation and spatial expansion of markets and market competition, underwrote bilateral agreements that prevented the expropriation of property owned by U.S. multinational firms in foreign countries, and embraced structural adjustment programs to contain the spread of the seventy-plus financial crises that erupted during the decade in low- and middle-income countries. Collectively, the agreements established a new legal framework that facilitated overseas capital investment, strengthened the international role played by U.S. currency and bonds, and underpinned five-fold increases in the number of U.S. law firms with overseas offices and U.S. lawyers in those offices. The measures set in place during the 1990s were not particularly effective at curbing crises, especially from the perspective of the East Asian countries and their residents in the late 1990s; however, the measures did succeed in keeping those countries in capital markets. Moreover, they encouraged the investment of more than 1.3 trillion dollars of private capital into the private sectors of the emerging markets in developing countries. The developing countries maintained high interest rates and pegged their currencies against the dollar to advertise their credentials in international financial markets. At the same time, massive inflows of capital into the United States cemented New York City's place in the global finance system. Spurred by the Federal Reserve's low interest rates and the ready availability of credit, household debt soared. Workers saw low interest and availability of credit as relief for delayed or deferred spending due to thirty-years of stagnant wages; however, the remedy was short-lived and lasted only a few years (Panitch and Gindin 2012:17–18, 223–271).

Others saw the Asian Crisis of 1997–1998 and the Dot.Com collapse of 1999–2001 as harbingers of the 2007–2012 global mortgage meltdown promoted by U.S. investment banks as the first crisis of the twenty-first century. On the one hand, Panitch and Gindin (2012:18–19) note that the crisis strengthened the role of the dollar and underwrote "the transformation in the global division of labor, the development of competitive networks of production, and a new financial architecture to facilitate accelerated financialization [of the global economy]." These, in turn, ensured "the US economy's continuing centrality in global capitalism, [and] … in the successful integration into it of the huge and fast-growing Chinese economy." It also marked "a new stage in the informal American empire's drive to realize a fully global capitalism." On the other hand, the crisis poured gasoline on the smoldering fires of resentment, antagonism, and protests (e.g. those in Seattle and Sao Paulo) fueled by the globalization of capital. The signs included (1) the anti-globalization demonstrations launched in 1999 at the Seattle summit of the WTO; (2) the militarized intervention in Afghanistan and Iraq during the Bush II presidency; (3) the U.S. Treasury's intervention to save domestic and foreign banks that were "too big to fail" in 2007 and the abject failure of the U.S. government to help homeowners who lost their homes through foreclosures, evictions, and underwater mortgages; (4) the normalization of wealth differences among countries; (5) the intensification of competition between firms and various levels of government; (6) the ongoing debates between proponents of free trade and those supporting protectionist policies; (7) the infusion of foreign capital and its incorporation into the national economy; (8) the disembedding of money capital from the productive economy; (9) the deleterious effects of the repeated implementation of structural adjustment programs at home and abroad; and (10) the continuous state intervention in more and more spheres of everyday life (Albo 2003; Panitch and Gindin 2012:275–340).

The proponents of the new imperialism and the informal American empire theses agree on some issues and disagree on others. Let us first consider the points of agreement. First, the structure of imperialism from the 1980s onward is different from the inter-imperialist rivalries and colonies described by Lenin and others in c. 1900 as well as from the dependency and uneven exchange relations depicted by the dependency theorists in the 1960s. Second, both argue that Hardt and Negri's claims are exaggerated. Third, both assert that the continuing influence of the United States after World War II marks a new era, although they characterize that era in different terms. Harvey and others see it as a second phase of bourgeois rule that crystallized between 1945 and the 1970s—one that speaks of economic growth and anti-colonialism behind the facade of democratic rule. In contrast, Panitch, Gindin, and others view this phase in terms of the emergence of an informal American empire that both reconstitutes and is reconstituted by the expansion and consolidation of global capitalism from the late 1970s onward. Fourth, there have been ongoing crises since the late 1960s.

There are differences between the advocates of the two positions as well. First, Harvey and others emphasize the importance of the internal dynamics of the capitalist mode of production (the concentration and centralization of capital) and a capitalist system of states, while Panitch and Gindin stress the importance of the historical contingency of the circumstances in which capitalism formed and would argue that the system of states in the capitalist world (not the states themselves) pre-date the emergence of capitalism. The question is whether the state system is a necessary feature or a contingent one (Callinicos 2009; Wood 2003). A second distinction is that Panitch and Gindin see the American empire as dominant or hegemonic in the global capitalist world today, while Harvey sees its influence as waning. Others, like Radika Desai (2013), see the United States as "first among equals" in a capitalist world dominated by the industrialized countries of North America, Western Europe, and East Asia.

These relations and circumstances have sometimes been called the "postmodern condition" or "postmodernity." Let us look more closely at such claims.

Postmodernism, Postmodernity, and Governmentality

The words "postmodernism" and "postmodernity" have a confusing array of meanings in everyday parlance—a confusion only magnified when they are used synonymously and interchangeably. The former refers to a style, content, or form, all of which have substantive criteria. The latter indicates the period of time during which those criteria prevailed. Both words are oppositional to "modernism" and "modernity." The term "governmentality" appeared in the late 1970s to explore "the forms of activity aiming to shape, guide or affect the conduct of some person or persons" (Gordon 1991:2). Let consider each of them in more detail.

Postmodernism

Postmodernism is a reaction to modernism. Postmodern theorists draw an analogy between culture and language. Cultures are like discourses—i.e. conversations or written exchanges among individuals that seem coherent at a specific moment in time. As such, discourses are representations of local knowledge, culture, identity, and politics. They have recognizable structures and make sense of what is known about the world. Events unfold at particular moments and points in a field of knowledge; the participants have clearly defined roles and shared sets of rules. Knowledge is established, reproduced, and generated in knowledge fields that include not only the discursive statements of conversations and texts but also objects, practices, programs, skills, performances, social networks, and institutions. Discourses—and, by extension, local cultures and knowledge fields—are dynamic and in continual flux or motion because the meanings attached to words and things are not necessarily fixed (Derrida 2000[1968]; Foucault 1972[1971]).

Jacques Derrida (1930–2004) and Michel Foucault (1929–1984), widely acknowledged as foundational figures of postmodern thought, explained the perpetual flux of discourses in different terms. On the one hand, Derrida (2000[1968]:242) argued that everyday language is "never innocent and neutral" because it carries with it diverse kinds of metaphysical presuppositions about reality that "are knotted into a system" and rarely examined very closely. Because discourses are able to project a sense of stability and leave room for a "structured" exchange, the fact that they have a temporal or linear flow means that examination of the differences in the presuppositions is postponed into the future. As a result, elements of the discourse only acquire meaning in relation to their past or future. Derrida refers to the traces, play, and movement of differences in the "becoming space" of discourse as *différance*. Phrased another way, neither the meanings nor the relations between the elements of discourse are stable. For Derrida, it is différance that produces systematic and regulated transformations in discourse. At these moments, the deferred element of the discourse "takes on or conveys meaning, only by referring to another past or future element in an economy of traces" (Derrida 2000[1968]:248). Culture, for some proponents of postmodernism, is analogous. In this context, it is perhaps worthy of note that Derrida (1994) wrote *Specters of Marx* in the mid-1990s.

On the other hand, Foucault saw new statements of truth and knowledge fields (*epistemes*) as generated and reconfigured during the temporal flow of a discourse. Power and knowledge are autonomous, intimately intertwined, mutually constitutive, and dynamic (Foucault 1991[1968]):

> Discourse transmits and produces power; it reinforces it, but also undermines and exposes it, renders it fragile and makes it possible to thwart it. In a like manner, silence and secrecy are a shelter for power, anchoring its prohibition; but they also loosen its hold and provide for relatively obscure areas of discourse.
>
> (Foucault 1978[1976]:101)

Before 1978, Foucault focused his attention on the practices of power—especially with regard to the formation of the individual body; disciplines like the human sciences; and institutions, like hospitals, asylums, or prisons. He deliberately eschewed looking at the state and its practices. His view of power has been characterized in various ways. For Jessop (2011:69), it resembles a strategic game: at one extreme, it is a struggle between free individuals in which some are trying to shape or determine the conduct of others; at the other extreme, it is domination in which some control, coerce, or have gained the consent of others. For Mark Kelly (2009:37–38), power (1) is impersonal and not guided by the will of individuals, (2) is always a relation between people and not a possession, (3) is not concentrated in a single individual or class, (4) is multidirectional, and (5) is independent from individuals and has its own dynamic. For Joseph Rouse (1994:109–110), power is dispersed across and through complex, diverse social networks and "is not something present at specific locations within those networks, but is instead always at issue in ongoing attempts to (re)produce effective social alignments, and conversely to avoid or erode their effects, often by producing various counteralignments." A given social alignment is effective and comprehensive when its coordinated practices are viewed as having control over things needed or desired by others (Wartenberg 1990:150).

Postmodernity

Postmodernity emerges in the wake of modernity. Temporal notions of modernity place its appearance variously during the Scientific Revolution of the seventeenth century, the Industrial Revolution of the late eighteenth century, or after World War II. Postmodernity, in contrast, is generally viewed as beginning in the 1970s and crystallizing in the 1980s. It was partly a reaction to (1) the turmoil and crises of the preceding twenty years and (2) the emergence of new political-economic and cultural logics. Postmodernism, from this perspective, is the "cultural logic of late capitalism" (i.e. multinational or consumer capitalism) and the "perfect complement for neoliberalism" with its endless quest for individual subjectivity, entrepreneurial sovereignty, and identity (Fine 2004:216; Jameson 1991).

Let us begin by considering the differences between modernity and postmodernity in more detail. Feminist philosopher of science Sandra Harding (1935–) notes that postwar accounts of modernity build on historical legacies from the eighteenth and nineteenth centuries and that they consistently focus

> ... on the emergence of a differentiated social structure with political, economic, religious/moral, and educational (including scientific) institutions which are independent of family structures; the separation, therefore, of public and private spheres; and such democratic institutions as representative government, free elections, and a free press. Such conceptions also focus on a secular worldview, the idealization of universal instrumental rationality, and a social orientation toward the future rather than the past. They also include several kinds of contradictory tendencies, such as the insistence on universal reason, yet also the recognition and even toleration of the pluralism of rationalities, and a critical and self-critical attitude along with severe restrictions on the appropriate targets of such criticism.
>
> (Harding 2008:11–12)

In her view, modernity is a legacy of Enlightenment and liberal thought as well as the perspectives of Marx, Durkheim, and Weber. It is reflected in the writing of the economic growth and modernization theorists in the 1950s.

Theorists of the postmodern era, by contrast, are reacting against notions of modernity. Marxist critic Terry Eagleton (1943–) wrote that postmodernity

> ... is a style of thought which is suspicious of classical notions of truth, reason, identity, and objectivity, of the idea of universal progress or emancipation, of single frameworks, grand narratives or ultimate grounds of explanation. Against these Enlightenment norms, it sees the world as contingent, ungrounded, diverse, unstable, indeterminate, a set of disunified cultures or interpretations which breed a degree of skepticism about the objectivity of truth, history, and norms, the givenness of natures and the coherence of identities. This way of seeing, so some would claim, has real material conditions: it springs from an historic shift in the West to a new form of imperialism—to the ephemeral, decentralized world of technology, consumerism, and the culture industry, in which the service, finance and information industries triumph over traditional manufacture, and classical class politics yield ground to a diffuse range of 'identity politics.'
>
> (Eagleton 1996:vii)

The rise of postmodern theory in the mid-1970s coincided with the beginning of the "cultural turn" in the social sciences and humanities (e.g. Bourdieu

1977[1972]; Foucault 1979[1975]; Geertz 1973). Substantively, this meant that economic activity, which had been separated from the other institutions of modern society, was enmeshed in a wider, more inclusive idea of culture. Societies were no longer constituted by distinct but interrelated economic, social, cultural, and psychological sub-systems or determined in the last instance by an economic base, as the structural-functionalists and modernization theorists had asserted repeatedly since the 1950s. While it might still be possible to analyze each of these realms or levels separately, they could, in fact, only be understood in terms of an expanded and determinant sphere of culture. In this view, culture consists of rules, norms, symbols, and images that have saturated and shaped the deepest recesses of everyday life; these allow people to communicate and make sense of the world. For theorists of postmodernity, culture

> … has expanded and become coterminous with market society in such a way that the cultural is no longer limited to its earlier, traditional or experimental forms …, but is consumed throughout daily life itself, in shopping, in professional activities, in the various televisual forms of leisure, in production for the market and in the consumption of those market products. … Social space is now completely saturated with the image of culture.
>
> (Jameson 1998:111)

Many postmodernist commentators are deeply skeptical of metaphysics (investigations of the most basic features of reality and the concepts used to talk about them—e.g. existence, essence, object, body, space, time, or contingency). Consequently, they reject the notions of abstraction and universality. They are nominalists and anti-essentialists whose comments are not framed in terms of general or abstract concepts but rather in terms of what exists in particular instances. For example, there is no such thing as a table because it is an abstraction without an essence, but we can describe myriad objects with horizontal surfaces and at least one vertical appendage. This implies that postmodern commentators are also anti-essentialists and relativists who proclaim that culture (in the singular, with capital "C") is an abstraction that does not exist in reality, but diverse, heterogeneous cultures (in the plural, with a small "c") constituted or constructed in particular times and places do occur. These tables or cultures can be described in terms of their differences (Eagleton 1995:112–128). Because the world is constituted, constructed, experienced, and intuited in different ways, the postmodernity theorists draw sharp distinctions between the natural and cultural realms. Nature is also constructed or viewed in different ways, depending on the cultures and perspectives of its observers. Thus, while postmodernity theorists reduced the economy and economic behavior and assigned them exclusively to the cultural sphere, their contemporaries in sociobiology and evolutionary psychology assigned them with equal vigor and in the same reductive manner to human nature or even nature itself (e.g. Wilson 1975).

Notions of history were also transformed by postmodern theorists as they argued that culture is constituted at particular times and places. Because of the diversity of cultures that exist in the modern world, history (with a capital "H")—which implies some sort of goal, directionality (progress or struggle), or contingency (interplay of factors), or one accident after another (chance)—simply does not exist. Instead, historical accounts (plural, with a small "h") are incommensurate because they are particular to different cultures and are only available in the form of competing narratives that reflected the positionality of their narrators in the unequal power relations of the present (multiculturalism). Because narratives are discourses shaped by the norms, symbols, and images of cultures, they can be investigated and explained in the same way as other discursive practices. A sense of temporal continuity with the past is eroded or erased altogether when these histories are reduced or seen merely as features of change—i.e. the expanded reproduction of capitalism. History becomes fragmented, discontinuous, and exists in a perpetually changing world that is continually being created, re-created, and reproduced at an ever-increasing pace in the present. Eagleton (1995:64) described history, in slightly different terms, as

> ... one of plurality, free play, plasticity, open-endedness ... [and] can be had right now, in culture, discourse, sex, or shopping mall, in the mobility of the contemporary subject or the multiplicities of social life. This false utopianism projects the future into the present, thus selling the future short and imprisoning the present in itself.

Postmodernists are concerned with the constant flux of today's neoliberal society.

Governmentality

Foucault reintroduced the term "governmentality" in the late 1970s when he shifted the focus of his analyses of power from the formation and production of individuals, local practices, and institutions to "the state's strategic role in the historical organization of power relationships and the establishment of global structures of domination" (Bröckling, Krasmann, and Lemke 2011:2). Earlier, he had deliberately not considered (i.e. bracketed) the practices of government in his studies. Governmentality, his new focus, consists of the complex ways in which states steer the conduct of individuals and collectives, "... working through their autonomy rather than through coercion even of a subtle kind" (Donzelot and Gordon 2008:48; Jessop 2011:56). In other words, how do the governmental practices and rationalities (reasoning) of modern states subsume the idea of freedom and the conduct of free subjects as part of their own moral sensibilities?

It is important to recognize the historical context of Foucault's new research on the governmental rationality of liberal states. It coincided with the crisis in the postwar "class compromise" based on a mass-production and consumption economic dynamic in the late 1960s; the proliferation of new social movements (anti-war, anti-nuclear, environmentalist, feminist, and sexual identity) at many sites of resistance, which were often based on identity politics and not reducible to class positionality; the resurgence of patriarchy and fundamentalism; and critiques of big business, unions, racial segregation, and bureaucracies. Calls for the study of governmentality were accompanied by calls to expand individual freedom, autonomy, and responsibility in every aspect of society (Jessop 2011:58). It also coincided with the growing influence of different forms of neoliberal thought, ideologies, and policies in Western capitalist countries—one in the United States and England and the other in Germany and the Scandinavian countries. France, where Foucault lived and worked, was exceptional because it was governed by socialist governments during the 1980s and 1990s. Foucault was quite explicit about the differences between the forms of neoliberalism in his 1978–1979 lectures at the Collège de France (Foucault 2008[2004]). It is also worth noting that a published summary of one lecture and commentaries on the lecture, as well as a selection of interviews and talks from the mid-1970s, sparked considerable interest in the English-speaking world (Burchell, Gordon, and Miller 1991; Donzelot and Gordon 2008; Foucault 1980, 1991[1978]). A French edition of the lectures was eventually published in 2004, twenty years after Foucault died and twenty-five years after he gave them; an English translation appeared four years later.

Governmentality, for Foucault (1991[1978]:102), is

the ensemble formed by the institutions, procedures, analyses and reflections, the calculations and tactics that allow the exercise of this very specific albeit complex form of power, which has as its target, as its principal form of knowledge political economy, and as its essential technical means apparatuses of security.

Commentators and critics took studies of governmentality in several directions in the 1990s.

One was the self-identified, Anglo-Foucauldian group that crystallized in English-speaking countries during the 1980s (Burchell, Gordon, and Miller 1991; Donzelot and Gordon 2008; Rose, O'Malley, and Valverde 2006). Its participants implicitly or explicitly rejected Marxian thought as economic reductionism or structural-functionalism; recast Gramsci as a prescient postmodernist; and de-institutionalized state apparatuses in order to examine "the logic, rationalities, and practices of government or governmentality in isolation from ... the state's role as a major site for the institutionalization and integration of power relations within the more general economy of power" (Jessop 2011:62). Jacques Donzelot (1943–) put it concisely:

We would have then not a power and those who undergo it, but, as Foucault shows, *technologies*, that is to say always local and multiple, intertwining, coherent or contradictory forms of activating and managing a population, and *strategies*, that is to say, formulae of government, 'theory-programmes'. ... Political economy, Marxism, Keynesianism are strategies, formulae of government, theories which explain reality only to the extent that they enable the implementation of a programme, the generation of actions; they provide their coherence as a 'practical object' ... for corrective intervention and governmental programmes of redirection.... The state would not be seen as a subject of history, but instead only 'a support for technologies' or only as 'an effect of governmental strategies'.

(Donzelot 1979:77)

In this view, language is an intellectual technology—"a mechanism for rendering reality amenable to certain kinds of action" (Miller and Rose 1990). While it does not create realities or identities, language, along with other signifying systems, is one element that allows reality to be governed. It is

... a key element in the process of forming networks through persuasion, rhetoric, and intrigue. In the assemblage of networks, authorities, groups, individuals, and institutions were enlisted, brought to identify their own desires and aspirations with those of others, so that they were or could become allies in governing. In particular, such networks made possible ... governing at a distance—that is to say, acting from a center of calculation, such as a government office or the headquarters of a nongovernmental organization, on the desire and activities of others who were spatially and organizationally distinct.

(Miller and Rose 1990; Rose, O'Malley, and Valverde 2006:89)

Language as an intellectual technology is important in understanding the constitution of the objects of politics—the relations between persons as well as between persons and things. Governmentality involves the formation of networks that bring people, organizations, and objectives together in ways that bring into existence the programs they desire to implement. Thus, the Anglo-Foucauldians have been concerned with the art of governing—i.e. the whole range of techniques and procedures of directing human behavior—that are derived from traditional virtues and common abilities. Their inquiries have yielded detailed, empirical studies of accounting, risk, insurance, and processes of subjectification in factories (e.g. Ewald 1991; Hacking 1991; Miller and O'Leary 1987; Power 1997; Rose 1988).

Foucault himself sketched a second line of inquiry that has a different emphasis from the Anglo-Foucauldians's micro-analyses of power:

I have not studied and do not want to study the development of the real governmental practice by determining the particular situations it deals with, the problems raised, the tactics chosen, the instruments employed, forged, or remodeled, and so forth. I want to study the art of governing, that is to say, the reasoned way of governing best and, at the same time, reflection on the best possible way of governing. ... I have tried to grasp the level of reflection in the practice of government and on the practice of government ... to grasp the way in which this practice that consists in governing was conceptualized within and outside government, and any-way as close as possible to governmental practice. ... We could call this the study of the rationalization of government practice in the exercise of political sovereignty.

(Foucault 2008[2004]:2)

Jessop (1946–) explains the difference between the two lines in terms of Fou-cault's distinction between strategic games, in which some try to determine the conduct of others, and states of domination (power). Between them are the techniques of government (the arts of governing) through which states of domination are established and maintained. Jessop pointed out that Foucault (2003[1997]:32–37, 2007[2004]:338, 347, 2008[2004]:220–222), in his later writ-ings, argued explicitly and implicitly that

... the state apparatus had a continuing importance as part of the general economy of power but also that its overall form, its specific organization, and its activities were shaped by the distinctive combination and relative primacy of different forms of exercising power within and beyond the state.

(Jessop 2011:62)

Jessop proceeds to argue that the Anglo-Foucauldians have focused mainly on "the logics, technologies, and practices of government ... in isolation from this broader concern with the state's role as a major site for the institutional integration of power relations within the general economy of power" (Jessop 2011:62, 69).

In sum, issues of governance and governmentality arose in the late 1970s amid growing concerns about the problems of states, their failures, and their unman-ageability. Suggestions for resolving these issues ranged from greater reliance on markets and lowered expectations to new ways of coordinating interdependence among autonomous actors and different levels or spheres of activity. While one focus was the liberal-democracies, the other was what was happening in the so-cialist countries.

The Dissolution of Socialism, the Rise of Post-Socialism

The disintegration of the Soviet state, the elections in the Eastern Bloc countries, and the development of export industries in southern China heralded by the Western media in the 1980s and 1990s have been interpreted in different ways. For many, these events marked the restoration of capitalism, globalization, and the triumph of market democracy in which elites compete for power to govern society and maintain social order. For right-wing commentators, they signaled the death of Communism and Marxism. For neoliberal convergence theorists, they indicated that the industrial countries of the world were once again fol-lowing the same path of global capitalist development. However, by the 1960s, Marxist scholars were already examining the conditions that would promote the "restoration of capitalism" in the socialist states and the changes that this would unleash (Esherick 1979).

The changes looming on the horizon in the 1980s renewed discussions about the meaning of civil society, democracy, and the state (e.g. Cohen and Arato 1992; Keane 1988; Rosenberg 1994). There were significant differences between how civil society was conceptualized historically and how it was being discussed at the present time. In the eighteenth century, civil society

> ... represent[ed] a separate sphere of human relations and activity, differentiated from the state but neither public nor private or perhaps both at once, embodying not only a whole range of social interactions apart from the private sphere of the household and the public sphere of the state, but more specifically a network of distinctively *economic* relations, the sphere of the market-place, the arena of production, distribution and exchange. A necessary but not sufficient condition for this conception of civil society was the modern idea of the state as an abstract entity with its own corporate identity... [and] the emergence of an autonomous 'economy', separated out of the unity of the 'political' and 'economic' which still characterized the absolute state.
>
> (Wood 1990:61, emphasis in the original)

The development of the concept of civil society in the eighteenth century was intimately linked with the development of capitalism. By contrast, in the 1990s, it referred to the non-economic realm of public and personal life outside the state in which autonomy, voluntary association, and plurality were presumed to be guaranteed by the kind of democracy that exists in the West. In other words, the current usage employed state oppression to oppose the freedom and pluralism. Moreover, it presumed that capitalism already existed and asserted that the exploitative social relations resulting from increased dependence on market relations are the same as those that shape participation in voluntary associations (Wood 1990:63–65).

The debate about civil society was linked with the dissemination and adoption of a peculiarly American notion of democracy, one rooted in the market and largely devoid of the egalitarian and moral ideals that had been central to liberal-democratic discourse since the mid-nineteenth century. This equilibrium-market theory of democracy treats citizens as a mass of apathetic consumers with conflicting, individual political interests. They attempt to optimize them by purchasing political goods from one of a small number of self-appointed entrepreneurs, who are compelled to perform social functions in order to sell their commodities in a competitive market in which a balance is maintained between the supply and demand of these items. Such a model does not require high levels of citizen participation, only a majority or plurality of the votes cast in an election. Numerous critics have pointed out that the equilibrium produced in such a market, in which purchasing power is based largely on money, is one of inequality because people are neither equally wealthy nor always rational in their behavior. Canadian political theorist Crawford B. Macpherson (1911–1987) suggested that a political theory based on utilitarian and equilibrium market assumptions can thrive only in capitalist democracies with expanding economies and that it can be no more than an academic luxury in those countries where political parties reflect real class interests rather than false consciousness (Macpherson 1973:170–194, 1977:77–92).

Let us now shift our focus from discussions of a conceptual apparatus to what happened in the socialist countries. The economic growth of the socialist countries slowed and stagnated in the 1970s. There were a number of reasons for this, including increased oil prices, the inefficiency of the countries' industrial planning and production bureaucracies, technology boycotts by the West, increased military expenditures, and explicit efforts by the U.S. government—National Security Council Directive 54 of 1982—to overthrow the Communist governments and parties of Eastern Europe and to reintegrate them into the capitalist world market (Chossudovsky 1997:2; Mandel 1989:56–67). The International Monetary Fund and the World Bank wreaked further havoc with the austerity measures they imposed. Taken collectively, these and other forces unleashed processes of primitive accumulation and accumulation by dispossession that persist to the present day; the rapid formation of capitalist and proletarian classes in a milieu built on the pillaging and plunder of public property and state assets by gangster capitalists and their cronies; the immiseration of hundreds of millions of people, who lost their guaranteed jobs, state-subsidized housing, health care—i.e. their futures; and the appearance of floating populations of poverty-stricken persons—150 million in China alone—continually moving from place to place to find work. These policies also provided a further rationale for the top-down, conservative revolutions that dismantled the institutions of centrally-planned, command economies and replaced them with the market (e.g. Holmstrom and Smith 2000; Meisner 1996, 1999; Walker 2006, 2008).

Class formation and class struggle shaped social development in the Soviet Union (USSR) and the Eastern Bloc from the 1970s onward. The processes appeared in the wake of World War II and gained momentum in the 1960s, especially after the revelations of Stalin's abuse of power. These disclosures threatened the legitimacy of state bureaucracies, composed mainly of Communist Party members, in both the USSR and the Eastern Bloc countries. They forced the party bureaucracies to share power, at least temporarily, with technocrats and members of the intelligentsia (Konrád and Szelényi 1979[1974]). However, by the 1970s and 1980s, bureaucrats were increasingly disinclined to make concessions to the intelligentsia or to share power with them; at the same time, they were more flexible in their dealings with private businesses and allowed "second economies" based on market production and exchange to flourish (Szelényi 1988:216–218).

The second economies emerged in response to industrialization policies imposed during the 1950s. Rapid industrialization had been achieved by simultaneously creating as many industrial jobs as possible; collectivizing agriculture; and reducing personal consumption and infrastructural investments, such as housing, schools, or shops but not public transportation. As a result, many of the first generation industrial workers left agriculture for urban industry. However, they retained control over their farm plots and continued to live in the countryside, traveling back and forth between their homes and job sites on public transportation. Because they had control over their lands, they enjoyed relatively high living standards and a degree of autonomy from their employers. By the 1970s, workers had stopped leaving the rural villages, and some of those who had immigrated to the cities earlier returned because of the entrepreneurial opportunities afforded by selling the agricultural produce they grew on their farms. By 1981, the 1.5 million family farms in Hungary grew a quarter of the country's food (Szelényi 1988:29–31).

Two class hierarchies co-existed in the socialist states by the late 1980s: an old established hierarchy, with party members and bureaucrats at the top and workers at the bottom, and a new emerging one tied to the capitalist market. In the new hierarchy, in which social mobility was tied to the possession of wealth and entrepreneurial skills, owners and entrepreneurs occupied the top rungs of the social ladder, and waged-workers occupied the bottom. The articulation of the two hierarchies yielded complex class structures in the Eastern Bloc countries. The ruling elite was fragmented, composed of a declining number of old-style party bureaucrats and an increasing number of intellectuals with technical skills. The entrepreneurial class was also fragmented: the petite bourgeoisie, whose members emerged out of the second economy; the managers and party members who used social and political connections to gain information and achieve goals—e.g. to acquire state or party assets offered for privatization or to enter joint ventures with Western firms; and, finally, the technocrats and intellectuals who possessed technical know-how and knowledge, and were employed by foreign-owned enterprises as foreign direct investment increased (Eyal, Szelényi, and Townsley 1997; Szelényi and Martin 1988; Szelényi and Szelényi 1991:123–126). The diverse interests of these groups and the alliances they forged underwrote the proliferation of political parties witnessed in the elections in the late 1980s and early 1990s.

Each of the transitions from the centrally planned economies of the socialist states to market socialism and then to market capitalism exacerbated already existing tensions and contradictions. The trajectories of development varied from one country to another, especially during the first decade or so of change. Let us briefly sketch the trajectories of two transitions: Russia's and China's.

The economic crisis of the Soviet Union intensified in the late 1980s. An example of the contradictions and unintended consequences it generated was Gorbachev's attempt to curb alcoholism in the country by increasing its price. This fueled the growth of the black market and criminal gangs that controlled the distribution and sale of spirits; these, in turn, deprived the state of billions of dollars of desperately needed revenues. By the end of 1991, the Soviet government officially declared itself dissolved and banned all activities of Communist Party organizations. The republics seceded from the union of socialist republics; several declared their independence, while others retained ties with the newly created Russian Federation. In January 1992, the Russian Federation launched the austerity programs imposed on it by the United States and the International Monetary Fund. What followed was a period of rampant primitive accumulation and accumulation by dispossession (gangster capitalism) of such unmatched magnitude and rapidity that it made the post-Civil War "robber barons" of the United States—John Rockefeller, Jay Gould, Carnegie, or J. P. Morgan—look like small-time petty crooks. Assets of the party organizations and three-quarters of all medium and large state-owned enterprises were sold to managers; gangsters; foreign investors; and, most importantly, to individuals whose loyalty was unquestioned by the Russian President.

The development of a capitalist market in these circumstances was a hotbed for the formation of a newly rich capitalist class. Simultaneously, the neoliberal policies implemented by the Russian Federation—the end of price controls on traded goods, scarcities, and the weakening state controls or subsidies—underwrote the formation of a poorly paid proletariat as well as vast numbers of unemployed persons who lacked access to the goods and services that were essential for their everyday life. It also fueled the growth of more than 8,000 major criminal gangs in the early 1990s, which controlled more than 50,000 companies and an estimated twenty five–forty percent of the gross national product by 1995 (Williams 1997). These gangs emerged in a milieu in which law enforcement was weak, government officials were underpaid and hence susceptible to bribes, and laws regulating contracts and criminal penalties for fictitious companies or phony bankruptcies were absent. These highly entrepreneurial organizations accumulated wealth by discouraging competition in the market; creating shortages of essential goods; reducing wages; evading workers' health insurance and other benefits; infiltrating banking and other enterprises; and establishing close ties with government officials at the local, state, and federal levels. They have stifled foreign direct investment in Russia and have invested only a small fraction of their wealth in country; the vast majority of their money is invested in foreign companies and real estate or deposited in safe havens—like Switzerland or the Cayman Islands (Holmstrom and Smith 2000; Williams 1997). Since 1994, capital flight from Russia has been about $150 billion each year, according to official sources, and may, in fact, be as high as a trillion dollars a year, according to independent analysts.

The assets of the USSR and Communist Party organizations had been privatized by 2000, when Vladimir Putin was elected President of Russia. There was a power struggle between Putin and the capitalist oligarchs who opposed his policies. He used the ambiguities of the legal system to expose their crimes and indiscretions—e.g. tax evasion—and confiscated their property before they were imprisoned or exiled. Their corporate assets were then redistributed to supporters in return for their loyalty and political silence. Thus, a new class of capitalists, loyal to Putin, was forged in the process; its members retained their wealth as long as they continued to support him (Szelényi 2015).

China has followed a different post-socialist path toward market socialism and neoliberal capitalism. It is still incomplete and highly contested. The changes began in the countryside in 1978, with policies that de-collectivized agriculture, privatized farm lands, and re-established the family farm as the basic production unit. The dismantling of the rural communes underwrote the rapid formation of a free capitalist market in land, which encouraged real estate speculation. It also promoted increasingly specialized agricultural production; a greater division of labor; rural class differentiation and formation; a continually expanding population of rural workers who floated from one job to the next; and the rapid development of enterprises operated by villages, cooperatives, or entrepreneurs. By the mid-1980s, the collective infrastructures of the communes (dams, bridges, and irrigation canals) and their assets (trucks, tractors, and equipment) had been either neglected, not replaced, or sold off as private property. The primary beneficiaries of these market-oriented reforms and commerce in the countryside were the rural bourgeoisie and local officials as well as their relatives and friends; the growth of the market afforded endless opportunities for bureaucratic corruption. At the same time, the peasantry saw the "five guarantees" of the Maoist era—food, shelter, clothing, fuel, and burial expenses—and rural families' need for labor put them on a collision course with the state's "one child per family" population control policy (Meisner 1996:234–250).

In the 1970s, seventy percent of the urban workforce of China was employed in state-owned enterprises. As Meisner (1996:258) noted,

> the economy was governed by a system of central state planning, which set detailed production targets for both the national economy as a whole and the individual factory, allocating supplies of materials and labor accordingly. The aim was to maximize economic rationality and the rate of growth. ... [T]he individual enterprise operated not on the basis of the capitalist principle of profitability but rather according to its assigned role in fulfilling social needs as dictated by the overall national economic plan ... [and] determined by central planners in Beijing.

Additional features of the state economic system were its commitment to full employment, job security, housing, insurance, pensions, and childcare facilities. This was the system that the reformers wanted to change; they claimed, falsely, that the workers were unproductive (Meisner 1996:258–259).

The market reforms introduced in 1979 by Deng Xiaoping and his allies in the government re-organized state-owned enterprises. They established harsher labor discipline and authoritarian management, no longer guaranteed job security, quickly eliminated workers' benefits, and soon imposed austerity measures. By the early 1980s, there was a free labor market, widespread unemployment, an explosive growth of the numbers of private-sector commercial and retail enterprises, a dramatic increase in crime, and corruption by bureaucrats and party officials. The state also created special economic zones (SEZs) on the southeast coast (Guangdong and Fujian), which led to the rapid growth of a market in land and rampant real estate speculation as the state developed the infrastructures of these largely rural areas using money obtained from various state banks. Foreign goods imported through private companies in the SEZs were resold illegally for foreign currency; seventy percent of the goods produced in the zones were sold illegally for profit in other parts of the country. In effect, the SEZs were trading centers for duty-free or smuggled foreign goods. Their failure was apparent by the mid-1980s as the state's foreign exchange reserves declined, and its trade deficit soared (Meisner 1996:260–284).

In 1984, the Central Committee of the Communist Party reformed urban economic policies along the lines of those it implemented five years earlier in the countryside. These were the substitution of central planning with enterprise profitability, the creation of a free labor market, the increased division of labor in the industrial sector, and the relaxation of price controls set by the state. While control over the economy was reformed or decentralized to provincial and local governments in many enterprises, the central government retained control over the production and prices of steel, coal, and oil. Enterprises were placed under trained managers who promoted capitalist rationality, increased efficiency, greater worker productivity, and the maximization of profits. The state gave more autonomy to provincial and municipal banks, while the central bank retained control over the banking system as a whole. Enterprises and local governments borrowed from provincial and local banks to expand the production of consumer goods that would yield quick profits and to purchase imported machinery through greater access to foreign exchange. This fueled the expansion of investment in light industry, financial investment, and wage increases for some. However, it also spurred double-digit inflation rates, widespread corruption, and shortages. New austerity measures were implemented in 1986 because of rising deficits, growing numbers of closed factories, rising unemployment, and growing inequality. Opposition to the reforms was intense among state industrial workers and party members who regarded job security and workers' welfare as moral obligations owed to all citizens by the socialist government (Meisner 1996:285–299).

While some city-dwellers saw substantial increases in their standard of living, the primary beneficiaries of the reforms were members of the higher echelons of the Communist Party bureaucracy and technocrats, who already enjoyed significant privileges—housing, travel, better health care, shops, and elite schools. Many of the new bourgeoisie that emerged in the 1980s were their sons and daughters—e.g. Deng Xiaoping's children. They profited directly or indirectly from the emerging capitalist market economy. They did so by plundering the state, influence-peddling, bribery, graft, profiteering, embezzlement, currency manipulation, kickbacks, and expropriating both state firms and property. They used their newly acquired wealth mainly for conspicuous consumption, to create more repressive labor systems, and overseas investment. Among the largest beneficiaries was the Peoples' Liberation Army (Meisner 1996:300–343; Walker 2006:1–6).

In the mid-1980s, the Democracy Movement was launched by university students, the children of privileged families, who called for greater autonomy for themselves and for reforms within the Communist Party that would facilitate their entry into the gangster capitalist class (Walker 2006). In 1989, they called for a general strike that defied the authority of the Communist Party. This set the stage for the massive demonstration called the Movement at Tiananmen Square and for the state's declaration of martial law. The center of gravity of the demonstration shifted from the students when massive numbers of workers arrived in the square to protest their own grievances against the government. Unlike the students who championed the market reforms and represented only a small fraction of the country's population (four million out of a population of nearly one billion), the several hundred million workers in China did have the capacity to disrupt production. Military units loyal to the government were ordered to suppress the demonstration as quickly as possible. Two to seven thousand demonstrators, mostly workers, were killed, and many more were jailed; the students, in contrast, were treated much more leniently (Meisner 1996:400–454).

Following the Tiananmen Square demonstrations, the austerity measures of the mid-1980s were eased, and high economic growth rates resumed. The early 1990s was a time characterized by double-digit growth; it was also a time of uneven development, growing inequality between and within the cities and the countryside, a floating (redundant or disposable) labor force of several hundred million people, increased insecurity felt by a majority of the working population because of the continued demands for greater efficiency and productivity, an upsurge in common crime in both the cities and countryside, and the massive degradation of the environment as its wealth and resources were plundered (Meisner 1999:532–537; Smith 1997).

In 1993, the party-state implemented a second phase of market reforms. The new policies asserted state control over fiscal resources, streamlined the state sector of the economy, and re-established austerity measures. These involved restructuring banking, reforming corporate governance, establishing regulatory agencies, eliminating corruption, and implementing tax reforms. What emerged out of the reforms is best conceptualized as a three-tier economy in which ownership is usefully distinguished from decision-making authority. The top tier consists of the assets of party-state enterprises, such as heavy industry, grain production, and finance, which are valued at trillions of dollars and are strategic to national economic and security concerns; control over these is exercised by state officials. The middle tier is comprised of enterprises owned by various state, provincial, and municipal entities—e.g. automobiles, pharmaceuticals, heavy machinery, biotechnology, and energy—which are overseen by a number of often overlapping and contradictory regulatory agencies. The lowest tier consists mainly of small and medium-sized manufacturing, retail, and service industries, many of which are owned by villages and towns and, after 2001, by enterprises with varying degrees of private and foreign direct investment; these are concentrated largely in the export sector and include firms like the ones supplying Walmart (Pearson 2015). The state encouraged foreign direct investment in order to gain access to technology, brands, and management skills. China's exports increased eightfold between 1994 and 2007, from $121 billion to $975 billion. The foreign-invested enterprises—subsidiaries of global multinationals and joint ventures with firms from the industrialized world—accounted for sixty five percent of the increase in Chinese exports during this period (Hart-Landsberg and Burkett 2004:89; Naughton 2015).

The state injected financial resources into the state banks in 1998 to prevent the spread of the East Asian financial crisis. It allowed thousands of small and medium-sized factories with non-producing loans to close. This put twenty million or so workers out on the streets, depriving them of job security, benefits, housing, and pensions. Since then, the Central Bank of China has held increasingly tight reins over the financial and banking sectors, which buffered the country to some extent from fluctuations in the global economy. The Central Bank has also wanted the yuan (renmindi) to become a globally recognized reserve currency, like the U.S. dollar. This is where another contradiction began to crystallize. For years, the Central Bank maintained a fixed exchange rate with the U.S. dollar; however, the value of the dollar appreciated relative to other fixed currencies (euro and yen) in mid-2014, which meant that the price of the goods produced in China increased for its major trading partners in East and Southeast Asia. This, in turn, meant that the value of its exports to those countries declined. In mid-August 2015, the Central Bank devalued the yuan. While this potentially boosted Chinese exports, it sent shock waves through financial markets around the world. It showed that countries whose currency is pegged to a standard, like the U.S. dollar or the euro, have difficulties managing their own economies.

Two immediate results of devaluation were that capital outflows from China quickly doubled or tripled and that the outbound direct investment far outpaced gains from maintaining a favorable trade balance (Victor Lippit, personal communication January 27, 2016). Individuals and Chinese companies—including state-owned ones—are investing overseas to secure the value of their assets. The government has threatened to crack down on "irrational overseas" investment tendencies and to scrutinize companies that invest outside their core business areas or that expand too rapidly. Further increases in the value of the dollar will likely exacerbate this situation (Roberts 2016).

The number of labor disputes rose dramatically after 1993. There were more than 325,000 labor disputes in 2000, some of which were settled through the legal system. However, there were also more than 8,000 collective actions and strikes that year, involving about 250,000 people. Five years later, in 2005, there were 87,000 strikes, protests, road blockades, and other disruptions, involving as many as five million people. These caused significant personal and property damage (Walker 2008:467). Ironically, the classes that the Chinese Communist Party claims to represent have become its worst and most feared enemy since the 1990s.

Nationalism, the Nation, and Nation-States

The worldwide political and economic turmoil since the late 1970s has been accompanied by the resurgence of nationalism, both in the former socialist countries and in liberal-democracies. Thus, the National Question is once again in the spotlight of world affairs (e.g. Anderson 1983; Gellner 1983; Nairn

1977, 1997; Wallerstein and Balibar 1991[1988]). The current debates are different from the earlier ones. They are not particularly concerned with the issues of national integration, national liberation, or the Cold War blocs of nations that dominated debates from c. 1920 to 1980 (see Chapters 4 and 5). Some theorists, attracted by globalization theory, emphasize the weakening of nation-states; the adoption of neoliberal policies; increased cosmopolitanism; the emergence of de-nationalized institutions, like the European Union or the WTO; and their consequences (e.g. Hardt and Negri 2000). Other commentators stress the crises that have been created by instability, secession, irredentism, the formation of new states, and their relation to issues of sovereignty, identity, and self-determination; still others are concerned with the processes underlying the rise of nationalism, ethnogenesis, ethnic/national revivals, populism, fundamentalism, fascism, ethnic conflict, and violence (Glick Schiller and Irving 2015; Kapferer and Bertelsen 2009). Thus, the current terrain of the National Question involves the constitution of the nation and its connections with (1) the closely related ideas of nationalism and nationality; (2) the formation of national education systems and collective identities; (3) modernity and modernization; (4) uneven development on a global scale; (5) civil society, democracy, and fascism; (6) cosmopolitanism and communitarianism; (7) social movements and populism; and (8) growing social inequality and structural violence. Many acknowledge the historical specificity and contingencies of the current conjuncture; some recognize the dialectical linkages of the conditions, relations, and processes that constitute this totality.

Nationalism and the Nation

Ernest Gellner (1925–1995) and Benedict Anderson (1936–2015), for example, focused on nationalism. In the mid-1960s, Gellner (1964) postulated that the rise of nationalism was linked with the uneven spread and experience of industrialization and modernization within a state, like Algeria. He insisted that an industrial society ultimately depends on literacy, a level of technical competence, and a common language—the products of a national educational system—which permit people to communicate with strangers. In his view, nationalism invents or fabricates nations. Anderson (1983) took a different tack. He argued that the nation and nationalism were cultural artifacts—imagined communities, sovereign, with finite boundaries that separated members from non-members (foreigners or others). The convergence of print technology with early capitalism created possibilities for new forms of imagined communities based on literacy. This set the stage for the formation of the modern nation. Nationalism emerged after creole states (Haiti and the United States) formed in the colonies of colonial countries. These movements were led by middle-class intelligentsias that spoke the same language and read the same books as the people against whom they fought. Moreover, there has since been a succession of nationalist forms—the last of which were the responses to the global imperialism made possible by industrial capitalism and were led by bilingual intelligentsias that had access to the experiences of earlier nationalist movements. Cosmopolitan intellectuals speak of nationalism as pathological—hatred, racism, and fear of Others. Those threatened by the new order (modernity)—its uncontrolled social and technological change, erosion of social order, weakening of religion, flattening of human aspirations, dehumanization, individuation, and distrust of institutions seen as agents of change—seek to revive the past by restoring waning social relations and fading expectations or desires for themselves and their families. This often involves an intensification of fundamentalism, structured violence, xenophobia, and fascism.

While Gellner and Anderson deployed the idea of the nation, neither really explored what a nation is. Nations, Étienne Balibar (1942–) writes, are a type of social formation that lasts for some period of time:

> They are held together by sentiments, collective memories, political ideologies and structures, the administration, economic interests, and other elements that have their own 'historicity.' It seems to me that the general rule is that historical nations at any given moment put to work *one of the existing possibilities* for uniting populations in the framework of the same institution. But it is never the only possibility, and other possibilities that seem open to new historical and political perspectives or to correspond to other relations of power can always recover their credibility—whence the frequency of 'divisions' or 'separations' and 'fusions' or 'federations.' To put it in terms of a concept borrowed from Marx ... in so far as nations are sets of codified relations between state and society, political community and individuals, social groups and public sphere, they can certainly acquire in the course of history a singular collective 'identity' (what Rousseau went so far as to call a 'common self' endowed with life and will) but only *on the condition of being reproduced* as such. ... The nation-form is a mode of combination of economic and ideological structures.
>
> (Balibar 2004:17, emphasis in original)

Balibar proceeds to point out that the nation-form is merely one way of articulating the administrative and ideological structures of a state in order to reduce complexity and forge homogeneity. What nation-states do is appropriate record-keeping, administrative functions, and the educational system that control communication and the definition of culture, history, nationality, and language. These practices occur historically only in contexts of uneven development. Balibar writes that

> a 'world-economy' that has developed in the form of a universal market cannot (contrary to the liberal myth) form a *homogeneous* whole; it must be divided into a plurality of *political unities* that allow for the concentration of economic power and the defense of positions of unearned income (*rente*) or 'monopoly' by extraeconomic means. There is no market without monopolies, no monopolies without instruments of political (or juridical)

compulsion, which in practice means national states. But if this is the case, we must go a step further for the condition required for the convergence of economic and political forces is *the political control of class struggles in and by the state*. To put it better: there must be *class struggles*, capable of representing or absorbing other forms of social conflict (such as tribalisms, illegalisms, regionalisms), but at the same time these *class struggles* must be controlled or regulated by force and, even more important, by means of specific political representation. It is thus necessary to invent institutions and discourses that allow class conflict to be subordinated to a relatively effective, durable, and 'equitable' 'general interest.'

(Balibar 2004:18, emphasis in original)

These are related to identity, to how individuals describe themselves and are described by others, and to notions of belonging or not. Every individual possesses multiple primary identities, qualities, and notions of belonging, qualities—like sex, gender, race, age, sexual preference, religion, occupation, and place of origin—that we deploy and that are deployed by others in everyday life—for example, grumpy, old white guy and retired worker from central Maine or orange, xenophobic narcissist from New York, to name two. Nation-states strive to create a secondary identity (a civic, national one)—American, Irish, or Peruvian—that competes for space in discourse and action with the primary identities of individuals as well as more or less coherent communities. These secondary identities are commemorated through the history classes we took in school, holidays (e.g. the Fourth of July, Thanksgiving, Columbus Day), monuments (the Capitol), symbols (flags), or unifying (patriotic) rhetoric in times of crisis (e.g. 9/11 or leading up to war). Of course, the secondary identities also compete for space and time in nationalist discourses and practices, where they revive the original meanings of the words "nation" or "ethnic group", which distinguish between those who do not belong—foreigners—and those who do.

Nationalism, of course, is based on rules of exclusion and preferential (unequal) access to rights depending on whether the individual is a national, not quite a national, or a foreigner altogether. Balibar continues by pointing out that multiple types of structural violence are involved in the processes of identification. One is the "multicultural problem" in which some languages and regional, religious, or national identities are not officially recognized as legitimate mediations of the state's secondary identity—e.g. African Americans. A second form of structural violence is the refusal to accept religious mediations of the secondary identity of the state—e.g. the exclusion of Jewish refugees from the United States before and during World War II or the potential ban on Muslims today. A third type of structural violence occurs when the institutions of the nation-state do not or cannot produce the kind of ideological integration necessary during times of crisis and

individuals find it increasingly difficult to inscribe themselves in subjective trajectories of formation of the personality and social integration. The risk then is that mediating function of primary identities within a hegemonic culture of historical *Sittlichkeit* [Hegel's notion of ethical life or order] will fall into what sociologists call 'anomie' or 'negative individuality,' even into what psychoanalysts call 'borderline' syndrome—in other words, the direct expression in social relations, of the ambivalence of identities, of the 'primary process' of affective displacement between love and hate. Not only 'civilization's discontent,' but its decomposition.

(Balibar 2004:29–30)

There has been a resurgence of nationalist sentiments and movements after the dissolution of socialist ideals in the late 1980s. For example, distinctions between Chinese nationals and foreigners became increasingly pronounced in the export processing zones of China's south coast. When Boris Yeltsin and his contemporaries weakened or dissolved the federated socialist states—the USSR, Yugoslavia, and Czechoslovakia—in the early 1990s without referenda, they left in place various national republics—Russia, Latvia, and Croatia, for instance—whose existences were already recognized in the federal constitutions. After the federations were dissolved and states seceded, the leaders of the dominant national groups in each of the successor states continued to exercise power. Where there were multinational populations, as in Latvia or Russia, the members of the politically dominant national group used their identity to secure their preferential treatment and access to scarce resources in a system marked by organized shortages.

Post-coloniality, Nationality, and Modernity

Anti-colonial and decolonization movements dominated the decades following World War II (Chapter 5). A debate began in the mid-1970s (e.g. Ahmad 1996[1985]; Alavi 1972; Saul 1974). It was framed in terms of "post-colonial." It was concerned with two questions: What was the historical specificity of post-colonial societies resulting from the experiences of imperialism and colonialism, and what changes occurred after liberation and independence because of the re-alignments of class forces in those countries? Hamsa Alavi (1972:62) wrote,

The state in post-colonial society is not the instrument of a single class. It is relatively autonomous, and it mediates between the competing interests of the three propertied classes, namely the metropolitan bourgeoisies, the indigenous bourgeoisie, and the landed classes, while at the same time acting on behalf of them to preserve the social order in which their interests are embedded, namely the constitution of private property and the capitalist mode as the dominant mode of production. ... In this situation the military-bureaucratic oligarchies, the apparatus of the state furthermore assumes also a new and relatively autonomous *economic* role which is not paralleled in the classical bourgeois state. The state in the post-colonial society directly appropriates a very large part of the economic surplus and deploys it in bureaucratically directed economic activity in the name of promoting economic development. ... The relationship [of politicians and political parties] with the bureaucratic-military is ... ambivalent; it is competitive as well as complementary. The ambivalence is greater where politicians who occupy high public office can influence the careers of individual members of the bureaucracy or the military.

Aijaz Ahmad (1996[1985]) disagreed and argued instead that the intermediate classes (e.g. small landowners, rural merchants, small manufacturers, retailers, and professionals—i.e. the petite bourgeoisie) also occupy strategic economic and political positions in post-colonial countries and, therefore, wield considerable power in their civil societies. Nationalism was often their preferred terrain of politics. It took a variety of forms: (1) opposition to colonial occupation and imperialist exploitation; (2) opposition to internal opponents or centralized state apparatuses—communal or separatist movements; (3) assimilative movements—such as Pan-Arabism, Pan-Islamism, or Pan-African—that involve collaborative projects; and (4) radical movements basing their claims on anti-imperialism and presenting themselves as a "third way" that was neither communist nor capitalist. Ahmad proceeded to argue that nationalism had no content before the particular historical circumstances in which post-colonial societies crystallized; the content of nationalist ideology depended on specific class alliances. "The nation" as a concept was attractive to the intermediate classes because of its ambiguity. It could be used to suppress questions about inequality and class structures and to pose them instead in terms of "the people" or even a classless state.

> It is precisely because of its supraclass appearance and its immense mobilizing power that the ideology of nationalism becomes the classic terrain for the construction of hegemony, on the part of any class which seeks to lead the other classes in civil society.
>
> (Ahmad 1996[1985]:68)

Thus, when we speak of these nations [i.e. the countries from the Indian subcontinent to North Africa] we are referring not so much to some set of supposedly permanent and primordial facts of ethnicity or race of religion, or of some idealized spiritual ethnos. We refer, rather ... to the mundane world of territorial boundaries, armies, markets, systems of taxation and governance, bodies of legislation, artefacts of ideology, facts and rights of residence, and so forth. That is to say: force, legality, hegemony. In other words, it is a characteristic of the capitalist era that nations and states tend to converge; that a nation is either created by or finds its material form in the existence of a state; and that consolidated nations arise only where a coherent power bloc is able, simultaneously, to fashion a nationalist and populist ideology as the principle of its own legitimation, as well as to construct a state that fixes the boundaries of what eventually becomes a nation.

No wonder, then, that precisely those class forces that are most prominent in the organization of the peripheral state are also the ones most prominent in articulating that whole set of ideological positions that appear ... under the rubric of 'the national question.' It is no exaggeration to say, I think, that every nationalist movement in these regions, whether assimilative or of the separatist kind, whether anticolonial and revolutionary or ethnocentric and chauvinist, is led primarily by personnel that originates in segments of the intermediate classes. This personnel is sometimes allied with fractions of capital and landed property, sometimes not; some might make a revolutionary choice ..., while others may settle down to be outright reactionaries. ... Neither their ideological outlook nor their alliances are preordained by their class origins. But their strategic location in the whole range of nationalist politics is at any rate beyond question.

(Ahmad 1996[1985]:70–71)

The ascendancy of the national bourgeoisies in the former colonies was short-lived. Once independence was attained, the dynamic of decolonization waned from the mid-1970s onward—except in settler colonies, like Israel and South Africa:

With the colonial relationship broken, the newly independent states were expected to combat imperialism with the nationalist *ideologies*, regardless of what classes were now in power and irrespective of the utter inadequacy of the nationalist ideology, as such, even at its best, to protect a backward capitalist country against the countless pressures of advanced capitalism, so long as the confrontation takes place within an imperialist structure, which is to say, on capitalist terms.

(Ahmad 1992:41)

In hindsight, the history of the colonial states in the 1970s was repeated during the 1990s in the wake of the dissolution, dismemberment, and secession of the socialist states in Eastern Europe. It is repeating itself again with rise of nationalist and populist movements in the advanced industrial countries of the European Union (Brexit) and in the United States (Donald Trump's election in 2016).

A new phenomenon—post-colonial studies—appeared in the late 1980s at the same time as the resurgence of nationalism and discourses about globalization; the collapse of the nation-state; and the emergence of a globalized, postmodern electronic culture. These, in fact, were aspects or facets of the same crisis. From Ahmad's (1995) perspective, post-colonial critics and theorists were not concerned with political-economic, social, and cultural dynamics underlying post-colonial states. Their foci instead were postmodern concerns with text and discourse, and the critique of the politics of representation and identities (e.g. subjectivities, race, gender, or class). These theorists sought to examine how European writers had portrayed colonial peoples; how their premises had crept into texts about the identities of colonial peoples written by authors from those colonies; the hybridity of writers who acknowledged and intermingled traditions from the worlds of both the colonizer and the colonized; and whether colonial people could, in fact, speak for themselves. The post-colonial theorists collapsed the specificity of the circumstances debated by Alavi, Ahmad, and others, replacing this with a generalized "post-colonial condition" in which the experiences of Andean peoples in the sixteenth century were somehow analogous or interchangeable with those living in the Indian subcontinent in the nineteenth century or in West Africa a century later. The theorists reduced the historicity, and tragedy, of the original debate to accidents of contingency.

Activist-critic David Lloyd has a different view about the importance of a comparative approach in understanding the effects of colonialism in post-colonial societies. He writes that

> Colonialism is an integrated phenomenon that operates across all the fields that in the West would constitute the public and the private, civil society and the state. No single event that occurs or institutional practice that is implemented is without effects across all domains of colonized societies, not least because the aim of colonialism is the utter transformation of the colonized culture: the eradication of its structures of feeling, the subjection of the population to the colonizers' notions of legality and citizenship, and the displacement of indigenous forms of religion, labour, patriarchy, and rule by those of colonial modernity. Again colonialism is also a rationalizing endeavor that leads to the frequent replication of similar institutions and practices across the widely spread and diverse colonies of each imperial power. Not least, colonialism produces power and fantasmatic ideologies that are no less fantastic for being woven and sustained through its quasiscientific studies in racial typology, history, and the economics of development. Nowhere more than under colonialism is the deep unreason of reason more compellingly in evidence.
>
> (Lloyd 2000:378)

While the policies and practices of imperial powers attempted to homogenize the structures of their colonies, no two were precisely the same. Their unevenness shaped their formation; it also calls into question colonializing or globalizing projects that are "founded in and still legitimated by Europe's delusion of universality" (Lloyd 2000:378). Lloyd advocates instead a differential analysis that recognizes the heterogeneity of the colonies and post-colonial states at the same time that it acknowledges that what happened in one might shed understanding on what happened in another without demanding that their histories be entirely congruent.

For Lloyd, the post-colonial studies that emerged from the late 1980s were a moral critique of the national bourgeoisies that crystallized in the wake of decolonization as well as their failures. Post-colonial studies challenged the integrity of established disciplines and fields of study in the industrial capitalist countries—e.g. the sciences, economics, history, literature, psychology, or anthropology—and were critical of the roles they played in buttressing imperialism and colonialism and that they continue to play in the globalizing processes of today. More importantly, they are a critique of universalized notions of rationality, objectivity, value-neutrality, sociohistorical development, and progressive features of modernity. They resuscitate and revitalize phrases from earlier in the twentieth century, such as "science is political" and "science for the people."

Feminist philosopher of science and critic Harding (2008:77–95, 124–129) goes even further. In her view, post-colonial and feminist studies, focused on the interaction between science and society, have signaled the emergence of a new kind of science, one that is sensitive to the particular sociohistorical contexts in which it is practiced, to the power relations that shape the interactions of its practitioners in those circumstances, and to the intersectionality of the multiple identities of those who are creating scientific knowledge (e.g. class, race, gender, mother, uncle, or retired worker, to name a few familiar ones). They break the connection between science and modernity; they challenge the identification of science and technology with some sort of progressive modernization; and they call into question the authority of scientists, their efforts to standardize scientific knowledge across different cultures, and their claims of having a monopoly on the production of scientific knowledge. They point instead to multiple pathways leading to multiple kinds of modernities. They erode the distinction between traditional and modern made by the modernization theorists, even though the arguments of the latter depend on the persistence of the former. They make it more difficult to generalize from one's own life experiences about individuals living in different conditions—i.e. to stand in their shoes and understand why they do what they do and why they believe what they do (to have empathy). While modern science has focused on value-neutrality, instrumental rationality, and the search for predictability, these studies point to the unpredictability and uncertainty of what the future will bring and to the anxiety and fear that they provoke in contemporary life.

Crisis, Identity, and Populism

In the 1970s, commentators noted new forms of social protest that were appearing in response to structural changes in the core industrial capitalist societies. They claimed that these *new social movements*—e.g. the women's, gay men's and lesbians', anti-war, peace, environmental, anti-nuclear, anti-tax, religious fundamentalist, and white power groups—were not rooted in class conflict as earlier ones had been. The questions they asked were how and why people in societies based on individualism, individualization, and alienation mobilize for collective action. They offered "... the concept of 'collective identities' as a way of explaining how people act in concert with the object of achieving a new, distinct, or semiautonomous kind of presence and cultural recognition... in the process of political activity" (Stephen 1997:20). They saw these largely urban-based, decentralized movements drawing members from various social classes who had diverse political and theoretical perspectives, ideas, and values. They saw the movements as giving voice to the grievances and sentiments of individuals and collectivities whose identities were weakly developed, blurred, subordinated, or suppressed by the dominant cultural, social, and political systems. The identities and grievances that the participants sought to preserve focused on cultural and social issues, and often involved expressions of personal, intimate aspects of their lives.

They argued that the movements were different from earlier forms of social protest because they were not concerned with the economic grievances of the working class nor did they question the basic tenets of capitalism itself. Support for the movements did not come from political parties, trade unions, or subordinated social strata but rather from middle-class individuals who opposed the institutions and practices of the welfare state. These individuals articulated certain values to gain and mobilize participants for political action. They frequently circumvented established political institutions because their participants felt marginalized or disenfranchised by political parties and other organizations that influenced state policies. Early theorists offered three sociological explanations for their appearance:

One explanation of the new social movements was sociologist Alain Touraine's (1925–) claim that they were the first manifestations of the appearance of post-industrial society (Touraine 1977[1973], 1981[1978]). The distinctive features of the new type of society were: (1) services had eclipsed the production of goods in the economic sphere, (2) a new professional and technical class had become pre-eminent, and (3) theoretical knowledge was the basis for innovation and policy formulation. Because a high degree of reflexivity characterized this emergent society, its political institutions, organizational practices, and cultural arrangements were often contested. While the members of the pre-eminent classes shared the same cultural orientation toward instrumental rationality and productivity, they disagreed over how this model should be deployed. For Touraine, the new social movements were expressions of this structural conflict.

A second explanation was that of critical theorist Jürgen Habermas (1929–) who argued that late capitalist states (i.e. those in the West or core countries) suffered from a crisis of legitimization; they had become disconnected from their communicatively constructed public spheres of debate (Habermas 1981). The public sphere is where states exercising their regulatory functions over the economy (narrowly defined in terms of instrumental rationality) had been invaded, overwhelmed, and remodeled by commercial interests that increasingly shaped public opinion and depoliticized political issues, treating them as technical problems. The new social movements arose as the same fate threatened the private sphere. The new social movements appeared in those areas of society concerned with cultural reproduction, social integration, and socialization. These extra-parliamentary forms of protest focused on issues concerning quality of life, self-realization, and human rights rather than economic, domestic, or military security. These highly particularistic movements seek to block formal, organized spheres of action by forging new structures of communication.

A third account, provided by Ernesto Laclau (1935–2014) and Chantal Mouffe (1943–), argued that the new social movements were based on the articulation of assembly-line production, interventionist state policies, and new cultural forms that unleashed complex processes (Laclau and Mouffe 1988). State intervention ensured capitalist reproduction by taming the capitalists' urge to lower wages and using regular cost-of-living wage increases to tie workers' demands to increased productivity. Capitalist relations penetrated almost every sphere of everyday life, commodifying and homogenizing culture, transforming people into consumers, underwriting the growing uniformity of everyday life that resulted from a media-imposed mass culture, and destroying the environment. Increasing state intervention in social life was accompanied by the steady growth of a professionalized bureaucracy as well as by antagonisms that underwrote the emergence of the new forms of protest. What was new about the new social movements for Laclau and Mouffe is that they emerged in spheres of everyday life that had only recently come under the domination of capital and the state. What the new social movements had in common was that they are not rooted in the class position of their participants. They were rooted instead in the appearance of antagonisms that were "... always discursively constructed" (Mouffe 1988:95). In other words, the collective subjects constituted by particular discourses (1) found that their identities and rights were negated by the emergence of new discourses and practices or (2) that they were constituted as subordinates by some discourses and as equals by others. Mouffe (1988:95–96) suggested that

> People struggle for equality not because of some ontological postulate but because they have been constructed as subjects in a democratic tradition that puts those values at the center of social life. ... Democratic discourse questions all forms of inequality and subordination.

As a result, opposition to subordination and inequality as well as efforts to democratize social life have taken diverse forms in the present situation. In this milieu, progressive movements are the ones whose members are capable of linking their own interests with those of other collective groups.

In a carefully argued response to their claims, Ellen Wood (1986:47, 62–68) pointed out that Laclau and Mouffe had dissolved social reality into discourse and politics into struggles for control over them. Because the collective identities constituted are autonomous from the relations of exploitation and domination rooted in the political economic structures of capitalist society—i.e. they are not organically linked to the members of a particular class—they can be de-linked from the ideology of one class and assimilated to that of another. In other words, these free-floating, class-neutral identities have no necessary relation to exploitation and domination. Thus, Laclau and Mouffe stripped these identities from the class relations and contexts in which they developed. Moreover, their liberal-democratic reconceptualization of the economic sphere displaced exploitation from its central position in capitalist social relations and separated the economic and political levels of society. Politics, in the process, became limited to relations among free and equal individuals.

Wood also raised another issue. If these identities are not related to class struggle and class position, then who really constitutes them: a plural subject; a popular force; no one; everyone; or some external agent or agency, like intellectuals standing partly or wholly outside the struggle? In Wood's view, class is central, and Laclau and Mouffe's perspective is a retreat. For Wood (1986:99–100), the economic sphere does have a bearing on the structure of social and political domination, the exploitative relations between capital and labor have had tangible effects on the working class, people who are exploited have an interest in and benefit from the abolition of exploitation, the destruction of the structures of domination is an essential part of the struggle for human emancipation, and the groups most exploited by capitalist accumulation and exploitation are the ones best situated to understand those relations.

Socialist, feminist anthropologist Karen Brodkin (1941–) also criticized explanations that relied on the analytical category of "collective identity." She asked instead how are political identities constructed, how do they crystallize into movements, and how have "participants in these movements connected their quests for personal and meaningful relationships to the world in which they lived to the activism in which they were engaged" (Brodkin 2003:7)? Since the early 1980s, her writing focused on political activism and the intersectionality of the multiple identities and experiences that each individual brings to or carries in the social world (Brodkin Sacks 1989; Brodkin 1998, 2000). Briefly, Brodkin argued (1) that one identity (e.g. gender) is not analytically separable from others because they are experienced simultaneously in historically specific social fields shaped by inequality and myriad forms of social hierarchy and (2) that, in the United States, these identities were constructed and internalized by participants during the intensification of liberal individualism and its linkages with postwar resistance to capitalism. As anthropologist Lynn Stephen (1997:20) noted, the collective identity of participants in a social movement are always constructed, contested, and negotiated in the process of political activism. Gavin Smith (1991), Marxian anthropologist, observed that participants frequently argue with one another and with others in the process. Their accounts of the cultural and historical specificity of the circumstances in which individuals construct and internalize their multiple selves contrast with the distinction that Balibar drew a few years later between primary and secondary identities (Balibar 2004).

Many new social movements have appealed or sought to represent the interests of the "common people" rather than those of "the elite." In this sense, they are populist movements; however, "populism" is a very fuzzy and elusive concept. Political theorist Michael Bray (2015) writes perceptively that populist movements arise during periods of social and economic transformation and destabilizing crises. He further notes that liberal-democratic notions of populist movements as narrowly political or ideological phenomena divorced from class sensibilities and class struggles are widely embraced, even by some leftist writers. Bray has a different view. He understands populism as

... a politicised antagonism to the increasingly dominant *economic* functions of the state, as well as a specific 'spatial-economic' that informs national-popular identities. Populism's bid for a more 'representative' government is also a demand for economic 'independence,' a demand mediated through the individualising and universalizing tendencies of state-discourse but articulating a nascent threat to them. ... [Bray sees] 'neoliberal populism' as an intrinsic aspect of the rise to hegemony of neoliberalism amidst the fragmentation of traditional class identities, such that contemporary populisms revolve around neoliberalism's reorientation of capital accumulation and its contradictory populist and de-democratising aspects.

(Bray 2015:31)

Bray bases his alternative to liberal-democratic views of populism on the work of earlier socialist critics, notably Laclau (1977) and Nicos Poulantzas (1975[1974], 1980[1978]). The latter had argued that the state is the central site at which the economic and political-ideological functions of the state are articulated and continually reproduced—i.e. capital accumulation and the political-ideological elements that underwrite exploitation at a society-wide level. This requires the state to train its citizens to believe that the market is a politically neutral place of consumption rather than the site of surplus extraction and capital accumulation. It also involves atomizing the body politic into individuals (the processes of individualization and isolation), which obscures class structures; hierarchically differentiating manual from intellectual laborers (workers or the "middle class" from technocrats) and thereby excluding vast numbers of individuals who presumably lack the knowledge required to manage complex systems; reproducing the image of a "people-nation" (i.e. Balibar's secondary identity) whose members have a common history and destiny; and proclaiming universal rights while simultaneously separating leaders from the governed and citizens from non-citizens.

Populism is an understanding of antagonisms materialized in the state. Crises of capital accumulation and class formation are moments when the state's functions are most visible and contested because of their failure. Populist movements reflect this disjunction between the traditional class structure and the political situations and circumstances configured by crises. They are times of transition when new class identities and interests have not crystallized. They are also times when states are potentially most open to pressures emanating from outside of their established institutions and to rules and demands to reconfigure or restructure their functions and objectives.

Socialist critic John Foster (2017a,b) takes a slightly different tack. He points out that populism is a "fuzzy concept"; he and others call what is taking place in the United States and Western Europe today "neofascism." In this view, there is a continuum between liberal-democracy and fascism. "Fascism is a political form that arises from interrelated crises of capitalism and the liberal-democratic state, undermining the latter and shoring up the former." An example is the bank bailouts following the collapse of U.S. financial institutions in 2007–2008; they were particularly beneficial to the finance, insurance, real estate, and energy sectors (Foster 2017a:9). The rising dominance of neofascism involves the appropriation (seizure) of the state apparatus, eliminating the separation of powers, privatizing state enterprises, and centralizing control under a strong executive (Foster 2017b:5).

Marxist anthropologist Christine Gailey (personal communication, 2016) argues that neofascism has been the political-economic project of neoliberalism since the 1970s. Bray (2015:47) points out that the project has involved reconfiguring capital accumulation. Globalization and the financialization of capital have (1) provoked an ongoing series of crises; (2) transformed production processes through computerization and automation, leading to large increases in corporate profits; (3) weakened the power of workers by "undermining unions, breaking the link between productivity and wage increases and throwing off increasing numbers of workers into low-paid service sectors or into the ranks of individuals who virtually drift about within the social structure, and who populate the interstices of society without finding any established position within it"; and (4) privatized and individualized the cost of social reproduction by linking the interests of individuals with those of capital.

The role of the state in the neoliberal project has been (1) to convince everyone that social reproduction is intimately tied to market growth by removing market exchange from human relations (and making it part of nature) and by assuring them that the market really is too complex to understand, except perhaps by highly skilled professionals; (2) to promote individualization, making each individual more dependent on market consumption and individually responsible for the reproduction of the wider society; (3) to weaken or eliminate traditional forms of collective resistance by "integrating dominated individuals into the systems of financial debt and risk or the equally pedagogical apparatuses of 'workfare'"; and (4) to persuade people that crises occur when governments or elites interfere in the natural functioning of the market (Bray 2015:47–49).

Different kinds of populist movements emerge in the core industrial countries and in the developing (semi-peripheral) states (Bray 2015; see also Goldfrank 1978; Roberto 2017). The reason is that the processes of individualization and enmeshment in market relations are greater in the former; remnants of communal relations of production and social reproduction still prevail in the latter. Thus, in the core industrial countries (e.g. the United States, France, or Great Britain), neofascist movements with transnational ties and racist, xenophobic, and nationalistic ideologies unite diverse groupings of the middle classes (e.g. small business owners) and privileged layers of the working class, who view themselves as increasingly marginalized in social hierarchies defined in terms of mental labor and advanced college degrees. They align themselves with members of the capitalist classes, whose primary interests remain capital accumulation, and their representatives in the government. This alliance opposes those working and middle-class interests that promote liberal cosmopolitan concerns about the effects of transnationalism and globalization. As Bray (2015:57–58) put it, they seek their

> own identity as a 'people', within the ambit of the state's juridical discourse on individualization, property and unity under the law and the neoliberal discourse of the (consumer) market as a site of freedom and independence. [They] tend towards merely 'political' resolutions—change of representatives, reduction of *visible* state interventions, attacks on abstract 'elitism', defences of property from (racially motivated) state intrusions, etc.—in which the collective identity of 'the people' remains constrained by individualistic terms. The 'people' appears as a collective of necessity, opposed to 'pathological' collectivisms, articulating its antagonistic core through national-popular pseudo-solutions: racism, xenophobia, anti-Semitism, etc. Thus, it is not surprising that neoliberal populism has its epicentres in the core, where neoliberal hegemony is strongest and where the dissolution of traditional notions of class impacts most strongly, since those notions were developed in relation to them.
>
> (Bray 2015:58)

In peripheral countries—e.g. Greece, Spain, Venezuela, or Bolivia—the persistence of communal forms provides bases for relations of production and social reproduction that are not grounded exclusively in market exchange. In these places,

> emphasis [is] on communities rather than workplaces; initial focus on the state as a site for demands, rather than private employers; experimentation with models of articulation that do not require the hegemony of one determinate class.... For the majority of the population, neoliberalism generally appears as an external imposition, fostering their dis-identification with elites who have collaborated in that imposition. Likewise, formally liberal systems of democratic equality and rights have been adapted, in their functioning, to collective or communal settings (including the corporate compromises involved in classical populism). Such settings also retain alternative forms of democratic practices such that class formation takes the form of a fundamental *democratisation*, 'reinstating the communal parameters of daily life as a point of departure for the development of a new autonomous social order.' Neo-colonial relations might also foster articulations of a transnational 'people.'
>
> (Bray 2015:58)

By the early 1990s, scholars from the developing countries had already begun to explore social movements emerging in response to the impact of neoliberal capitalism on the internal crises of their countries (Wignaraja 1993). Unlike some of their counterparts in the West, they retained a much clearer awareness of the relations between those movements and the political and economic structures that gave rise to them.

Global Capitalism and World Environmental Crisis

In the preceding sections, we have discussed global capitalism, its monetary politics, its predatory investment tactics, its engagement in financial speculation, and its reliance on military force. We have not considered its plunder of the earth's resources or its destruction of the environment. The social and natural worlds are intimately intertwined. Changes in one lead to changes in the other. For example, dumping lead or other toxic chemicals into rivers or streams poisons the water, alters the kinds of plants and fish that can survive in the new habitat, and sickens the people who rely on the rivers and streams for water and food—e.g. Flint, Michigan. Cutting rainforest for timber or clearing land for mining in Brazil has turned vast swaths of jungle into semi-arid grasslands. Rising temperatures in the polar regions, caused by enormous releases of carbon dioxide and particulates among other pollutants, have increased the rate at which icecaps and glaciers are melting, thereby increasing sea levels and threatening low-lying cities, like New Orleans or Miami, and even whole countries, like Bangladesh or the Seychelles Islands.

Since the 1960s, environmental movements in advanced capitalist countries, those of the Third World or periphery, and the Soviet Union made ecological destruction a social issue. At this point, there is no question about whether climate and environmental changes have taken place and are continuing to do so at an increasing pace. There are overwhelming amounts of different kinds of empirical and historical evidence showing that this is indeed the case. The issue, then, is not whether change is occurring but rather what the nature of the connections between human society and the natural world is. How do our presuppositions about society and change affect our understanding of those environmental changes?

In his *Perspectives on Ecology: A Critical Essay*, Koula Mellos (1988) observed that many understandings of the human-nature relation are portrayed in terms of neo-Malthusian, expansionist, eco-development, or radical ecological perspectives, each of which makes certain assumptions about human nature and posits a direct, socially unmediated relation between the individual and nature. Their presuppositions simultaneously link the various perspectives and differentiate them. They understand how the advocates of each standpoint comprehend the connections, how they constitute ecology, and what kinds of political action they prescribe to rectify ecological problems. Let us briefly consider each of them.

First, *neo-Malthusians*—such as Ester Boserup (1965) and Mark Cohen (1977)—view the world in terms of a late-eighteenth-century theory of crisis based on scarcity: Misery occurs when the size of a population with a given level of development of productive forces exceeds the capacity of nature to provide an adequate food supply. Crises occur when the finite resources of nature are overused by masses of people with insatiable appetites and desires. The condition of the environment is a consequence of the relationship between the almost unfettered consumption of nature and the limited or deteriorating capacity of nature to replenish itself in the face of overexploitation and pollution. Neo-Malthusian explanations gained momentum in the 1960s—roughly coinciding with decolonization and the wholesale environmental destruction of Vietnam and its neighbors by the United States (Coontz 1957; Ehrlich 1968; Ophuls 1977). From this perspective, population growth is limited by wars, epidemics, famines, and other controls, and by various preventive checks—e.g. birth control, abortion, infanticide, or abstinence—that lower birth rates. Since the neo-Malthusians view human societies as undifferentiated masses of people, their understanding of the relationship between nature and society is unmediated. This prevents them from asking questions about social relations, class structures, or the impact of various culturally informed practices and relations on the environment. In their view, ecological crises are resolved by constraining population growth, reducing the demand for key raw materials, and diminishing waste and pollution. Thus, political policies rooted in neo-Malthusian are concerned with restraining consumption.

Second, *expansionists*—like Ester Boserup (1965), Herman Kahn (1979), and the World Bank (1972)—believe that the infinitely expandable appetites of people are not a problem because there is no contradiction between unfettered consumption and the capacity of nature to reproduce itself. They emphasize the enormous extent of nature's wealth and assert that scarcity must always be understood in terms of the limitations imposed by particular socioeconomic contexts and levels of development. Throughout history, they argue, people have repeatedly overcome shortages and created new needs through technological innovation. From their perspective, ecology is ultimately crisis-free. The appearance of problems in the connection between society and nature—like the contamination or destruction of nature—creates the conditions for future solutions because of the steadily increasing tempo of technological innovation. For example, manufacturing pollution devices or providing services—like cleaning up toxic waste sites, buildings with asbestos, or severely damaged nuclear reactors—became major growth industries in the 1980s. Expansionist political praxis claims that the proper role of government is not to regulate the activities of innovative individuals but rather to protect the conditions that permit them to pursue the private appropriation and accumulation of capital with as little oversight or interference as possible.

Third, *eco-developmentalists*—e.g. Ernest Schumacher (1973)—argue (1) that human beings produce and consume in order to satisfy basic needs, which are constituted at the level of the asocial individual; (2) that the relationship between a community and nature is a consequence of technologies that embody different ways of appropriating nature rather than an effect of social relations; (3) that the centralization of economic and political power at a global level distributes individuals, societies, and states along a rich-poor axis; (4) that, as a result of the concentration of power, the activities of the rich are guided by a desire to accumulate and expand, while those of the poor are guided by concerns about subsistence; and (5) that the activities of the rich and poor destroy or modify the environment in different ways. They advocate self-reliance—severing the connection with other communities and decentralizing political and economic power in order to eliminate the distinctions between the rich and the poor, and to restore the viability of the environment. Production, consumption, and self-reliance are the critical and problematic features for the eco-developmentalists. They view production and consumption as a single undifferentiated activity (need satisfaction) that involves the appropriation of nature, either as a directly consumable object or as the source of raw materials for producing usable objects. Because the consumption of nature is not mediated by social relations, the relationship between a community and nature is determined exclusively by its technology of appropriation. Hence, technology is the source of social and ecological problems. These problems are resolved when communities become self-reliant and satisfy their needs in ways that are compatible with a stable ecological order and do not involve external assistance. The difficulties encountered by a theory of action based on this perspective are twofold: It lacks a theory of community beyond one defined merely as an aggregate of individuals, and it does not consider how such aggregates assert their political and economic autonomy from the existing world order.

Fourth, *radical ecologists*—such as Murray Bookchin (1980), André Gorz (1980), or William Leiss (1976)—are concerned with the devastating effects of hierarchical social relations and the tendencies toward accumulation generated by capitalism. Capitalist relations rooted in the market exchange of commodities simultaneously create artificial wants and degrade the environment; at the same time, they prevent individuals from realizing their human potential, from satisfying their authentic needs, and from establishing harmonious relations with nature. The radical ecologists explore the contradictions between exploitative social relations, on the one hand, and environmental destruction, on the other. They understand these contradictions in terms of a connection, an exchange, between asocial individuals and nature that is not mediated by social relations. In their view, the satisfaction of authentic needs and self-sufficiency or self-management are critical; these capabilities derive from the species essence of human beings, when the efforts of individuals are free from outside interference or intervention. Authentic needs are satisfied by the individualized activities of persons who are self-sufficient managers of their own destinies. This means that those individuals, who aggregate and constitute a community, relate to nature in a variety of ways. By producing use-values, which satisfy genuine needs, rather than commodities from exchange in the market, which create artificial wants, they establish diversity and equality. Such activities replicate the structure of nature and thereby restore balanced relations with it. Like the eco-developmentalists, the radical ecologists have not adequately explored how aggregates of asocial individuals assert their autonomy and self-sufficiency in a world dominated by capitalist social relations.

Fifth, in the mid-1990s, *Marxian critics*—notably John Bellamy Foster (2000) and Paul Burkett (1999)—began to comment on the linkages between human societies and nature. They describe it in terms of the metabolic interaction and interdependence of human societies and the earth. They view the current crisis in terms of a growing rift in the metabolism underwritten by capitalist accumulation and privatization (theft) of natural resources—the earth's wealth. They recall the dialectic connections that Marx described between the simultaneous appropriation of agricultural land by capitalist landlords engaged in large-scale commercial farming on the outskirts of London; displacement of individuals and families that had tended those lands; migration of these individuals to the city; increased pollution of the Thames River, which was an open sewer for its residents; and depletion of soils' nutrients on capitalist farms—soils that had previously been nourished by the waste products now dumped into the river. The metabolism involves the exchange between human communities and the earth. In systems of capitalist production and accumulation, there is a growing rift or contradiction. People are alienated from the earth and the wealth it provides to all of its inhabitants. This wealth is appropriated by capitalist corporations and transformed into commodities and then profits. In this perspective, the linkage between people and nature, the metabolic rift, is mediated by capitalist social relations. Its focus, then, is not reductively environmental change per se but rather global capitalism, which is destroying the world as a place for human habitation through its relentless drive for "ever-expanding capital accumulation and exponential economic growth" (Foster and Clark 2015:2).

Foster and Brett Clark (2015) explore the differences in these perspectives by examining the reviews of Naomi Klein's (2014) path-breaking book *This Changes Everything: Capitalism vs the Climate*. Klein argues that climate change is taking place; the cause of the environmental crisis associated with it "is not the planet, which operates according to natural laws, but rather the [capitalist] economic and social system in which we live, which treats natural limits as mere barriers to surmount" (Foster and Clark 2015:1). She asserts that climate change loomed as a problem in the 1980s and became critical a decade later. Instead of addressing the issue, the capitalist "world turned to neoliberal globalization, notably through the creation of the World Trade Organization … [which] removed most constraints on the operations of capitalism, and the negative effects that this had on all attempts to address the climate problem" (Foster and Clark 2015:3). Succinctly, Klein's central thesis is that rich countries, like the United States, should revert to the standard of living that prevailed in the 1970s; however, the population needs to be mobilized to see the benefits of forging a collective or community for themselves and for the rest of the world.

The political Right sees this as an either/or question—capitalism or climate change; it defends the former by denying scientific explanations based on correspondence or realist theories of truth, accepting authoritarian truth claims, or relying on "alternative facts" created by corporations and the media to sow confusion or manufacture consent. Centrists and liberals take different tacks. For example, public intellectuals associated with the Breakthrough Institute, like Bruno Latour, argue that technological innovations leading to a high energy planet—based on cheap energy sources like nuclear fuel—can ameliorate global warming and poverty, and should not be regulated by the state. This is a twenty-first century restatement of the expansionist and eco-developmentalist views of the 1980s. A *New York Times* reviewer praises Klein's book and then points to a serious flaw: She is really not writing about capitalism in general but rather about neoliberal capitalism and the era of extreme extraction that it has promoted. A *Huffington Post* reviewer asserts that the book's sub-title opens Klein up to accusations that she is promoting a sort of Soviet-style state planning and that the real villain is the extreme exploitation of non-renewable resources. A commentator in the *New York Review of Books* writes that human nature will prevent people from adopting managed degrowth. A reviewer in the *Los Angeles Times* claims that Klein is too optimistic in her faith in humanity because she has not consulted polls about which kinds of climate justice programs might work. A *Daily Beast* writer calls her "clueless [because] she rejects capitalism, market mechanisms, and even seemingly, profit motives and corporate governance." A Nobel laureate in economics and regular columnist for the *New York Times* argues that there needs to be market regulation to curb the climate crisis. Finally, an economist reviewing the book in the *Literary Review of Canada* suggests that Klein ignores market mechanisms and that legislation reducing greenhouse gas emissions has not been as threatening as she assumes. The list of liberal reservations grows longer with each subsequent review (Foster and Clark 2015:9–15).

Discussion

We live in a time of crisis—the breakdown of postwar democratic capitalism since the 1970s. Following is a dialectical process rooted in the contradictions between democratic social life and the imperatives of market-driven capitalism, economic growth, and the financialization of capital. It has unfolded over time and involves the shifting balance of force (power) between workers and the owners of capital as this is mediated by nation states. The social relations and institutions formed during the process, "especially in the spheres of politics and economics, thus appeared as constant objects of contention, inherently contradictory, and only provisionally, if all, in equilibrium, involving no more than temporary compromises between fundamentally incompatible action orientations and social systems" (Streeck 2014:x).

The tempo of the process is uneven and has varied from one country to another, reflecting simultaneously its position in an increasingly global capitalist economy and the historical circumstances in which the contradictions appeared and festered. The contradictions and the issues they raised were already noted by Smith and Jean-Jacques Rousseau in the mid-eighteenth century, by Marx in the middle of the nineteenth century, and by Durkheim and Weber at the beginning of the twentieth century. Their legacies are evident in virtually everything written about social change during the last hundred years.

Consider briefly the waxing and waning of the contradiction in an imperialist country, like the United States:

- *1870s to mid-1930s.* The owners of capital, supported by the state, reigned supreme. The labor movement, efforts to organize workers, and strikes were suppressed, often violently, by law enforcement agencies at all levels of government as well as by private security firms (e.g. Haymarket Square in Chicago and Ludlow, Colorado). Income inequality grew rapidly in an economy fueled by venture capital. The whole edifice collapsed when the stock market crashed in 1929, profits declined, and unemployment soared.

- *Mid-1930s to c. 1970.* The federal government forged a marriage between capitalists and workers to stabilize the economy in the 1930s, promising full employment for workers and regular profits for capitalists. It created publicly financed projects (building infrastructure) and jobs through centrally planned and organized projects, new investment opportunities (the nascent military-industrial complex), government regulation of the economy, and a highly graduated (progressive) income tax structure; importantly, it also opened the door for the formation of labor unions. The capitalist classes were under a worldwide attack in the immediate postwar years. However, they and the government renewed their attack on labor in the late 1940s and steadily eroded its power, especially in the early 1980s. At the same time, the government promised full employment, regular profits, and lower federal income taxes, especially for the upper brackets. The state and capitalist firms used the relative economic and political stability of the 1950s and early 1960s to ensure economic growth and capital accumulation through expanded markets and popular allegiance to consumption-oriented projects; to advance the ideology of the American Dream—a secure job, a home, and two cars in every driveway; and, not incidentally, to run up the public debt at the expense of capital accumulation.

- *1970s to the Present.* The Dream began to unravel from the 1970s onward because of inflation, chronic high unemployment, and the waning power of organized labor. Rates of profit were declining, and public debt was growing steadily after tax cuts for the capitalist classes in the early 1960s. The social programs of the Great Society in the mid-1960s were juxtaposed against the rising costs of government, wars (which fueled the profits of the military-industrial complex), and the soaring public debt. The state attempted to resolve the growing fiscal crisis by printing more money, which reduced the real value of its bonds; it sought alternatively to reduce the public debt by eliminating social programs and to raise the debt by supporting undeclared wars. Along with capital-dependent firms (like banks), it expanded credit, which further financialized the economy and dramatically increased household debt, both of which laid the foundation for the stock market and home foreclosure crises of the first decade of the twenty-first century. In essence, the state with support from capitalist classes steadily privatized the economy from the 1970s onward; made the population increasingly dependent on "self-regulating"; de-regulated the market; and actively promoted neoliberalism as an ideology, policy, and, ultimately, as an understanding of the economy, social relations, and human nature: "the stock market and statistics reflect the economic health of the society"; "it is a dog eat dog world," with "winners" and "losers"; "inequality is inevitable"; and "everyone has to take care of himself."

The process has been called the separation of democracy from capitalism and of the economy from democracy (Streeck 2014).

Focusing only on one facet of this process to the exclusion of others misses the complexity, interrelatedness, and unevenness of what is taking place in the world today. Let us consider a second one and add complexity to the analysis. Colonialism, imperialism, and globalization promoted the movement of people around the globe. Under these regimes of capital accumulation, people moved for various reasons—work, education, escape, safety, and family are only a few— and relocated under quite different conditions and circumstances. For example, immigration to the United States after 1870 was actively opposed by the early 1890s and effectively ended in 1914 with the beginning of World War I; however, there was a small but steady trickle of immigrants from English-speaking countries who became resident aliens or even gained citizenship from the 1920s through the mid-1960s. The government changed its immigration policy in 1965 to reunite immigrant families and to attract skilled workers—e.g. engineers and scientists (the "brain drain"). The policy was opposed almost immediately, with claims that "the immigrants are taking American jobs." It was supported by agri-business, food-processing, and other business sectors that relied on "unskilled" labor and areas in the states where these were important to the economy—e.g. California or North Carolina. The country's immigration policy has been contested for the past fifty years. Equally important, however, are the conditions under which immigrants arrived in the United States; where they came from; the assistance, if any, they received; and how they were integrated into or fared in the labor market (Lamphere, Stepick, and Grenier 1994).

People are mobile; however, focusing just on their movement and ignoring the specificity and contingency underlying their circumstances and motives runs the risk of conflating the experiences of the tourist, the academic from Africa, or the Asian CEO's wife residing in San Francisco with those of the teenage girls brought from remote villages in Thailand to serve as sex workers in Kuwait or those of undocumented women who cross the United States-Mexico border to sew clothing with real and fake designer labels in Los Angeles. In other words, class and cultural capital matter. So does how they intersect with other identities—like gender, race, or nationality—that they appropriate and that are assigned by others.

As you recall, the Northeast and the Great Lakes states were de-industrialized in the 1970s and 1980s. Workers lost secure, well-paying jobs in factories where they were preceded by their fathers and grandfathers before them. Production facilities were closed, moved, or upgraded with new, more efficient machines. Unemployment (i.e. the size of the reserve army of labor) soared. With it, the ability of the unemployed person's ability to realize or sustain their version of the American Dream was called into question. Some people moved to where the jobs were; others found work locally, usually at lower wages. If there were jobs, other household members—women and children—previously not employed or only occasionally working for wages entered the labor force. Levels of stress, poverty, illness, abuse, alcoholism, abandonment, and divorce rose as the availability of jobs and services declined (Weis 1990; Willis 1981[1977]).

The public education system of the United States has been remarkably successful in some regards. By tracking students into different programs from an early age, it helped to create and reproduce a two-tiered workforce in the early part of the twentieth century. Blue-collar workers toiled in factories and fields. White-collar workers—managers, teachers, ministers, doctors, scientists, or government officials—worked with their minds. An American sociologist labeled them the "working class" and the "middle class." While there was often a significant overlap in their incomes, the status and cultural capital of the highly paid heavy equipment operator was not the same as that typically accorded the less-well-paid schoolteacher nor did they receive the same level of deference and respect. Individuals who move socially from working-class to middle-class status lose something in the process. They are no longer *of* the working class but rather are *from* it. They spend the remainder of their lives unable or unwilling to forget completely their roots as they "live awkwardly in the shoes of others." The opposite is also true for those who have experienced job-loss and downward mobility as they entered the ranks of the marginally or self-employed, and wondered why this happened and who was responsible. How communities and individuals experience these processes is further shaped by both their identities and the identities assigned to them by others (Susser 1982). This adds complexity to their social relations. It also points to the unevenness, interrelatedness, and contradictions of what is happening in the world today.

The educational system, along with the media, also succeeded in promoting phrases like "better living through the miracles of science" or "progress through technological innovation." These were potent claims in the 1950s. A consequence was increasing deference to the authority of "experts" in knowledge-based fields because of their insights and opinions on various issues. However, since the 1980s, the effects of technological innovations—e.g. computerization, automation, and robotics—have destroyed the livelihoods of many households. The relative size of the middle class shrank, the number of marginally employed workers (the reserve army of labor) expanded, and income disparities between the capital-dependent classes and the rest grew explosively. At the same time, faith in educational and governmental institutions and belief that experts (technocrats) can solve problems have waned.

Conjunctures like this are hotbeds for the crystallization of social movements that attempt to explain what is taking place and change it. They propose courses of action, and action can have consequences. At a basic level, developing plans of action involves assessing and understanding, as fully and accurately as possible, what is actually taking place. The question, then, is how do we actually do this? Some accept the views of authorities—like Marx or Weber—without critically examining their claims, the evidence they use to support their arguments, or the presuppositions that underlie their assertions. Others argue that there should be a correspondence between the empirical evidence (facts) whose existence is independent of our perceptions and our experience of them—e.g. a person gets struck by a car when walking across a busy street at rush hour because he believes neither cars nor traffic exist. While we cannot actually see some things that happened in the past, like the "big bang" or the construction of an ancient pyramid in Peru, we know they occurred because of the signatures, or traces of evidence, they left. Still others adopt an argument because it coheres or is consistent with other statements held to be true by the members of a community.

It is useful to think of social theory as a conversation between people with different viewpoints. It is sometimes easier to talk with people whose views correspond to facts, as you understand them, and are consistent with your own comprehension; it is often more difficult to have a meaningful conversation with people who are not clear on the implicit and explicit assumptions underlying their points of view or who eschew facts, social theory, and their own presuppositions altogether. Not surprisingly, it is also relatively easy to have a productive conversation with someone with whom you disagree, especially when you both understand one another's theoretical perspectives and presuppositions.

It is also useful to keep in mind that arguments about human social relations, change, and history are always constructed in light of particular theoretical frameworks. For example, arguments about the exploitation of one group by another only make sense in the context of a theory that recognizes exploitation as a social relation that exists in certain kinds of societies and not in others; it makes little sense at all if this relation is viewed through the lens of a social theoretical tradition that either denies that exploitation is a meaningful analytical category, is confused about its significance, or values eclecticism without paying too much attention to the inconsistencies and contradictions of the product that gets cobbled together.

This survey of social change theories shows that they are not static and that present-day commentators and critics continually rework the views of their predecessors to explain the present and to envision the future. As a conclusion, I have three suggestions: (1) beware of explanations that reductively locate motors of social and historical change in biology or human nature; (2) examine whose interests are served by championing particular explanations and understandings; and (3) let the past inform you about the present, and think about a future in which you, your family and friends, and others might want to live. The question posed by the commentators we have discussed is how do *we* get there?

Notes

1 Fordism is a system of production that emerged in the capitalist states bordering the Atlantic Ocean in the late nineteenth and early twentieth centuries. It involves the production of large quantities of standardized goods in large factories located in urban areas. It took advantage of economies of scale and employed mostly male workers on a continuous, full-time basis. Fordist production was sustained by the continued existence of mass markets and by Keynesian economic policies that stabilized the production system and enabled the capitalist class to exploit its full potential. The shift to post-Fordism occurred because of changes in the market when the demand for standardized goods diminished as customized goods became more available.

2 Hardt and Negri's argument presupposes (1) the globalization of capital, (2) the unification of the world market, (3) the unevenness of capitalist development, (4) the entry of great masses of people into the regime of modern capitalist production, (5) the appearance of new forms of labor migration, (6) the formation of significant supranational institutions, and (7) the assertion that imperialism will lead to the collapse of capitalism rather than to the appearance of a new phase of capitalism (Green 2002:35–52).

References

Abu-Lughod, Janet L. (1989) *Before European Hegemony: The World System A.D. 1250–1350*. Oxford, UK: Oxford University Press.

Aglietta, Michel (1979[1976]) *A Theory of Capitalist Regulation: The US Experience*. London, UK: Verso.

Ahmad, Aijaz (1992) *In Theory: Classes, Nations, Literatures*. London, UK: Verso.

—— (1995) The Politics of Literary Postcoloniality. *Race and Class* 36(3):1–20.

—— (1996[1985]) Class, Nation, and State: Intermediate Classes in Peripheral Societies. In *Lineages of the Present: Political Essays*, edited by Aijaz Ahmad, pp. 44–72. New Delhi, India: Tulika.

—— (2001) Introduction. In *Karl Marx and Frederick Engels on the National and Colonial Questions*, edited by Aijaz Amhad, pp. 1–20. New Delhi, India: LeftWord Books.

Aimard, Guy (1962) *Durkheim et la Science Economique*. Paris, France: Presses Universitaire de France.

Alavi, Hamsa (1965) Peasants and Revolution. In *Socialist Register 1965*, edited by Ralph Miliband and John Saville, pp. 241–277. New York: Monthly Review.

—— (1972) The State in Post-Colonial Societies: Pakistan and Bangladesh. *New Left Review* 74:59–81.

Alavi, Hamsa and Teodor Shanin (1988) Introduction to the English Edition: Peasantry and Capitalism. In *The Agrarian Question*, edited by Karl Kautsky, vol. 1, pp. xi–xxxix. London, UK: Zwan Publications.

Albo, Gregory (2003) The Old and New Economies of Imperialism. In *Socialist Register 2004: The New Imperial Challenge*, edited by Leo Panitch and Colin Leyes, pp. 88–113. New York: Monthly Review Press.

Albrow, Martin (1990) *Max Weber's Construction of Social Theory*. New York: St. Martin's Press.

Alchon, Guy (1985) *The Invisible Hand of Planning: Capitalism, Social Science, and the State in the 1920s*. Princeton, NJ: Princeton University Press.

Alexander, Jeffrey (1982) *Theoretical Logic in Sociology*, vol. 2, *The Antinomies of Classical Thought*. Berkeley: University of California Press.

—— (1983) *Theoretical Logic in Sociology*, vol. 4, *The Modern Reconstruction of Classical Thought: Talcott Parsons*. Berkeley: University of California Press.

Amin, Samir (1974[1970]) *Accumulation on a World Scale: A Critique of the Theory of Underdevelopment*. New York: Monthly Review Press.

—— (1976[1973]) *Unequal Development: An Essay on the Social Formations of Peripheral Capitalism*. New York: Monthly Review Press.

Amsden, Alice (1990) Third World Industrialization: "Global Fordism" or New Model? *New Left Review* 182:5–32.

—— (1991) Diffusion of Development: The Late-Industrializing Model of Greater East Asia. *The American Economic Review* 81(2):282–286.

Anderson, Benedict (1983) *Imagined Communities: Reflections on the Origin and Spread of Nationalism*. London, UK: Verso.

Anderson, Kevin (1995) *Lenin, Hegel, and Western Marxism: A Critical Study.* Chicago, IL: The University of Chicago Press.

—— (2002) Marx's Late Writings on Non-Western and Precapitalist Societies and Gender. *Rethinking Marxism* 14(4):84–96.

—— (2010) *Marx at the Margins: On Nationalism, Ethnicity, and Non-Western Societies.* Chicago, IL: The University of Chicago Press.

Appadurai, Arjun (1990) Disjuncture and Difference in the Global Cultural Economy. *Theory, Culture and Society* 7(2):295–310.

Appelbaum, Richard and Jeffrey Henderson (1992) *States od Development in the Asian Pacific Rim.* Newbury Park, CA: Sage Publications.

Apter, David (1965) *The Politics of Modernization.* Chicago, IL: The University of Chicago Press.

Aristotle (1984) [c. 350 B.C.] Politics. In *The Complete Works of Aristotle,* edited by Jonathan Barnes, vol. 2, pp. 1986–2129. Princeton, NJ: Princeton University Press.

Arkush, R. David (1981) *Fei Xiaotong and Sociology in Revolutionary China.* Cambridge, MA: Council on East Asian Studies, Harvard University.

—— (1988) A Conversation with Fei Xiaotong. *Current Anthropology* 29(4):637–662.

Arnove, Robert, ed. (1982) *Philanthropy and Cultural Imperialistm: The Foundations at Home and Abroad.* Bloomington, IN: Indiana University Press.

Arrighi, Giovanni (1994) *The Long Twentieth Century: Money, Power, and the Origins of Our Times.* London, UK: Verso.

Arrighi, Giovanni, Beverly J. Silver, and Benjamin D. Brewer (2003) Industrial Convergence, Globalization, and the Persistence of the North-South Divide. *Studies in Comparative Economic Development* 31(1):3–31.

Assadourian, Carlos Sempat (1973) Modos de producción, capitalismo y subdesarrollo en América Latina. In *Modos de producción en América Latina,* edited by Carlos Assadourian, Ernesto Laclau, Ciro S. F. Cardoso, and Juan Carlos Garavaglia, pp. 47–81. Mexico City, Mexico: Siglo XXI.

Aston, Trevor H. and C. H. E. Philpin, eds. (1985) *The Brenner Debate: Agrarian Class Structure and Economic Development in Pre-Industrial Europe.* Cambridge, UK: Cambridge University Press.

Augustine of Hippo (1984 [c. 427]) *Concerning the City of God against the Pagans.* London, UK: Penguin Books.

Bacevich, Andrew J. (2003) *American Empire: The Realities and Consequences of U.S. Diplomacy.* Cambridge, MA: Harvard University Press.

Bacon, Francis (2000 [1620]) *The New Organon.* Cambridge, UK: Cambridge University Press.

Baert, Patrick J. N. (2006) Time. In *The Blackwell Dictionary of Modern Social Thought,* edited by William Outhwaite, pp. 693–697. Oxford, UK: Blackwell Publishing.

Balassa, Bela (1989) *New Directions in the World Economy.* New York: New York University Press.

Balibar, Etienne (1970[1965]) Elements for a Theory of Transition. In *Reading Capital,* edited by Louis Althusser and Étienne Balibar, pp. 273–324. London, UK: New Left Books.

—— (1977) *On the Dictatorship of the Proletariat.* London, UK: Verso.

—— (2004) *We, the People of Europe? Reflections on Transnational Citizenship.* Princeton, NJ: Princeton University Press.

Banaji, Jairus (1972) For a Theory of Colonial Modes of Production. *Economic and Political Weekly* 7(52):2498–2502.

—— (1973) Backward Capitalism, Primitive Accumulation and Modes of Production. *Journal of Contemporary Asia* 3(4):393–413.

—— (1976) Chayanov, Kutsky, Lenin: Considerations toward a Synthesis. *Economic and Political Weekly* 9(40):1594–1607.

—— (1990) Illusions about the Peasantry: Karl Kautsky and the Agrarian Question. *Journal of Peasant Studies* 17(2):288–307.

—— (2002) *Agrarian Change in Late Antiquity: Gold, Labour, and Aristocratic Dominance.* Oxford, UK: Oxford University Press.

Banerjee, Diptendra (1985) In Search of a Theory of Pre-Capitalist Modes of Production. In *Marxian Theory and the Third World*, edited by Diptendra Banerjee, pp. 13–40. New Delhi, India: Sage Publications.

——— (1986) The Historical Problematic of Third World Development. *Social Scientist: Monthly Journal of the Indian School of Social Sciences* 15(8–9):3–45.

Baran, Paul (1957) *The Political Economy of Growth*. New York: Monthly Review Press.

——— (1969[1952]) On the Political Economy of Backwardness. In *Essays toward a Critique of Political Economy*, edited by John O'Neill, pp. 249–270. New York: Monthly Review.

——— (1969[1953]) Economic Progress and Economic Surplus. In *Essays toward a Critique of Political Economy*, edited by John O'Neill, pp. 271–307. New York: Monthly Review.

Barnard, Frederick M. (1965) *Herder's Social and Political Thought*. Oxford, UK: Oxford University Press.

——— (2003) *Herder on Nationality, Humanity, and History*. Montreal, QC: McGill-Queen's University Press.

Barnet, Richard J. and Ronald E. Muller (1974) *Global Reach: The Power of Multinational Corporations*. New York: Simon and Schuster.

Baron, Hans (1938) A Sociological Interpretation of the Early Renaissance in Florence. *The South Atlantic Quarterly* 38(4):427–448.

——— (1939) The Historical Background of the Florentine Renaissance. *History* 22(4):315–327.

——— (1959) The *Querelle* Between the Ancients and the Moderns as a Problem for Renaissance Scholarship. *Journal of the History of Ideas* 20(1):3–22.

Bauer, Otto (1978[1907]) The Concept of the "Nation." In *Austro-Marxism*, edited by Tom Bottomore and Patrick Goode, pp. 102–109. Oxford, UK: Oxford University Press.

——— (1979[1907]) *La Cuestión de las Nacionalidades y la Socialdemocracia*. Mexico D.F., Mexico: Siglo Veintiuno.

Beer, Max (2011[1897]) Modern English Imperialism. In *Discovering Imperialism: Social Democracy to World War I*, edited by Richard B. Day and Daniel Guido, pp. 95–108. Chicago, IL: Haymarket Books.

Beetham, David (1985) *Max Weber and the Theory of Modern Politics*. Cambridge, UK: Polity Press.

——— (1994) Max Weber and the Liberal Political Tradition. In *The Barbarism of Reason: Max Weber and the Twilight of Enlightenment*, edited by Asher Horowitz and Terry Maley, pp. 99–112. Toronto, ON: University of Toronto Press.

Beiser, Frederick C. (1992) *Enlightenment, Revolution, and Romanticism: The Genesis of Modern German Thought, 1790–1800*. Cambridge, MA: Harvard University Press.

Bell, Daniel (1987) The World and the United States in 2013. *Daedalus* 116(3):1–32.

Bello, Walden (1998) The End of the Asian Miracle. *The Nation* 266(2):16–21

——— (2010) Will China Save the World from Depression? In *The Great Credit Crash*, edited by Martijn Konings, pp. 276–288. London, UK: Verso.

Bendix, Reinhard (1967) Tradition and Modernity Reconsidered. *Comparative Studies in Society and History* 9(3):292–346.

——— (1979) *Max Weber: An Intellectual Portrait*. Berkeley: University of California Press.

Benkemoune, Rabah (2009) Charles Dunoyer and the Emergence of the Idea of an Economic Cycle. *History of Political Economy* 41(2):271–295.

Benton, Ted (1977) *Philosophical Foundations of the Three Sociologies*. London, UK: Routledge and Kegan Paul.

Berger, John (1972) *Ways of Seeing*. London, UK: Penguin Books.

Bernal, Martin (1987) *Black Athena: The Afro-Asiatic Roots of Classical Civilization*, vol. 1, *The Fabrication of Ancient Greece 1785–1985*. London, UK: Free Association Books.

Bernheimer, Richard (1952) *Wild Men in the Middle Ages: A Study in Art, Sentiment, and Demonology*. Cambridge, MA: Harvard University Press.

Bernstein, Eduard (1909) *Die Revisionismus in der Sozialdemokratie*. Amsterdam, the Netherlands: Martin Cohen.

——— (1961[1898]) *Evolutionary Socialism: A Criticism and Affirmation*. New York: Schocken Books.

Bernstein, Henry (1971) Modernization Theory and the Sociological Study of Development. *Journal of Development Studies* 7(2):141–160.

Bettelheim, Charles (1972[1969]) Theoretical Comments. In *Unequal Exchange: A Study of the Imperialism of Trade*, edited by Arghiri Emmanuel, pp. 271–322. New York: Monthly Review Press.

—— (1975[1968]) *The Transition to Socialist Economy*. Hassocks, UK: the Harvester Press.

—— (1976[1974]) *Class Struggles in the USSR, First Period: 1917–1923*. New York: Monthly Review Press.

—— (1978[1977]) *Class Struggles in the USSR, Second Period: 1923–1930*. New York: Monthly Review Press.

Bisley, Nick (2007) *Rethinking Globalization*. Basingstoke, UK: Palgrave Macmillan.

Bleaney, Michael (1976) *Underconsumption Theories: A Historical and Critical Analysis*. New York: International Publishers.

Boas, Franz (1887a) The Occurrence of Similar Inventions in Areas Widely Apart. *Science* 9:485–486.

—— (1887b) Museums of Ethnology and Their Classification. *Science* 9:587–589.

—— (1894) The Half-Blood Indian, An Anthropometric Study. *Popular Science Monthly* 45(10): 761–770.

—— (1911a) Changes in the Bodily Form of Descendants of Immigrants. *Senate Document 208, 1911, 61st Congress, 2d Session*. Washington, DC: Government Printing Office.

—— (1911b) *The Mind of Primitive Man*. New York: Macmillan.

—— (1940[1922]) Report of an Anthropometric Investigation of the Population of the United States. In *Race, Language, and Culture*, by Franz Boas, pp. 28–59. Chicago, IL: The University of Chicago Press.

Bock, Kenneth E. (1963) Evolution, Function, and Change. *American Sociological Review* 28(2): 229–237.

Bodin, Jean (1945[1586]) *Method for the Easy Comprehension of History*. New York: Columbia University Press.

Boeke, Julius H. (1953) *Economies and Economic Policy of Dual Societies as Exemplified by Indonesia*. New York: Institute of Pacific Relations.

Bois, Guy (1984[1976]) *The Crisis of Feudalism: Economy and Society in Eastern Normandy c. 1300–1550*. Cambridge, UK: Cambridge University Press.

—— (1985) Against the Neo-Malthusian Orthodoxy. In *The Brenner Debate: Agrarian Class Structure and Economic Development in Pre-Industrial Europe*, edited by Trevor H. Aston and C. H. E. Philpin, pp. 107–118. Cambridge, UK: Cambridge University Press.

Bookchin, Murray (1980) *Toward an Ecological Society*. Montreal, QC: Black Rose Press.

Boserup, Ester (1965) *The Conditions of Agricultural Growth: The Economics of Agrarian Change under Population Pressure*. Chicago, IL: Aldine.

Bottomore, Tom (1981) Introduction to the Translation. In *Finance Capital: A Study of the Latest Phase of Capitalist Development*, by Rudolf Hilferding and edited by Tom Bottomore, pp. 1–17. London, UK: Routledge and Kegan Paul.

—— (1984) *Sociology and Socialism*. New York: St. Martin's Press.

—— (1988) *Interpretations of Marx*. Oxford, UK: Basil Blackwell.

—— (2006) Socialism. In *The Blackwell Dictionary of Modern Social Thought*, edited by William Outhwaite, pp. 631–633. Oxford, UK: Blackwell Publishing.

Bottomore, Tom and Patrick Goode, eds. (1978) *Austro-Marxism*. Oxford, UK: Oxford University Press.

Bourdeau, Michel (2013) Auguste Comte. *Stanford Encyclopedia of Philosophy*. Stanford, CA: Center for the Study of Language and Information, Stanford University. http://plato.stanford.edu/entries/comte/.

Bourdieu, Pierre (1977[1972]) *Outline of a Theory of Practice*. Cambridge, UK: Cambridge University Press.

Bray, Michael (2015) Rearticulating Contemporary Populism: Class, State, and Neoliberal Society. *Historical Materialism* 23(3):27–64.

Brenner, Robert (1977) The Origins of Capitalist Development: A Critique of Neo-Smithian Marxism. *New Left Review* 104:25–92.

—— (1985[1976]) Agrarian Class Structure and Economic Development in Pre-Industrial Europe. In *The Brenner Debate: Agrarian Class Structure and Economic Development in Pre-Industrial Europe*, edited by Trevor H. Aston and C. H. E. Philpin, pp. 10–63. Cambridge, UK: Cambridge University Press.

—— (1997) Property Relations and the Growth of Agricultural Productivity in Late Medieval and Early Modern Europe. In *Economic Development and Agricultural Productivity*, edited by Amit Bhaduri and Rune Skarstein, pp. 9–41. Cheltenham, UK: Edward Elgar.

—— (2001) The Low Countries in the Transition to Capitalism. *Journal of Agrarian Change* 1(2):169–242.

—— (2006) *The Economics of Global Turbulence*. London, UK: Verso.

Brewer, Anthony (1990) *Marxist Theories of Imperialism: A Critical Survey*. 2nd ed. London, UK: Routledge.

Bröckling, Ulrich, Susanne Krasmann, and Thomas Lempke (2011) From Foucault's Lectures at the Collège de France to Studies of Governmentality: An Introduction. In *Governmentality: Current Issues and Future Challenges*, edited by Ulrich Bröckling, Susanne Krasmann, and Thomas Lempke, pp. 1–33. London, UK: Routledge.

Brodkin, Karen (1998) *How Jews Became White Folks and What That Says about Race in America*. New Brunswick, NJ: Rutgers University Press.

—— (2000) Global Capitalism: What's Race Got To Do With It? *American Ethnologist* 27(2): 237–256.

—— (2003) *Making Democracy Matter: Identity and Activism in Los Angeles*. New Brunswick, NJ: Rutgers University Press.

Brookfield, Harold (1973) *Interdependent Development*. Pittsburgh, PA: Pittsburgh University Press.

Broué, Pierre (2006[1971]) *The German Revolution, 1917–1923*. Chicago, IL: Haymarket Books.

Brown, Richard (1973) Anthropology and Colonial Rule: Godfrey Wilson and the Rhodes-Livingstone Institute, Northern Rhodesia. In *Anthropology and the Colonial Encounter*, edited by Talal Asad, pp. 173–198. Atlantic Highlands, NJ: Humanities Press.

Brubaker, Rogers (1984) *The Limits of Rationality: An Essay on the Social and Moral Thought of Max Weber*. London, UK: George Allen and Unwin.

Bukharin, Nikolai (1971[1920]) *Economics of the Tranformation Period, with Critical Remarks by Lenin*. New York: Bergman Publishers.

—— (1973[1915]) *Imperialism and the World Economy*. New York: Monthly Review Press.

—— (1982[1920]) Toward a Theory of the Imperialist State. In *Selected Writings on the State and the Transition to Socialism*, edited by Richard B. Day, pp. 6–38. Armonk, NY: M. E. Sharpe.

—— (1982) *Selected Writings on the State and the Transition to Socialism*. Edited by Richard B. Day. Armond, NY: M. E. Sharpe.

Burke, Edmund (1993[1790]) *Reflections on the French Revolution*. Oxford, UK: Oxford University Press.

Burns, James H., ed. (1988) *Medieval Political Thought, c. 350–c. 1450*. Cambridge, UK: Cambridge University Press.

Burns, James H. and Mark Goldie, eds. (1991) *Political Thought, 1450–1700*. Cambridge, UK: Cambridge University Press.

Burchell, Graham, Colin Gordon, and Peter Miller, eds. (1991) *The Foucault Effect: Studies in Governmentality*. Chicago, IL: The University of Chicago Press.

Burkett, Paul (1999) *Marx and Nature: A Red and Black Perspective*. New York: St. Martin's Press.

Byres, Terence J. (1991) The Agrarian Question and Differing Forms of Capitalist Agrarian Transition: An Essay with Reference to Asia. In *Rural Transformation in Asia*, edited by Jan Breman and Sudipto Mundle, pp. 3–76. Oxford, UK: Oxford University Press.

—— (1996) *Capitalism from Above and Capitalism from Below: An Essay in Comparative Political Economy*. New York: St. Martin's Press.

—— (2005) Neoliberalism and Primitive Accumulation in Less Developed Countries. In *Neoliberalism: A Critical Reader*, edited by Alfred Saad-Filho and Deborah Johnston, pp. 83–90. London, UK: Pluto Press.

—— (2006) Differentiation of the Peasantry under Feudalism and the Transition to Capitalism: In Defence of Rodney Hilton. *Journal of Agrarian Change* 6(1):17–68.

Cabral, Amílcar (1969) *Revolution in Guinea: Selected Texts*. New York: Monthly Review Press.

—— (1973) *Return to the Source: Speeches and Writings*. New York: Monthly Review Press.

—— (1979) *Unity and Struggle: Speeches and Writings*. New York: Monthly Review Press.

Cain, Peter (1999) *Empire and Imperialism: The Debate of the 1870s*. South Bend, IN: St. Augustine Press.

—— (2002) *Hobson and Imperialism: Radicalism, New Liberalism, and Finance, 1887–1938*. Oxford, UK: Oxford University Press.

Calhoun, Craig (1997) *Nationalism*. Minneapolis, MN: University of Minnesota Press.

Callinicos, Alex (2009) *Imperialism and Global Political Economy*. Cambridge, UK: Polity Press.

Cantor, Norman F. (1991) *Inventing the Middle Ages: The Lives, Works, and Ideas of the Great Medievalists of the Twentieth Century*. New York: W. Morrow.

Caponigri, A. Robert (1968) *Time and Idea: The Theory of History in Giambattista Vico*. Notre Dame, IN: Notre Dame University Press.

Cardoso, Enrique and Enzo Faletto (1979[1969]) *Dependency and Development in Latin America*. Berkeley: University of California Press.

Carneiro, Robert L. (1981) Leslie White. In *Totems and Teachers: Perspectives in the History of Anthropology*, edited by Sydel Silverman, pp. 208–252. New York: Columbia University Press.

Carr, Edward H. (1953) *A History of Soviet Russia*, vol. 3, *The Bolshevik Revolution, 1917–1923*. London, UK: The Macmillan Company.

—— (1979) *The Russian Revolution from Lenin to Stalin (1917–1929)*. London, UK: Macmillan.

—— (1982) *Twilight of the Comintern, 1930–1935*. New York: Pantheon Books.

Cartledge, Paul (1999) *Democritus*. London, UK: Routledge.

Castells, Manuel (1996) *Rise of Network Society*, vol. 1, *The Information Age: Economy, Society and Culture*. Oxford, UK: Blackwell Publishers.

Chabal, Patrick (1983) *Amílcar Cabral: Revolutionary Leadership and People's War*. Cambridge, UK: Cambridge University Press.

Chakrabarti, Anjan and Stephen Cullenberg (2003) *Transition and Development in India*. London, UK: Routledge.

Chapple, Eliot D. (1953) Applied Anthropology in Industry. In *Anthropology Today: An Encyclopedic Inventory*, edited by Alfred L. Kroeber, pp. 819–831. Chicago, IL: The University of Chicago Press.

Chayanov, Alexander V. (1986[1924]) On the Theory of Non-Capitalist Economic Systems. In *The Theory of Peasant Economy*, edited by Daniel Thorner, Basile Kerblay, and R. E. F. Smith, pp. 1–28. Madison, WI: The University of Wisconsin Press.

—— (1986[1926]) Peasant Farm Organization. In *The Theory of Peasant Economy*, edited by Daniel Thorner, Basile Kerblay, and R. E. F. Smith, pp. 29–270. Madison, WI: The University of Wisconsin Press.

Chibber, Vivek (2004) The Return of Imperialism to Social Science. *European Journal of Sociology* 45(3):427–441.

Chilcote, Ronald H. (1991) *Amílcar Cabral's Revolutionary Theory and Practice: A Critical Guide*. Boulder, CO: Lynne Rienner Publishers.

Childe, V. Gordon (1942) *What Happened in History*. Harmondsworth, UK: Penguin Books.

—— (1951[1936]) *Man Makes Himself*. New York: New American Library.

Chomsky, Noam (2003) *Hegemony or Survival: America's Quest for Global Dominance*. New York: Metropolitan Books.

Chossudovsky, Michel (1997) Dismantling Former Yugoslavia: Recolonising Bosnia. *Capital and Class* 62:1–12.

Cirese, Alberto M. (1982) Gramsci's Observation on Folklore. In *Approaches to Gramsci*, edited by Anne Showstack Sassoon, pp. 22–248. London, UK: Writers and Readers Publishing Cooperative.

Cladis, Mark S. (2005) Beyond Solidarity? Durkheim and Twenty-first Century Democracy in a Global Age. In *The Cambridge Companion to Durkheim*, edited by Jeffrey C. Alexander and Philip Smith, pp. 383–409. Cambridge, UK: Cambridge University Press.

Clark, John (1984) *The Anarchist Moment: Reflections on Culture, Nature and Power*. Montreal, QC: Red Rose Books.

Clarke, Simon (1982) *Marx, Marginalism and Modern Sociology from Adam Smith to Max Weber*. London, UK: The Macmillan Press.

——— (1994) *Marx's Theory of Crisis*. Basingstoke, UK: The Macmillan Press.

——— (2003) Globalisation and the Subsumption of the Soviet Mode of Production under Capital. In *Anti-Capitalism: A Marxist Introduction*, edited by Alfredo Saad-Filho, pp. 187–198. London, UK: Pluto Press.

——— (2012) Crisis Theory. In *The Elgar Companion to Marxist Economics*, edited by Ben Fine and Alfredo Saad-Filho, pp. 90–95. Cheltenham, UK: Edward Elgar Publishing.

Coates, David (1991a) Reformism. In *A Dictionary of Marxist Social Thought*, edited by Tom Bottomore, 2nd ed., pp. 460–461. Oxford, UK: Blackwell Publishers.

——— (1991b) Revisionism. In *A Dictionary of Marxist Social Thought*, edited by Tom Bottomore, 2nd ed., pp. 475–476. Oxford, UK: Blackwell Publishers.

Cohen, Jean and Andrew Arato (1992) *Civil Society and Political Theory*. Cambridge, MA: The MIT Press.

Cohen, Mark N. (1977) *The Food Crisis in Prehistory*. New Haven, CT: Yale University Press.

Cole, Thomas (1967) *Democritus and the Sources of Greek Anthropology*. Cleveland, OH: Western Reserve University Press.

Conant, Charles A. (1898) The Economic Basis of "Imperialism." *The North American Review* 167(502):326–340.

Coontz, Sydney H. (1957) *Population Theories and Their Economic Interpretation*. London, UK: Routledge and Kegan Paul.

Cox, Terry (1984) Class Analysis of the Russian Peasantry: The Research of Kritsman and His School. In *Kritsman and the Agrarian Marxists*, edited by Terry Cox and Gary Littlejohn, pp. 11–60. London, UK: Frank Cass.

Crisp, Olga (1976) *Studies in the Russian Economy before 1914*. London, UK: The Macmillian Press.

Crowell, Steven G. (1998) Neo-Kantianism. In *A Companion to Continental Philosophy*, edited by Simon Critchley and William R. Schroeder, pp. 185–197. Oxford, UK: Blackwell Publishing.

Crowther, Ian (1997) Conservatism. In *The Blackwell Dictionary of Modern Social Thought*, edited by William Outhwaite, pp. 111–112. Oxford, UK: Blackwell Publishing.

Curd, Patricia (2012) Presocratic Philosophy. In *Stanford Encyclopedia of Philosophy*. Stanford, CA: Center for the Study of Language and Information, Stanford University. http://plato.stanford.edu/entries/presocratics/.

Curry, James (1993) The Flexibility Fetish: A Review Essay on Flexible Specialization. *Capital and Class* 50:99–126.

Darwin, Charles (1859) *On the Origin of Species by Means of Natural Selection, Or the Preservation of Favoured Races in the Struggle for Life*. London, UK: John Murray.

——— (1874) *The Descent of Man and Selection in Relation to Sex*. London, UK: Murray.

Davidson, Neil (2006) From Uneven to Combined Development. In *100 Years of Permanent Revolution: Results and Prospects*, edited by Bill Dunn and Hugo Radice, pp. 10–26. London, UK: Pluto Press.

——— (2014) *Holding Fast to an Image of the Past: Explorations in the Marxist Tradition*. Chicago, IL: Haymarket Books.

Davis, Allison, Burleigh B. Gardner, and Mary R. Gardner (1941) *Deep South: A Social Anthropological Study of Caste and Class*. Chicago, IL: The University of Chicago Press.

Day, Richard B. (1982) The New Leviathan: Bukharin's Contribution to the Theory of the State and the Transition to Socialism. In *N. I. Bukharin: Selected Writings on the State and the Transition to Socialism*, edited by Richard B. Day, pp. xxi–lviii. Armonk, NY: M. E. Sharpe.

———— (2004) Translator's Introduction: Pavel V. Maksakovsky's *The Capitalist Cycle*. In *The Capitalist Cycle: An Essay on the Marxist Theory of the Cycle*, edited by Pavel V. Maksakovsky, pp. ix–xlviii. Leiden, the Netherlands: Brill.

Day, Richard B. and Daniel Gaido (2011) Introduction. In *Discovering Imperialism: Social Democracy to World War I*, edited by Richard B. Day and Daniel Gaido, pp. 1–93. Chicago, IL: Haymarket Books.

de Coulanges, Numa D. Fustel (1980 [1864]) *The Ancient City: A Study on the Religion, Laws, and Institutions of Greece and Rome*. Baltimore, MD: The Johns Hopkins University Press.

Deane, Herbert A. (1963) *The Political and Social Ideas of St. Augustine*. New York: Columbia University Press.

Defert, Daniel (1982) The Collection of the World: Accounts of Voyages from the Sixteenth to the Eighteenth Centuries. *Dialectical Anthropology* 7(1):11–20.

Derrida, Jacques (1994) *Specters of Marx: The State of the Debt, the Work of Mourning and the New International*. New York: Routledge.

———— (2000[1968]) Semiology and Grammatology: Interview with Julia Kristeva. In *The Routledge Language and Cultural Theory Reader*, edited by Lucy Burke, Tony Crowley, and Alan Girvin, pp. 241–248. London, UK: Routledge.

Desai, Radika (2013) *Geopolitical Economy: After US Hegemony, Globalization, and Empire*. London, UK: Pluto Press.

Descartes, René (1998 [1637]) *Discourse on Method*. Indianapolis, IN: Hackett Publishing Company.

Despain, Hans G. (2011) *The Political Economy of Maurice Dobb: History, Theory, and the Economics of Reproduction, Crisis, and Transformation*. Ph.D. Dissertation in Economics, University of Utah, Salt Lake City, UT.

Deutsch, Karl W. (1963) Some Problems in the Study of Nation-Building. In *Nation-Building*, edited by Karl W. Deutsch and William J. Foltz, pp. 1–16. New York: Atherton Press.

Deyo, Frederick, ed. (1987) *The Political Economy of the New Asian Industrialism*. Ithaca, NY: Cornell University Press.

Diamond, Jared (2005) *Collapse: How Societies Choose or Fail to Succeed*. New York: Viking.

Diamond, Josephine (1992) Montaigne's "Des Cannibales": Savage Society and Wild Writing. In *Dialectical Anthropology: Essays in Honor of Stanley Diamond*, edited by Christine W. Gailey, vol. 1, pp. 37–56. Gainesville, FL: University Presses of Florida.

Diamond, Stanley (1974) *In Search of the Primitive: A Critique of Civilization*. New Brunswick, NJ: Transaction Books.

Dobb, Maurice H. (1946) *Studies in the Development of Capitalism*. London, UK: Routledge and Kegan Paul.

———— (1966) *Soviet Economic Development since 1917*, 6th ed. London, UK: Routledge and Kegan Paul.

———— (1976 [1950]) A Reply. In *The Transition from Feudalism to Capitalism*, edited by Rodney Hilton, pp. 57–67. London, UK: New Left Books.

Donzelot, Jacques (1979) The Poverty of Political Consciousness. *Ideology and Consciousness* 5:73–86.

Donzelot, Jacques and Colin Gordon (2008) Governing Liberal Studies—The Foucault Effect in the English-Speaking World. *Foucault Studies* 5:48–62.

Douglass, Frederick (1857) *My Bondage and My Freedom*. Auburn, NY: Miller, Orton.

Drake, St. Clair and Horace Cayton (1945) *Black Metropolis: A Study of Negro Life in a Northern City*, 2 vols. New York: Harcourt, Brace and Company.

Du Bois, W. E. B. (1898) The Study of Negro Problems. *Annals of the American Academy of Political and Social Science* 11(219):1–23.

———— (1969 [1903]) *The Souls of Black Folk*. New York: New American Library.

Dudley, Edward and Maximilian E. Novak, eds. (1972) *The Wild Men Within: An Image in Western Thought from the Renaissance to Romanticism*. Pittsburgh, PA: University of Pittsburgh Press.

Duménil, Gérard and Dominque Lévy (2004) *Capital Resurgent: Roots of the Neoliberal Revolution*. Cambridge, MA: Harvard University Press.

———— (2005) The Neoliberal (Counter-) Revolution. In *Neoliberalism: A Critical Reader*, edited by Alfred Saad-Filho and Deborah Johnston, pp. 9–19. London, UK: Pluto Press.

———— (2011) *The Crisis of Neoliberalism*. Cambridge, MA: Harvard University Press.

Durkheim, Émile (1886) Les Études de Science Sociale. *Revue Philosophique* 22:61–80.

———— (1887) La Science Positive de la Morale en Allemagne. *Revue Philosophique* 24:33–58, 113–143, 275–284.

———— (1888) Cours de Science Social: Leçon d'Ouverture. *Revue Internationale de L'Enseignement* 15:23–48.

———— (1898) Preface. *L'Année Sociologique* 1:i–vii.

———— (1938[1895]) *The Rules of Sociological Method*. New York: The Free Press.

———— (1951[1897]) *Suicide: A Study in Sociology*. Glencoe, IL: Free Press.

———— (1958[1895–1896]) *Socialism and Saint-Simon*. Yellow Springs, OH: The Antioch Press.

———— (1961[1925]) *Moral Education: A Study in the Theory and Application of the Sociology of Education*. New York: The Free Press.

———— (1964[1893]) *The Division of Labor in Society*. New York: The Free Press.

———— (1965[1912]) *The Elementary Forms of Religious Life*. New York: The Free Press.

———— (1977) *The Evolution of Educational Thought: Lectures on the Formation and Development of Secondary Education in France*. London, UK: Routledge and Kegan Paul.

———— (1992[1898–1900]) *Professional Ethics and Civil Morals*. London, UK: Routledge.

———— (2013[1901]) Two Laws of Penal Evolution. In *Durkheim and the Law*, edited by Steven Lukes and Andrew Scull, pp. 80–102. London, UK: Palgrave Macmillan.

Eagleton, Terry (1996) *The Illusions of Postmodernism*. Oxford, UK: Blackwell Publishers.

Ehrlich, Paul R. (1968) *The Population Bomb*. New York: Ballatine Books.

Eisenstadt, Shmuel (1973) Social Change and Development. In *Readings in Social Evolution and Development*, edited by Shmuel Eisenstadt, pp. 3–33. Oxford, UK: Oxford University Press.

Emmanuel, Arghiri (1972[1969]) *Unequal Exchange: A Study of the Imperialism of Trade*. New York: Monthly Review Press.

Engels, Frederick (1952[1882]) Nationalism, Internationalism, and the Polish Question. In *The Russian Menace to Europe by Karl Marx and Friedrich Engels*, edited by Paul W. Blackstock and Bert F. Hoselitz, pp. 116–120. Glencoe, IL: The Free Press [Letter to Karl Kautsky 7 February 1882. In *Karl Marx, Frederick Engels Collected Works*, vol. 46, pp. 191–195. New York: International Publishers, 1992].

———— (1975[1845]) The Condition of the Working Class in England. From Personal Observation and Authentic Sources. In *Karl Marx, Frederick Engels Collected Works*, vol. 4, pp. 295–596. New York: International Publishers.

———— (1977[1849]) Democratic Pan-Slavism. In *Karl Marx, Frederick Engels Collected Works*, vol. 8, pp. 362–378. New York: International Publishers.

———— (1987[1877]) Anti-Dühring: Herr Eugen Dühring's Revolution in Science. In *Karl Marx and Frederick Engels: Collected Works*, vol. 25, pp. 5–590. New York: International Publishers.

———— (1990[1884]) On the Decline of Feudalism and the Rise of National States. In *Karl Marx, Frederick Engels Collected Works*, vol. 26, pp. 556–565. New York: International Publishers.

———— (1990[1885]) On the History of the Prussian Peasants. Introduction to Wilhelm Wolff's Pamphlet *The Silesian Milliard*. In *Karl Marx, Frederick Engels Collected Works*, vol. 26, pp. 341–352. New York: International Publishers.

———— (1990[1894]) The Peasant Question in France and Germany. In *Karl Marx, Frederick Engels Collected Works*, vol. 27, pp. 481–502. New York: International Publishers.

Erlich, Alexander (1960) *The Soviet Industrialization Debate, 1924–1928*. Cambridge, MA: Harvard University Press.

Esherick, Joseph W. (1979) On the "Restoration of Capitalism": Mao and Marxist Theory. *Modern China* 5(1):41–78.

Ewald, François (1991) Insurance and Risk. In *The Foucault Effect: Studies in Governmentality*, edited by graham Burchell, Colin Gordon, and Peter Miller, pp. 197–210. Chicago, IL: The University of Chicago Press.

Eyal, Gil, Iván Szelényi, and Eleanor R. Townsley (1997) The Theory of Post-Communist Managerialism. *New Left Review* 222:60–92.

Fanon, Frantz (1965[1959]) *A Dying Colonialism*. London, UK: Pelican Books.

—— (1967[1952]) *Black Skin, White Masks*. London, UK: MacGibbon and Kee.

—— (1967[1961]) *The Wretched of the Earth*. London, UK: Penguin Books.

Featherstone, Mike (1990) *Global Culture: Nationalism, Globalization and Modernity*. London, UK: Sage Publications.

Febvre, Lucien and Henri-Jean Martin (1976) *The Coming of the Book: The Impact of Printing*. London, UK: New Left Books.

Fei, Xiaotong (1939) *Peasant Life in China: A Field Study of Country Life in the Yangtze Valley*. New York: Durham.

Fine, Ben (2004) Examining the Ideas of Globalisation and Development Critically: What Is the Role for Political Economy? *New Political Economy* 9(2):213–231.

Finley, Moses I. (1973) *The Ancient Economy*. Berkeley: University of California Press.

Fisher, Donald (1983) The Role of Philanthropic Foundations in the Reproduction and Production of Hegemony: Rockefeller Foundations and the Social Sciences. *Sociology* 17(2):206–233.

—— (1993) *Fundamental Development of the Social Sciences: Rockefeller Philanthropy and the United States Social Science Research Council*. Ann Arbor, MI: The University of Michigan Press.

Forbes, Robert J. (1968) *The Conquest of Nature*. New York: The New American Library.

Forsyth, Donald W. (1983) The Beginnings of Brazilian Anthropology: Jesuits and Tupinamba Cannibalism. *Journal of Anthropological Research* 39(2):147–178.

Fortes, Meyer (1938) Culture Contact as a Dynamic Process. In *Methods of Study of Culture Contact in Africa*, edited by Lucy P. Mair, pp. 60–91. Oxford, UK: Oxford University Press.

Foster, George M. (1967) Introduction: What Is a Peasant? In *Peasant Society: A Reader*, edited by Jack M. Potter, May N. Diaz, and George M. Foster, pp. 15–24. Boston, MA: Little, Brown and Company.

Foster, John Bellamy (2000) *Marx's Ecology: Materialism and Nature*. New York: Monthly Review Press.

—— (2017a) Neo-Fascism in the White House. *Monthly Review* 68(11):1–30.

—— (2017b) This is not Populism. *Monthly Review* 69(2):1–24.

Foster, John Bellamy and Brett Clark (2015) Crossing the River of Fire: The Liberal Attack on Naomi Klein and This Changes Everything. *Monthly Review* 65(9):1–17.

Foster-Carter, Aidan (1978a) The Mode of Production Controversy. *New Left Review* 107:47–78.

—— (1978b) Can We Articulate "Articulation"? In *The New Economic Anthropology*, edited by John Clammer, pp. 210–249. New York: St. Martin's Press.

Foucault, Michel (1972[1971]) The Discourse on Language. In *The Archaeology of Knowledge and the Discourse of Knowledge*, pp. 215–237. New York: Pantheon Books.

—— (1978[1976]) *The History of Sexuality*, vol. 1, *Introduction*. New York: Pantheon Books.

—— (1979[1975]) *Discipline and Punish: The Birth of the Prison*. New York: Vintage Books.

—— (1980) *Power/Knowledge: Selected Interviews and Other Writings 1972–1977*. New York: Pantheon Books.

—— (1991[1968]) Politics and the Study of Discourse. In *The Foucault Effect: Studies in Governmentality*, edited by Graham Burchell, Colin Gordon, and Peter Miller, pp. 53–72. Chicago, IL: The University of Chicago Press.

—— (1991[1978]) Governmentality. In *The Foucault Effect: Studies in Governmentality*, edited by Graham Burchell, Colin Gordon, and Peter Miller, pp. 87–104. Chicago, IL: The University of Chicago Press.

—— (2003[1997]) *Society Must Be Defended: Lectures at the Collège de France 1975–1976*. London, UK: Palgrave Macmillan.

—— (2007[2004]) *Security, Territory, Population: Lectures at the Collège de France 1977–1978*. London, UK: Palgrave Macmillan.

—— (2008[2004]) *The Birth of Biopolitics: Lectures at the Collège de France 1978–1979*. London, UK: Palgrave Macmillan.

Frank, André G. (1967) *Capitalism and Underdevelopment in Latin America: Historical Studies of Chile and Brazil*. New York: Monthly Review Press.

——— (1969) *Development and Underdevelopment in Latin America*. New York: Monthly Review Press.

——— (1969[1966]) The Development of Underdevelopment. In *Latin America: Development or Revolution*, edited by André G. Frank, pp. 4–17. New York: Monthly Review Press.

——— (1972) Sociology of Development and Underdevelopment of Sociology. In *Dependence and Underdevelopment: Latin America's Political Economy*, edited by James D. Cockcroft, André G. Frank, and Dale E. Johnson, pp. 321–398. Garden City, NY: Doubleday and Company.

Frey, Raymond G. (2006) Utilitarianism. In *The Blackwell Dictionary of Modern Social Thought*, edited by William Outhwaite, pp. 714–716. Oxford, UK: Blackwell Publishing.

Friedman, Milton (1962) *Capitalism and Freedom*. Chicago, IL: The University of Chicago Press.

Fröbel, Folker, Jürgen Heinrich, and Otto Kreye (1977) The Tendency towards a New International Division of Labor. *Review* 1(1):73–88.

——— (1982) *The New International Division of Labour*. Cambridge, UK: Cambridge University Press.

Fukuyama, Frances (1989) The End of History? *The National Interest*, Summer. www.wesjones/com/eoh/htm.

Furley, David J. (1999) Aristotle the Philosopher of Nature. In *From Aristotle to Augustine*, edited by David J. Furley. Routledge History of Philosophy, vol. 2, pp. 9–39. London, UK: Routledge.

Furtado, Celso (1963[1959]) *The Economic Growth of Brazil: A Survey from Colonial to Modern Times*. Berkeley: University of California Press.

——— (1964[1955]) The Historic Process of Underdevelopment. In *Development and Underdevelopment: A Structural View of the Problems of Developed and Underdeveloped Countries*, edited by Celso Furtado, pp. 77–114. Berkeley: University of California Press.

——— (1964[1958]) Elements of a Theory of Underdevelopment. In *Development and Underdevelopment: A Structural View of the Problems of Developed and Underdeveloped Countries*, by Celso Furtado, pp. 115–140). Berkeley: University of California Press.

——— (1965[1964]) *Dialéctica del desarrollo: diagnóstico de la crisis del Brasil*. Mexico City, MX: Fondo de la Cultura Económica.

——— (1970) *Economic Development of Latin America: Historical Background and Contemporary Problems*. Cambridge, UK: Cambridge University Press.

Gailey, Christine W. (1987) *Kinship to Kingship: Gender Hierarchy and State Formation in the Tongan Islands*. Austin, TX: University of Texas Press.

Garcia Pelayo, Manuel (1979) *La Tema de las Nacionalidades en la Teoría de la Nación en Otto Bauer*. Madrid, Spain: Editorial Pablo Iglesias.

Garrod, J. Z. (2015) A Critique of Panitch and Gindin's Theory of American Empire. *Science and Society* 79(1):38–62.

Gay, Peter (1962) *The Dilemma of Democratic Socialism: Eduard Bernstein's Challenge to Marx*. New York: Collier Books.

Gayton, Anna H. (1932) The Ghost Dances of 1870 in South-Central California. In *University of California Publications in American Archaeology and Ethnology*, vol. 28, pp. 57–82. Berkeley: University of California Press.

Geary, Dick (1987) Max Weber, Karl Kautsky and German Social Democracy. In *Max Weber and His Contemporaries*, edited by Wolfgang J. Mommsen and Jürgen Osterhammel, pp. 335–366. London, UK: Allen and Unwin.

Geertz, Clifford (1956) *The Development of the Javanese Economy: A Socio-Cultural Approach*. Massachusetts Institute of Technology: Center for International Studies, Economic Development Program, document C/56-18.

——— (1963) The Integrative Revolution: Primordial Sentiments and Civil Politics in the New States. In *Old Societies and New States: The Quest for Modernity in Asia and Africa*, edited by Clifford Geertz, pp. 105–157. Glencoe, IL: The Free Press.

——— (1973) *The Interpretation of Cultures: Selected Essays*. New York: Harper Books.

Gellner, Ernest (1964) Nationalism. In *Thought and Change*, edited by Ernest Gellner, pp. 158–169. London, UK: Weidenfeld and Nicholson.

―――― (1983) *Nations and Nationalism*. Oxford, UK: Basil Blackwell.

Geras, Norman (1976) *The Legacy of Rosa Luxemburg*. London, UK: Verso.

Gerschenkron, Alexander (1962[1952]) Economic Backwardness in Historical Perspective. In *Economic Backwardness in Historical Perspective: A Book of Essays*, pp. 5–20. Cambridge, MA: The Belknap Press of Harvard University Press.

Giddens, Anthony (1990) *Consequences of Modernity*. Cambridge, UK: Polity Press.

Gilman, Nils (2003) *Mandarins of the Future: Modernization Theory in Cold War America*. Baltimore, MD: The Johns Hopkins University Press.

―――― (2011) *The Right Kind of Revolution: Modernization, Development, and U.S. Foreign Policy from the Cold War to the Present*. Ithaca, NY: Cornell University Press.

Giroux, Henry A. (2017) Trump's America: Rethinking *1984* and *Brave New World*. *Monthly Review* 69(1):20, 21.

Girvan, Norman (1973) The Development of Dependency Economies in the Caribbean and Latin America: Review and Comparison. *Social and Economic Studies* 22(1):1–33.

Gisberg, Pascual (1959) Social Facts in Durkheim's System. *Anthropos* 54(3):353–369.

Glick Schiller, Nina and Andrew Irving, eds. (2015) *Whose Cosmopolitanism? Critical Perspectives, Relationalities and Discontents*. New York: Berghahn Books.

Godwin, William (1976[1793]) *An Enquiry Concerning Human Justice and its Influence on General Virtue and Happiness*. London, UK: Penguin Books.

―――― (1998[1794]) *Things as They Are: The Adventures of Caleb Williams*. London, UK: Penguin Books.

Goldfrank, Walter L. (1978) Fascism and World Economy. In *Social Change in the Capitalist World Economy*. London, UK: Sage Publications.

Goldmann, Lucien (1973) *The Philosophy of Enlightenment: The Christian Burgess and the Enlightenment*. Cambridge, MA: The MIT Press.

Goldthorpe, John (1971) Theories of Industrial Society: Reflections on the Recrudescence or Historicism and the Future as Futurology. *Archives Européenes de Sociologie* 12(2):263–288.

Gordon, Colin (1991) Governmental Rationality: An Introduction. In *The Foucault Effect: Studies in Governmentality*, edited by Graham Burchell, Colin Gordon, and Peter Miller, pp. 1–52. Chicago, IL: The University of Chicago Press.

Gorz, André (1980) *Ecology as Politics*. Boston, MA: South End Press.

Graham, Daniel W. (1997) Heraclitus's Criticism of Ionian Philosophy. *Oxford Studies in Ancient Philosophy* 15:1–50.

―――― (2003) A New Look at Anaximenes. *History of Philosophy Quarterly* 20(1):1–20.

―――― (2008) Heraclitus: Flux, Order and Knowledge. In *The Oxford Handbook of Presocratic Philosophy*, edited by Patricia Curd and Daniel W. Graham, pp. 169–188. Oxford, UK: Oxford University Press.

Gramsci, Antonio (1967[1926]) The Southern Question. In *The Modern Prince and Other Writings*, pp. 28–51. New York: International Publishers.

―――― (1971[1930–1932]) State and Civil Society. In *Selections from the Prison Notebooks of Antonio Gramsci*, edited by Quintin Hoare and Geoffrey N. Smith, pp. 206–276. New York: International Publishers.

―――― (1971[1931]) Americanism and Fordism. In *Selections from the Prison Notebooks*, edited by Quintin Hoare and Geoffrey N. Smith, pp. 277–318. New York: International Publishers.

―――― (1971[1933]) The Intellectuals. In *Selections from the Prison Notebooks*, edited by Quintin Hoare and Geoffrey N. Smith, pp. 3–23. New York: International Publishers.

―――― (1971[1933–1937]) The Study of Philosophy. In *Selections from the Prison Notebooks of Antonio Gramsci*, edited by Quintin Hoare and Geoffrey N. Smith, pp. 321–377. New York: International Publishers.

―――― (1977[1916]) The Revolution against "Capital." In *Selections from Political Writings, 1910–1920*, edited by Quintin Hoare, pp. 34–37. New York: International Publishers.

―――― (1992[1929]) Types of Periodicals. In *Antonio Gramsci Prison Notebooks*, edited by Joseph A. Buttigieg and Antonio Callari, vol. 1, pp. 125–136. New York: Columbia University Press.

Gray, John (2000) *Two Faces of Liberalism*. New York: The New Press.

Green, Peter (2002) The Passage from Imperialism to Empire: A Commentary on *Empire* by Michael Hardt and Antonio Negri. *Historical Materialism* 10(1):29–78.

Grossmann, Henryk (1992[1929]) *The Law of Accumulation and Breakdown of the Capitalist System, Being Also a Theory of Crises*. London, UK: Pluto Press.

———— (2000[1919]) The Theory of Economic Crises. *Review of Political Economy* 18:171–180.

Habermas, Jürgen (1981) New Social Movements. *Telos* 49:33–37.

Habib, Irfan (1995[1983]) The Peasant in Indian History. In *Essays in Indian History: Towards a Marxist Perspective*, edited by Irfan Habib, pp. 109–160. New Delhi, India: Tulika.

Hacking, Ian (1991) How Should We Do the History of Statistics? In *The Foucault Effect: Studies in Governmentality*, edited by Graham Burchell, Colin Gordon, and Peter Miller, pp. 181–196. Chicago, IL: The University of Chicago Press.

Hall, Edith (1989) *Inventing the Barbarian: Greek Self-Definition through Tragedy*. Oxford, UK: Clarendon Press.

Halliday, Fred (2002) The Pertinence of Imperialism. In *Historical Materialism and Globalization*, edited by Mark Rupert and Hazel Smith, pp. 75–89. London, UK: Routledge.

Harding, Sandra (2008) *Sciences from Below: Feminism, Postcolonialities, and Modernities*. Durham, NC: Duke University Press.

Hardt, Michael and Antonio Negri (2000) *Empire*. Cambridge, MA: Harvard University Press.

———— (2004) *Multitude: War and Democracy in an Age of Empire*. London, UK: Penguin Books.

Harman, Chris (1992) The Return of the National Question. *International Socialism* 56:3–62.

Harrod, Roy F. (1939) An Essay in Dynamic Theory. *The Economic Journal*, vol. 49, no. 193, pp. 14–33. London.

Hart-Landsberg, Martin and Paul Burkett (2004) *China and Socialism: Market Reforms and Class Struggle*. New York: Monthly Review Press.

Haupt, Georges, Michael Löwy, and Claudie Weill, eds. (1974) *Les marxistes et la question nationale, 1848–1918: études et textes*. Paris, France: François Maspero.

Harvey, David (1989) *The Condition of Postmodernity: An Enquiry into the Origins of Cultural Change*. Oxford, UK: Basil Blackwell.

———— (2003) *The New Imperialism*. Oxford, UK: Oxford University Press.

———— (2011) *The Enigma of Capital and the Crises of Capitalism*. Oxford, UK: Oxford University Press.

Havighurst, Alfred, ed. (1958) *The Pirenne Thesis: Analysis, Criticism, and Revision*. Boston, MA: D. C. Heath and Company.

Hayek, Friedrich A. (1960) *The Constitution of Liberty*. Chicago, IL: The University of Chicago Press.

Hearn, Frank (1985) Durkheim's Political Sociology: Corporatism, State Autonomy and Democracy. *Social Research* 52(1):115–177.

Hegel, Georg W. F. (1952[1821]) *Philosophy of Right*. Oxford, UK: Oxford University Press.

———— (1967[1807]) *The Phenomenology of Mind*. New York: Harper and Row, Publishers.

———— (1975[1830]) *Lectures on the Philosophy of World History. Introduction*. Cambridge, UK: Cambridge University Press.

Held, David and Anthony McGrew (2003) The Great Globalization Debate: An Introduction. In *The Global Transformations Reader: An Introduction to the Globalization Debate*, edited by David Held and Andrew McGrew, 2nd ed., pp. 1–50. Cambridge, UK: Polity Press.

Held, David, Anthony McGrew, David Goldblatt, and Jonathan Perraton (1999) *Global Transformations: Politics, Economics, and Culture*. Cambridge, UK: Polity Press.

Hennis, Wilhelm (1987) A Science of Man: Max Weber and the Political Economy of the German Historical School. In *Max Weber and His Contemporaries*, edited by Wolfgang J. Mommsen and Jürgen Osterhammel, pp. 25–58. London, UK: Allen and Unwin.

Herold, Marc W. and Nicholas Kozlov (1987) A New International Division of Labor: The Caribbean Case. In *The Year Left 2: An American Socialist Yearbook*, edited by Mike Davis, Manning Marable, Fred Pfeil, and Michael Sprinker, pp. 218–241. London, UK: Verso.

Herskovits, Melville J. (1938) *Acculturation: The Study of Culture Contact*. New York: J. J. Augustin Publisher.

Hilferding, Rudolf (1902–1903) Der Funktionswechsel des Schutzzolles. Tendenz der modernen Handelspolitik. *Die Neue Zeit* 21(2):274–281.

——— (1981[1910]) *Finance Capital: A Study of the Latest Phase of Capitalist Development*. London, UK: Routledge and Kegan Paul.

Hilton, Rodney (1976[1953]) A Comment. In *The Transition from Feudalism to Capitalism*, edited by Rodney Hilton, pp. 102–108. London, UK: New Left Books.

——— (1985[1976]) Reasons for Inequality among Medieval Peasants. In *Class Conflict and the Crisis of Feudalism*, edited by Rodney Hilton, pp. 139–151. London, UK: The Hambledon Press.

Ho, Chi Minh (1922) Some Considerations on the Colonial Question. www.marxists.org/reference/archive/ho-chi-minh/works/1922/05/25.html.

Hobbes, Thomas (1968[1651]) *Leviathan*. London, UK: Penguin Books.

Hobsbawm, Eric J. (1964) Introduction. In *Pre-Capitalist Economic Formations*, edited by Karl Marx, pp. 9–65. London, UK: Lawrence and Wishart.

——— (1968) *Industry and Empire*. Harmondsworth, UK: Penguin Books.

——— (1976[1962]) From Feudalism to Capitalism. In *The Transition from Feudalism to Capitalism*, edited by Rodney Hilton, pp. 159–164. London, UK: New Left Books.

——— (1979) *The Age of Capital, 1848–1879*. New York: Mentor Books.

——— (1987) *The Age of Empire, 1875–1914*. New York: Pantheon Books.

——— (1996) *The Age of Extremes: A History of the World, 1914–1991*. New York: Vintage Books.

Hobson, John A. (1965[1902]) *Imperialism: A Study*. Ann Arbor, MI: University of Michigan Press.

Hodgen, Margaret T. (1964) *Early Anthropology in the Sixteenth and Seventeenth Centuries*. Philadelphia, PA: University of Pennsylvania Press.

Hollis, Martin (2006) Rationality and Reason. In *The Blackwell Dictionary of Modern Social Thought*, edited by William Outhwaite, pp. 556–557. Oxford, UK: Blackwell Publishing.

Holmstrom, Nancy and Richard Smith (2000) The Necessity of Gangster Capitalism: Primitive Accumulation in Russia and China. *Monthly Review* 51(9):1–12.

Hoppensbrouwers, Pete and Jan L. van Zanden, eds. (2001) *Peasants into Farmers? The Transformation of Rural Economy in the Low Countries during the Later Medieval and Early Modern Periods in Light of the Brenner Debate*. CORN Publication Series, no. 4. Turnhout, Belgium: Brepols Publishers.

Horowitz, Asher (1987) *Rousseau, Nature and History*. Toronto, ON: University of Toronto Press.

Hou, Xiaoshuo (2013) *Community Capitalism in China: The State, the Market, and Collectivism*. Cambridge, UK: Cambridge University Press.

Howard, Michael C. and John E. King (1989) *A History of Marxian Economics*, vol. 1, *1883–1929*. Princeton, NJ: Princeton University Press.

Howard, Michael C. and J. E. King (1992) *A History of Marxian Economics*, vol. 2, *1929–1990*. Princeton, NJ: Princeton University Press.

Hudson, Michael (2003) *Super-Imperialism: The Origin and Fundamentals of U.S. World Dominance*, 2nd edn. London, UK: Pluto Press.

Hughes, H. Stuart (1977) *Consciousness and Society: The Reorientation of European Social Thought, 1890–1930*. New York: Vintage Books.

Hunter, Monica (1936) *Reaction to Conquest: Effects of Contact with Europeans on the Pondo of South Africa*. Oxford, UK: Oxford University Press.

——— (1938) Contact between European and Native in South Africa: 1. Pondoland. In *Methods of Study of Culture Contact in Africa*, edited by Lucy P. Mair, pp. 9–24. Oxford, UK: Oxford University Press.

Huntington, Samuel P. (1965) Political Development and Political Decay. *World Politics* 17(3):386–430.

Huppert, George (1971) The Idea of Civilization in the Sixteenth Century. In *Renaissance Studies in Honor of Hans Baron*, edited by Anthony Milho and John A. Tedeschi, pp. 757–769. DeKalb, IL: Northern Illinois University Press.

Hussain, Athar and Keith Tribe (1981) *Marxism and the Agrarian Question*, vol. 2, *Russian Marxism and the Peasantry 1861–1930*. Atlantic Highlands, NJ: Humanities Press.

Hussey, Edward (1985) Thucydidean History and Democritean Theory. In *Crux: Essays in Greek History Presented to G. E. M. de Ste. Croix*, edited by Paul Cartledge and F. D. Harvey, pp. 118–138. London, UK: Gerald Duckworth.

Hutchinson, John and Anthony D. Smith, eds. (1994) *Nationalism*. Oxford, UK: Oxford University Press.

Hymer, Stephen (1968) La grande "corporation" multinationale: analyse de certaines raisons qui poussent à l'intégration international des affaires. *Revue Économique* 19(6):949–973.

——— (1970) The Efficiency (Contradictions) of Multinational Corporations. *The American Economic Review* 60(2):441–448.

——— (1972a) The Multinational Corporation and the Law of Uneven Development. In *Economics and World Order from the 1970's to the 1990's*, edited by Jagdish N. Bhagwati, pp. 113–140. London, UK: The Macmillan Company.

——— (1972b) The Internationalization of Capital. *Journal of Economic Issues* 6(1):91–111.

——— (1976[1960]) *The International Operations of National Firms: A Study of Direct Foreign Investment*. Cambridge, MA: The MIT Press.

Hymer, Stephen and Stephen Resnick (1971) International Trade and Uneven Development. In *Trade, Balance of Payments and Growth: Papers in International Economics in Honor of Charles P. Kindleberger*, edited by Jagdish N. Bhagwati, Ronald W. Jones, Robert A. Mundell, and Jaroslav Vanek, pp. 473–493. Amsterdam, the Netherlands: North-Holland Publishing Company.

Ibn Khaldun (1967 [1377]) *The Muqaddimah: An Introduction to History*. Princeton, NJ: Princeton University Press.

Irele, Abiola (1973a) Negritude or Black Cultural Nationalism. *The Journal of Modern African Studies* 3(3):321–348.

——— (1973b) Literature and Ideology. *The Journal of Modern African Studies* 3(4):499–526.

Ishay, Micheline R. (1995) Introduction. In *The Nationalism Reader*, edited by Omar Dahbour and Micheline R. Ishay, pp. 1–19. Atlantic Highlands, NJ: Humanities Press International.

Israel, Jonathan R. (2001) *Radical Enlightenment: Philosophy and the Making of Modernity, 1650–1750*. Oxford, UK: Oxford University Press.

Jacob, Margaret C. (1988) *The Cultural Meaning of the Scientific Revolution*. Philadelphia, PA: Temple University Press.

Jameson, Frederic (1991) *Postmodernism and the Cultural Logic of Late Capitalism*. London, UK: Verso.

——— (1998) *The Cultural Turn: Selected Essays on the Postmodern, 1983–1998*. London, UK: Verso.

Jaspers, Karl (1953[1949]) *The Origin and Goal of History*. New Haven, CT: Yale University Press.

Jenkins, Rhys (1984) Divisions over the International Division of Labor. *Capital and Class* 22:28–57.

——— (1987) *Transnational Corporation and Uneven Development*. London, UK: Methuen.

Jessop, Bob (1982) *The Capitalist State*. New York: New York University Press.

——— (2011) Constituting Another Foucault Effect: Foucault on States and Statecraft. In *Governmentality: Current Issues and Future Challenges*, edited by Ulrich Bröckling, Susanne Krasmann, and Thomas Lempke, pp. 56–73. London, UK: Routledge.

Johnson, Monte R. (2005) *Aristotle on Teleology*. Oxford, UK: Clarendon Press.

Joll, James (1955) *The Second International, 1889–1914*. London, UK: Routledge and Kegan Paul.

Jones, Greta (1980) *Social Darwinism and English Thought: The Interaction between Biological and Social Theory*. Brighton, UK: Harvester.

Jones, Richard F. (1961) *Ancients and Moderns: A Study of the Rise of the Scientific Movement in Seventeenth-Century England*. Berkeley: University of California Press.

Jones, Robert A. (2003) Émile Durkheim. In *The Blackwell Companion to Major Classical Social Theorists*, edited by George Ritzer, pp. 193–238. Oxford, UK: Blackwell Publishing.

Kahn, Herbert (1979) *World Economic Development: 1979 and Beyond*. Boulder, CO: Westview Press.

Kalberg, Stephen (2003) Max Weber. In *The Blackwell Companion to Major Classical Social Theorists*, edited by George Ritzer, pp. 132–192. Oxford, UK: Blackwell Publishing.

Kant, Immanuel (1996[1797]) *The Metaphysics of Morals*. Cambridge, UK: Cambridge University Press.

Kapferer, Bruce and Bjørn Enge Bertelsen, eds. (2009) *Crisis of the State: War and Social Upheaval*. New York: Berghahn Books.

Kautsky, Karl (1887) Die moderne Nationalität. *Die Neue Zeit* 5:3920405, 442–451.

―――― (1908) Nationalität under Internationalität. *Die Neue Zeit* 1(1):1–25.

―――― (1971[1892]) *The Class Struggle*. New York: W. W. Norton and Company.

―――― (1988[1899]) *The Agrarian Question*, 2 vols. London, UK: Zwan Publications.

Keane, John (1988) *Democracy and Civil Society: On the Predicaments of European Socialism, the Prospects for Democracy, and the Problem of Controlling Social and Political Power*. London, UK: Verso.

Kelly, Mark G. E. (2009) *The Political Philosophy of Michel Foucault*. London, UK: Routledge.

Kennedy, Tony (1992) Henryk Grossmann and the Theory of Capitalist Collapse. In *The Law of Accumulation and Breakdown of the Capitalist System, Being also a Theory of Crises*, pp. 1–27. London, UK: Pluto Press.

Kerblay, Basile (1986[1966]) A. V. Chayanov: Life, Career, Works. In *The Theory of Peasant Economy*, edited by Daniel Thorner, Basile Kerblay, and R. E. F. Smith, pp. xxv–lxxv. Madison, WI: The University of Wisconsin Press.

Kerr, Clark (1960) Changing Social Structure. In *Labor Commitment and Social Change in Developing Areas*, edited by Wilbert E. Moore and Arnold S. Feldman, pp. 348–359. New York: Social Science Research Council, Committee on Economic Growth.

Keynes, John M. (1919) *The Economic Consequences of Peace*. London, UK: Macmillan and Company.

―――― (1933) *The Means to Prosperity*. New York: Harcourt, Brace and Company.

―――― (1936) *The General Theory of Employment, Interest and Money*. London, UK: Macmillan and Company.

―――― (1940) *How to Pay for War: A Radical Plan for the Chancellor of the Exchequer*. London, UK: Macmillan and Company.

Kiely, Ray (1994) Development Theory and Industrialisation: Beyond the Impasse. *Journal of Contemporary Asia* 24(2):133–160.

―――― (2005) *The Clash of Globalisations: Neo-Liberalism, the Third Way, and Anti-Globalisation*. Leiden, NL: Brill.

―――― (2007) *The New Political Economy of Development: Globalization, Imperialism, Hegemony*. London, UK: Palgrave Macmillan.

Kinser, Samuel (1971) Ideas of Temporal Change and Cultural Process, 1470–1535. In *Renaissance Studies in Honor of Hans Baron*, edited by Anthony Molho and John Tedeschi, pp. 703–755. DeKalb, IL: Northern Illinois University Press.

Klein, Naomi (2014) *This Changes Everything: Capitalism vs the Climate*. New York: Simon and Schuster.

Kluckhohn, Clyde (1943) Covert Culture and Administrative Problems. *American Anthropologist* 45(2):213–227.

Koebner, Richard and Helmut D. Schmidt (1965) *Imperialism: History and Significance of a Political Word 1840–1960*. Cambridge, UK: Cambridge University Press.

Kolakowski, Leszek (1968) *Postivist Philosophy: From Hume to the Vienna Circle*. Harmondsworth, UK: Penguin Books.

―――― (1981) *Main Currents of Marxism*, vol. 2, *The Golden Age*. Oxford, UK: Oxford University Press.

Kolko, Gabriel (1968) *The Politics of War: The World and United States Foreign Policy, 1943–1945*. New York: Random House.

Kolko, Joyce (1972) *The Limits of Power: The World and United States Foreign Policy, 1945–1954*. New York: Harper and Row.

Kolko, Joyce and Gabriel Kolko (1972) *The Limits of Power: The World and United States Foreign Policy, 1945–1954*. New York: Harper and Row.

Konrád, György and Iván Szelényi (1979[1974]) *The Intellectuals on the Road to Class Power*. New York: Harcourt Brace Jovanovich.

Kritsman, L.N. (1984[1926]) Class Stratification of the Soviet Countryside. In *Kritsman and the Agrarian Marxists*, edited by Terry Cox and Gary Littlejohn, pp. 85–143. London, UK: Frank Cass and Company.

Kuhn, Rick (2004) Economic Crises and Socialist Revolution: Henryk Grossman's Law of Accumulation, Its First Critics and His Responses. *Research in Political Economy* 21:181–221.

———— (2005) Henryk Grossman and the Recovery of Marxism. *Historical Materialism* 13(3): 57–101.

Kula, Witold (1976[1962]) *An Economic Theory of the Feudal System: Towards a Model of the Polish Economy 1500–1800*. London, UK: New Left Books.

Kumar, Krishnan (2006) Modernity. In *The Blackwell Dictionary of Modern Social Thought*, edited by William Outhwaite, pp. 404–405. Oxford, UK: Blackwell Publishing.

Kurihara, Kenneth (1968) The Dynamic Impact of History on Keynesian Theory. In *Events, Ideology and Economic History: The Determinants of Progress in the Development of Economic Analysis*, edited by Robert V. Eagly, pp. 127–158. Detroit, MI: Wayne State University Press.

Laclau, Ernesto (1971) Feudalism and Capitalism in Latin America. *New Left Review* 37:19–38.

———— (1977) *Politics and Ideology in Marxist Theory: Capitalism, Fascism, Populism*. London, UK: New Left Books.

Laclau, Ernesto and Chantal Mouffe (1988) *Hegemony and Socialist Strategy: Towards a Radical Democratic Politics*. London, UK: Verso.

Lamphere, Louise, Alex Stepick, and Guillermo J. Grenier, eds. (1994) *Newcomers in the Workplace: Immigrants and the Restructuring of the U.S. Economy*. Philadelphia, PA: Temple University Press.

Lapavitsas, Costas (2005) Mainstream Economics in the Neoliberal Era. In *Neoliberalism: A Critical Reader*, edited by Alfred Saad-Filho and Deborah Johnston, pp. 30–40. London, UK: Pluto Press.

Larrain, Jorge (1983) *Marxism and Ideology*. Atlantic Highlands, NJ: Humanities Press.

Leacock, Eleanor B. (1982) Marxism and Anthropology. In *The Left Academy: Marxist Scholarship on American Campuses*, edited by Bertell Ollman and Edward Vernoff, pp. 242–276. New York: McGraw-Hill Book Company.

Leiss, William (1976) *The Limits to Satisfaction*. Toronto, ON: University of Toronto Press.

Lenin, Vladimir I. (1960[1893]) New Economic Developments in Peasant Life (On V. Y. Postnikov's *Peasant Farming in South Russia*). In *V. I. Lenin Collected Works*, vol. 1, pp. 11–74. Moscow, USSR: Progress Publishers.

———— (1960[1899a]) Karl Kautsky, *Die Agrarfrage: eine Übersicht über die Tendenzen der modernen Landwirtschaft und die Agrarpolitik der Sozialdemokratie*. In *V. I. Lenin Collected Works*, vol. 4, pp. 84–99. Moscow, USSR: Progress Publishers.

———— (1960[1899b]) The Development of Capitalism in Russia: The Process of the Formation of a Home Market for Large-Scale Industry. In *V. I. Lenin Collected Works*, vol. 3, pp. 21–607. Moscow, USSR: Progress Publishers.

———— (1961[1902]) What Is to Be Done? Burning Questions of Our Movement. In *V. I. Lenin Collected Works*, vol. 5, pp. 347–530. Moscow, USSR: Progress Publishers.

———— (1962[1906]) Revision of the Agrarian Programme of the Workers' Party. In *V. I. Lenin Collected Works*, vol. 10, pp. 165–195. Moscow, USSR: Progress Publishers.

———— (1962[1907]) The Agrarian Program of Social-Democracy in the First Russian Revolution, 1905–1907. In *V. I. Lenin Collected Works*, vol. 13, pp. 217–431. Moscow, USSR: Progress Publishers.

———— (1963[1908a]) Inflammable Material in World Politics. In *V. I. Lenin Collected Works*, vol. 15, pp. 182–188. Moscow, USSR: Progress Publishers.

———— (1963[1908b]) The Agrarian Question in Russia toward the Close of the Nineteenth Century. In *V. I. Lenin Collected Works*, vol. 15, pp. 69–147. Moscow, USSR: Progress Publishers.

———— (1963[1913]) The Awakening of Asia. In *V. I. Lenin Collected Works*, vol. 19, pp. 85–86. Moscow, USSR: Progress Publishers.

———— (1964[1914]) The Right of Nations to Self-Determination. In *V. I. Lenin Collected Works*, vol. 20, pp. 393–454. Moscow, USSR: Progress Publishers.

———— (1964[1915]) New Data on the Laws Governing the Development of Capitalism in Agriculture, Part One. *Capitalism and Agriculture in the United States of America*. In *V. I. Lenin Collected Works*, vol. 22 pp. 13–102. Moscow, USSR: Progress Publishers.

———— (1964[1916a]) The Junius Pamphlet. In *V. I. Lenin Collected Works*, vol. 22, pp. 305–319. Moscow, USSR: Progress Publishers.

———— (1964[1916b]) The Discussion on Self-Determination Summed Up. In *V. I. Lenin Collected Works*, vol. 22, pp. 320–360. Moscow, USSR: Progress Publishers.

———— (1964[1917a]) Imperialism, The Highest Stage of Capitalism: A Popular Outline. In *V. I. Lenin Collected Works*, vol. 22, pp. 185–304. Moscow, USSR: Progress Publishers.

———— (1964[1917b]) The Socialist Revolution and the Rights of Nations to Self-Determination. *Theses*. In *V. I. Lenin Collected Works*, vol. 22, pp. 143–156. Moscow, USSR: Progress Publishers.

———— (1964[1917c]) State and Revolution: The Marxist Theory of the State and the Tasks of the Proletariat in the Revolution. In *V. I. Lenin Collected Works*, vol. 25, pp. 385–498. Moscow, USSR: Progress Publishers.

———— (1965[1919]) Eighth Congress of the R.C.P.(B.), March 18–23, 1919. In *V. I. Lenin Collected Works*, vol. 29, pp. 143–225. Moscow, USSR: Progress Publishers.

———— (1965[1921a]) The New Economic Policy and the Tasks of Political Education Departments. In *V. I. Lenin Collected Works*, vol. 32, pp. 60–80. Moscow, USSR: Progress Publishers.

———— (1965[1921b]) Report on the New Economic Policy. In *V. I. Lenin Collected Works*, vol. 33, pp. 83–101. Moscow, USSR: Progress Publishers.

———— (1965[1922]) The Tax in Kind. In *V. I. Lenin Collected Works*, vol. 33, pp. 329–365. Moscow, USSR: Progress Publishers.

———— (1966[1920]) Preliminary Draft Theses on the Agrarian Question. In *V. I. Lenin Collected Works*, vol. 31, pp. 152–165. Moscow, USSR: Progress Publishers.

———— (1968[1912–1917]) Notebooks on Imperialism. In *V. I. Lenin Collected Works*, vol. 39, pp. 29–791. Moscow, USSR: Progress Publishers.

Lerner, Daniel (1958) *The Passing of Traditional Society: Modernizing the Middle East*. New York: The Free Press.

Lerner, Ralph and Muhsin Mahdi (1963) *Medieval Political Philosophy: A Sourcebook*. Glencoe, IL: The Free Press.

Lesser, Alexander (1985[1939]) Evolution in Social Anthropology. In *History, Evolution, and the Concept of Culture: Selected Papers by Alexander Lesser*, edited by Sidney W. Mintz, pp. 78–91. Cambridge, UK: Cambridge University Press.

Letelier, Orlando (1976) The Chicago Boys in Chile: Economic Freedom's Awful Toll. *The Nation*, August 28. www.ditext.com/letelier/chicago.html.

Levins, Richard and Richard Lewontin (1985) *The Dialectical Biologist*. Cambridge, MA: Harvard University Press.

Lewin, Moishe (1968) *Russian Peasants and Soviet Power: A Study of Collectivization*. New York: W. W. Norton.

———— (1974) *Political Undercurrents in Soviet Economic Debates: From Bukharin to the Modern Reformers*. Princeton, NJ: Princeton University Press.

———— (1985) *The Making of the Soviet System: Essays on the Social History of Interwar Russia*. New York: Pantheon Books.

———— (1985[1965]) The Immediate Background of Soviet Collectivization. In *The Making of the Soviet System: Essays in the Social History of Interwar Russia*, by Moshe Lewin, pp. 91–120. New York: Pantheon Books.

Linton, Ralph, ed. (1940) *Acculturation in Seven American Indian Tribes*. New York: D. Appleton-Century Company.

Littlejohn, Gary (1977) Peasant Economy and Society. In *Sociological Theories of the Economy*, edited by Barry Hindess, pp. 118–156. New York: Holmes and Meier Publishers.

———— (1984) The Agrarian Marxist Research in its Political Context: State Policy and the Development of the Soviet Rural Class Structures in the 1920s. In *Kritsman and the Agrarian Marxists*, edited by Terry Cox and Gary Littlejohn, pp. 61–84. London, UK: Frank Cass.

Llobera, Josep R. (1981) Durkheim, the Durkheimians and Their Collective Misrepresentation of Marx. In *The Anthropology of Pre-Capitalist Societies*, edited by Joel S. Kahn and Josep R. Llobera, pp. 214–240. London, UK: The Macmillan Press.

———— (1994) Durkheim and the National Question. In *Debating Durkheim*, edited by William S. F. Pickering and H. Martins, pp. 134–158. London, UK: Routledge.

Lloyd, David (2000) Ireland after History. In *A Companion to Postcolonial Studies*, edited by Henry Schwarz and Sangeeta Ray, pp. 377–395. Oxford, UK: Blackwell Publishers.

Love, John R. (1991) *Antiquity and Capitalism: Max Weber and the Sociological Foundations of Roman Civilization*. London, UK: Routledge.

Love, Joseph L. (1990) The Origins of Dependency Analysis. *Journal of Latin American Studies* 22(1):143–168.

Lowe, Donald M. (1982) *History of Bourgeois Perception*. Chicago, IL: The University of Chicago Press.

Löwith, Karl (1982[1960]) *Max Weber and Karl Marx*. London, UK: George Allen and Unwin.

Löwy, Michael (1971) Le Problème de l'Histoire. In *Les Marxistes et la Question Nationale, 1848–1914*, edited by Georges Haupt, Michael Löwy, and Claudie Weill, pp. 370–391. Paris, France: Maspero.

—— (1981) *The Politics of Combined and Uneven Development: The Theory of Permanent Revolution*. London, UK: Verso.

—— (1999[1980]) Introduction: Points of Reference for a History of Marxism in Latin America. In *Marxism in Latin America from 1909 to the Present*, edited by Michael Löwy, pp. xiii–lxv. Amherst, NY: Humanity Books.

Löwy, Michael and Robert Sayre (2001) *Romanticism: Against the Tide of Modernity*. Durham, NC: Duke University Press.

Lukács, Georg (1971[1923]) *History and Class Consciousness*. Cambridge, MA: MIT Press.

Lukes, Steven (1973) *Émile Durkheim: His Life and Work: A Historical and Critical Study*. Harmondsworth, UK: Penguin Books.

—— (2006a) Anomie. In *The Blackwell Dictionary of Modern Social Thought*, edited by William Outhwaite, pp. 7–19. Oxford, UK: Blackwell Publishing.

—— (2006b) Power. In *The Blackwell Dictionary of Modern Social Thought*, edited by William Outhwaite, pp. 516–517. Oxford, UK: Blackwell Publishing.

Luxemburg, Rosa (1970[1900]) Reform or Revolution. In *Rosa Luxemburg Speaks*, edited by Mary-Alice Walker, pp. 33–90. New York: Pathfinder Press.

—— (1970[1906]) The Mass Strike, the Political Party, and the Trade Unions. In *Rosa Luxemburg Speaks*, edited by Mary-Alice Walker, pp. 153–218. New York: Pathfinder Press.

—— (1971[1899]) Speech to the Hanover Congress. In *Selected Writings of Rosa Luxemburg*, edited by Dick Howard, pp. 44–51. New York: Monthly Review Press.

—— (1972[1921]) The Accumulation of Capital—An Anti-Critique. In *The Accumulation of Capital—An Anti-Critique, by Rosa Luxemburg. Imperialism and the Accumulation of Capital by Nikolai Bukharin*, pp. 45–150. New York: Monthly Review Press.

—— (1976[1908–1909]) The National Question and Autonomy. In *The National Question: Selected Writings by Rosa Luxemburg*, edited by Horace B. Davis, pp. 101–287. New York: Monthly Review Press.

—— (2003[1913]) *The Accumulation of Capital*. London, UK: Routledge.

—— (2013[1909–1910]). Introduction to Political Economy. In *The Complete Works of Rosa Luxemburg*, vol. 1, *Economic Writings 1*, edited by Peter Hudis, pp. 89–301. London, UK: Verso.

Machiavelli, Niccolò (1988[1525]) *Florentine Histories*. Princeton, NJ: Princeton University Press.

Macpherson, Crawford B. (1973) *Democratic Theory: Essays in Retrieval*. Oxford, UK: Oxford University Press.

—— (1977) *The Life and Times of Liberal Democracy*. Oxford, UK: Oxford University Press.

Magdoff, Harry (1969) *The Age of Imperialism: The Economics of U.S. Foreign Policy*. New York: Monthly Review Press.

Makdisi, George (1981) *The Rise of Colleges: Institutions of Learning in Islam and the West*. Edinburgh, UK: Edinburgh University Press.

Maksakovsky, Pavel V. (2004[1928]) *The Capitalist Cycle: An Essay on the Marxist Theory of the Cycle*. Leiden, NL: Brill.

Malinowski, Bronislaw (1938) Introductory Essay: The Anthropology of Changing African Cultures. In *Methods of Study of Culture Contact in Africa*, edited by Lucy P. Mair, pp. vii–xxxviii. Oxford, UK: Oxford University Press.

———— (1945) *The Dynamics of Culture Change: An Inquiry into Race Relations in Africa.* New Haven, CT: Yale University Press.

Mandel, Ernest (1978[1972]) *Late Capitalism.* London, UK: Verso.

———— (1989) *Beyond Perestroika: The Future of Gorbachev's USSR.* London, UK: Verso.

Mann, Michael (2003) *Incoherent Empire.* London, UK: Verso.

Mannoni, Octave (1964[1950]) *Prospero and Caliban: The Psychology of Colonization.* New York: Frederick A. Praeger.

Mao, Zedong (1965[1926]) Analyses of the Classes in Chinese Society. In *Selected Works of Mao Tse-ting,* vol. 1, pp. 13–22. Peking, China: Foreign Languages Press.

———— (1965[1927]) Report on an Investigation of the Peasant Movement in Hunan. In *Selected Works of Mao Tse-ting,* vol. 1, pp. 23–62. Peking, China: Foreign Languages Press.

———— (1965[1933]) How to Differentiate Classes in Rural Areas. In *Selected Works of Mao Tse-ting,* vol. 1, pp. 137–140. Peking, China: Foreign Languages Press.

———— (1965[1937]) On Contradiction. In *Selected Works of Mao Tse-tung,* vol. 1, pp. 311–347. Peking, China: Foreign Language Press.

———— (1990[1930]) *Report from Xunwu.* Stanford, CA: Stanford University Press.

———— (1994[1923]) Resolution on the Peasant Question. In *Mao's Road to Power: Revolutionary Writings 1912–1949,* vol. 2, *National Revolution and Social Revolution, December 1920–June 1927,* edited by Stuart R. Schram, pp. 164–165. Armonk, NY: M. E. Sharpe.

———— (1994[1925]) Analysis of All Classes in Chinese Society. In *Mao's Road to Power: Revolutionary Writings 1912–1949,* vol. 2, *National Revolution and Social Revolution, December 1920–June 1927,* edited by Stuart R. Schram, pp. 249–262. Armonk, NY: M. E. Sharpe.

Marable, Manning (1995) *Beyond Black and White: Transforming African-American Politics.* London, UK: Verso.

Maravall, José A. (1986 [1975]) *Culture of the Baroque: Analysis of a Historical Structure.* Theory and History of Literature 25. Minneapolis, MN: University of Minnesota Press.

Marcuse, Herbert (1960[1941]) *Reason and Revolution: Hegel and the Rise of Social Theory.* Boston, MA: Beacon Press.

Mariátegui, José C. (1971[1928]) *Seven Interpretive Essays on Peruvian Reality.* Austin, TX: University of Texas Press.

———— (1999[1928]) The Indigenous Question in Latin America. In *Marxism in Latin America from 1909 to the Present,* edited by Michael Löwy, pp. 33–36. Amherst, NY: Humanity Books.

Martinussen, John (1997) *Society, State, and Market: A Guide to Competing Theories of Development.* London, UK: Zed Books.

Marshall, Alfred (1920[1890]) *Principles of Economics: An Introductory Volume.* New York: Macmillan and Company.

Marx, Karl (1963[1875]) *Ouevres. Economie,* vol. 1. Paris, France: Gallimard.

———— (1970[1859]) A Contribution to the Critique of Political Economy. In *Karl Marx and Frederick Engels: Collected Works,* vol. 29, pp. 257–417. New York: International Publishers.

———— (1973[1857–1858]) *Grundrisse: Foundations to the Critique of Political Economy.* New York: Vintage Books.

———— (1975[1844]) The Economic and Philosophic Manuscripts of 1844. In *Karl Marx and Frederick Engels: Collected Works,* vol. 3, pp. 229–348. New York: International Publishers.

———— (1976[1845]) Theses on Feuerbach. In *Karl Marx and Frederick Engels: Collected Works,* vol. 5, pp. 3–5. New York: International Publishers.

———— (1977[1863–1867]) *Capital: A Critique of Political Economy,* vol. 1. New York: Vintage Books.

———— (1978[1850]) The Class Struggles in France, 1848 to 1850. In *Karl Marx and Frederick Engels: Collected Works,* vol. 10, pp. 45–145. New York: International Publishers.

———— (1978[1884]) *Capital: A Critique of Political Economy,* vol. 2. New York: Vintage Books.

———— (1979[1852]) The Eighteenth Brumaire of Louis Bonaparte. In *Karl Marx and Frederick Engels: Collected Works,* vol. 11, pp. 97–199. New York: International Publishers.

———— (1981[1864–1894]) *Capital: A Critique of Political Economy,* vol. 3. New York: Vintage Books.

————— (1982[1843]) *Critique of Hegel's Philosophy of Right*. Cambridge, UK: Cambridge University Press.

————— (1983[1877]) A Letter to the Editorial Board of *Otechestvennye Zapiski*. In *Late Marxism and the Russian Road: Marx and "The Peripheries of Capitalism,"* edited by Teodor Shanin, pp. 134–137. New York: Monthly Review Press [*Karl Marx and Frederick Engels: Collected Works*, vol. 24, pp. 196–201. New York: International Publishers, 1989].

————— (1983[1881]) Marx-Zasulich Correspondence: Letters and Drafts. In *Late Marxism and the Russian Road: Marx and "The Peripheries of Capitalism,"* edited by Teodor Shanin, pp. 97–129. New York: Monthly Review Press [*Karl Marx and Frederick Engels: Collected Works*, vol. 24, pp. 346–371. New York: International Publishers, 1989].

————— (1985[1860]) Letter to Frederick Engels, 19 December 1860. In *Karl Marx and Frederick Engels: Collected Works*, vol. 41, pp. 231–233. New York: International Publishers.

————— (1985[1875]) *Le Capital, Livre 1, Sections V à VIII*. Paris, France: Éditions Flammarion.

————— (1986[1871]) The Civil War in France. In *Karl Marx and Frederick Engels: Collected Works*, vol. 22, pp. 307–359. New York: International Publishers.

————— (1987[1869]) Letter to Ludwig Kugelmann, 29 November 1869. In *Karl Marx and Frederick Engels: Collected Works*, vol. 43, pp. 390–391. New York: International Publishers.

————— (1989[1877]) Letter to the Editorial Board of *Otechestvennye Zapiski*. In *Karl Marx and Frederick Engels: Collected Works*, vol. 24, pp. 196–201. New York: International Publishers.

————— (1992[1881]) Letter to Vera Zasulich, 8 March. In *Karl Marx and Frederick Engels: Collected Works*, vol. 46, pp. 71–72. New York: International Publishers.

Marx, Karl and Frederick Engels (1976[1845–1846]) The German Ideology. In *Karl Marx and Frederick Engels: Collected Works*, vol. 5, pp. 19–452. New York: International Publishers.

————— (1976[1848]) Manifesto of the Communist Party. In *Karl Marx and Frederick Engels: Collected Works*, vol. 6, pp. 477–519. New York: International Publishers.

————— (1989[1882]) Preface to the Second Russian Edition of the *Manifesto of the Communist Party*. In *Karl Marx and Frederick Engels: Collected Works*, vol. 24, pp. 425–426. New York: International Publishers.

Mauss, Marcel (1958[1895–1896]) Introduction to the First Edition. In *Socialism and Saint-Simon*, by Émile Durkheim, pp. 1–4. Yellow Springs, OH: The Antioch Press.

McClelland, David (1961) *The Achieving Society*. Princeton, NJ: Van Nostrand.

————— (1964[1962]) Business Drive and National Achievement. In *Social Change: Sources, Patterns and Consequences*, edited by Amitai Etzioni and Eva Etzioni, pp. 165–178. New York: Basic Books.

McCulloch, Jock (1983a) *Black Soul, White Artifact: Fanon's Clinical Psychology and Social Theory*. Cambridge, UK: Cambridge University Press.

————— (1983b) *In the Twilight of Revolution: The Political Theory of Amilcar Cabral*. London, UK: Routledge and Kegan Paul.

McCune Smith, James (2006[1841]) Lecture on the Haytien Revolution. In *The Works of James McCune Smith: Black Intellectual and Abolitionist*, edited by John Stauffer, pp. 25–47. Cambridge, MA: Harvard University Press.

McEachern, Doug (1976) The Mode of Production in India. *Journal of Contemporary Asia* 6(4):444–457.

Medearis, John (2001) *Joseph Schumpeter's Two Theories of Democracy*. Cambridge, MA: Harvard University Press.

————— (2013[2009]) *Joseph A. Schumpeter*. New York: Bloomsbury Academic.

Meek, Ronald L. (1976) *Social Science and the Ignoble Savage*. Cambridge, UK: Cambridge University Press.

Mehta, Uday S. (1999) *Liberalism and Empire: A Study in Nineteenth-Century British Liberal Thought*. Chicago, IL: The University of Chicago Press.

Meisner, Maurice (1986) *Mao's China and After: A History of the People's Republic*. New York: Free Press.

—— (1996) *The Deng Xiaoping Era: An Inquiry into the Fate of Chinese Socialism, 1978–1994.* New York: Hill and Waing.

—— (1999) *Mao's China and After: A History of the People's Republic.* 3rd ed. New York: The Free Press.

Mellos, Koula (1988) *Perspectives on Ecology: A Critical Essay.* New York: St. Martin's Press.

Merchant, Carolyn (1980) *The Death of Nature: Women, Ecology, and the Scientific Revolution.* New York: Harper and Row, Publishers.

Mészáros, István (1995) *Beyond Capital: Towards a Theory of Transition.* New York: Monthly Review Press.

Miller, Peter and Ted O'Leary (1987) Accounting and the Construction of the Governable Person. *Accounting, Organizations and Society* 12(1):235–265.

Miller, Peter and Nikolas Rose (1990) Governing Economic Life. *Economy and Society* 19(1):1–31.

Mintz, Sidney (1953) The Folk-Urban Continuum and the Rural Proletarian Community. *American Sociological Review* 59(2):136–143.

—— (1973) A Note on the Definition of Peasantries. *Journal of Peasant Studies* 1(1):91–106.

—— (1974) The Rural Proletariat and the Problem of Rural Proletarian Consciousness. *Journal of Peasant Studies* 1(4):291–325.

Mirowski, Philip and Dieter Plehwe (2009) *The Road from Mont Pèlerin: The Making of the Neoliberal Thought Collective.* Cambridge, MA: Harvard University Press.

Modelski, George (1972) *Principles of World Politics.* New York: The Free Press.

Molina Enríquez, Andrés (1978[1909]) *Los grandes problemas nacionales.* Edited by Arnaldo Córdoba. Mexico, D.F., Mexico: Ediciones Era.

Mommsen, Wolfgang J. (1974) *Max Weber and German Politics 1890–1920.* 2nd ed. Chicago, IL: The University of Chicago Press.

—— (1980) *Theories of Imperialism.* Chicago, IL: The University of Chicago Press.

—— (1984) *Max Weber and German Politics 1890–1920.* Chicago, IL: The University of Chicago Press.

—— (1989) *The Political and Social Theory of Max Weber.* Chicago, IL: The University of Chicago Press.

Mommsen, Wolfgang J. and Jürgen Osterhammel, eds. (1987) *Max Weber and His Contemporaries.* London, UK: Allen and Unwin.

Montaigne, Michel de (1965[1588]) On Cannibals. In *The Complete Essays of Montaigne,* edited by Donald M. Frame, pp. 150–159. Stanford, CA: Stanford University Press.

Mooney, James E. (1896) The Ghost-Dance Religion and the Sioux Outbreak of 1890. *Fourteenth Annual Report of the Bureau of American Ethnology, 1892–1893,* pt. 2, pp. 635–1136. Washington, DC: Government Printing Office.

Moore, Barrington, Jr. (1966) *Social Origins of Dictatorship and Democracy: Lord and Peasant in the Making of the Modern World.* Boston, MA: Beacon Press.

Morgan, Lewis H. (1963[1877]) *Ancient Society, Or Researches in the Lines of Human Progress from Savagery through Barbarism to Civilization,* edited by Eleanor B. Leacock. New York: World Publishing Company.

Morishima, Michio (1969) *Theory of Economic Growth.* Oxford, UK: Clarendon Press.

Moser, Stephanie (1998) *Ancestral Images: The Iconography of Human Origins.* Ithaca, NY: Cornell University Press.

Mouffe, Chantal (1988) Hegemony and New Political Subjects: Toward a New Concept of Democracy. In *Marxism and the Interpretation of Culture,* edited by Cary Nelson and Lawrence Grossberg, pp. 89–104. Urbana, IL: University of Illinois Press.

Moulakis, Athanasios (2011) Civic Humanism. In *Stanford Encyclopedia of Philosophy.* Stanford, CA: Center for the Study of Language and Information, Stanford University. http://plato.stanford.edu/entries/humanism-civic/.

Muller, Jerry Z., ed. (1997) *Conservatism: An Anthology of Social and Political Thought from David Hume to the Present.* Princeton, NJ: Princeton University Press.

Munck, Ronaldo (1986) *The Difficult Dialogue: Marxism and Nationalism.* London, UK: Zed Books.

Nairn, Tom (1977) *The Break-up of Britain: Crisis and Neo-Nationalism*. 2nd ed. London, UK: New Left Books.

———— (1997) *Faces of Nationalism: Janus Revisited*. London, UK: Verso.

Nash, Philleo (1937) The Place of Religious Revitalism of the Intercultural Community on Klamath Reservation. In *The Social Anthropology of North American Tribes*, edited by Fred Eggan, pp. 377–442. Chicago, IL: The University of Chicago Press.

Naughton, Barry (2015) The Transformation of the State Sector: SAAC. The Market Economy, and the New National Champions. In *State Capitalism, Institutional Adaptation, and the Chinese Miracle*, edited by Barry Naughton and Kellee S. Tsai, pp. 46–71. Cambridge, UK: Cambridge University Press.

Needham, Joseph (1969) *The Grand Titration: Science and Society in East and West*. London, UK: Allen and Unwin.

Nehru, Jawaharlal (1946) *The Discovery of India*. New York: The John Day Company.

Nettl, J. Peter (1966) *Rosa Luxemburg*. 2 vols. Oxford, UK: Oxford University Press.

Nimni, Ephraim (1991) *Marxism and Nationalism: Theoretical Origins of a Political Crisis*. London, UK: Pluto Press.

Nisbet, Robert A. (1969) *Social Change and History: Aspects of the Western Theory of Development*. Oxford, UK: Oxford University Press.

———— (1978) Conservatism. In *A History of Sociological Analysis*, edited by Tom Bottomore and Robert Nisbet, pp. 80–117. New York: Basic Books.

———— (1980) *History of the Idea of Progress*. New York: Basic Books.

Nove, Alec (1965) Introduction. In *The New Economics*, edited by Evgeny Preobrazhensky, pp. vii–xvii. Oxford, UK: Clarendon Press.

———— (1969) *An Economic History of the U.S.S.R.* London, UK: Penguin Books.

Oakes, Guy (1987) Weber and the Southwest German School: The Genesis of the Concept of the Historical Individual. In *Max Weber and His Contemporaries*, edited by Wolfgang J. Mommsen and Jürgen Osterhammel, pp. 434–446. London, UK: Allen and Unwin.

O'Brien, Philip J. (1975) A Critique of Latin American Theories of Dependency. In *Beyond the Sociology of Development*, edited by Ivar Oxaal, Tony Barnett, and David Booth, pp. 7–27. London, UK: Routledge and Kegan Paul.

O'Connor, James (1985) *The Meaning of Crisis: A Theoretical Introduction*. Oxford, UK: Basil Blackwell.

Ohmae, Kenicki (1990) *The Borderless World: Power and Strategy in an Interlinked Economy*. New York: HarperCollins Publishers.

Ophuls, William (1977) *Ecology and the Politics of Scarcity: Prologue to a Political Theory of the Steady State*. San Francisco, CA: W. H. Freeman.

Ostergaard, Geoffrey (2006) Anarchism. In *The Blackwell Dictionary of Modern Social Thought*, edited by William Outhwaite, pp. 12–14. Oxford, UK: Blackwell Publishing.

Owen, Robert (1991[1817]) *A New View of Society*. New York: AMS Press.

Oxaal, Ivar, Tony Barnett, and David Booth, eds. (1975) *Beyond the Sociology of Development*. London, UK: Routledge and Kegan Paul.

Panitch, Leo (1994) Globalisation and the State. In *Social Register 1994: Between Globalism and Nationalism*, edited by Ralph Miliband and Leo Panitch, pp. 60–93. London, UK: Merlin Press.

Panitch, Leo and Sam Gindin (2002) Gems and Baubles in Empire. *Historical Materialism* 10(2):17–44.

———— (2012) *The Making of Global Capitalism: The Political Economy of American Empire*. London, UK: Verso.

Panofsky, Erwin (1957) *Gothic Architecture and Scholasticism*. Cleveland, OH: The World Publishing Company.

Parsons, Talcott (1949[1937]) *The Structure of Social Action*, vol. 2, *Weber*. Glencoe, IL: The Free Press.

———— (1951) *The Social System*. New York: Free Press.

———— (1961a) Some Considerations on the Theory of Social Change. *Rural Sociology* 26(3):219–239.

——— (1961b) An Outline of the Social System. In *Theories of Society: Foundations of Modern Sociological Theory*, edited by Talcott Parsons, Edward Shils, Kaspar D. Naegele, and Jesse R. Pitts, vol. 1, pp. 30–79. Glencoe, IL: The Free Press.

——— (1961c) Differentiation and Variation in Social Structure: Introduction. In *Theories of Society: Foundations of Modern Sociological Theory*, edited by Talcott Parsons, Edward Shils, Kaspar D. Naegele, and Jesse R. Pitts, vol. 1, pp. 239–264. Glencoe, IL: The Free Press.

——— (1966) *Societies: Evolutionary and Comparative Perspectives*. Englewood Cliffs, NJ: Prentice-Hall.

——— (1967[1964]) Evolutionary Universals in Society. In *Sociological Theory and Modern Society*, edited by Talcott Parsons, pp. 490–536. New York: The Free Press.

——— (1971) Comparative Studies and Evolutionary Change. In *Comparative Methods in Sociology*, edited by Ivan Vallier, pp. 97–139. Berkeley: University of California Press.

Patnaik, Utsa, ed. (1990) *Agrarian Relations and Accumulation: The "Mode of Production" Debate in India*. Bombay, India: Oxford University Press.

Patterson, Thomas C. (2009) *Karl Marx, Anthropologist*. Oxford, UK: Berg Publishers.

Peace, William (1993) Leslie White and Evolutionary Theory. *Dialectical Anthropology* 18(2): 123–152.

Pearce, Frank (1989) *The Radical Durkheim*. London, UK: Unwin Hyman.

Pearson, Margaret M. (2015) State-Owned Business and Party-State Regulation China's Modern Political Economy. In *State Capitalism, Institutional Adaptation, and the Chinese Miracle*, edited by Barry Naughton and Kellee S. Tsai, pp. 27–45. Cambridge, UK: Cambridge University Press.

Pelczynski, Zbigniew A. (1981) Nation, Civil Society, State: Hegelian Sources of the Marxian Non-Theory of Nationality. In *Hegel's Political Philosophy*, edited by Zbigniew A. Pelczynski, pp. 262–278. Cambridge, UK: Cambridge University Press.

——— (1984) Nation, Civil Society, State: Hegelian Sources of the Marxian Non-Theory of Nationality. In *The State and Civil Society: Studies in Hegel's Political Philosophy*, edited by Zbigniew A. Pelczynski, pp. 262–278. Cambridge, UK: Cambridge University Press.

Periwal, Sukumar, ed. (1995) *Notions of Nationalism*. Budapest, Hungary: Central European University Press.

Perkins, J. A. (1984) The German Agricultural Worker, 1815–1914. *The Journal of Peasant Studies* 11(3):3–27.

Pickering, William S. F. (1984) *Durkheim's Sociology of Religion: Themes and Theories*. London, UK: Routledge and Kegan Paul.

Piore, Michael and Charles Sabel (1984) *The Second Industrial Divide: Possibilities for Prosperity*. New York: Basic Books.

Pirenne, Henri (1914) The Stages in the Social History of Capitalism. *American Historical Review* 19(3):494–515.

——— (1939) *A History of Europe from the Invasions to the XVI Century*. London, UK: Allen Unwin.

——— (1952[1925]) *Medieval Cities: Their Origins and the Revival of Trade*. Princeton, NJ: Princeton University Press.

Pitts, Jennifer (2005) *A Turn to Empire: The Rise of Imperial Liberalism in Britain and France*. Princeton, NJ: Princeton University Press.

Pletsch, Carl E. (1981) The Three Worlds, or the Division of Social Scientific Labor, circa 1950–1975. *Comparative Studies in Society and History* 23(4):565–590.

Polanyi, Karl (1957[1944]) *The Great Transformation: The Political and Economic Origins of Our Time*. Boston, MA: Beacon Press.

Pollert, Anna (1988) Dismantling Flexibility. *Capital and Class* 34:42–75.

Pomerantz, Kenneth (2000) *The Great Divergence: China, Europe, and the Making of the Modern World Economy*. Princeton, NJ: Princeton University Press.

Popkin, Richard H. (1979) *The History of Scepticism from Erasmus to Spinoza*. Berkeley: University of California Press.

Poulantzas, Nicos (1975[1974]) *Classes in Contemporary Capitalism*. London, UK: New Left Books.

——— (1980[1978]) *State, Power, Socialism*. London, UK: Verso.

Power, Michael (1997) *The Audit Society: Rituals of Verification*. Oxford, UK: Clarendon Press.

Prebisch, Raúl (1949) *El desarrollo económico de América Latina y algunos de sus principales problemas*. Santiago, Chile: Comisión Económica para de América Latina (ECLA).

—— (1950) *The Economic Development of Latin America and its Principal Problems*. New York: United Nations.

Preobrazhensky, Evgeny (1965[1926]) *The New Economics*. Oxford, UK: Clarendon Press.

Proudhon, Pierre-Joseph (1966[1840]) *What is Property? Or, an Inquiry into the Principle of Right or Government*. New York: H. Fertig.

Raatgever, Reini (1985) Analytical Tools, Intellectual Weapons: The Discussion among French Marxist Anthropologists about the Identification of Modes of Production in Africa. In *Old Modes of Production and Capitalist Encroachment: Anthropological Explorations in Africa*, edited by Wim van Binsbergen and Peter Geschiere, pp. 290–330. Cambridge, UK: Cambridge University Press.

Radkey, Oliver H. (1958) *The Agrarian Foes of Bolshevism: Promise and Default of the Russian Socialist Revolutionaries, February to October, 1917*. New York: Columbia University Press.

Ratner, Carl (2015) Co-optation of Leading Co-op Organizations, and a Socialist Counter-Politics of Cooperation. *Monthly Review* 66(9):18–30.

Redfield, Robert (1956) *Peasant Society and Culture: An Anthropological Approach to Civilization*. Chicago, IL: The University of Chicago Press.

—— (1962[1930]) The Regional Aspect of Culture. In *The Papers of Robert Redfield*, vol. 1, *Human Nature and the Study of Society*, edited by Margaret P. Redfield, pp. 145–151. Chicago, IL: The University of Chicago Press.

—— (1962[1934]) Culture Changes in Yucatán. In *The Papers of Robert Redfield*, vol. 1, *Human Nature and the Study of Society*, edited by Margaret P. Redfield, pp. 160–172. Chicago, IL: The University of Chicago Press.

—— (1962[1935]) Folkways and City Ways. In *The Papers of Robert Redfield*, vol. 1, *Human Nature and the Study of Society*, edited by Margaret P. Redfield, pp. 172–182. Chicago, IL: The University of Chicago Press.

—— (1962[1939]) Primitive Merchants of Guatemala. In *The Papers of Robert Redfield*, vol. 1, *Human Nature and the Study of Society*, edited by Margaret P. Redfield, pp. 200–210. Chicago, IL: The University of Chicago Press.

—— (1962[1942]) The Folk Society. In *The Papers of Robert Redfield*, vol. 1, *Human Nature and the Study of Society*, edited by Margaret P. Redfield, pp. 221–253. Chicago, IL: The University of Chicago Press.

Redfield, Robert, Ralph Linton, and Melville J. Herskovits (1936) 1936 Memorandum for the Study of Acculturation. *American Anthropologist* 38(1):149–152.

Rey, Pierre-Philippe (1971) *Colonialisme, néo-colonialisme, et transition au capitalisme: exemple du "Comilog" au Congo-Brazzaville*. Paris, France: Maspero.

—— (1979) Class Contradiction in Lineage Societies. *Critique of Anthropology* 13–14:41–60.

—— (1982[1973]) Class Alliances. *International Journal of Sociology* 12(2):1–120.

Richardson, Theresa and Donald Fisher, eds. (1999) *The Development of the Social Sciences in the United States and Canada: The Role of Philanthropy*. Stamford, CT: Ablex Publishing.

Riesebrodt, Martin (1989) From Patriarchalism to Capitalism: The Theoretical Context of Max Weber's Agrarian Studies. In *Reading Weber*, edited by Keith Tribe, pp. 131–157. London, UK: Routledge.

Rivers, William H. R. (1906) *The Todas*. London, UK: Macmillan and Company.

—— (1917) The Government of Subject Peoples. In *Science and the Nation: Essays by Cambridge Graduates*, edited by Albert. C. Seward, pp. 302–328. Cambridge, UK: Cambridge University Press.

Roberto, Michael J. (2017) The Origins of American Fascism. *Monthly Review* 69(2):26–42.

Roberts, Dexter (2016) Beijing Moves to Curb Overseas Investments. *Bloomberg Businessweek* December 19–25, p. 17.

Roberts, Michael (2009) *The Great Recession: Profit Cycles, Economic Crisis: A Marxist View*. London, UK: Lulu Enterprises.

—— (2016) *The Long Depression: How It Happened, Why It Happened, and What Happens Next.* Chicago, IL: Haymarket Books.

Robinson, Joan (2003[1951]) Introduction. In *The Accumulation of Capital*, edited by Rosa Luxemburg, pp. xxi–xxxvii. London, UK: Routledge.

Rodinson, Maxime (1987[1980]) *Europe and the Mystic of Islam.* Seattle, WA: University of Washington Press.

Rodney, Walter (1974[1972]) *How Europe Underdeveloped Africa.* Washington, DC: Howard University Press.

Rosdolsky, Roman (1980[1964]) *Friedrich Engels y el Problema de los Pueblos "Sin Historia:" La Cuestión de las Nacionalidades en la Revolución de 1848–1849 a la Luz de la "Neue Rheinische Zeitung."* Mexico, D.F.: Ediciones Pasado y Presente.

Rose, Nikolas (1988) Calculable Minds and Manageable Individuals. *History of the Human Sciences* 1(2):179–200.

Rose, Nikolas, Pat O'Malley, and Mariana Valverde (2006) Governmentality. *Annual Review of Law and the Social Sciences* 2:83–104.

Roseberry, William (1993) Beyond the Agrarian Question in Latin America. In *Confronting Historical Paradigms: Peasants, Labor, and Capitalist World Systems in Africa and Latin America*, edited by Frederick Cooper, Allen F. Isaacman, Florencia E. Mallon, William Roseberry, and Stephen J. Stern, pp. 318–368. Madison, WI: The University of Wisconsin Press.

Rosenberg, Justin (1994) *The Empire of Civil Society: A Critique of the Realist Theory of International Relations.* London, UK: Verso.

—— (2000) *The Follies of Globalisation.* London, UK: Verso.

—— (2005) Globalization Theory: A Post Mortem. *International Politics* 42(1):2–74.

Ross, Dorothy (1991) *The Origins of American Social Science.* Cambridge, UK: Cambridge University Press.

Rossi-Landi, Ferruccio (1990) *Marxism and Ideology.* Oxford, UK: Oxford University Press.

Rostow, Walt W. (1971) *Politics and the Stages of Growth.* Cambridge, UK: Cambridge University Press.

—— (1971[1960]) *The Stages of Economic Growth: A Non-Communist Manifesto.* Cambridge, UK: Cambridge University Press.

Rotenstreich, Nathan (1971) The Idea of Progress and Its Assumptions. *History and Theory* 10(2):197–221.

Roth, Guenther (1971a) Weber's Generational Rebellion and Maturation. In *Scholarship and Partisanship: Essays on Max Weber*, edited by Reinhard Bendix and Guenther Roth, pp. 13–34. Berkeley: University of California Press.

—— (1971b) The Historical Relationship to Marxism. In *Scholarship and Partisanship: Essays on Max Weber*, edited by Reinhard Bendix and Guenther Roth, pp. 227–252. Berkeley: University of California Press.

—— (1971c) The Genesis of the Typological Approach. In *Scholarship and Partisanship: Essays on Max Weber*, edited by Reinhard Bendix and Guenther Roth, pp. 253–265. Berkeley: University of California Press.

Roth, Guenther and Wolfgang Schluchter (1979) *Max Weber's Vision of History: Ethics and Methods.* Berkeley: University of California Press.

Rouse, Joseph (1994) Power/Knowledge. In *The Cambridge Companion to Foucault*, edited by Gary Gutting, pp. 92–114. Cambridge, UK: Cambridge University Press.

Rousseau, Jean-Jacques (1962[1764]) *Lettres écrites de la Montagne* Neuchâtel, FR: Ides et Calendes.

—— (1973[1750]) A Discourse on the Arts and Sciences. In *The Social Contract and the Discourses*, edited by George D. H. Cole, pp. 1–26. London, UK: J. M. Dent and Sons.

—— (1973[1755]) A Discourse on the Origin of Inequality. In *The Social Contract and the Discourses*, edited by George D. H. Cole, pp. 27–114. London, UK: J. M. Dent and Sons.

Rowe, John H. (1964) Ethnography and Ethnology in the Sixteenth Century. *Kroeber Anthropological Society Papers* 30:1–20.

—————— (1965) The Renaissance Foundation of Anthropology. *American Anthropologist* 67(1):1–20.

Rubin, Vera, ed. (1959) *Plantation Systems in the New World*. Social Science Monograph, no. 7. Washington, DC: Division of Social Science, Pan-American Union.

Saad-Filho, Alfredo (2005) From Washington to Post-Washington Consensus: Neoliberal Agendas for Economic Development. In *Neoliberalism: A Critical Reader*, edited by Alfredo Saad-Filho and Deborah Johnston, pp. 113–119. London, UK: Pluto Press.

Saad-Filho, Alfred and Deborah Johnston (2005) Neoliberalism. In *Neoliberalism: A Critical Reader*, edited by Alfred Saad-Filho and Deborah Johnston, pp. 1–6. London, UK: Pluto Press.

Sacks, Karen Brodkin (1989) Toward a Unified Theory of Class, Race, and Gender. *American Ethnologist* 16(3):534–550.

Said, Edward (1979) *Orientalism*. New York: Vintage Books.

Saint-Simon, Claude-Henri de (1976[1804–1825]) *The Political Thought of Saint-Simon*. Oxford, UK: Oxford University Press.

Sandel, Michael, ed. (1984) *Liberalism and Its Critics*. Oxford, UK: Basil Blackwell.

Saul, John (1974) The State in Post-Colonial Societies: Tanzania. In *Social Register 1974: A Survey of Movements and Ideas*, edited by Ralph Miliband and John Saville, pp. 349–372. London, UK: Merlin Press.

Schram, Stuart R. (1994) Introduction. In *Mao's Road to Power: Revolutionary Writings 1912–1949*, vol. 2, *National Revolution and Social Revolution, December 1920–June 1927*, edited by Stuart R. Schram, pp. xv–lv. Armonk, NY: M. E. Sharpe.

Schumacher, Ernest F. (1973) *Small Is Beautiful: Economics as if People Mattered*. New York: Harper and Row.

Schumpeter, Joseph A. (1951[1919]) The Sociology of Imperialism. In *Imperialism and Social Classes*, edited by Paul M. Sweezy, pp. 3–130. New York: Augustus M. Kelley.

—————— (1981) *History of Economic Analysis*. Oxford, UK: Oxford University Press.

—————— (1983[1911]) *The Theory of Economic Development: An Inquiry into Profits, Capital, Credit, Interest, and the Business Cycle*. New Brunswick, NJ: Transaction Books.

Semmel, Bernard (1970) *The Rise of Free Trade Imperialism: Classical Political Economy, the Free Empire of Free Trade and Imperialism, 1750–1850*. Cambridge, UK: Cambridge University Press.

Seth, Sanjay (1992) Lenin's Reformulation of Marxism: The Colonial Question as a National Question. *History of Political Thought* 13(1):99–128.

Shadle, Stanley F. (1994) *Andrés Molina Enríquez: Land Reformer of the Revolutionary Era*. Tucson, AZ: University of Arizona Press.

Shaikh, Anwar (1979) Foreign Trade and the Law of Value, Part I. *Science and Society* 43(3):281–302.

—————— (1980) Foreign Trade and the Law of Value, Part II. *Science and Society* 44(1):27–57.

—————— (2016) *Capitalism: Competition, Conflict, Crises*. Oxford, UK: Oxford University Press.

Shanin, Teodor (1971) Peasantry: Delineation of a Sociological Concept and a Field of Study. *Archives Européenes de Sociologie* 12(3):289–300.

—————— (1983) Measuring Peasant Capitalism: The Operationalization of Concepts of Political Economy: Russia's 1920s—India's 1970s. In *Peasants in History: Essays in Honour of Daniel Thorner*, edited by Eric Hobsbawm, Witold Kula, Ashok Mitra, K. N. Raj, and Ignacy Sachs, pp. 83–104. Calcutta, India: Oxford University Press.

—————— (1986) *The Roots of Otherness: Russia's Turn of Century*, vol. 2, *Russia 1905–07: Revolutions as a Moment of Truth*. New Haven, CT: Yale University Press.

——————, ed. (1983) *Late Marx and the Russian Road: The Peripheries of Capitalism*. New York: Monthly Review Press.

—————— (2006) Peasantry. In *The Blackwell Dictionary of Modern Social Thought*, edited by William Outhwaite, 2nd ed., pp. 467–469. Oxford, UK: Blackwell Publishing.

Shils, Edward A. (1960a) Political Development in the New States—Alternative Courses of Political Development. *Comparative Studies in Society and History* 11(2):265–292.

—————— (1960b) Political Development in the New States—The Will to Be Modern. *Comparative Studies in Society and History* 11(3):379–411.

—— (1963) On the Comparative Study of the New States. In *Old Societies and New States: The Quest for Modernity in Asia and Africa*, edited by Clifford Geertz, pp. 1–26. Glencoe, IL: The Free Press.

Silverman, Sydel (1979) The Peasant Concept in Anthropology. *Journal of Peasant Studies* 7(1):49–69.

Simmel, Georg (1997[1903]) The Metropolis and Mental Life. In *Simmel on Culture*, edited by David Frisby and Mike Featherstone, pp. 174–186. London, UK: Sage Publications.

Singer, Hans (1949) Economic Progress in Underdeveloped Countries. *Social Research* 16(1):1–11.

Sklar, Martin J. (1988) *The Corporate Reconstruction of American Capitalism, 1890–1916: The Market, The Law, and Politics.* Cambridge, UK: Cambridge University Press.

Smelser, Neil J. (1961) Mechanisms of Change and Adjustment to Change. In *Industrialization and Society*, edited by Bert F. Hoselitz and Wilbert E. Moore, pp. 32–54. Paris, France: UNESCO-Mouton.

Smith, Adam (1976[1776]) *An Inquiry into the Nature and Causes of the Wealth of Nations.* Chicago, IL: The University of Chicago Press.

—— (1982[1762–1763]) *Lectures on Jurisprudence.* Indianapolis, IN: Liberty Press.

Smith, Anthony D. (1986) *The Ethnic Origins of Nations.* Oxford, UK: Basil Blackwell.

Smith, Gavin (1991) The Production of Culture in Local Rebellion. In *Golden Ages, Dark Ages: Imagining the Past in Anthropology and History*, edited by Jay O'Brien and William Roseberry, pp. 180–207. Berkeley: University of California Press.

Smith, Richard (1997) Creative Destruction: Capitalist Development and China's Environment. *New Left Review* 222:3–42.

Solomon, Susan G. (1977) *The Soviet Agrarian Debate: A Controversy in Social Science, 1923–1929.* Boulder, CO: Westview Press.

Solow, Robert (1956) A Contribution to the Theory of Economic Growth. *Quarterly Journal of Economics* 70(1):65–94.

Spencer, Herbert (1852) A Theory of Population Deduced from the General Law of Animal Fertility. *The Westminster Review* 57(112):468–501.

—— (1876) *The Principles of Sociology.* vol. 1, pt. 2. London, UK: Williams and Norgate.

—— (1880[1862]) *First Principles.* New York: A. L. Barr.

—— (1896) *The Principles of Sociology.* vol. 3, pt. 8. London, UK: Williams and Norgate.

Spicer, Edward A. (1977) Early Applications of Anthropology in North America. In *Perspectives in Anthropology 1976*, edited by Anthony F. C. Wallace, J. Lawrence Angel, Richard Fox, Sally McLendon, Rachael Sady, and Robert Sharer, pp. 116–141. Washington, DC: American Anthropological Association.

Ste. Croix, Geoffrey E. M. de (1972) *The Origins of the Peloponnesian War.* London, UK: Gerald Duckworth.

—— (1981) *The Class Struggle in the Ancient Greek World from the Archaic Period to the Arab Conquests.* Ithaca, NY: Cornell University Press.

—— (1984) Class in Marx's Conception of History, *Ancient and Modern.* New Left Review 146:94–111.

Stedman Jones, Gareth (1991) Utopian Socialism. In *A Dictionary of Marxist Thought*, edited by Tom Bottomore, pp. 561–563. Oxford, UK: Blackwell Publishers.

Steenson, Gary P. (1978) *Karl Kautsky, 1854–1938: Marxism in the Classical Years.* Pittsburgh, PA: University of Pittsburgh Press.

Stephen, Lynn (1997) *Women and Social Movements in Latin America: Power from Below.* Austin, TX: University of Texas Press.

Stern, Steve J. (1985) Review: New Directions in Andean Economic History: A Critical Dialogue with Carlos Sempat Assadourian. *Latin American Perspectives* 12(1):133–148.

Steward, Julian H. (1949) Cultural Causality and Law: A Trial Formulation of the Development of Early Civilizations. *American Anthropologist* 51(1):1–27.

—— (1950) Area Research: Theory and Practice. *Social Science Research Council Bulletin* 63:1–164.

——— (1955[1950]) The Concept and Method of Cultural Ecology. In *Theory of Culture Change*, by Julian H. Steward, pp. 43–63. Urbana, IL: The University of Illinois Press.

——— (1977) Limitations of Applied Anthropology: The Case of the Indian New Deal. In *Evolution and Ecology: Essays on Social Transformation by Julian Steward*, edited by Jane C. Steward and Robert F. Murphy, pp. 333–346. Urbana, IL: The University of Illinois Press.

——— (1977[1941]) Determinism in Primitive Society. In *Evolution and Ecology: Essays on Social Transformation by Julian Steward*, edited by Jane C. Steward and Robert F. Murphy, pp. 150–157. Urbana, IL: The University of Illinois Press.

Steward, Julian H. and Frank M. Setzler (1938) Function and Configuration in Archaeology. *American Antiquity* 4(1):4–10.

Stocking, George W., Jr. (1995) *After Tylor: British Social Anthropology 1888–1951*. Madison, WI: The University of Wisconsin Press.

Streeck, Wolfgang (2014) *Buying Time: The Delayed Crisis of Democratic Capitalism*. London, UK: Verso.

Streeten, Paul (1972) *The Frontiers of Development Studies*. London, UK: Palgrave Macmillan.

Sullivan, Paul (1989) *Unfinished Conversations: Mayas and Foreigners between Two Wars*. Berkeley: University of California Press.

Sum, Ngai-Ling and Bob Jessop (2013) *Towards a Cultural Political Economy: Putting Culture in its Place in Political Economy*. Cheltenham, UK: Edward Elgar.

Susser, Ida (1982) *Norman Street: Poverty and Politics in an Urban Neighborhood*. Oxford, UK: Oxford University Press.

Sutcliffe, Bob (2002) How Many Capitalisms? Historical Materialism in the Debates about Imperialism and Globalization. In *Historical Materialism and Globalization*, edited by Mark Rupert and Hazel Smith, pp. 40–58. London, UK: Routledge.

Swedberg, Richard (1998) *Max Weber and the Idea of Economic Sociology*. Princeton, NJ: Princeton University Press.

——— (2005) *The Max Weber Dictionary: Key Words and Central Concepts*. Palo Alto, CA: Stanford University Press.

Sweezy, Paul (1970[1942]) *The Theory of Capitalist Development*. New York: Monthly Review Press.

——— (1976[1950]) A Critique. In *The Transition from Feudalism to Capitalism*, edited by Rodney Hilton, pp. 33–56. London, UK: New Left Books.

——— (1991) Socialism. In *A Dictionary of Marxist Thought*, edited by Tom Bottomore, pp. 500–502. Oxford, UK: Blackwell Publishers.

——— (1997) More (or Less) Globalization. *Monthly Review* 49(4):1–4.

Sweezy, Paul M. and Charles Bettelheim (1971) *On the Transition to Socialism*. New York: Monthly Review Press.

Szelényi, Iván (1988) *Socialist Entrepreneurs: Embourgoisement in Rural Hungary*. Madison, WI: The University of Wisconsin Press.

——— (2015) Capitalisms after Communism. *New Left Review* 96:39–51.

Szelényi, Iván and Bill Martin (1988) The Three Waves of New Class Theories. *Theory and Society* 17(4):645–667.

Szelényi, Iván and Szonya Szelényi (1991) The Vacuum in Hungarian Politics: Classes and Parties. *New Left Review* 187:121–138.

Szëll, György (2006) Workers' Council. In *The Blackwell Dictionary of Modern Social Thought*, edited by William Outhwaite, 2nd ed., pp. 742–744. Oxford, UK: Blackwell Publishing.

Tabb, William K. (1982) *The Long Default: New York City and the Urban Fiscal Crisis*. New York: Monthly Review Press.

Takahashi, Kohachiro (1976[1952]) A Contribution to the Discussion. In *The Transition from Feudalism to Capitalism*, edited by Rodney Hilton, pp. 68–97. London, UK: New Left Books.

Tarbuck, Kenneth J. (1972) Introduction. In *The Accumulation of Capital—An Anti-Critique, by Rosa Luxemburg. Imperialism and the Accumulation of Capital by Nikolai Bukharin*, pp. 14–43. New York: Monthly Review Press.

Tenbruck, Friedrich (1987) Max Weber and Eduard Meyer. In *Max Weber and His Contemporaries*, edited by Wolfgang J. Mommsen and Jürgen Osterhammel, pp. 234–267. London, UK: Allen and Unwin.

Thomas, Peter D. (2010) *The Gramscian Moment: Philosophy, Hegemony and Marxism*. Chicago, IL: Haymarket Books.

Thompson, Edward P. (1963) *The Making of the English Working Class*. New York: Vintage Books.

———— (1997) *The Romantics: England in a Revolutionary Age*. New York: The New Press.

Thorner, Alice (1982) Semi-Feudalism or Capitalism? Contemporary Debate on Classes and Modes of Production in India. *Economic and Political Weekly* 17(49–51):1911–1968, 1993–1999, 2061–2066.

Thorner, Daniel T. (1986[1966]) Chayanov's Concept of Peasant Economy. In *The Theory of Peasant Economy*, edited by Daniel Thorner, Basile Kerblay, and R. E. F. Smith, pp. xi–xxiv. Madison, WI: The University of Wisconsin Press.

Tipps, Dean C. (1973) Modernization Theory and the Comparative Study of Societies: A Comparative Perspective. *Comparative Studies in Society and History* 15(2):199–226.

Tönnies, Ferdinand (1996[1887]) *Community and Society*. New Brunswick, NJ: Transaction Publishers.

Touraine, Alain (1977[1973]) *The Self-Production of Society*. Chicago, IL: The University of Chicago Press.

———— (1981[1978]) *The Voice and the Eye: An Analysis of Social Movements*. Cambridge, UK: Cambridge University Press.

Toye, John and Richard Toye (2003) The Origins and Interpretation of the Prebisch-Singer Thesis. *History of Political Economy* 35(3):437–467.

Tracy, James D., ed. (1990) *The Rise of Merchant Empires: Long-Distance Trade in the Early Modern World, 1350–1750*. Cambridge, UK: Cambridge University Press.

Tribe, Keith (1989a) Introduction. In *Reading Weber*, edited by Keith Tribe, pp. 1–14. London, UK: Routledge.

———— (1989b) Prussian Agriculture—German Politics: Max Weber 1892–7. In *Reading Weber*, edited by Keith Tribe, pp. 85–130. London, UK: Routledge.

———— (1995) *Strategies of Economic Order: German Economic Discourse, 1750–1950*. Cambridge, UK: Cambridge University Press.

Trigger, Bruce G. (1989) *A History of Archaeological Thought*. Cambridge, UK: Cambridge University Press.

Trompf, Garry W. (1979) *The Idea of Historical Recurrence in Western Thought: From Antiquity to the Reformation*. Berkeley: University of California Press.

Trotsky, Leon (1969[1906]) Results and Prospects. In *The Permanent Revolution and Results and Prospects*, pp. 29–122. New York: Pathfinder Press.

———— (1969[1930]) The Permanent Revolution. In *The Permanent Revolution and Results and Prospects*, pp. 125–281. New York: Pathfinder Press.

———— (1973[1907–1909]) *1905*. Harmondsworth, UK: Penguin Books.

———— (1980[1932–1933]) *The History of the Russian Revolution*. New York: Monad Press.

Turner, Jonathan H. (1985) *Herbert Spencer: A Renewed Appreciation*. Beverly Hills, CA: Sage Publications.

Valcárcel, Luis (1914) *La cuestión agrarian en el Cuzco*. Bachiller's Thesis in Political and Administrative Sciences, Universidad de San Antonio Abad, Cuzco, Peru.

———— (1981) *Memorias*. Lima, Peru: Instituto de Estudios Peruanos.

Veblen, Thorsten (1939[1916]) *Imperial Germany and the Industrial Revolution*. New York: Viking Press.

Vernengo, Matias (2006) Technology, Finance, and Dependency: Latin American Radical Political Economy in Retrospect. *Review of Radical Political Economics* 38(4):551–568.

Vico, Giambattista (1970 [1725]) *The New Science of Giambattista Vico*. Ithaca, NY: Cornell University Press.

Vogt, William P. (1991) Political Connections, Professional Advancement, and Moral Education in Durkheimian Sociology. *Journal of the History of the Behavioral Sciences* 27(1):56–75.

Walker, Kathy L. (1999) *Chinese Modernity and the Peasant Path: Semicolonialism in the Northern Yangzi Delta*. Stanford, CA: Stanford University Press.

——— (2006) "Gangster Capitalism" and Peasant Protest in China: The Last Twenty Years. *The Journal of Peasant Studies* 33(1):1–33.

——— (2008) From Covert to Overt: Everyday Peasant Politics in China and the Implications for Transnational Agrarian Movements. *Journal of Agrarian Change* 8(2–3):462–488.

Walker, Martin (1993) *The Cold War and the Making of the Modern World*. London, UK: Fourth Estate.

Wallerstein, Immanuel (1966) Introduction. In *Social Change: The Colonial Situation*, edited by Immanuel Wallerstin, pp. 1–8. New York: John Wiley and Sons.

——— (1974) *The Modern World-System: Capitalist Agriculture and the Origins of the European World-Economy in the Sixteenth Century*. New York: Academic Press.

——— (1979[1976]) Semiperipheral Countries and the Contemporary World Crisis. In *The Capitalist World-Economy: Essays by Immanuel Wallerstein*, pp. 95–118. Cambridge, UK: Cambridge University Press.

——— (2000[1974]) The Rise and Future Demise of the World Capitalist System: Concepts for Comparative Analysis. In *The Essential Wallerstein*, pp. 72–205. New York: The New Press.

——— (2000[1975]) Class Formation in the Capitalist World-Economy. In *The Essential Wallerstein*, pp. 315–323. New York: The New Press.

——— (2011) *The Modern World-System*, vol. 4, *Centrist Liberalism Triumphant, 1789–1914*. Berkeley: University of California Press.

Wallerstein, Immanuel and Étienne Balibar (1991[1988]) *Race, Nation, Class: Ambiguous Identities*. London, UK: Verso.

Wallwork, Ernest (1972) *Durkheim: Morality and Milieu*. Cambridge, MA: Harvard University Press.

——— (1984) Religion and Social Structure in The Division of Labor. *American Anthropologist* 86(1):63–66.

Wartenberg, Thomas (1990) *The Forms of Power: From Domination to Transformation*. Philadelphia, PA: Temple University Press.

Weber, Max (1946[1915]) The Social Psychology of World Religions. In *From Max Weber: Essays in Sociology*, edited by Hans Gerth and C. Wright Mills, pp. 129–146. New York: Oxford University Press.

——— (1949[1903–1917]) *The Methodology of the Social Sciences*. Edited by Edward A. Shils and Henry A. Finch. New York: The Free Press.

——— (1958[1904–1905]) *The Protestant Ethic and the Spirit of Capitalism*. New York: Charles Scribner's Sons.

——— (1958[1921]) *The City*. Glencoe, IL: Free Press.

——— (1976[1896]) The Social Causes of the Decline of Ancient Civilization. In *The Agrarian Sociology of Ancient Civilizations*, pp. 35–411. London, UK: New Left Books.

——— (1976[1898]) The Agrarian History of the Major Centres of Ancient Civilization. In *The Agrarian Sociology of Ancient Civilizations*, pp. 35–386. London, UK: New Left Books.

——— (1978[1922]) *Economy and Society: An Outline of Interpretive Sociology*. Edited by Guenther Roth and Claus Wittich, 2 vols. Berkeley: University of California Press.

——— (1981[1923]) *General Economic History*. New Brunswick, NJ: Transaction Books.

——— (1989[1894]) Developmental Tendencies in the Situation of East Elbian Rural Labourers. In *Reading Weber*, edited by Keith Tribe, pp. 158–187. London, UK: Routledge.

——— (1989[1895]) The Nation State and Economic Policy. In *Reading Weber*, edited by Keith Tribe, pp. 188–209. London, UK: Routledge.

——— (1989[1897]) Germany as an Industrial State. In *Reading Weber*, edited by Keith Tribe, pp. 210–220. London, UK: Routledge.

——— (2003[1889]) *The History of Commercial Partnerships in the Middle Ages*. Lanham, MD: Rowman and Littlefield, Publishers.

——— (2008[1889]) *Roman Agrarian History: In its Relation to Roman Public and Civil Law*. Claremont, CA: Regina Books.

Weis, Lois (1990) *Working Class without Work: High School Students in a De-Industrializing Economy.* London, UK: Routledge.

Weiss, Linda (1997) Globalization and the Myth of the Powerless State. *New Left Review* 225:3–27.

——— (1998) *The Myth of the Powerless State.* Cambridge, UK: Polity Press.

Weiss, Roberto (1988) *The Renaissance Discovery of Classical Antiquity.* Oxford, UK: Basil Blackwell.

West, Cornel (2001) *Race Matters.* New York: Vintage Books.

White, Leslie A. (1943) Energy and the Evolution of Culture. *American Anthropologist* 45(4):335–356.

White, Stephen A. (2008) Milesian Measures: Time, Space, and Matter. In *The Oxford Handbook of Presocratic Philosophy,* edited by Patricia Curd and Daniel W. Graham, pp. 89–133. Oxford, UK: Oxford University Press.

Whyte, Willam F. (1987) Organizational Behavior Research: Changing Styles of Research and Action. In *Applied Anthropology in America,* edited by Elizabeth M. Eddy and William L. Partridge, 2nd ed., pp. 159–183. New York: Columbia University Press.

Wiener, Norbert (1954[1950]) *The Human Use of Human Beings: Cybernetics and Society,* 2nd ed. Garden City, NY: Doubleday and Company.

Wignaraja, Ponna, ed. (1993) *New Social Movements in the South: Empowering People.* London, UK: Zed Books.

Williams, Phil, ed. (1997) *Russian Organized Crime: The New Threat?* London, UK: Frank Cass.

Willis, Paul (1981[1977]) *Learning to Labour: How Working Class Kids Get Working Class Jobs.* New York: Columbia University Press.

Wilson, Edward O. (1975) *Sociobiology: The New Synthesis.* Cambridge, MA: Belknap Press of Harvard University Press.

Wilson, Godfrey B. and Monica H. Wilson (1954[1945]) *The Analysis of Social Change.* Cambridge, UK: Cambridge University Press.

Wolf, Eric R. (1955) Types of Latin American Peasantry: A Preliminary Discussion. *American Anthropologist* 57(3):452–471.

——— (1956) Aspects of Group Relations in a Complex Society: Mexico. *American Anthropologist* 58(6):1065–1078.

——— (1957) Closed Corporate Communities in Mesoamerica and Central Java. *Southwestern Journal of Anthropology* 13(1):1–18.

——— (1966) *Peasants.* Englewood Cliffs, NJ: Prentice-Hall.

——— (1969) *Peasant Wars of the Twentieth Century.* New York: Harper and Row.

Wolf, Eric R. and Sidney W. Mintz (1957) Haciendas and Plantations in Middle America and the Antilles. *Social and Economic Studies* 6(3):382–412.

Wolff, Richard D. and Stephen A. Resnick (1987) *Economics: Marxian versus Neoclassical.* Baltimore, MD: The Johns Hopkins University Press.

——— (2012) *Contending Economic Theories: Neoclassical, Keynesian, and Marxian.* Cambridge, MA: MIT Press.

Wolpe, Harold (1980) Introduction. In *The Articulation of Modes of Production: Essays from Economy and Society,* edited by Harold Wolpe, pp. 289–320. London, UK: Routledge and Kegan Paul.

——— (1980[1972]) Capitalism and Cheap-Labour in South Africa: From Segregation to Apartheid. In *The Articulation of Modes of Production: Essays from Economy and Society,* edited by Harold Wolpe, pp. 1–43. London, UK: Routledge and Kegan Paul.

——— (1985) The Articulation of Modes and Forms of Production. In *Marxian Theory and the Third World,* edited by Diptendra Banerjee, pp. 89–103. New Delhi, India: Sage Publications.

——— (1988) *Race, Class, and Apartheid State.* Martlesham, UK: James Currey.

Wood, Ellen Meiksins (1986) *The Retreat from Class: A New "True" Socialism.* London, UK: Verso.

——— (1990) The Uses and Abuses of "Civil Society." In *Socialist Register 1990: The Retreat of the Intellectuals,* edited by Ralph Miliband, Leo Panitch, and John Saville, pp. 60–84. London, UK: Merlin Press.

——— (2003) *Empire of Capital.* London, UK: Verso.

Woodfield, Andrew (1976) *Teleology.* Cambridge, UK: Cambridge University Press.

World Bank (1972) *The Limits of Growth: Report of the Club of Rome on the State of Mankind*. London.

Worsley, Peter M. (1961) The Analysis of Rebellion and Revolution in Modern British Social Anthropology. *Science and Society* 21(1):26–37.

———— (1964) *The Third World*. London, UK: Weidenfeld and Nicolson.

———— (1984) *The Three Worlds: Culture and World Development*. Chicago, IL: The University of Chicago Press.

Wylie, Alison (2004) Why Standpoint Matters. In *The Feminist Standpoint Theory Reader: Intellectual and Political Controversies*, edited by Sandra Harding, pp. 339–352. London, UK: Routledge.

———— (2012) Feminist Philosophy of Science: Standpoint Matters. Presidential Address—Pacific Division. *Proceedings and Address of the American Philosophical Association* 86(2):47–76.

Zilsel, Edgar (2003) *Social Origins of Modern Science*. Boston Studies in the Philosophy of Science, vol. 200. Dordrecht, the Netherlands: Kluwer Academic Publishers.

Index

acculturation 157
accumulation: primitive 106–107; by
    dispossession 224–226
Acosta, J. 22
Aeschylus
Agrarian Question 57–61, 99–106
Alavi, H. 196–197
American Empire 227–232
Amin, S. 174–175
anarchism 4
Anaximenes 4
Anglo-Foucauldians 238–239
Aristotle 18–19
articulation of modes of
    production138–142, 172, 178–182
Augustine 19

Bacon, F. 24
Balibar, E. 249–251
Banaji, J. 177
Baran, P. 165–167
Bauer, O. 91–92
Bernstein, E. 121–123
Bettelheim, C. 199–200
Boas, F. 90
Bodin, J. 23
Boeke, J. 141
Bois, G. 186–187
Brenner, R. 186–187
Brenner Debate 186
Brodkin, K. 268
Bukharin, N. 79–81
Burke, E. 4
business cycles 116

Cabral, A. 191–192
capitalism 1–9, 44–49, 72–85
capitalist accumulation 106–107, 224–226
capitalist economic crises 120–129,
    203–232, 255–265
change, metaphors of: cyclical renewal
    14–17; development 26; evolution

31–35; growth 17–20; human nature
    or nature 30–35; progress or becoming
    modern 20–30; telelology 17–20
Chayanov, A. 130–133
China 134–137, 243–247
civil society 240–241
civilization 3–4, 31–35
class structure 40–42, 48, 69
class struggle 42, 142–151, 194–199
class warfare 200–201, 206–208
Cold War 153–200
colonial mode of production 177–178
colonialism 69
Colonial Question 72–99
combined and uneven development
    106–109, 178–182
communitarianism 210
conservativism 4, 142–151, 263–270
commodity 45–46
criminal organizations 242–243
crisis 6–8, 46–47, 115–129, 142–151,
    263–270
cultural turn 234–235

decolonization, see also national liberation
    153–200
Democritus 24
dependency theory 164–171
Derrida, J. 232–233
Descartes, R. 24
developmental contingency 35, 43–44
dissolution of socialist states 239–247
Dobb, Maurice 182–184
Du Bois, W. E. B. 90
dual economies 141, 169–170, 174
Durkheim, É. 36–37: anomie 51–53; change
    51, 53; individual 50; 49–57; modern
    industrial society 51–53; organic
    solidarity 51–52; primitive society 51;
    religion 52, 55–57; social pathology
    50–51, 53–55; social order 53–57; social
    solidarity 51–53; state 53–55

Eagleton T. 234–236
economic growth theories 116–120, 155–158
economy of transition 199–200
Emmanuel, A. 173–174
Empedocles 17
end of history thesis 209–210
Engels, F. 40, 101–102
Enlightenment 20–21
ethnocide 110
ethnogenesis 110
environmental crisis 262–266
exploitation 40–42, 48, 69

Fanon, Frantz 190–192
fascism 255–262
Fei, X. 177
feudal society 182–188
finance capital 76–77
First World War 71–113
folk-urban continuum 147–149
Fortes, M. 145
Foucault, M. 233–234
Fourier, C. 30
Frank, A. G. 167–169

gangster capitalism 242–243
Geertz, C. 155–164, 193–194, 235
globalization theory 217–232
governmentality 236–239
Gramsci, A. 136–139
Great Depression 115–120
Green Revolution 177–182
Great Transformation 1
Grossmann, H. 119–120

Harding, S. 234
Harvey, D. 222–232
Hegel, G. 6–7
Heraclitus 15
Herder, J. 86
Hesiod 13
Hilferding, R. 76–77
Hilton, R. 185
Ho, C. 98
Hobbes, T. 251
Hobson, J. 74–75
Homer 13
Hymer, S. 175–177

idealism 235
identity 85–92, 247–251, 255–261
imperialism 69, 72–85
international trade 175–177

indigenous people 106–110
individual subject 67
industrial society 30, 38
information and computer technologies 8
International Monetary Fund 153–164, 214

Kant, I. 86
Kautsky, K. 91–92, 99, 102–103
Kerr, C. 153–163
Keynes J. 6
Keynesianism 10
Kritsman, L. 131–132

Laclau, E. 178–179
language 238
Le Roy, L. 23
Lenin, V. 82–84, 93–98, 121–122, 130–138
liberalism 3–4
Luxemburg, R. 78–79, 98, 121

Machiavelli, N. 17
Maksakovsky, P. 120
Malinowski, B. 70, 144–145
Mandel, E. 178
Mao Z. 98, 35–137
Mariátegui, J. 98–99, 140–141
Marx, K. 36–37: Asiatic societies 42–43; alienation 40; capitalist economic crises 46–47, 117–120; capitalist mode of production 44–47; crises of capitalism 46–47; critique of political economy 39–41; development of capitalism 43–49; dynamics of change 42–43, 49; imperialism 47–49; peasant village communes 43, 47–48; mode of production 40–43
Meisner, M. 243–246
metaphors of change 7–9
middle peasant thesis 196–198
Mintz, S. 195–196
modernity 247–251
modernization theories 69, 116–120, 208–210
modes of production 177–182
Montaigne, M. 25–26
Mooney, J. 111–112
Moore, B. 198–199
Morgan, L. 31–32
multinational corporate capitalism 175–177

nation 85–92, 247–251
national liberation movements 89–93, 153–155, 188–194

national minority 89–93, 96, 138–142
National Question 85–99
national state 138–142, 164–177,
    247–251
nationalism 72–85, 138–152, 247–262
neocolonialism 185
neoclassical economy theory 6
neoconservatism 210
neoliberalism 209, 212–217
Neo-Kantianism 58, 124
New Economic Policy 126–127
new imperialism 188–194, 227–232
new social movements 236, 253–257

Panitch, L. and S. Gindin 227–232
Parsons, T. 160–165
peasants 133–137, 194–200
philanthropic foundations 140–142
Plato 17
postcolonial studies 243–255
postcoloniality 251–55
postmodernism 209, 232–233
postmodernity 233–236
post-socialism 239–247
Prebisch, R. 164
Preobrazhensky, E. 133–134
Proudhon, P. 4–5

Radcliffe-Brown, A. 70
rationality 24, 26
Redfield, R. 147–149
reification 70
religion 56 62–64
Rey, P. 179–181
Rivers, W. 112–113
romanticism 3–4, 27–28
Rostow, W. 158–160
Rousseau, J. 2–4
rural class formation 103–105, 129–138,
    194–199
Russia 103–105, 121
Russian Federation 242–243
Russian Revolution 121–128

Saint-Simon, C. 30, 38
scientific method 24

Schumpeter, J. 84–85, 117–118
Scottish Historical Philosophers 29–30
Second World War 153–155
Sempat Assadourian, C. 179
settler colonies 72–73, 95–97
Smith, A. 2–4, 29–30
Smith, G. 268
Social Darwinism 34–35
social evolution 31–35
social identities 255–262
socialism 4–5, 121–128, 239–247
Southern Question 137–139
Spencer, H. 32–35
standpoint theory 2–4
Stephen, L. 268
Steward, J. 156–158
Stalin, J. 128, 134
Sweezy, P. 183–184, 199–200

Takahashi, K. 184
Third World 154–155, 177–182
transition 182–200
Trotsky L. 108

underdevelopment 164–172
unequal exchange 172–177
uneven development 78–81, 83
Union of Soviet Socialist Republics
    120–129, 154, 200
United States 199–201, 266–267

Vico, Giambattistia 26–27

Wallerstein I. 170
Weber, M. 36–37, 57–66; agrarian
    question 57, 60; capitalism 58–61;
    class and state formation 62–66;
    development of capitalism 58–61,
    65; nation-state 6–66; race 60; rural
    transformation 58–61, 101; social
    stratification 62–64
Wilson, G. and M. Wilson 145–147
Wolf, E. 195–198
Wolpe, H. 181–182
World Bank 153–154, 214
world systems theory 170–172